# Accountancy and Empire

# Routledge New Works in Accounting History

EDITED BY GARRY CARNEGIE, *Melbourne University Private, Australia*, JOHN RICHARD EDWARDS, *Cardiff University, UK*, SALVADOR CARMONA, *Instituto de Empresa, Spain* AND DICK FLEISCHMAN, *John Carroll University, USA*

**1. The Institute of Accounts**
Nineteenth Century Origins of Accounting Professionalism in the United States
Stephen E. Loeb and Paul J. Miranti, Jr.

**2. Professionalism and Accounting Rules**
Brian P. West

**3. Accounting Theory:**
Essays by Carl Thomas Devine
Edited by Harvey S. Hendrickson and Paul F. Williams

**4. Mark to Market Accounting**
"True North" in Financial Reporting
Walter P. Schuetze, edited by Peter W. Wolnizer

**5. A History of Auditing**
The Changing Audit Process in Britain from the Nineteenth Century to the Present Day
Derek Matthews

**6. Contemporary Issues in Financial Reporting**
A User-Oriented Approach
Paul Rosenfield

**7. The Development of the American Public Accountancy Profession**
Scottish Chartered Accountants and the Early American Public Accountancy Profession
T. A. Lee

**8. Two-Hundred Years of Accounting Research**
Richard Mattessich

**9. Double Accounting for Goodwill**
A Problem Redefined
Martin Bloom

**10. Accountancy and Empire**
The British Legacy of Professional Organization
Edited by Chris Poullaos and Suki Sian

# Accountancy and Empire

## The British Legacy of Professional Organization

**Edited by**
**Chris Poullaos and Suki Sian**

Routledge
Taylor & Francis Group
New York London

First published 2010
by Routledge
270 Madison Avenue, New York, NY 10016

Simultaneously published in the UK
by Routledge
2 Park Square, Milton Park, Abingdon, Oxon OX14 4RN

*Routledge is an imprint of the Taylor & Francis Group, an informa business*



Typeset in Sabon by IBT Global.
Printed and bound in the United States of America on acid-free paper by IBT Global.



*Library of Congress Cataloging-in-Publication Data*

Poullaos, Chris.
Accountancy and empire / by Chris Poullaos and Suki Sian.
p. cm. — (Routledge new works in accounting history ; 10)
Includes bibliographical references and index.
1. Accounting—History. I. Sian, Suki, 1969– II. Title.
HF5605.P68 2010
657.09171'241—dc22
2009046616

ISBN13: 978-0-415-45771-2 (hbk)
ISBN13: 978-0-203-85154-8 (ebk)

# Contents

# Tables

# Key Acronyms

## ACCOUNTING ASSOCIATIONS

| | |
|---|---|
| AACA | Association of Chartered Accountants of Alberta |
| AACPA | American Association of Certified Public Accountants |
| AAEA | Association of Accountants in East Africa |
| AAJ | Association of Accountants of Jamaica |
| AAM | Association of Accountants in Montreal (see Note 1) |
| ACCA | Association of Certified Corporate Accountants (UK- see Note 2) |
| ACPA | Australasian Corporation of Public Accountants |
| AICPA | American Institute of Certified Public Accountants |
| ANAN | Association of National Accountants of Nigeria |
| CICA | Canadian Institute of Chartered Accountants |
| CIMA | Chartered Institute of Management Accountants (UK) |
| CIPFA | Chartered Institute of Public Finance and Accountancy (UK) |
| CSAA | Cape Society of Accountants and Auditors |
| CSCA | Canadian Society of Cost Accountants |
| DACA | Dominion Association of Chartered Accountants (see Note 3) |
| FASB | Financial Accounting Standards Board (US) |
| IAAG | Institute of Accountants and Actuaries in Glasgow |
| IAAPQ | Institute of Accountants and Auditors of the Province of Quebec |
| IAB | Indian Accountancy Board |
| IASB | International Accounting Standards Board |
| ICABC | Institute of Chartered Accountants in British Columbia |
| ICAC (Ch. 7) | Institute of Chartered Accountants of the Caribbean |
| ICAC (Ch. 6) | Institute of Chartered Accountants of Ceylon |
| ICAEW | Institute of Chartered Accountants in England and Wales |
| ICAI (Ch. 9) | Institute of Chartered Accountants of India |
| ICAI | Institute of Chartered Accountants of Ireland |

| | |
|---|---|
| ICAJ | Institute of Chartered Accountants of Jamaica |
| ICAM | Institute of Chartered Accountant of Manitoba |
| ICAN | Institute of Chartered Accountants of Nigeria |
| ICANS | Institute of Chartered Accountants of Nova Scotia |
| ICAO | Institute of Chartered Accountants of Ontario |
| ICAS (Ch. 2,3) | Institute of Chartered Accountants of Saskatchewan |
| ICAS | Institute of Chartered Accountants in Scotland |
| ICASL | Institute of Chartered Accountants of Sri Lanka (see Note 4) |
| ICATT | Institute of Chartered Accountants of Trinidad and Tobago |
| ICPAK | Institute of Certified Public Accountants of Kenya |
| ICWA | Institute of Cost and Works Accountants (UK—see Note 5) |
| IFAC | International Federation of Accountants |
| IMTA | Institute of Municipal Treasurers and Accountants (UK—see Note 6) |
| KASNEB | Kenyan Accountants and Secretaries National Examination Board |
| LAA | London Association of Accountants |
| MACPA | Malaysian Association of Certified Public Accountants |
| MIA | Malaysian Institute of Accountants |
| NACA | National Association of Cost Accountants (US) |
| NSA | Natal Society of Accountants |
| SAA | Society of Accountants in Aberdeen |
| SAAOFS | Society of Accountants and Auditors in the Orange Free State |
| SAE | Society of Accountants in Edinburgh |
| SCAJ | Society of Chartered Accountants in Jamaica |
| SCAPGH | Society of Chartered Accountants in the Province of the Cape of Good Hope |
| SEC | Securities and Exchange Commission (US) |
| SIAA | Society of Accountants and Auditors (UK—see Note 7) |
| SMAC | Society of Management Accountants of Canada |
| TSA | Transvaal Society of Accountants |

## OTHER ACRONYMS

| | |
|---|---|
| CA/CAs | Chartered accountant/chartered accountants |
| 'CA' | 'Chartered Accountant' as designation (used generically, not necessarily reflecting the designations of particular associations) |
| 'CASA' | 'Chartered Accountant (South Africa)' as designation |

| | |
|---|---|
| CMA | Certified Management Accountant (designation used in Canada from 1977) |
| CO | Colonial Office |
| DO | Dominions Office |
| IFRS | International Financial Reporting Standard |
| MAFs | Multinational accounting firms |
| PCO/PC | Privy Council Office/Privy Council |
| T&T | Trinidad and Tobago |

## NOTES

| | |
|---|---|
| Note 1 | Name changed to Society of Chartered Accountants of the Province of Quebec (SCAPQ) in English and La Société des Comptables Agréés de la Province de Québec in French in 1927. |
| Note 2 | The ACCA was renamed the Association of Certified Accountants in 1971, then the Chartered Association of Certified Accountants (CACA) in 1984 and latterly the Association of Chartered Certified Accountants. |
| Note 3 | The DACA was renamed Canadian Institute of Chartered Accountants (CICA) in 1951. |
| Note 4 | Previously the Institute of Chartered Accountants of Ceylon. |
| Note 5 | The ICWA was renamed the Institute of Cost and Management Accountants (ICMA) in 1972 and then the Chartered Institute of Management Accountants in 1986. |
| Note 6 | The IMTA was renamed the Chartered Institute of Public Finance Accountants (CIPFA) in 1973. |
| Note 7 | Name changed to Society of Incorporated Accountants and Auditors in 1908. |

# Preface

Since the revival of imperial history in the 1980s a number of hitherto neglected aspects of Britain's imperial past have been more fully illuminated. Much of the emphasis has been on cultures of colonialism, and the intersections of race, gender and sexuality in legitimizing empire. However, there was a clear need to apply these new cultural perspectives to economic and business history in order to gain a more nuanced understanding of the mechanisms of imperial power. This comprehensive collection of chapters incorporates insights from the 'new' imperial history in extending our understanding of connexions between the accountancy profession and the empire. It builds on earlier pioneering work by Dean Neu and others into the indispensable role of taxation and accountancy in imperial contexts as a Foucaultian mechanism of 'disciplining' and 'moralizing' indigenous peoples to facilitate colonial rule. Additionally several contributions push the boundaries further to include the legacies of empire.

These chapters, authored by key academics working in the field, have been judiciously selected by the editors to cover developments in the accountancy profession in different parts of the empire and in different colonial and post-colonial contexts in the twentieth century. Together they reveal the extent to which the profession was embedded in complex networks of power that spanned the white settler, non-white settler or 'tropical' colonies and the metropolitan centre, and secured the stability and perpetuation of the empire. In charting the development of the training of accountants and the validation of professional bodies in the colonial context, the collection also illuminates the interrelationship between power and knowledge and demonstrates that accountancy was not simply a tool of good governance and auditing of empire and imperial businesses but also a form of cultural imperialism.

A study of the accountancy profession may, on the surface, seem to be a specialist area but this collection has wider appeal in that the organization and training for the profession reflected the entrenched race, class and ethnic divisions that sustained imperial divide and rule policies across the extensive British Empire. Moreover, as Alan Richardson points out in his chapter in this volume on Canada, accounting was intertwined with different forms of imperialism—economic, military, political and cultural. Modern European empires in the twentieth century were characterized by complex bureaucracies and systems of taxation to fund administration, and colonial economies developed, in theory if not always in practice, to render colonies profitable for the imperial state and private business sector. Accountants and auditors were essential to ensuring that colonial administrations and economies worked in metropolitan interests. The chapters in this collection thus illuminate the relations between the state (imperial, colonial and post-colonial) and the accountancy profession and reveal how the development of the profession mirrored developments in imperial power relations. Of particular significance here is the increasing economic and cultural dominance of the US as Britain declined as an imperial power, which facilitated the global reach of American accountancy multinationals and subsequent Westernization of the profession.

Additionally, interesting insights emerge into post-colonial problems of continued Western dominance of the profession and the gate-keeping mechanisms of British-based professional organizations such as the Association of Chartered Certified Accountants (ACCA) and the Institute of Chartered Accountants in England and Wales (ICAEW). In building independent societies nationalist governments wanted to localize the profession and entry into it. But, as the contributions focusing on Jamaica, Nigeria and Malaya demonstrate, attempts at localism were scuppered by assumptions that locally obtained accountancy qualifications were inferior to the gold standard of professional training and practice recognized by British professional bodies. The prioritization of British-trained chartered accountants (CAs) over those locally trained was based on assumptions of the superiority of European culture that endured after independence. Hence multinationals preferred to employ British-trained CAs and, as Chibuike Uche points out in his chapter in this volume on the colonial heritage in the accounting profession in Nigeria, this led to neglect of the needs of small, local businesses. In the words of the editors, Suki Sian and Chris Poullaos, this continued bias against localism in the profession constituted 'a new accounting imperialism'.

A number of chapters in this collection also reveal the extent to which race and class inequalities and assumptions of white superiority were institutionalized during the colonial era and persisted after the end of formal empire. This is demonstrated in Suki Sian's study in this volume of colonial Kenya and Marcia Annisette's analysis of the race-based discrimination faced by indigenous accountants in colonial and post-colonial Trinidad and Tobago. It was only in the white settler colonies of Canada, New Zealand, South Africa and Australia that a strong local profession emerged and that was dominated by Europeans—indigenous peoples were excluded. Before the Second World War, most accountants in the non-settler colonies were from Britain or from her white empire. Apart from India, where 'Indianization' of the civil service and professions began from the late nineteenth century in response to the growth of Indian nationalism, the colonized were racially excluded from the accountancy profession until after independence. Indeed, common to colonial discourse was the assumption that it was only white men of 'character', to use Peter Cain's term, who had the moral fibre and probity to manage money and finances. These were regarded as masculine characteristics and this was reflected in the fact that women were largely excluded from the development of the profession in Britain and the empire. This superior imperial masculinity was compared to inferior colonial masculinities. Colonized men were characteristically represented as feckless, corrupt and incapable of handling their own finances. Colonized women were invisible, although we know that women in European and colonial societies often managed family finances and had their own systems of saving. This invisibility points to the need for more extensive research into indigenous accounting systems and how men and women in colonial and ex-colonial societies mediated, and continue to grapple with, the cultural differences between their own perceptions of financial management and the modernity of Western practices. Such research arguably constitutes a more difficult task in terms of archival sources. Nevertheless, it is vital to critiquing assumptions of 'West is best', which this present collection addresses. This volume also provides pointers towards productive new debates and academic enquiry.

Professor Barbara Bush
Sheffield Hallam University

# Acknowledgments

We would like to thank Dick Edwards and our academic referees for supporting this project at the proposal stage. We would also like to express our gratitude to Laura Sterns, Terry Clague and Sarah Hastings from Routledge for their guidance and advice on how to negotiate the production process; and their patience while it proceeded.

We owe a special debt to our contributors. They have participated in the project in an enthusiastic, co-operative and friendly manner, and the intellectual exchanges with them have been a great learning experience for the both of us.

We acknowledge also the bountiful moral support, unfailing good humour and encouragement provided by Alannah, Jaspal and Aman, other family members, friends and colleagues.

Chris Poullaos and Suki Sian

# 1 Accountancy and Empire
## Setting the Stage

*Suki Sian and Chris Poullaos*

For much of the nineteenth and twentieth centuries, the British built and maintained a vast empire that extended from North America to Australia and included the Indian subcontinent, much of the Caribbean and parts of South-East Asia and the Middle East. Various rationales have been forwarded for this determined expansion: the rise of European democracy and competition between the imperial powers, the military imperative, the economic imperative and the moral imperative (Marshall 1996). Historians are by no means agreed on the relative significance of these driving forces. Britain employed the might of its military and naval forces to establish and defend its territories from competing powers, maintain order within them and facilitate relations of production, investment and trade with them, to its advantage. Commercial penetration and political influence combined with arms to provide the British with opportunities to incorporate complementary economies into the empire and the broader world capitalist system and it came to function as a closely integrated trading network, reaching its height between 1900 and 1930 (Osterhammel 1997; Cain and Hopkins 2002). This historical occupation of foreign lands left a lasting legacy and dramatically shaped the modern world.[1] The creation and expansion of the formal British Empire[2] not only influenced the developmental paths of

1. Conventionally, key periods in the history of the British Empire are identified as: (a) 1630–1680, when the Caribbean plantation economy was perhaps the first 'periphery' of the Eurocentric world economy; (b) 1760–1830, when the loss of most of Britain's colonies in North America was formally recognized and a second wave of colony formation was initiated involving expansion into India by the East India Company and settlement in Australia and New Zealand; (c) 1880–1900, during which a 'new imperialism' emerged involving the partition of Africa via the Berlin Act of 1885; (d) 1900–1930, the heyday of colonial settlement in the existing outposts and expansion into the Middle East; (e) 1945–1960s, the era of decolonization in many countries (Marshall 1996; Osterhammel 1997).

2. Gallagher and Robinson (1953) distinguished between formal (colonial rule) and informal empire. Whilst formal empire entailed sovereign control and the political, social and economic organization of the colonies, informal empire involved control by other means: 'British policy followed the principle of extending control informally if possible and formally if necessary . . . [W]hatever the method British interests were steadily safeguarded and extended. The usual summing of the policy

the territories that were ruled through the introduction of new systems of government, education, language, societal organization, religion and even sport, but also physically transformed the land through farming and mining, the construction of infrastructure assets and the introduction of diseases (Marshall 1996).

Although the British wielded power over their vast empire they could not do so by exercising direct supervision and coercive powers alone given the number of administrators per head of population in most colonies. Thus 'managerial devices' (Marshall 1996, 147) were widely deployed and institutions established to effect imperial rule. In particular, the imposition of British law and administration conferred a degree of protection upon investors (both shareholders and creditors), which did much to encourage capital formation and flow and without which entrepreneurial endeavour could not flourish (Ferguson 2003).

While there is a vast literature on the British Empire, relatively little attention has thus far been directed to the imperial fingerprint upon the development of colonial institutions, particularly those with a role in the regulation of commercial and entrepreneurial activity in the colonies and integral to the operation of commercial/financial 'managerial devices'. This volume aims to address this gap by tracing the rise of professional accountancy in selected colonial outposts and examining the role of the institutions regulating it, within the context of the empire experience. It is no coincidence that the expansion of professional accountancy throughout Britain and her self-governing colonies occurred in the late nineteenth and early twentieth centuries during the height of Britain's imperial power (Johnson and Caygill 1971; Johnson 1973, 1982), given accountants' close relationship to British capital and given that British professional organization served as a blueprint for such organization in the colonies.

British accountants were often dispatched to far-flung territories to assist with colonial administration. More relevant for our purposes: others emigrated in search of economic opportunities to provide accounting services to British organizations (both those operating locally and those in Britain with offshore investment interests) and local enterprises. British accountants in the colonies were keen to replicate their British status and *modus operandi* (as 'professional accountants') and were a means through which their 'home' societies became imperial bodies with imperial interests while 'the expansion and consolidation of the British imperial state was associated with the imperial involvement of emergent professional associations

---

of the free trade empire as "trade not rule" should read "trade with informal control if possible; trade with rule when necessary"' (1953, 13). Thus imperialism can exist without (formal) empire and although the latter ended with the achievement of political independence for the colonies, imperialism, it may be argued, might continue in various forms. The rise of the US could be described as a new variety of informal empire.

in a form which significantly affected the profession/state relationship in Britain itself' (Johnson 1982, 197). The empire became a site of competition between British accounting associations, some of which were active in promoting local branches while others relied on their members overseas, their links to market and state in the imperial centre and their close association with British capital abroad to negotiate the age of empire. British accountancy associations trained colonial accountants both in Britain and in the colonies, as well as inspiring the formation of similar-but-different versions of themselves by colonial accountants (aided and abetted, at times, by British immigrant accountants). Mimesis and mutation aside, however, the interests of colonial accountants (and the state agents who regulated them) by no means coincided with those of British accountants: competition, after all, was still competition and domination was still domination. The resultant engagements between imperial and colonial accountants (and their allies within imperial and colonial state agencies) resulted in the formation of an imperial accountancy arena (Chua and Poullaos 2002) and contributed ultimately to the formation of a 'world-wide system of examining, recognition and reciprocation' (Johnson 1982, 198).

The aim of this volume is to analyze a rich variety of those engagements and to reflect upon their consequences. It brings together, for the first time, studies of the professionalization of accountancy in key constituent territories of the British Empire, its particular ambition being to provide historical insight by focusing on selected ex-colonies that provide contrasting examples of the uptake of the 'British model' ('models', more strictly speaking). It thus provides an opportunity to highlight the peculiarities of the professionalization processes in variant social, economic and political environments linked together by the relays of empire, prompting reflection on both the common and disparate dynamics involved. Further, the adopted approach provides a platform to facilitate broad-based discussion on the significance of the empire experience for both the periphery and the imperial centre.

The key question posed is: how has the organization of accountants in Britain's (former) colonies and in the imperial centre itself been affected by the 'empire' experience? In addressing this question, the volume builds upon the pioneering work of Terry Johnson and Marjorie Caygill (1971) and Bob Parker (1989); extends and complements more recent work by Briston and Kedslie (1997), Chua and Poullaos (2002) and Parker (2005) which has the empire as its focus; and adds to our knowledge of how the empire experience has impacted upon individual countries. We stress *first* that the invited contributors were given the option of exploring the legacy effects of empire after formal decolonization and many of them have taken it up; and *second*, that when we talk about the 'organization of accountants' we are not referring to accounting practices or standards or audit methodologies—rather our focus is in the formation, training and collective organization of embodied practitioners into occupational groupings, typically self-identifying and socially accepted as 'professionals'.[3]

Our contributors have previously written about the organization of accountancy in 'their' countries (often being places where they were born and/or domiciled), but all have been encouraged to specifically focus on the 'empire' angle for the purposes of this volume so as to address the question posed in the previous paragraph. They were presented with a list of possible themes and issues extracted from the broader accounting professionalization literature and asked to make a choice as to which to pursue (given the aims of this book) and for which period. There was no expectation that all themes could be pursued across time in all chapters. We hope, nevertheless, that readers will be prompted to reflect upon how the accountants in their vicinity are trained and otherwise organized—perhaps these things are not a simple reflection of, or response to, their locales alone. We hope also that our academic colleagues will be stimulated to fill in the gaps through further research.

We have found it useful to cluster the chapters around two broad categories of (former) colonies: the (white), 'self-governing', settler colonies (Canada, South Africa and Australia) where locally trained accountants of British stock were 'professionalizing' themselves at roughly the same time (with a slight lag) as their counterparts in Britain in the late nineteenth and early twentieth centuries; and the racially/ethnically diverse (mainly non-settler) colonies which were subject to colonial administration from Britain for much longer, not attaining formal independence until after—in some cases well after—the Second World War. It is striking that, on the whole, locally trained accountants in the latter category of colonies did not have an opportunity to organize *themselves* until decolonization. Clearly different dynamics were at work between our two broad categories of colonies while there were also variations within them. The remaining chapters in this volume will attempt to unravel these differences and to identify some of their major effects. To *illustrate*: varying motivations for professionalization existed in different locales at different times, with groups utilizing assorted tactics and forming unique alliances to (for example) secure exclusion and closure. Some professional projects were strongly influenced by British institutions and adopted British designations and notions of professional training and conduct, whilst others rejected these outright and sought new ones, perhaps heralding (or hoping for) a decisive break from empire. In particular, the 'chartered accountant' designation ('CA') was

3. '[Important] aspects of an accountancy community's activities and rewards have been affected by efforts to construct a collective occupational identity and to then "keep up a continual effort to maintain and if possible enhance the position of the group" (Macdonald 1995, 188). The "continual effort"—the accountancy professional project—is what researchers of accounting professionalization are interrogating, with process being given as much attention as outcome' (Poullaos 2009, 249).

much coveted throughout the empire, both during and after colonial occupation, and many chapters in this volume allude to the tussles surrounding its appropriation. Finally, in some territories, professionalization projects were, to a greater or lesser extent, afflicted with issues of race and other cultural precepts. In more recent times, changes in the global political economy, American hegemony, the advance of American informal power and the internationalization of accountancy have all impacted upon professional organization and structure in former British colonies. It is with these challenges in mind that this volume was conceived; it attempts to unravel the complexities and legacies of the metropole/periphery relationship as reflected in the professionalization of accountancy.

In Chapter 2 of this volume Chris Poullaos examines how the fluidity of relations between Britain and the self-governing colonies/dominions after the First World War impacted upon relations between accountants in the imperial centre and those in the dominions. It argues that during the 1920s organized dominion accountants (supported by local state agents) were able to leverage the increasing autonomy of the dominions to either solidify (in the case of Canada) or gain access to the 'CA' designation (South Africa and Australia) against the wishes (more or less) of the CAs' bodies in England and Scotland. 'CA' had by then become a form of symbolic capital widely perceived as an advantage in the market for accountancy services. Although their tactics varied, the dominion accountants all successfully appropriated 'CA'; however, somewhat paradoxically, in the process and as a result, the linkages between the various members of the imperial accountancy community became denser, thereby contributing to the integration of the imperial accountancy arena. Included in the analysis is an account of the failure of an attempt by the Institute of Chartered Accountants in England and Wales (ICAEW) to create examination and training facilities throughout the empire; an outcome which helps to explain why colonial accountants outside the dominions subsequently had (until the decolonization era) to travel to Britain to become CAs. The relative ease with which dominion accountants achieved their major aims contrasts markedly with the experiences of their professional brethren in the racially diverse non-settler colonies, as shown in later chapters.

In his synoptic analysis of Canada's 'empire' experience(s) in Chapter 3 of this volume, Alan Richardson highlights the point that Canada has been subject to French and American influences as well as British. The compromises made with the French community in Quebec enabled the evolution of 'statist' code-based regulation of accountancy in that province which has created something of a disconnect (manageable but noticeable) with the organization of accountants in other provinces. Furthermore, although Canadian institutions were derived from British traditions of professional training and credentialing, they developed in the shadow of US economic and cultural hegemony. This chapter explores the dual influence of heritage and hegemony on the Canadian accounting project, identifying the Scottish influence on the form of the Canadian accounting profession, the leadership role of British expatriates and the accommodation by the profession of the emergence of US accounting firms and accounting regulation. The American influence on the Canadian profession is found predominantly in the adoption of American accounting literature and standards that influence the information flowing across the border for the benefit of American investors in Canada; rather than in the training of those producing it. Richardson sees in Canada's involvement (as a 'middle power') in international standard-setting a trajectory of looking back to the UK as a buffer against American standard-setting hegemony.

Attention then turns to the racially-diverse, non-self-governing colonies of Nigeria, Malaysia, Sri Lanka, Jamaica and Trinidad and Tobago where, although local professional bodies were established after independence under the auspices of state-sponsored legislation, the colonial legacy remained strong, notwithstanding the commitment of new post-independence governments to a nationalist ethos. Chibuike Uche's analysis of Nigeria in Chapter 4 of this volume observes that although a British commercial presence in Nigeria during the colonial period gave rise to a demand for accounting services, an indigenous professional accounting association (the Institute of Chartered Accountants of Nigeria [ICAN]) was only formed via statute after independence. Originally designed to avoid race-based discrimination and professional status differences (as between members of various British accounting associations) according to a formula combining openness of entry with monopoly over (the most lucrative areas of) practice, ICAN has subsequently fought a failing rearguard action against an increasing number of both home-grown and foreign associations. The former have been nurtured by the inadequate production by ICAN of qualified accountants to meet the economic demands of the newly independent nation. The latter (in particular the British-based Association of Chartered Certified Accountants [ACCA]) have offered the temptation of an internationally recognized qualification which appeals to multinational businesses operating in Nigeria but neglects the accounting needs of small businesses; culminating in what might be termed a new accounting imperialism.

A different type of legacy is highlighted in Devi Susela's analysis of the Malaysian profession in Chapter 5 of this volume. The post-independence Malaysian state pursued an active and sustained development agenda but the elite accountants that supported it were British-trained (and Australian-trained) CAs who replicated the forms of professionalism within which they had themselves been trained. The twist is that the elite largely consisted of Malaysian accountants of Chinese descent whose forebears were bought to Malaysia during the colonial period to supply manual labour; while the *bumiputra* accountants, mostly members of the ACCA, only gained leverage by activating the moribund state-sponsored Malaysian Institute of Accountants (MIA). Thus British associational rivalry and racial division resulting from British colonial policy are still playing out, even as the forces of globalization loom on the horizon. The case of Sri Lanka, too, analyzed by Senarath Yapa in Chapter 6 of this volume, shows how British rule had an enduring effect upon the professionalization process there. Yapa details the struggle between the two main groups—the 'elite accountants', advantaged with British accountancy qualifications, British-style education and links to local power elites, who modeled the Institute of Chartered Accountants of Sri Lanka (ICASL) on the ICAEW; and the 'non-elite', consisting of the registered accountants who took the examinations of the local accountancy board and (later) graduates from local universities, coming from the lower social strata. Eager to maintain British traditions, the elite accountants borrowed closure strategies from the ICAEW in order to marginalize the non-elite group. The elite's focus on public practice has, furthermore, created a vacuum in other areas of accountancy which British accounting associations (the ACCA included) have been happy to fill.

The ACCA has been more active in the Caribbean than it has in South-East Asia. In Jamaica, a typical racially-diverse non-settler colony until independence, the ostensibly nationalist post-independence accountancy profession divided, initially, on the basis of ICAEW versus ACCA training and subsequently on 'local' versus 'internationalization' lines. As articulated by Owolabi Bakre in Chapter 7 of this volume, the supporters of localization (in both the accountancy and the broader Jamaican communities) imagined an accountancy community geared to local needs through basic training at the University of the West Indies (UWI) and subsequent professional qualification through membership of the Institute of Chartered Accountants of Jamaica (ICAJ). The internationalization group were allied with the ACCA, favouring an internationally recognized qualification over a local one, effectively undermining the nationalist ethos of the early era of independence and pushing the ICAJ into the background. In Bakre's view, this outcome can only be fully understood with reference to the conflict of identity experienced by the indigenous leaders of the profession and their strong and continuing allegiance to the UK professional bodies.

In Chapter 8 of this volume Marcia Annisette extends her seminal work on the accountancy profession in Trinidad and Tobago (T&T) which focused on strong dependence of the local Institute of Chartered Accountants of Trinidad and Tobago (ICATT) on the ACCA for the internationally recognized professional education and certification of the country's accountants and on the race-based discrimination faced by indigenous accountants in both colonial and post-colonial T&T. In her contribution to this volume, she highlights an underlying 'practice link' between the major local and foreign accounting firms. The local firms began as local branches of British firms but were gradually incorporated into large multinational accounting firms (MAFs) whose origins were British but which are now US-dominated, in keeping with the supplanting of British capital by American capital as the driving force behind global capitalism. Her argument is that the local accounting firms were willingly incorporated into the MAFs so that they could gain access to 'highly valued accountancy knowledge products centred around standardization' (Annisette, this volume, p. 187); seeing in this motivation the continuation of a process of psychological/cognitive subordination evident during the era of British rule. Reflecting further upon the practice link, she further contends that the particular knowledge-generating practices of the MAFs may help to explain the more general gap between the practice and academic arms of accountancy.

Whilst the final two countries, India and Kenya, have much in common with the preceding non-settler, racially diverse, non-self-governing colonies they also exhibit characteristics in their professionalization trajectories evident in the white-settler, self-governing colonies. In Chapter 9 of this volume, Shraddha Verma focuses on the development of the accounting profession in India from 1947 to 1960; in particular, on relations between the newly independent Indian state apparatus and local accountants. In contrast to other racially diverse colonies, the race factor does not appear to have prevented indigenous Indians from entering the profession long before a local institute was established; indeed, the British may well have encouraged it as a form of 'divide and rule'. The case of India also highlights another anomaly: the new Indian government embraced an essentially socialist ideology involving economic central planning while the Indian accountants proactive in the formation of the Institute of Chartered Accountants of India (ICAI) modeled it on the 'autonomous' British accounting associations. Verma shows how the aspirations of the local accounting elite were not always aligned with the political and economic strategies of the new government, which, paradoxically, was sufficiently concerned about its relations with Britain to keep in check the desire of the ICAI's promoters to take a hard line against British accountants on the issue of mutual recognition.

Kenya is another country that does not seem to fit either the settler or the non-settler mould. In Chapter 10 of this volume, Suki Sian presents evidence of the existence of a white-dominated professional organization during the colonial period; an indigenous professional body was not created until 1977, some 14 years after independence. This chapter charts the rise of professional accountancy in Kenya, beginning with the arrival of the earliest expatriate British accountants through to exclusionary reversal after independence and finally indigenous professionalization in the 1970s. In doing so, it also draws attention to the racial divisions in colonial society, rivalries amongst the professional bodies represented in Kenya and the role of the state as factors influencing the local professionalization trajectory. In a significant development, Sian shows how external pressure was exerted on the colonial professional body not only by the colonial state, but also the British government and the Indian profession (supported by the Indian government), forcing it to reconsider its position on Indian accountants operating in Kenya. Such events highlight further the interconnected nature of the empire and perhaps reinforce Chua and Poullaos's conceptualization of an imperial accountancy arena.

In the final chapter we reflect upon the varied contributions to this volume to comment upon the ways in which the organization of accountancy has been affected or constituted by the (British) empire experience, in both the colonial periphery and imperial centre, highlighting not only common patterns but also variations, and offering suggestions for further research. Such research might support (or confound) our belief that the global accounting profession, as we know it today, is to a significant degree the product of Britain's imperial age. In our view, the interactions between centre and periphery highlighted in the chapters that follow provide preliminary evidence that such a proposition is plausible.

## REFERENCES


Briston, R.J., and M.J.M. Kedslie (1997) 'The internationalisation of British professional accounting: The role of the examination exporting bodies. *Accounting, Business & Financial History* 7(2): 175–94.

Cain, P.J., and Hopkins, A.G. (2002) *British Imperialism, 1688–2000*. 2nd ed. Harlow, UK: Pearson Education.

Chua, W.F., and Poullaos, C. (2002) 'The empire strikes back? An exploration of centre-periphery interaction between the ICAEW and accounting associations in the self-governing colonies of Australia, Canada and South Africa, 1880–1907'. *Accounting, Organizations and Society* 27:409–45.

Ferguson, N. (2003) *Empire: How Britain Made the Modern World*. London: Penguin.

Gallagher, J., and Robinson, R. (1953) 'The imperialism of free trade'. *Economic History Review* 6:1–15.

Johnson, T.J. (1973) 'Imperialism and the professions: Notes on the development of professional occupations in Britain's colonies and the new states'. In *Professions and Social Change (Sociological Review Monograph 20)*, ed. P. Halmos. Keele: University of Keele.

———. (1982) 'The state and the professions: peculiarities of the British'. In *Social Class and the Division of Labour*, ed. A. Giddens and G. McKenzie. Cambridge: Cambridge University Press.

Johnson, T.J., and Caygill, M. (1971) 'The development of accountancy links in the commonwealth'. *Accountancy and Business Research* (Spring): 155–73.

Macdonald, K.M. (1995) *The Sociology of the Professions*. London, Thousand Oaks, CA, and New Delhi: Sage.

Marshall, P.J. (1996) *British Empire*. Cambridge: Cambridge University Press.

Osterhammel, J. (1997) *Colonialism: A Theoretical Review*. Princeton, NJ: Markus Wiener Publishers.

Parker, R.H. (1989) 'Importing and exporting accounting: the British experience'. In *International Pressures for Accounting Change*, ed. A. Hopwood. Hertfordshire: Prentice Hall International and ICAEW.

———. (2005) 'Naming and branding: Accountants and accountancy bodies in the British Empire and commonwealth, 1853–2003'. *Accounting History* 10:7–46.

Poullaos, C. (2009) 'Professionalisation'. In *Routledge Companion to Accounting History*, ed. R. Edwards and S. Walker. London and New York: Routledge.

# 2 The Self-Governing Dominions of South Africa, Australia and Canada and the Evolution of the Imperial Accountancy Arena During the 1920s

*Chris Poullaos*

> We have heard that the man coming here from overseas by using the term chartered accountant establishes a sort of magnificence for himself? Naturally he does. That is part of the game.
>
> (*Report of the Select Committee on the South African Society of Accountants [Private] Bill*, 1924, 164)

## INTRODUCTION

In the late nineteenth and the early twentieth centuries the formal organization of accountants from Scotland spread not just to England, Wales and Ireland, but also to the self-governing (white-dominated) dominions of Canada, Australia and South Africa (among others). By 1910 dominion accounting associations, largely modeled on British bodies, had managed to provoke the British chartered accountancy bodies into engaging with them, in part by leveraging the capacity of local legislators to exclude or impose onerous obligations on the members of British bodies undertaking work locally. In their turn, the British bodies turned to the Colonial Office (CO) for assistance, invoking their connexion to British capital and their elite status as expert accountants. An imperial accountancy arena, in which centre and periphery mutually acted upon each other to bring about a degree of co-ordination (if not integration) of professional accountancy across large distances, had emerged (Chua and Poullaos 2002). 'A web of negotiations, spun around the relays of empire, had been set up and it was not likely to end soon' (Poullaos 2009b, 259).[1]

1. See Chua and Poullaos (2002) for an overview of the relevant literature on the period to 1907. On the meaning of 'self-governing' see Chua and Poullaos (2002, note 4). Appendix A lists the accounting associations relevant to the present chapter. The Dominions Office (DO) was split off from the CO in July 1925 but both came under the same secretary of state. The former became responsible for 'business relating to the self-governing Dominions (Canada, Australia, New

Building upon the seminal work of Johnson and Caygill (1971),[2] this chapter extends the analysis in Chua and Poullaos (2002) to the evolution of the imperial accountancy arena during the 1920s. The analytical focus remains cross-border profession–state interaction between the imperial centre (Britain) and (part of) the colonial periphery (Canada, Australia and South Africa). The empirical focus is on a group of nested issues: the access of dominion accountants to British designations, the conditions under which British accountants could practise in the dominions, the negotiating of reciprocity between British and colonial associations and an (unsuccessful) attempt by the Institute of Chartered Accountants in England and Wales (ICAEW) to modify its charter to allow it to run examinations throughout the empire for which local apprentices of ICAEW members practising locally could sit; thereby becoming ICAEW members without travelling to England or Wales.

With respect to the last point, this chapter supports and expands upon Johnson and Caygill's claim (1971, 168) that the 'failure of this attempt . . . was due to the protests of the Canadian and South African professions who saw a threat to their own independence if the "great parent body" were to extend its overseas activities'. This chapter provides an account of the ICAEW's motivation for instituting the attempt, the escalating pressure from the dominions which prompted it, the elaborate cross-border tactics of the key players and the eventual outcome. The chapter thus helps to explain why locals in *other* places and times were unable to qualify locally as ICAEW members, an observation made elsewhere in this volume. In highlighting cross-border engagements, however, this chapter does not seek to comprehensively capture the internal dynamics of professionalization in Britain, Canada, Australia and South Africa. That is, it does not provide a history of professionalization in those locales.

Broadly speaking, the shift in the imperial accountancy arena sketched here is the enhancement of the capacity of the periphery to impact upon the centre. Chua and Poullaos (2002, 439) cautioned, with respect to the situation circa 1907, that 'it is important not to overstate the strength of the periphery or the difficulties faced by the ICAEW'. By 1930 the ICAEW had a lot more to worry about.

---

Zealand, the Union of South Africa and Newfoundland), the Irish Free State and the Imperial Conference[,] the self-governing colony of Southern Rhodesia and the South African High Commission' (Jeffries 1956, 26). 'Race thinking' expanded in conjunction with both professionalization and empire (Poullaos 2009a). Although tentative attempts were made by non-whites to join British accounting associations during the 1920s in the imperial centre they did not get far; the negotiations by or on behalf of South African, Australian and Canadian accountants were effectively carried out on behalf of white accountants.

2. See also Johnson (1982), Parker (1989, 2005) and Briston and Kedslie (1997). The notion of an 'imperial accountancy arena' implies moving beyond focusing just upon Britain, or an individual dominion or the bilateral relationship between a dominion and Britain to imagining an empire-wide space of interaction characterized by 'the mutual and joint impact of a number of colonial arenas on each other . . . and on the imperial centre' (Chua and Poullaos 2002, 437).

## BACKGROUND AND CONTEXT

Britain emerged from World War I in better economic/financial shape than her European allies and rivals. Her geopolitical and naval pre-eminence were still in place, the extensity of her formal empire actually expanded after the war and, even in 1929, 'Britain was still probably the world's greatest overseas investor' (Cain and Hopkins 2002, 440). Nevertheless:

> The war disrupted the international economy, enabled the United States to emerge as a competitor on a global scale and seriously damaged Britain's ability to act as banker to the world. Thereafter, the slow and incomplete recovery of international trade hampered Britain's efforts to return to 'normality' and checked her influence overseas. Exports and foreign investment dwindled during the war, and failed in the 1920s to recover the levels attained in 1913. . . . Returning [to the gold standard in 1925 after its abandonment in 1919] involved an immense effort which probably accelerated Britain's relative decline. (Ibid., 405–6)

By war's end Britain was a sizable debtor to America. Furthermore, the latter's considerable advantages in economic capacity and holdings of gold and 'dollar diplomacy' prevented Britain from remaking the international financial system as she saw fit.[3] It was under these circumstances that 'trade with the empire, and more especially with the white Dominions of Canada, Australia, New Zealand and Australia' became of 'increased importance' in the interwar period (ibid., 431), the dominions' contribution to the war effort was appreciated and war-time co-operation had for the time being revived the imperial union movement (Dawson 1965; Poullaos 1994, 178–79). Concurrently, Britain and the dominions negotiated their post-war relationship during the 1920s, seeking a mutually acceptable balance between loose and tight coupling as war co-operation segued to a resurgence of nationalism in the dominions, especially in South Africa and Canada (Dawson 1965, 36–124). The report of the interimperial relations committee of the 1926 imperial conference chaired by Lord Balfour declared that the self-governing dominions were:

> autonomous Communities within the British Empire, equal in status, in no way subordinate one to another in any aspect of their domestic or external affairs . . . Every self-governing member of the Empire is now the master of its destiny. In fact, if not always in form, it is subject to no compulsion whatever. (Cited in Dawson 1965, 106)

3. On the extent of Britain's decline and her relations with America during the 1920s, see Cain and Hopkins (2002), Schulzinger (2002), Ferris (1991), McKercher (1988), Watt (1984), Darwin (1980), Parrini (1978), Costigliola (1977), Goldberg (1973) and Feis (1950).

The Balfour declaration was a way of 'bringing the theory of the Empire up to the point where it corresponded with the facts' (ibid., 105), especially in relation to matters internal to the individual dominions (the regulation of accountancy included). On Darwin's (1980, 662) interpretation, the declaration reflected 'the deep-rooted British assumption that, however fragile the constitutional bond, the dominions would remain bound to Britain because the facts of dominion politics and economics dictated that they must'. Similarly, Cain and Hopkins observe that South Africa and Australia, at least, relied on Britain for defence, trade and money supply (2002, 491). Money supply 'was determined largely by the state of the London balances of their banks which depended, in turn, upon the level of exports and the ability to borrow' (ibid., 492). For Cain and Hopkins, the Balfour declaration was 'in many ways . . . no more than a polite fiction' (ibid., 491). Australia borrowed heavily from Britain in the 1920s thereby tightening Britain's informal rein on nationalist aspirations (ibid., 497). During the 1920s, Britain provided around 40 per cent of net investment in the South African economy and remained a significant trading partner (ibid., 506). 'National Party politicians [led by General Hertzog] often took advantage of Afrikaaner sentiment to demand greater local autonomy but they had to take care not to scare off the capital which made white prosperity possible, and they also had to live with continued British trading and financial dominance' (ibid., 507).

In short, there was a tension between formal equality and autonomy on the one hand, and informal dependence on the other. This chapter explores the playing out of that tension in accountancy circles during the 1920s. Broadly speaking, the South African accountants aggressively promoted an autonomous position locally which they then sought to defend from the counter-attack of their British confreres. In contrast, Australian accountants went to Britain (for the third time), royal charter application in hand,[4] before attempting to mollify the counter-attack of excluded accountants in the Antipodean periphery. The case of Canada is different again. The Canadians could rely on American protection from international predators and 'they habitually kept their reserves in New York rather than in London' (ibid., 514). During the 1920s, America 'substantially increased her lead over Britain as a provider of Canadian imports and overtook her as a market for the Dominion's exports. More fundamentally, the United States became Canada's chief source of capital after 1914' (ibid.).[5] Furthermore, Canadian accountants had already successfully struggled (1908–1912) to maintain control of the 'chartered accountant' ('CA') designation, previously established through

4. On previous unsuccessful attempts to gain a royal charter, see Chua and Poullaos (1993) and Poullaos (1994). As a detailed account of the third attempt is provided in Poullaos (1994), the current chapter only surveys the Australian experience selectively to provide a contrast with South Africa and Canada.

5. 'In 1914, Britain still owned three-quarters of all the foreign investment in Canada and the United States one-fifth. By 1930 the British share had fallen to one-third and the American had risen to two-fifths' (Cain and Hopkins 2002, 514).

local legislative processes, in the face of protests of British CAs channelled through the CO (Creighton 1984; Poullaos 2008). What Canada, Australia and South Africa had in common was a desire to produce local 'CAs',[6] and to do so they all had to negotiate with the British state–profession axis. The next section provides an account of those negotiations.

## PROFESSION–STATE INTERACTION OF BRITAIN WITH SOUTH AFRICA, AUSTRALIA AND CANADA DURING THE 1920S

### Australia and Canada to 1923

One mode of interaction evident during the 1920s was the pursuit by dominion accountants of some form of formal relationship with the British chartered bodies that would indicate that they were roughly in the same league. This movement, evident early in the twentieth century, continued into the era of war. In 1915 F.N. Yarwood, a stalwart of the Australian efforts to obtain a royal charter, wrote to the ICAEW's Sir William Plender to propose that:

> the present time is very opportune for doing something with regard to an Imperial Charter for Public Accountancy throughout the Empire, and as only at your end can the venture be first mooted I have been asked to write to you to see if you think there is anything in the idea, and also whether anything can be done.[7]

In a similar vein the Institute of Chartered Accountants of Saskatchewan (ICAS) thought 'the time was opportune' to approach the ICAEW with a view to establishing reciprocal relations (*Canadian Chartered Accountant*—hereafter *CCA*—July 1915, 67). The ICAEW had apparently acknowledged that it was 'very natural, at a time like this . . . that closer ties should be sought with the Mother Institute, and [was] . . . fully sympathetic regarding the overtures'. It also acknowledged the generosity of the Canadian bodies in providing ready entry to British CAs. The ICAEW had 'had the question of reciprocal relations between England and Canada well in mind for some years past, but at the present time it is impossible for Parliament to deal with a question of this nature'. The ICAS nevertheless proclaimed that 'the

6. In the rest of this chapter 'CA' denotes the designation while CA or CAs refers to persons using it. 'CA' as a designation is used generically in that no discrimination is made between different versions as used by, say, the Scots and the ICAEW (e.g., 'CA' versus 'ACA').

7. Yarwood to Plender, 2 February 1915, in ICAEW 14–3-3. Details of acronyms used in the main text for primary sources and/or their locations are provided in the references.

matter is . . . not to be lost sight of', that the time 'was opportune' for the ICAEW to reciprocate. The ICAS wondered, 'Why not an Imperial Institute of Chartered Accountants? This war is teaching us to think imperially and not provincially' (ICAS report, *CCA*, January 1916, 226–29).

Yarwood kept the momentum going in Australia by asserting in November 1920 that the ICAEW had been sympathetic to his claim that although it (the ICAEW) thought the Australasian Corporation of Public Accountants (ACPA)[8] 'was running upon satisfactory lines', he, as an ACPA member, would not be considered fit to be a CA in England unless he restarted his training, an outcome he considered 'absurd' (*Public Accountant*, 1920, 148). Within a year the ACPA had signalled that it was making another royal charter attempt. Its president, Thomas Brentnall, made the same point as Yarwood with softer language, referring to the 'urgent demand for fuller recognition of the equality of English-speaking peoples' and highlighted the economic cost of 'CA' deficiency: 'Some of us have on occasions lost valuable business simply because the instructions from the other side [i.e., Great Britain] stipulated for the service of a "Chartered Accountant" although the representatives were fain to admit that qualifications and experience and character were beyond question'.[9]

By late 1922 the CO was considering its options. The intervention of Sir Mark Sheldon, a prominent Australian businessman connected to Yarwood and active in imperial economic diplomacy (Poullaos 1994, 182–83), prompted the CO and the Privy Council Office (PCO) to take the ACPA's application seriously. Sheldon also emphasized the economic loss argument, the contribution of ACPA members to Australian business and the delicate state of negotiations between Britain and the dominions. Support for the ACPA's application, he asserted, 'would have a most important bearing upon Imperial unity and anything that can be done to cement this unity is something to be desired', while rejection 'may ultimately lead to a feeling of grievance and a certain amount of cleavage in Empire commercial and business relations' (cited in Poullaos 1994, 183; see also 177–84). By the end of 1923 the ACPA had negotiated its way through the concerns of the ICAEW, the Scottish chartered bodies[10] and the Society of Incorporated Accountants and Auditors (SIAA). The British bodies were concerned to ensure easy entry to the proposed Australian chartered institute for their members in Australia, now and in the future; with the ICAEW willing to support a process of colonial status enhancement it considered preferable

8. The ACPA was the body through which the second and third Australian royal charter attempts was enacted. It was explicitly modeled on the ICAEW (Poullaos 1994).

9. Cited in Poullaos (1994, 180). Claims of economic loss to Australian non-CAs also surfaced in the first two charter attempts.

10. These were the Society of Accountants in Edinburgh (SAE), the Institute of Accountants and Actuaries in Glasgow (IAAG) and the Society of Accountants in Aberdeen (SAA).

to those previously adopted in Canada or the Transvaal (Poullaos 1994, 184–86; Chua and Poullaos 2002, 434). Furthermore, when approached by Sheldon in February 1923, ICAEW president William Cash had allegedly opined that if the Australians 'were placed under the same obligations as their English brethren . . . the way would paved to what [in] Mr. Cash's opinion was a desirable consummation, namely a Society for both Accountants [i.e., Australian and English]' (meeting notes, cited in Poullaos 1994, 185). The prospect of a status-enhancing link with the ICAEW was now dangled before the Australians as well.

There was, however, a darker counterpoint to this imperial *bonhomie*. A memorandum prepared in April 1922 by Robert Nesbitt of Markby, Stewart and Wadesons (ICAEW solicitors, hereafter Markbys) while Cash was ICAEW president suggests[11] that there was under contemplation in 1922 a supplemental charter allowing, *inter alia*, members practising abroad to take on articled clerks who could also sit ICAEW examinations locally.[12] Nesbitt cautioned that the CO might require the Canadian societies to receive notice of such proposals. He also noted that some British CAs desired a situation where they could use the 'CA' designation 'throughout the British Dominions' whereas dominion CAs (e.g., the Canadians) would, when using 'CA', be required to add something to their designation (e.g., 'Canada') *even in the dominions*, indicating that they were not members of a British chartered body. This was going too far, thought Nesbitt, although it was likely that Canadian CAs could be required to so indicate should they come to practise in England and Wales. However, the ICAEW general purposes committee decided in July 1922 not to proceed with the supplemental charter proposal (28435/2).[13] The significance of the 1922 discussion, for present purposes, is twofold. First, the service-abroad and examinations-abroad proposals ran totally counter to the 'equality' argument put forward by the Canadians and Australians and purportedly regarded sympathetically by the ICAEW. Second, although not being pursued when Cash spoke to Sheldon in 1923 (in equality mode), they were to reappear in 1926–1927. To understand why we need to understand what

11. Nesbitt's memorandum is attached to a letter by Cash, 10 August 1938, to the ICAEW's then secretary R.W. Bankes (both in 28435/2).

12. In 1903 the ICAEW (and the Scots) had rejected requests from members in Southern Africa to take on apprentices locally thereby pushing those members into further involvement with local associations and SIAA branches (Chua and Poullaos 2002, 424). A number ended up promoting or defending local measures that upset their 'Home' societies (see ibid., 425–27 and later in this chapter).

13. Reflecting (in 1938) upon the events of 1922, Cash recalled that 'certain members of the Council were not prepared to consider any revision mainly on the ground that the Charter had worked well and there might be some danger in "tampering" with its provisions, and that any alterations would probably be of a minor character. There was also a fear that a Supplemental Charter might arouse opposition and endanger the position of the Institute' (Cash to Bankes, 10 August 1938, 28435/2).

was happening in South Africa while the ACPA was in negotiation with its opponents in Australia (Poullaos 1994, 190–95).

## South Africa 1924–1927

### *The South African Society of Accountants (Private Bill) 1924*

In 1910 the separate colonies of Transvaal, Natal, Cape Colony and the Orange Free State were rolled into the Union of South Africa. In 1913 an unsuccessful attempt was made to create a national accounting association by joining together the 'Union Societies', namely, the Transvaal Society of Accountants (TSA), the Natal Society of Accountants (NSA), the Cape Society of Accountants and Auditors (CSAA) and the Society of Accountants and Auditors in the Orange Free State (SAAOFS).[14] The 1913 bill was similar to its 1924 successor but it differed in containing a list of approved societies (other than the Union societies themselves) whose members could be added to the register of accountants as a matter of right. Societies not included on the list protested and 'the storm raged until it was withdrawn'.[15] In 1924 the Union societies tried again as promoters of the South African Society of Accountants (Private Bill) of 1924. They sought to create a national accountancy body (the South African Society of Accountants) into which they would be folded. It would have powers over public accountancy equivalent to those obtained in the Transvaal and Natal but they would apply to the Cape and the Orange Free State as well (see note 14). The aim of the bill was to 'provide for the registration of persons publicly practising or entitled to practise publicly as accountants in the Union of South Africa so as to distinguish qualified from unqualified persons, and to debar unregistered persons from so publicly practising' (original preamble). This time no list of approved societies was included in the bill. Existing members of the Union Societies would be added to the register automatically. The merits of other bodies would be considered subsequently and provision

14. The TSA was set up under a 1904 ordinance which created a register of persons who could hold themselves out as 'accountant', 'public accountant' or 'auditor' and allowed persons on the register to call themselves 'Registered Public Accountant (Transvaal)'. The TSA was also enabled to determine which foreign accountants could be added to the register without having to satisfy local entry requirements. Members of the British chartered bodies and the SIAA were eventually accorded this privilege, but only after considerably lobbying (see Chua and Poullaos 2002, 425–27). The Natal Accountants Act of 1909, under which the NSA was formed, followed the Transvaal model. In that sense both the TSA and the NSA were 'statutory' bodies but the CSAA and SAAOFS were purely 'voluntary' (although incorporated); that is, they lacked the powers granted to the TSA and NSA.

15. Testimony of Samuel Thompson *(Report of the Select Committee on the South African Society of Accountants (Private Bill), 1924* (hereafter *RSC1924*), 21; copy available in 28457. See also pages 94 and 97.

made for entry of their members under bye-laws. Registrants *could* call themselves 'registered public accountants' and, unless they were members of foreign (e.g., British) associations approved under the proposed Society's future bye-laws,[16] they could not use any other designation—unless it was approved by the Society's council.[17] That was the original plan anyway.

In late 1923 a conference of delegates representing unhappy members of the Union societies met in Johannesburg to develop amendments to the bill to be put to the select committee of Parliament due to consider the bill in the first session of 1924.[18]

> It was the unanimous opinion of the conference that the name [of the proposed society] and designation of members inserted in the Bill was [sic] unsuitable and did not provide for the future generation of accountants a sufficient guarantee that the South African trained and graduated accountant would be recognised as equally qualified with the members of any other Society in the Empire. (Anon. 1924, 3)

The conference resolved that delegates go back to their respective associations and seek specific suggestions to be put to an upcoming conference in Cape Town to be held while Parliament was sitting (ibid.). A special general meeting of CSAA members held on 28 December 1923 suggested that the name of the Society be changed to '"The S.A. Society of Chartered Accountants" and that "Chartered Accountant S.A." be the designation of members', with the CSAA Council being left to carry out the motion as

16. Thus members of the British chartered bodies and the SIAA could designate themselves as 'chartered' or 'incorporated', respectively.

17. Although expressed as a prohibition, this last provision effectively gave the Society's council scope to change the designation usable by the general membership, as the ICAEW and its advisers readily observed.

18. The coverage of the bill here is restricted to issues most directly relevant to the themes of this chapter, the use of 'CA' in particular. Issues not discussed in detail here include: whether the bill was a device for closing off the profession for the benefit of practitioners rather than the public, the merits of service with an accountant in public practice, the rights of entry of government accountants and other accountants not in public practice, the protection of the livelihoods of accountants in practice who were not members of the South African societies as of 1924 and the availability of affordable accountancy services outside the cities (*RSC1924*). Most of these issues had arisen in Britain, Australia and Canada (see Chua and Poullaos 2002, notes 12 and 14, for references). Local issues arose from the fact that, as elsewhere in the imperial accountancy arena, it would be necessary to be relatively open to protect the interests of unaffiliated/'unqualified' accountants in the Cape and the Orange Free State in the early days of the proposed South African Society. Thus, people who would not otherwise have been allowed entry to the TSA or NSA in 1924 could enter the South African society in the Cape or Orange Free State and then move to Natal or the Transvaal. In the end, ongoing disagreement as to the extent of openness of entry into the proposed Society brought about the demise of the bill.

they saw fit (ibid.). The suggestion followed '*the precedent of five separate State Acts of the Dominion of Canada*' (ibid.; emphasis added).[19] By late March 1924 the ICAEW had been informed that the Union societies had all 'by large majorities passed Resolutions in favour of pirating the title "Chartered Accountant"' even though 'the majority of the four Councils are against the proposition'[20] (Markbys to ICAEW, 19 March 1924, in 28457). This expression of desire for (a designation signifying) imperial arena-strength professional status was on par with that of the Australian royal charter–seekers.

The *Memorandum* of January 1924 usefully anticipates claims debated at length before the select committee (in March 1924). It was necessary, claimed the anonymous author, to distinguish between public accountants of 'skill and ability' and those 'unscrupulous persons' who certify 'as correct statements which they have not examined minutely—or worse—which they know to be false' (Anon. 1924, 2). The Union societies had laboured for 15 to 20 years to raise 'the status of S.A. Accountants in the minds of the public', having in recent years co-operated to set up a general examining board whose examinations 'it is generally admitted . . . [are] . . . as difficult as any accountancy test in the Empire' (ibid., 4). Furthermore, the 'training in this country is in every material way equal to and as arduous as the training given in England. . . . In addition . . . a knowledge of certain branches of South African law is required here which an accountant from overseas would not have' (ibid., 6). Why, then, did the South African societies want 'CA'?

> Professional accountants, whatever their Society or status, to a vast number of the uninitiated are believed to be "Chartered Accountants," that name conveying to the man in the street . . . the same meaning as the simple words "Accountant" or "Auditor." "Chartered Accountant" is the hall-mark of the profession, and no other name carries with it the same prestige . . . [In] accountancy . . . the value of an unknown signature can only be gauged by the signatory's qualification or rank. . . . "Chartered Accountant" has become through usage a term . . . denoting efficiency in the art of accountancy. (Ibid., 4, 7)

Why did South Africans not join an existing CA body and what harm would they suffer if they did not?

---

19. It 'was pointed out by one of the members that in Canada five Societies not possessed of a Royal Charter had, by Acts of Parliament, been incorporated under the description of "Chartered Accountants" and it was accordingly proposed that this designation should be recommended for adoption in the place of that of "Registered Accountant". The meeting seized on the suggestion with eagerness and the [proposal] was carried by an overwhelming majority' (Markbys to PCO, 26 March 1924, in CO532/284:14862).

20. Some British CAs were themselves involved in promoting the bill as officers of local associations, while councillors in general were probably aware that the British CA bodies and the CO would protest.

> There is no Chartered Society in South Africa, and before a South African youth can obtain equality with his competitors even in his own country, it is incumbent upon him to proceed to England or Canada and enter into articles . . . for a term of five years in a Chartered Accountant's office and pay a very large premium to his employer there. . . . Why then, should the South African student who may not be able to afford to go to England and live there at his own or his father's expense for five years, or who, for other reasons, cannot go, be for ever forbidden the best fruits of his study and relegated to the rank of a third-rate accountant . . . for it is a fact that many institutions and corporate bodies in England stipulate in their constitutions that their accounts may only be audited by Chartered or Incorporated Accountants. If, and when these institutions open branches in the Union, the members of the South African Society . . . would be ineligible as auditors. . . . [If the bill becomes law then in 15–20 years time] a youth coming out from England having just completed his training and passed his exams, would have a higher status in South Africa than a South African accountant who passed his exams twenty years previously, and has the additional qualification which is only gained in the hard school of experience. (Ibid., 6)

The British and Canadian chartered societies had all adopted 'CA', continues the *Memorandum*, without objection inter se,[21] and the former had no good grounds to complain about their designation being 'filched' so long as the South Africans maintained the highest standards and allowed entry to members of other CA bodies (ibid., 7). The 'established [British] Societies' were exhibiting 'a selfish and short-sighted desire to preclude younger [South African] men from competing with them'. South Africa was 'a new field and a splendid outlet for the surplus of young accountants trained in England' with 'little opportunity for advancement there' and that it was natural for their societies 'to endeavour to keep this promising field of ours as their reserve' (ibid., 5–6). With a discursive finger pointed squarely at the local politicians and their nationalist constituents, the *Memorandum* asked: 'Is South Africa weak enough in its institutions to tolerate such injustice to its youth and manhood?' (ibid., 6).The Australians would have agreed with many elements of the *Memorandum*'s case.[22] Yet they had the support of the British for their royal charter application while the South Africans were on the receiving end of a concerted operation to prevent them from getting

21. Per contra, the ICAEW had complained bitterly about the Canadians before (Chua and Poullaos 2002; Poullaos 2008; cf. van Rensburg, cited in Parker 2005, 32) and would do so again.

22. Australian politicians, both state and federal (national) bureaucrats were so wary of ceding authority over accountancy in Australia that, during the ACPA's first charter attempt, the latter developed a 'neutral' position of neither recommending nor opposing the application. The federal government had claimed for years that it had power to legislate for accountants, the implication being that a

'CA' through local legislation (such as the Canadians had had for decades). The ICAEW was aware of the CSAA's proposed 'chartered accountant S.A.' amendment by the end of January 1924; its secretary declared 'it most unfair and improper for any body of Accountants to endeavour to take a professional designation which indicates in the public mind the status of other Accountants' (ICAEW to Gibson, 31 January 1924, in 28457). Nesbitt began poring over the files on Canada, declaring, 'I do not think that the Canadian legislation should be treated as a precedent'. Reporting back on 4 February, Markbys opined that the objects of the bill *per se* were not objectionable, but the appropriation of 'CA' was 'highly objectionable', the position in Canada was 'very unsatisfactory' and that 'two wrongs do not make a right' (Markbys to ICAEW, 4 February 1924, in 28457).

A hastily forged network consisting of the ICAEW, Markbys and their South African agents Fairbridges, the Scottish and Irish chartered bodies, and individual CAs in South Africa worked feverishly throughout February and March 1924 to lodge petitions against the South African bill and to be represented before the select committee established to review it.[23] They were suspicious of the lack of specific provisions for the entry of British CAs working in South Africa. In March 1924 the SIAA (in London) advised the ICAEW that:

> in the view of both our Cape Town and Johannesburg Agents no Overseas Societies will be recognised in future if the Bill is passed in its present form. I previously communicated the advice of my Council to South Africa by mail. In these circumstances a cable has been sent instructing our Agents to press for recognition by Bye-Law, failing which the Society will oppose the Bill.[24]

---

royal charter from Britain was unnecessary, undesirable or both. Even after the courts and the electorate refused to sanction this view, the neutrality position was maintained well into the 1920s (Poullaos 1994). In short, an Australian equivalent to the South African bill was not feasible. Indeed, it took an unusual combination of factors, most notably the preparedness of Prime Minister Bruce, to set aside neutrality to formally support the ACPA's petition for the ACPA to succeed. Without this move the DO would not have supported it (Poullaos 1994, 195–206, 288). In Canada, the eventual reluctance of federal bureaucrats and politicians to cede authority over local accountants led to the Canadians keeping CA, whereas in Australia over the same period (circa 1908–1913) the same reluctance stopped Australian accountants from gaining it (Poullaos 2008, 31, note 48).

23. See correspondence between Markbys and the ICAEW and the ICAI and ICAEW in 28457; 28420/2, 186–87; JCSMB1, 347–48; SAECMB4, 143–44, 151; SAACMB2, 170–71; ICAIMB2 re Quarterly Council Meeting 14 February 1924. The virtually identical petitions in opposition to the bill submitted on behalf of the ICAEW and A.S. Hooper of Deloitte, Plender, Griffiths, Annan & Co. are available both in 28457 and *RSC1924*. By the end of 1924 the British chartered bodies had spent almost £950 in opposing the bill (JCSMB2, 20–21).

24. SIAA to ICAEW, 7 March 1924. See also Markbys to ICAEW, 28 March 1924, both documents in 28457. The SIAA had branches in South Africa and had

Both the ICAEW (for the British chartered bodies) and the SIAA apparently managed to secure an understanding along the suggested lines (SAECMB4, 156–57; *Incorporated Accountants' Journal*—hereafter *IAJ*—June 1924, 238). The committee was also persuaded to allow appeals to be made to the governor-general by 'any foreign Society aggrieved at its non-recognition in the said bye-laws' (revised section 34 [3]). This would purportedly 'prevent a majority of members in South Africa from endeavouring to exclude such foreign Societies at their discretion' (Markbys to ICAEW, 15 April 1924, in 28457). Sections 6 (1) and 9, furthermore, provided protection from discrimination against (among others) British CAs already resident in South Africa who had not already joined one of the Union societies, by providing that they could apply to the provisional council of the proposed South African society for entry within nine months from the enactment of the bill; with the Union auditor-general sitting on the provisional council along with another person, nominated by the Minister of the Interior, from those not entitled to membership of the proposed body; both appointees ostensibly keeping watch over the fairness of the council's deliberations.[25] The committee also rejected the suggestion that the proposed body be called a 'Society of Chartered Accountants'.[26] The big-ticket item, however, as far as the British chartered bodies were concerned, was the appropriation of 'CA'.

The major supporting arguments for 'CA South Africa' presented to the committee were those anticipated by the *Memorandum* of 9 January 1924, as noted earlier. There were some interesting twists, however. The appeal of 'chartered' was in part a reflection of the failure of 'registered'. Allegedly it: 'has never been popular' (*RSC1924*, 46); 'resembled too much . . . that you had to register a dog and to put "registered" in front of your name was not very nice' (ibid., 83); 'was not a nice sounding title' (ibid., 113); had been a 'dismal failure', rarely used by those overseas accountants who had joined local associations and dropped 'altogether' by many locals (ibid., 134)—'no one was wholly in love with it' (ibid., 172; but compare 186). Second, N.S. Wood, a prominent CSAA member and trenchant advocate for 'Chartered Accountant (South Africa)' ('CASA'),[27] claimed that *some*

---

been heavily involved in the formation of the TSA (Johnson and Caygill 1971). The South African branches ran examinations and SIAA members could take on apprentices locally. The simplest way for British CAs to do likewise was to join the SIAA, given that they had been forbidden by their 'home' associations from doing so (Cooper Brothers to ICAEW, 5 January 1926, enclosing letter from G.H. Fry, 3 January 1926, in 28457; Chua and Poullaos 2002; Poullaos 2009a).

25. However, members of foreign accounting associations admitted in the future would be required to pass an examination in South African law (revised section 18 [1] [b]).

26. There is, surprisingly, very little debate about the name of the proposed society in *RSC1924*.

27. An immigrant from Britain (ibid., 134) and a possible candidate for the anonymous author of the *Memorandum*.

*British CAs/overseas accountants and incorporated accountants were supporting him* (ibid., 138; emphasis added). He even claimed that 'CASA' 'was not my original suggestion at all: three chartered accountants [had] suggested that all the members of the four societies should be taken in and called "chartered accountants"' (ibid., 149). Third, British CAs involved in the governance of the Union societies were put in the difficult position of arguing for 'CASA'. According to Markbys the:

> four principal witnesses called by the Promoters, one from each Province, were all Chartered Accountants and although each put forward the contention of his Society . . . they individually when cross examined did not approve of the assumption [of 'CA'] while sheltering themselves under the opinion that if the words 'South Africa' were added they did not think there would be any confusion or injustice. (Markbys to ICAEW, 8 April 1924, in 28457)

Fourth, like the Australians and Canadians before them, the supporters of the bill used the opportunity to probe the prospects of reciprocity with the British chartered bodies (*RSC1924*, 123–24, 154, 176–77, 193–94, 207–8 and 250). The reply was that exact reciprocity was not feasible as the British bodies, being 'voluntary' bodies (which did not administer a state-sanctioned register that public accountants had to join) were different from the South African statutory bodies (which did—see *RSC1924*, 61–63, 94 and 231). The British could neither include nor exclude the South Africans on/from a register but they (the British) could not work in South Africa if the bill was enacted unless they were on a South African register. (What the proponents of 'CASA' wanted, of course, was the designation itself, for use in South Africa.) Fifth, the belated knowledge that the Canadians had acquired 'CA' by legislation not only put them on the South African accountancy map; it also provided a long-established exemplar and strengthened the claim that a 'charter' could be given under legislation (as opposed to the argument that the only real charter was one obtained in Britain at the discretion of authorities in the imperial centre), a position that the proponents of 'CASA' wanted to make in any case (see *RSC1924*, 123, 149, 174–75, 195, 198 and 252).

The opponents of 'CASA' (not all of whom were British CAs) put forth a suite of related propositions. The supporters of 'CASA' were unfairly or unscrupulously taking advantage of the hard work put in by British bodies and their members over many years in raising standards and establishing reputation. In improperly seeking equivalence to the British bodies (through their adoption of 'CA') they would cause confusion or, worse still, be misleading or deceptive. It was up to South Africans to work hard to make their own reputations under their own designation. The provisions of entry to the proposed South African society were so generous that it was inevitable that 'incompetents' would gain 'CA', thereby defeating the purpose of the bill and lowering the standing of the designation generally.[28] And while local examinations might be sufficiently arduous, there was no general provision for five years of service under articles (as per the British bodies), and the training opportunities were not as great in South Africa given the greater sophistication of British industry and commerce. That is, the standard of training was lower in South Africa. In response, the proponents of 'CASA' claimed that: 'CA' had gained a generic status as the 'hallmark' of high-quality accountancy throughout the dominions;[29] that it was not the possession of the British bodies alone (as Canada had shown) and that it was unfair to South African accountants (young ones in particular) that they be excluded from the top ranks of imperial accountancy, even in their own country, irrespective of the quality of their qualification and work; the ICAEW's charter restricted its authority to England and Wales;[30] the addition of 'SA' would preclude or limit any deception or error of interpretation (*vis-à-vis* the public) or unfairness to British CAs; the ICAEW's borrowing of 'CA' from the Scots was comparable to the South Africans borrowing it from the British; and that the ICAEW had had itself to open its doors widely in its early days—it was the long-term future of public accountancy in South Africa that the bill was trying to secure. There was considerable debate about the extent to which it was the accounting association (representing the occupational group) or the individual that determined the success of the designation (or vice versa).[31]

Consequentially, there was sharp disagreement as to the extent of the economic loss suffered by South African accountants because they did not have 'CA'. Proponents—and some critics—of 'CASA' claimed/conceded that 'the public' or the local business sector or British capitalists investing in South Africa were, other things being equal, likely to prefer a 'CA' to a non-'CA', whether they were knowledgeable about providers of accountancy services or not—notwithstanding that there were many non-CAs who had had successful careers (see *RSC1924*, 57, 137, 142–51, 155, 161–66, 173, 200, 204–5, 249, 251–54). Wood even claimed to have used a CA himself 'when I wanted someone to represent my firm in this country' (ibid., 144). Critics tended to deflect the success of CAs (and non-CAs for that matter) to their personal qualities or training rather than their access to 'CA' (or

---

28. The original bill tried to deal with this issue by establishing the category of 'statutory' accountants but the select committee effectively excised it. It is also worth noting that the London Association of Accountants (LAA) participated in the committee's review as an advocate of openness (*RSC1924*, especially 223–39).

29. Per contra, a memorandum prepared by a group of public accountants as of 6 August 1924 (in 28457) described 'CA' as being more like a 'private trade-mark' than a (generic) 'hall-mark'.

30. A point also highlighted in Australia and Canada (Chua and Poullaos 2002; Poullaos 2008).

31. For articulation and contestation of these various positions see *RSC1924* (47–52, 57, 60–61, 67, 83–85, 93, 98–100, 114–16, 118, 134, 136, 139, 141–51, 155, 163–64, 171–76, 186–93, 194, 197–208, 244–49, 253–55).

not) *per se* (e.g., see ibid., 173, 189, 191–92, 199–205, 245–46). In order to highlight the diversity and nuances of opinion on this matter, the last word may be left to Mr. D.M. Brown, a British CA with a local practice (in the Cape) and a South African politician to boot. He thought it foolish to deny the market value of 'CA': 'the word "Chartered" carries weight and very great weight'. He gave one example from his own experience where 'a most competent man' but not a CA would have lost 'an audit for an English firm' if he (Brown) had not signed the audit certificate as a CA. He had also heard from fellow public accountants of five audits being lost (two of which he labelled 'English audits') because of 'CA'-lack (*RSC1924*, 251). He also referred to a court case where a 'licensed . . . practising accountant in Cape Town was refused expert fees and only paid the ordinary witness's fee on the ground that he was not a Chartered Accountant' (ibid., 251–52).[32]

Brown also had a reply to the argument (ibid., 162, 171–72, 191) that the market value of 'CA' could be seen to be exaggerated from the fact that the number of CAs in South Africa was tiny in relation to the total number of public accountants in South Africa (28 out of 554 overall, ibid., 139, 191–92). Responding with respect to Cape Town (with three CAs) Brown remarked: 'Look at the class of business they are doing. These firms have a reputation and do good business' (ibid., 255). The implication was that the CAs got the lucrative work. Presumably, 'English audits' fell into this category. His overall judgment was that 'South Africa has suffered through not having it ['CA'] as against their British opponents' (ibid.). And yet he was *opposed* to 'CASA': 'I think we can establish our own name . . . [subject] to other men not coming in and flaunting a flag larger than South Africa's' (ibid., 254). What, then, was his solution to South African accountants' deficiency of symbolic capital? There were two parts. First, pick a local designation and make everybody use it, and it only, even CAs: 'Take it ['CA'] off the brass plates and letter paper, and their merits will carry them through' (ibid., 255). Second, press offshore CA bodies for reciprocity: if they didn't recognize the South African qualification then South Africa shouldn't recognize theirs (ibid., 250).

Notwithstanding Brown's views, the select committee reported as of 1 April 1924 that it had agreed to the bill 'with certain amendments', one of them being the replacement of 'Registered Public Accountant' with 'Chartered Accountant (South Africa)' (ibid., v). The amended bill still had to be formally passed by Parliament before it became law.

In the week before the select committee came out with its recommendation, Markbys in London wrote to the PCO on the ICAEW's behalf, pointing out the past and proposed misdeeds of the Canadians and South

32. When the prospect of 'CA' for South African accountants came up again in 1926–1927 the promoters went to some trouble to identify further cases of economic hardship attributable to 'CA'-deficiency. See Union of South Africa House of Assembly (1927)—hereafter *RSC1927*—(8–10, 13–16, 20, 22–26, 39, 43–44, 47–49, 58–59).

Africans with respect to 'CA' and suggesting that it 'indicate to the proper Authorities in South Africa that no body of persons should be empowered to use the word "Chartered" unless they are entitled to do so by virtue of a Royal Charter granted by His Majesty' (Markbys to PCO, 26 March 1924, in CO532/284:14862). The PCO immediately referred the matter to the CO. Nesbitt interviewed seemingly sympathetic PCO and CO staff trying to move things along (Markbys to ICAEW, 27 and 28 March 1924, in 28457). This was an important play. The PCO and CO were the vehicles through which the formal might of the imperial centre might be directed at the colonial periphery. On 1 April Nesbitt again pressed the PCO to take action, having heard that the South African select committee was favouring 'CASA', and the very next day Markbys wrote again to the PCO confirming the committee's support for 'CASA' (Markbys to ICAEW, 2 April 1924; Markbys to PCO, 1 and 2 April 1924, in 28457 and CO532/284:14862). On 2 April Nesbitt wrote to the CO noting (*inter alia*) that the Australian royal charter application, having given the British chartered bodies the opportunity to 'safeguard the privileges, rights and interests of [their] members', was 'the course which should be pursued by Accountants in any other part of the Empire who desire ['CA']' (Markbys to CO, 2 April 1924, in 28457). On the same day, however, Markbys reported to the ICAEW the gloomy news that a senior CO official they had interviewed was having:

> great difficulty with regard to the legislation which has already been passed in Canada: . . . [The CO] had made representations . . . in 1908 and 1910, but without any good result; in fact he told us privately that [those representations] . . . appear only to have stiffened the back of the Colonial legislature and inasmuch as the Canadian Accountants have secured the designation by Statute the [CO] are in great difficulty about putting forward a good and valid reason why the Accountants in South Africa should not acquire a similar designation. (Markbys to ICAEW, 2 April 1924, in 28457)

A week later the CO confirmed that the 'correspondence relating to this Canadian legislation which took place some years ago with the [ICAEW] and the Canadian Government has been carefully reviewed and the Secretary of State regrets to inform you that having regard to all the circumstances he doesn't feel that he could usefully intervene in the matter' (CO to Markbys, 9 April 1924, in 28457). As Nesbitt of Markbys had feared, the Canadian legislation *was* being used as a precedent. Deloittes (Johannesburg) were similarly of the view that 'an attempt to move through the [CO] to get the Bill vetoed by the Governor General would, we are afraid, be impracticable under the present constitutional conditions' (Deloittes to ICAEW, 24 April 1924; see also Markbys to ICAEW, 26 April 1924, in 28457). The view of both Fairbridges and Deloittes in South Africa was that the lobbying efforts had achieved as much as was achievable under the circumstances. There seemed little prospect of (even future British CA immigrants) being excluded while the addition of 'South Africa' after 'CA' would offer reasonable protection (ibid.). The addition was reportedly supported by the 'more moderate members' of the select committee while the 'Nationalist and Labour Members' wanted 'CA' without the 'SA'. The moderates had won out 'and for this small mercy we must be as thankful as we can' (Deloittes to ICAEW, 24 April 1924, in 28457). A.S. Hooper of Deloittes (Cape Town), heavily involved in the lobbying, found another silver lining: 'there is no doubt that Chartered Accountants have never had so fine an advertisement in this country before' (Deloittes to ICAEW, 14 April 1924, enclosing letter from Hooper, 28 March 1924, in 28457).

From this point on, however, the British chartered bodies were on the back foot as far as intervention in South African accountancy politics was concerned. In late April 1924 Markbys had little doubt that the bill would 'pass into law in the near future' (Markbys to ICAEW, 26 April 1924, in 28457). Fairbridges advice (circa early June 1924) was not to oppose further, pending the outcome of the forthcoming South African election and further moves by the bill's promoters (Markbys to ICAEW, 5 May 1924, in 28457), while Deloittes (Johannesburg) had advised that further opposition would be 'fruitless' (Deloittes, London, to ICAEW, 30 June 1924, in 28457). In November 1924 the Scots were also of the view that nothing further could be done, having been advised by a South African CA that 'it would be wiser to let well alone so far as the Chartered Societies were concerned' (JCSMB2, 4).

*Nevertheless*, the momentum in favour of the bill dissipated as the local state–profession relationship deteriorated. The dynamic was mostly internal to South Africa.[33] The select committee added a new section 19, specifying conditions under which government accountants could be placed on the proposed register. In broad terms what was at issue here was: how wide would the door be opened? Section 19 was a particular expression of the broader view, pushed hard by Labour members on the select committee and the LAA that (a) accountants not in public practice and (b) public accountants who were not members of the South African societies should be given the greatest possible scope (i.e., the least conditionality) for entry into the proposed Union society. The statutory societies (the TSA and NSA) were also put under heavy pressure to 're-open their registers', that is, to let in (b) if not (a) on the same generous terms as the CSAA and the SAAOFS. The stresses involved were ramped up after a Nationalist-Labour coalition swept to power in June 1924 under Herzog. A resident British CA later colourfully alluded to (i) the 'the Nationalists hatred of the "imported snobs" as they genially call us' and (ii) 'the Labour hatred of any monopoly other than that of a Labour Union'

33. However, the LAA was involved. The LAA was a relatively low-status body which followed the SIAA's lead in developing an active imperial policy to compensate for the dominance of the chartered bodies and the SIAA at 'home' (Johnson and Caygill 1971; Parker 1989, 2005; Briston and Kedslie 1997). It is a predecessor to today's Association of Chartered Certified Accountants (ACCA).

(Cooper Brothers to ICAEW, 5 January 1926, enclosing letter from G.H. Fry, 3 January 1926, in 28457). In light of (i), the British chartered societies were well advised to keep their heads down; while (ii) amplified the pressure on the TSA and NSA. Eventually they buckled under the strain.[34] On 1 December 1925, the *IAJ* (85) publicly reported 'private advice' that the bill had been withdrawn. A fortnight later Deloittes (London) wrote to the ICAEW, passing on the views of Deloittes (Johannesburg) that the bill was 'dead':

> Both the [TSA and NSA] have by extraordinary resolutions of their members, decided to withdraw from further participation in the measure, owing to the amendments which have been introduced, or which were threatened to be introduced, of a nature seriously undermining the position of accountants already registered in those two provinces . . .
>
> The net result therefore of this unfortunate venture is that the various South African Societies have spent practically the whole of their funds and have achieved nothing.
>
> In view of this financial outcome, it may be safely taken for granted that in future no private attempt will be made to promote legislation of a similar nature at any rate for many years to come. (Deloittes to ICAEW, 15 December 1925)[35]

Not for the first time, a player close to the action had made a bad call, as will be shown later. A succession of linked events cascaded over each other, pushing the ICAEW into applying for a supplemental charter.

### *Aftermath of the 1924 Bill: Formation of Institutes of Chartered Accountants 'South Africa Ltd' by CAs resident in South Africa*

The day after Deloittes (London) wrote to inform the ICAEW of the death of the bill they wrote again, enclosing a letter from Deloittes (Johannesburg), to say that another movement was alive. Its starting premise was:

> that it is the avowed intention of the general body of accountants in South Africa to obtain the designation 'chartered accountant' by hook or by crook, and as evidence of this we are informed that, in the event

34. See (from 28457): Union House of Assembly debates 1 and 8 August 1924; Markbys to ICAEW, 26 April 1924; Deloittes (London) to ICAEW, 30 June and 23 September 1924; memoranda re the (South African) Accountants Registration Bill by 'Saml. Thomson, Chartered Accountant' and Walker, Jacobsohn & Le Roux, 'Parliamentary Agents for the Promoters' of 4 and 7 August 1924 respectively; Brown to ICAEW, 10 September 1924; NSA Annual Report of Council for 1924–1925, 13 February 1925; and Deloittes (Cape Town) to Deloittes (London,) 12 June 1925. See also report of ICAEW Parliamentary and Law Committee re meeting of 7 January 1926 (ICAEWC10).

35. See also Deloittes to ICAEW, 16 December 1925 (both documents in 28457).

of the Bill being rejected, the Cape Society . . . had intended to apply to Parliament to obtain the right to call their members 'Chartered Accountants, South Africa'. As a consequence certain members of the British Societies of Chartered Accountants resident in Johannesburg, in an endeavour to protect the indiscriminate use of their title, have registered separate Limited Companies under the name of the Institute of Chartered Accountants in South Africa, in each of the four provinces of the Union, viz: Transvaal, Cape, Free State and Natal. . . .

Before proceeding . . . resident Chartered Accountants wish to obtain the views and, if possible, the approval of their Home Societies. They are anxious not to encroach upon the rights of the Home Societies to ['CA'] . . .

[Their] object . . . is to safeguard the title from indiscriminate adoption and to ensure its being confined to themselves (all home Chartered Accountants) and to such *practising* [original emphasis] members of the profession as they choose to admit by virtue of their experience and qualifications.

Needless to say the promoters would rather not admit any such outside accountants at all if they could possibly avoid it, but it is felt that by such expedient alone is it possible to satisfy the growing demand in this country [for 'CA'] and so stave off its much wider and indiscriminate bestowal by legislation.

It is realised that the Home Societies may possibly be unable to take up any attitude other than to say that they cannot "sanction" the proposed course. We, both here and in Cape Town, identified ourselves with the scheme in its early stages when it was proposed to confine membership to home Chartered Accountants only; now that the scheme has expanded . . . into one involving the granting of the title to approved others the promoters would like to know that the home bodies will at least not "object" to the proposal. (Deloittes, London, to ICAEW, 16 December 1925, enclosing letter from Deloittes, Johannesburg, 18 November 1925, in 28457)

Samuel Thomson, a Scottish CA and chairman of the CA companies, also wrote to the ICAEW (and other British chartered bodies) and expressed similar arguments. He also provided useful background. The chairman and secretary of the Transvaal branch of the SIAA had tried to set up an accountants' society under the companies act which could grant 'CA' but had been rejected 'on the ground, it is understood, that the applicants were not chartered accountants'. Furthermore, one of the South African societies (probably the CSAA) had expressed an intention to alter their constitution so that they could use 'CA'. It was in this context that the British CAs had formed the CA companies.[36] And, reflecting the division between CAs

36. Thomson to ICAEW, 30 November 1925 (28457). Thomson noted that the legal adviser to the Crown in the Transvaal had insisted that the Transvaal CA company be restricted to British CAs on the grounds that only members of societies

evident in *RSC1924*, Thomson reported that at a meeting of CAs held in Johannesburg to discuss the CA company proposal, the majority held that 'CA' has, in English-speaking countries:

> come to have a dictionary significance, meaning a highly trained professional accountant; that local practitioners are prejudiced when they have to deny in public, membership of a Chartered Society and acknowledge a designation which does not carry the same weight though earned in the same way; that if the coveted title is placed within the reach of those who have qualified by training and examination it will be a strong incentive to the younger men to support the Chartered Accountants in their endeavours to raise the status of the profession in this country; and that as the title is used by nine Societies in Canada and is being agitated for *in Australia*[37] there seems to be no real objection to its use in South Africa. In support . . . they quoted the opinion of a leading K.C. [Kings Counsel] obtained by the promoters of the [1924] Bill. His opinion was that there was no legal objection as the British Institutes have no legal standing in this country and therefore could not interfere.
>
> Some strongly supported the views expressed by the Legal Adviser to the Crown [in the Transvaal—see note 36] . . . and held that it would be an act of piracy to use the term, even with the addition 'SOUTH AFRICA', and morally indefensible. (Thomson to ICAEW, 30 November 1925, in 28457)

The British CAs were reprising the 1924 debate but presuming that their claim was more legitimate than that of the Union societies precisely because they were CAs. As Markbys noted in December 1925 the actions of the British CAs had placed the ICAEW 'very much on the horns of a dilemma'. If the South African CA companies admitted (as was proposed):

> persons who are not Chartered Accountants in the sense of being Members of [the British chartered societies] and such a course is sanctioned by [those societies], it may be used as an argument all over the world that the expression 'Chartered Accountant' in its original and proper sense . . . has been abandoned and is to be used as being practically equivalent to Public Accountant. (Markbys to ICAEW, 21 December 1925, in 28457)

---

incorporated under royal charter could validly use 'CA'—the ICAEW's perennial argument to anyone who would listen. Presumably this was the same adviser who knocked back the application of the chairman and secretary of the SIAA Transvaal branch.

37. Emphasis added. The South African end of the imperial grapevine was now linked to Australia (there having being no awareness of the Australian charter application in *RSC1924*).

In short, the stakes were high. The British CAs were effectively asking the British chartered bodies to abandon the last rhetorical weapon in their armoury against the appropriation of 'CA'. Were they prepared to do so? As the ICAEW Parliamentary and Law Committee (chaired by Plender of Deloittes) put it in January 1926, 'approval of this step':

> would be directly opposed to the present policy of the Council, which is to protect the title Chartered Accountant throughout the British Empire and elsewhere, communications on this matter being in fact in progress with the Board of Trade on the subject of the unauthorised use of the expression 'Chartered Accountant' by Chinese in China. (Report re meeting of 7 January 1926, in ICAEWC10)

Consistent with this view, the ICAEW's reply to Johnson stated categorically that the council:

> dissent entirely from any suggestion that the words ['CA'] have obtained a secondary or dictionary meaning representing merely a certain standard of qualification. They must insist and maintain that ['CA'] means and means only a member of a body incorporated by Royal Charter . . .
>
> [Further] . . . the voluntary association of members of such bodies with other persons not being members of the same or in an association containing provisions which would enable other persons to be come associated with them is open to the strongest objection as tending to mislead the public. (Markbys to ICAEW, 12 January 1926, in 28457)

The Scottish and Irish chartered bodies agreed (See JCSMB2, 107–9; ICAIMB2 re meeting of 17 February 1926). In short: while the British CAs in South Africa felt that they were protecting British 'CA', the chartered bodies in the imperial centre felt that CAs were behaving like the non-CAs in seeking to water down the meaning and value of 'CA'. In taking this position, the ICAEW may have been influenced by information and opinion from CAs in South Africa. G.H. Fry (of Cooper Brothers) claimed, among other things, that the CA companies were bound to lead to a reaction from those excluded, that the Nationalist and Labour politicians would be sympathetic and that, inevitably, the 1924 bill would be revived:

> Parliament will note that we have abandoned our claim to the designation as a proprietary brand and acquiesced in the Bill's supporters' view that it is a hall mark: if we grant this, surely Parliament is better entitled to regulate its use than a handful of individuals who happen to have obtained it for themselves elsewhere.[38]

38. Fry to Cooper Brothers (London), 3 January 1926, enclosed in Cooper Brothers to ICAEW, 5 January 1926 (both in 28457).

In February 1926, a Mr. B. Halsey was interviewed in London. Among other things, he observed that, although wishing to retain their ICAEW membership in South Africa (and 'CA'), practicality (e.g., access to articled clerks) dictated that they join the SIAA, the members of which, he suspected, secretly harboured a desire for 'CA'. The CSAA was, in addition, likely to try again to get it through legislation. Under the circumstances he felt that:

> it is absolutely imperative that the Institute should obtain further powers. [Having asked] him why the Accountants in South Africa did not apply for a Charter themselves . . . his reply was that they had been legally advised that they had to apply for one to the Governor General. Mr. Halsey is wrong, as a matter of practice, for the Australian Accountants are at this moment applying to the Privy Council for a Royal Charter. It is probably not wrong in practice [however] because a Royal Charter would only be granted if there were a recommendation from the local Governor and this, in the present circumstances would probably not be forthcoming in South Africa. (Meeting notes, 1 February 1925, in 28457)

The reference to 'taking further powers' was in effect a recommendation that the ICAEW revive its supplemental charter process. The 'present circumstances' were that it was extremely unlikely that the Nationalist-Labour government would have supported a South African royal charter application,[39] particularly as the Union societies did, indeed, seek 'CA' through legislation.

### *The South African Designation Bill 1927*

In early May 1926, S.C. Carruthers, the secretary of the South African CA companies, wrote to the ICAEW, enclosing a copy of a private bill promoted by the Union societies and adding that as 'others have taken steps to obtain ['CA'] . . . it seems useless to spend any more of our money to protect the name' (Carruthers to ICAEW, 7 May 1926, in 28457). The short bill basically provided that members of the Union societies[40] on the one hand, and the British chartered bodies and the SIAA on the other, could use 'CASA'—so long as the latter group continued to be recognized under the bye-laws of the former. Anyone else who tried to do so would be guilty

39. Even the relatively tame Australian (federal) government was still unprepared to support the Australian charter application at this time (see note 22).

40. The non-CAs in the Cape, led by N.S. Wood, seem to have been particularly desperate to get 'CA'. At the same time as the designation bill was being promoted, Wood and others had registered a Society of Chartered Accountants in the Province of the Cape of Good Hope (SCAPGH) in March 1926. Hooper of Deloittes (Cape Town) tried, unsuccessfully, to stop the registration (Carruthers to ICAEW, 27 April 1926, in 28457). SCAPGH's fortunes are not tracked in detail here. It became irrelevant once the designation bill gained momentum (Deloittes to ICAEW, 31 May 1926, in 28457).

of an offence and liable on conviction to be fined. That is, it was a designation bill not a registration bill. By the end of May, Plender had forwarded to the ICAEW advice from Deloittes (Johannesburg) that, should the bill become law:

> the home Chartered bodies and their various members in this country will be powerless in the matter, as, with the present development of the constitutional relationship between Great Britain and the Dominions, it is scarcely to be expected that the Government at home would be willing to instruct the Governor-General here to veto any such measure.[41]

The 'present development' referred to was the build-up to the 1926 Imperial Conference, with South African Prime Minister Herzog pushing for a clear statement of the autonomy of the dominions from the imperial centre (see Fairbridges to Markbys, 21 January 1927, in 28457; Dawson 1965).

In June/July/August 1926 the British chartered bodies reactivated the network which had fought the 1924 bill[42] notwithstanding that the chances of keeping 'CA' to themselves were slim (Markbys to ICAEW, 3 August 1926, ICAEW to Deloittes, 11 August 1926, in 28457; JCSMB2, 132–33). In November, Hooper, Fairbridges and Mars (the Kings Counsel used in 1924) all agreed that outright opposition might provoke the promoters into removing 'South Africa' from the designation and that it would be wise to negotiate with the promoters to forestall this possibility (Deloittes, Cape Town, to Deloittes, London, 26 November 1926 in 28457). In January 1927 it became clear that the PCO, although very supportive of the argument that 'CA' not based on a royal charter was illegitimate, could not budge the DO, especially now that the Balfour declaration had been made public. 'The attitude of the [DO] appears to be that the respective Dominion Legislatures can practically do as they please and that the assent of the [DO] to any legislation is almost a matter of course' (Markbys to ICAEW, 5 January 1927; see also PCO to Markbys, 3 January 1927, in 28457). The British chartered bodies were running out of leverage. In late January Fairbridges even advised against aggressively pushing the maintenance of 'South Africa' ('SA'), so strong was the feeling locally that 'SA' should be removed. Hooper wanted assurance that if 'SA' was dropped and the British CAs were still able to add 'England', 'Scotland' (etc.) to their designations, that their home societies would not object. (That way they could still be distinguished from South African CAs.) Alternately if the bill was changed to require everybody (including British CAs) to use 'CASA' only, would the home societies be agreeable? Under the

---

41. Deloittes (Johannesburg) to Plender, 12 May 1926, enclosed in Plender to ICAEW, 31 May 1926 (28457).

42. See (for example) from 28457: JCCASS to ICAEW, 5 June and 10 June 1926; ICAEW to JCCCASS, 7 June 1926; ICAI to ICAEW, 7 June 1926; and Markbys to ICAEW, 19 July 1926. See also JCSMB2 (124–25).

circumstances, it was preferable not to oppose the bill for the time being. If the version approved by the forthcoming select committee or Parliament was objectionable then the British bodies could press for a new bill altogether (Markbys to ICAEW, 20 January 1927, Fairbridges to Markbys, 21 February 1927, in 28457). The ICAEW agreed, on behalf of all the British CA bodies (Markbys to ICAEW, 24 January 1927, in 28457).

By the time Hooper and the British chartered bodies completed their petitions opposing the bill (as of 11 February 1927), their only substantive complaint was that the penalty provisions of section 1(2) did not seem to catch the case of an accountant entitled to use 'CASA' who just used 'CA' (i.e., dropped 'SA').[43] The ICAEW also followed advice that it should not join those excluded from using 'CA' in opposing the bill for fear of provoking retaliation (the Union societies could remove the British societies from their approved lists—see Fairbridges to Markbys, 8 and 18 February 1927, in 28457). And, although the promoters of the bill conceded the deficiency in section 1(2) they began to stonewall rather than move to fix it, leading Fairbridges to speculate that the deficiency was deliberate.[44] Only under the pressure of a select committee and subsequent parliamentary debate did the promoters relent in order to minimize opposition to the bill.[45]

By the end of February 1927 it was clear that the largely local movement to maximize openness of entry to the register in 1924 was still strong. With respect to the 1927 bill it translated into a movement to (a) extend 'CA' much more widely than the Union societies had anticipated, and (b) to loosen entry to those bodies.[46] Consequently, the bill was not enacted until June 1927 (Deloittes [Cape Town] to ICAEW, 10 June 1927, in 28457). Overall, the British chartered bodies had barely managed to maintain the extant status of their own members, let alone keep 'CA' to themselves. It had become clear, furthermore, that in the future they would have to tread very softly in South Africa, as highlighted all too starkly when the South Africans started to focus on the ICAEW's supplemental charter process. It had been rolling for over a year before the designation bill became law and had been made public the month before.

43. See *RSC1927* (appendix iii–v); also Fairbridges to Markbys, 8 February 1927, both documents in 28457.

44. Fairbridges to Markbys, 18 February 1927 (28457). The suspicion was subsequently confirmed (Fairbridges to Markbys, 25 February 1927, in 28457).

45. Negotiations with the promoters and the select committee eventually resulted in amendments removing the deficiency in the penalty provisions and protecting the rights of CAs coming to South Africa in the future (Markbys to ICAEW, 21 and 28 March 1927, Deloittes [Cape Town] to ICAEW, 25 March 1927, *RSC1927*, xv–xvi, all in 28457). As the Scots pointed out, however, it was still possible for a 'CA' created by legislation (e.g., Canadian) to just use 'CA' without adding 'South Africa' so long at the relevant association was recognized by one of the South African societies (JCSMB3, 8).

46. See, for example, *RSC1927* and the material on Pearce's bill in 28457. The LAA was again involved in trying to expand the range of people entitled to use 'CA'.

## The ICAEW's Supplemental Charter and the Self-Governing Dominions 1926–1930

In March 1926 the ICAEW secretary suggested it was time to think again about a supplemental charter to extend its examination and articles arrangements offshore (Colville to unnamed recipients, possibly ICAEW councillors, 17 March 1926, in 28457). He specifically cited the 1924 South African bill and 'cases recently reported to the Parliamentary and Law Committee in which Foreigners have adopted the title "Chartered Accountant", and to its being impossible for this Institute to take legal action to prevent them using the title'.[47]

In April 1926 the matter was referred to the general purposes committee (28411/9, 113) which duly set up a subcommittee to consider the matter (28416/5, 154). The frantic South African attempts to attain 'CA' hurried things along. By mid-May the ICAEW had heard of the formation of the SCAPGH (see note 40) and was rallying the troops for another protest to the PCO (ICAEW to ICAI and JCCASS, 19 May 1926; ICAI and JCCASS to ICAEW, 21 May 1926, in 28457). The SCAPGH project caused the ICAEW president for 1926–1927, Sir Arthur Whinney, 'considerable perturbation' and accentuated 'the urgency of the question of the supplemental charter'.[48] By early June 1926 the South African designation bill had also been incorporated into the proposed protest to the PCO; along with the unsuccessful 1924 South African bill, ICAF (see note 47), the Chinese—and even the Canadians with Alberta being mentioned specifically, notwithstanding that the Association of Chartered Accountants of Alberta (AACA) had been incorporated 16 years earlier.[49] The PCO referred the matter to the DO, which replied in late July 1926. Internally the DO pored over its unsuccessful attempts to influence the Canadians in 1911 and the South Africans in 1924 and concluded that it 'is quite obvious that in view of the constitutional position of the Dominions, we can do nothing in the way of helping the Institute in this matter' (Minutes to DO35/6:D6358; see also copy letter to PCO, 31 July 1926).

---

47. The most notable case was China. See Markbys to ICAEW, 8 and 29 August 1924 (ICAEWC10); JCSMB2, 12, 24, 88; 28416/5, 114–15; 282420/2, 204, 216; *Accountant*, 9 May 1925, 755–60; ICAEW Parliamentary and Law Committee, 7 January 1926 (ICAEWC10); ICAEW Annual Report for 1925 (ICAEWC10); *Accountant*, 8 May 1926, 664–69; also Xu and Xu (2003). See also the correspondence in 28456 on the Institute of Chartered Accountants (California), hereafter ICAF.

48. Whinney to Carruthers, 19 May 1926 (28457). Whinney was also on the general purposes committee subcommittee referred to earlier, as was Plender of Deloittes (London).

49. JCCASS to ICAEW, 5 June 1926; ICAEW to JCCASS, 7 June 1926; ICAI to ICAEW, 7 June 1926; ICAEW 'Memorandum re the use of the word "CHARTERED" for consideration of the PCO', 10 June 1926 (all in 28457); see also JCSMB2 (122–26). The ICAEW complained of ICAF that it 'has been formed on a purely commercial and voluntary basis' and that under its bye-laws '[m]embers are entitled to use the initials "F.C.A." and "A.C.A."'.

With the DO unwilling/incapable of intervening in a rapidly deteriorating situation in South Africa (from the ICAEW's point of view), Whinney addressed the institute's Autumnal meeting in October 1926. Covering the same ground as the ICAEW's memorandum to the PCO, he referred to 'the improper and misleading use in foreign countries and in the Dominions of the word "Chartered" by members of Societies or Associations which are not incorporated by Royal Charter'. The efforts of the South Africans, the Chinese, the Canadians (e.g., Alberta) and the promoters of ICAF were not only 'unfair . . . but also calculated to mislead and deceive the public who are thus led to believe that they are dealing with a member of a body which has established a reputation for efficiency, honour and fair dealing' (*Accountant*, 23 October 1926, 563). He also hinted that a possible solution was brewing:

> I should remind you that by the terms of our Charter, our operations, and the jurisdiction of the Council, are confined to England and Wales. No doubt at the time when the Charter was obtained, it was little thought that Chartered Accountants would be practising in all parts of the world. There is little doubt that the fact that our operations were confined to England and Wales was in order to meet the wishes of the Scotch bodies. Since those days however, the ever-increasing employment of British capital in all parts of the world has caused the Chartered Accountant's practice to become world-wide. This gives rise to many questions of difficulty, all of which are engaging the attention of the Council, and it may be that a way will be found of strengthening our position in this connection. (Ibid.)

By late October 1926 the ICAEW had been advised that:

> any application which may be made for a Supplemental Charter will in no way imperil or affect the existing Charter, but will be considered and dealt with entirely on its merits. The Officials at the Privy Council are most willing, and indeed anxious, to assist Chartered bodies to obtain all the powers which may be regarded as necessary for the proper conduct of their affairs. There are precedents for such a Supplemental Charter as is suggested and any opposition could only come from some body which might consider that it was injuriously affected by the further powers asked for, such opposition would have to be by means of a formal Petition to the Privy Council of which due notice would be given to the Institute.[50]

50. File memorandum, 25 October 1926, in 28457. The memorandum deals with a number of other issues not relevant to this chapter. It is, however, worth mentioning that one of them was the addition of provision explicitly allowing ICAEW members to use 'CA'. There was no such provision in its original charter, a factor used against it in the debates over the 1924 South African bill (*RSC1924*, 194–95).

In early November 1926, with the South African situation becoming even more dire, the imperial conference in session and the Balfour declaration within a fortnight of being formally approved (Marshall 2001) the ICAEW made a last desperate bid to get some assistance from the DO through the PCO, with the PCO itself pushing hard on its own initiative, having been initially fobbed off by the DO.[51] But, as reported earlier, the DO would not budge; indeed, it dug in its heels even deeper. To the PCO's key point it responded: 'It may be that the Crown in the Dominions has not the inherent right to incorporate bodies by charter . . . But this defect could be remedied by legislation and no objection could be taken to such legislation'. It also claimed that the 'SA' in the South African designation bill gave the ICAEW adequate protection. Further, that bill had been modeled on the Canadian legislation whose validity could scarcely be challenged at this stage. Indeed, although the Australians had agreed to add 'Australia' after 'CA' in their petition, they could have refused to so. All in all, the DO trusted that the PC would 'accept . . . that there is no action which [H.M. Govt.] could usefully take on the representations of the [ICAEW]' (CO to PCO, 17 December 1926, in DO35/6:D12527). The signal was clear: enough is enough!

In March 1927 Hooper (of Deloittes, Cape Town), who had sat through the 1924 and 1927 select committee hearings in South Africa and was then in the middle of delicate negotiations regarding the designation bill, wrote to the ICAEW arguing forcefully for the extension of the ICAEW's training activities to the dominions. Not only would this:

> be a very graceful and generous act on the part of the Home Societies to the youth of this or any other Country but it would be a most tactful decision in that it would satisfy our Legislators and any other enquirers that there *is* [original emphasis] an open door, though from your point of view fully safeguarded, by which the Colonial youth may attain a very coveted degree and it would at the same time, cement the bonds in our profession between the Mother Country and the Colonies giving the Chartered men abroad support and increasing influence which they at present lack, for their influence declines as the other Societies grow in numbers.

Hooper highlighted the difficulties of sending South African 'lads' to Britain to train, and the growing piracy of 'CA' around the world. Why not, he asked, allow the '"real" product' to expand? There could be no more opportune time, surely, than 'just now . . . when a better status for the Dominions is in the air . . . [and] self Government and equal rights have

51. DO to PCO, 18 November 1926; PCO to DO, 25 November 1926 (both in DO35/6:D12527). Balfour was himself 'Lord President' of the PC at this time. 'It is curious that Lord Balfour or Sir M. Hankey or both shd. so completely disregard the whole tenor of the Inter Impl. Relations Cmm's Report' (Minutes to DO35/6:D12527).

just been declared'.[52] As seen below, however, South Africans did not view competition with the ICAEW as a bonding experience.

While Hooper's letter was in transit, a draft supplemental charter was being finalized (28416/5, 184). On 6 April 1927 it was approved for submission to a general meeting of members (28411/9, 186). It was aired publicly by the *Accountant* (30 April 1927, 641–43, 652) and passed at a general meeting of members on 4 May held immediately following the ICAEW's annual meeting. Whinney's argument in support was an amalgam of positions noted earlier, the difficulties of long-suffering CAs abroad included (ibid., 7 May 1927, 706–11; see also coverage of the annual meeting and Whinney's presidential address on pp. 695–706). The relevant clauses pertaining to the extension of examinations and service under articles to the 'parts of the Empire' other than Scotland or Ireland survived unscathed. The major remaining task, in a formal sense, was to gain the approval of the Privy Council (PC). The ICAEW leadership decided to settle any differences with the dominions before submitting the supplemental charter to it. With its petition for royal charter still being negotiated in Australia, the ACPA was potentially still vulnerable to ICAEW interference and never complained about the supplemental charter. The disputes were with the Canadians and the South Africans.

### *Negotiating with the Canadians*

In Canada the supplemental charter proposal fell on ground somewhat fouled by Whinney's address of October 1926. Frank M. Harvey, a former AACA president, was the first (in December 1926) to take offence. Why, he asked, had Whinney associated the Canadians, the AACA in particular, with propositions about attempting to mislead and deceive and with a society that sold designations commercially (see note 49)? The Canadian incorporation and training processes was as valid as the ICAEW's, and Canadian CAs were, in Canada, held in as high regard as their British counterparts. There was nothing deceptive about their 'CA' (F.M. Harvey to the *Accountant*, 16 December 1926, published 5 February 1927, 181–82)! The *Accountant* (ibid., 173–74) tried to hose things down. No disparagement was intended—the real point was that 'CA' should only be used by members of bodies incorporated by royal charter. This only bought forth a vituperative response from R.R. Thompson, an ICAEW member, professor of accountancy at the University of Montreal and an examiner for the local CA body. Without going into the details of Thompson's letter here, the practical sting was in an unveiled threat:

> It is a thousand pities that such an insult should have emanated from the Old Country, especially when it is directed against a body of men who are amongst the most loyal to the Flag. One cannot insult people

52. All quotes are from Deloittes (Cape Town) to ICAEW, 25 March 1927. See also the support offered by Deloittes (Johannesburg) in a letter to ICAEW 16 March (both documents in 28457).

> and at the same time preserve their friendship. If the Canadian bodies took general notice of it, a very nasty reaction would certainly be produced here, and nothing but harm could result. Some consideration should be given by the [ICAEW president] to the lot of young English Chartered Accountants trying to get settled in Canada. He and you, Sir, discriminated in your statements against Canadian bodies; do you wish to invite discrimination of some kind against English Chartered Accountants?[53] (R.R. Thompson to the *Accountant*, 19 March 1927, published 23 April 1927, 608–9)

Whinney was sufficiently concerned to state publicly (and disingenuously) on the day the ICAEW membership voted to proceed with supplemental charter that his 'remarks, of course, were not intended to apply to bodies the members of which have by statutory authority become entitled to use the term "Chartered Accountant"'.[54]

On 31 May 1927 (28435/2) Thompson wrote to the ICAEW again, succinctly capturing Canadian concerns addressed in subsequent negotiations. In Canada it was the provincial CA bodies that controlled 'CA'. A clerk completing ICAEW exams and service under articles in Canada would still have to join one of those bodies to use it.

> Very naturally the provincial body concerned would want to know why he, working in that province as an accountant's clerk, had not made his arrangements so that he could sit for the provincial body's own examinations. I fear that there is grave probability that such a request would be refused, and your new member be permanently penalised. Several years ago I heard objections from young Canadian chartered accountants against the admission into provincial bodies, of chartered accountants trained in the British Isles. I fear that the provincial bodies will certainly refuse to admit local men, who have passed an examination held locally by the English Institute
>
> (a) in order to protect the rights and privileges granted to the provincial bodies by the provincial parliaments, and

53. Thompson was alluding here to the fact that the Canadian CA bodies had long provided easy entry for British CAs—a sensitive point considering what was happening contemporaneously in South Africa. For the *Accountant's* defensive response see the issue of 23 April 1927. On 1 April 1927 the Association of Accountants in Montreal (AAM) had changed its name to the Society of Chartered Accountants of the Province of Quebec (SCAPQ) in English and La Société des comptables agréés de la province de Québec in French. Under its new act it retained control of 'CA' (bilingually) and could 'admit as members such persons as it sees fit' (Laws of Quebec, chapter 101, section 4).

54. *Accountant* (7 May 1927, 703). The ICAEW replied that Whinney's remarks were personal and that he could not withdraw them 'as unfortunately he is dead' (ICAEW to Thompson, 14 July 1927, see also Deloittes [London] to Thompson, 29 June 1927, and Cash to Thompson, 30 June 1927, all documents in 28435/2; Whinney died on 30 May 1927).

(b) because of the feeling, which has already been aroused [in part by Whinney's speech], and will be much more serious, if the English Institute holds examinations locally in Canada, with a view to the making of chartered accountants who can practice in Canada.

The admission into the Provincial bodies of chartered accountants trained in the British Isles is already regarded as a concession, and will become increasingly difficult by your proposed action.

May I also point out that the Provincial Governments would be certain to question the desirability of a body in London, England, where the practice is different in many respects to that in Canada, setting examinations for the admission of men to the accounting profession in Canada. . . .

It is certain that the Canadian governments, Dominion and Provincial, will never allow another body to over-ride their legislation in their own domains.

The ICAEW was sufficiently concerned by Thompson's letter to appoint a subcommittee to deal with the issues it raised. The committee's report (of 11 July 1927, in 28435/2) was delivered with a suggested letter of reply. For present purposes the most relevant part (maintained in the final version of 15 July) was the claim that the real target of the supplemental charter was not Canada but South Africa, where the SIAA was growing but the ICAEW could not. It 'would be invidious . . . to make distinctions between one part of the Empire and another. It may also be pointed out that if examinations were held in Canada—which is extremely doubtful—special papers would have to be set under competent advice, dealing with local legislation and practice'.[55] The committee also recommended that the ICAEW delay further action so that legal opinion could be sought in both London and Canada.

Thompson, however, would not be mollified. He refused to believe that Whinney's views were not those of the institute[56] and that Whinney's speech:

55. ICAEW to Thompson, 14 July 1927 (28435/2). It was not clear, however, why young Canadians wouldn't seek English 'CA' if it was readily available locally. The ICAEW committee asserted disingenuously that no cases were known of Canadians seeking articles with an ICAEW member as such—but if so, this was probably because examinations (and service) would have had to be undertaken in England or Wales—precisely the obstacle the supplemental charter sought to remove. Cash's letter to Thompson of 30 June 1927 (28435/2) states that the 'question of holding local examinations is . . . dependent on the question of whether sufficient local candidates would desire to become members of the English Institute'.

56. In his address on 2 May 1928, ICAEW president R.G. March made a point of stressing that 'I should like to make it clear that for any observations which I may make, I only am responsible. This address has not been submitted to my colleagues, and I mention this because an unfortunate misunderstanding has arisen with one

has been taken in Canada (*and South Africa*) as evidence of a certain suspicious and disdainful attitude of mind on the part of the English Institute towards Canadian and South African bodies. The proposed [supplemental charter] . . . has been taken as a natural outcome of that attitude of mind. . . .

Since writing on May 31st, it has come to my knowledge that both Canadian and South African groups of Chartered Accountants have protested, through their respective Governments, against the action of the English Institute, and have asked for the exclusion of Canada and South Africa from the scope of the proposed Supplemental Charter.

May I answer here your question of how the proposed [supplemental charter] would obstruct, over-ride or encroach upon legislation already made by the Dominion or Provincial governments of Canada. Provision has already been made by the governments of Canada for the granting of the title 'chartered accountant' only to such persons as are qualified to bear it. . . . The [supplemental charter] . . . would encroach upon that legislation. Because of the location of the English Institute, Canadian bodies, and, I believe, South Africans to do not regard it as a body, as competent as they are, to decide who are fitted to practise as chartered accountants in Canada and South Africa. . . .

The opinion held here very strongly is that the Privy Council will not grant a charter covering the self-governing Dominions, unless requested to do so by the Dominions. . . .

Under these circumstances, gentlemen, I respectfully suggest that you exclude Canada and South Africa from the proposed charter, just as Scotland and Ireland are excluded already.[57]

The Dominion Association of Chartered Accountants (DACA), however, was not prepared to take as hard a line as Thompson at its annual meeting in September 1927. Thompson had made available copies of the correspondence between himself and the ICAEW, Plender and Cash (see notes 54 and 55). The DACA 'committee on the president's report' was prepared to take the views expressed in the latter correspondence at face value

---

our professional brethren in the Dominion of Canada' (*Accountant*, 5 May 1928, 644). See also the placatory remarks of the next ICAEW president, Sir Nicholas Waterhouse, in October 1928, including: 'Surely it would be more than a pity and little less than a disaster to our world-wide expansion and prestige if through some false move on our part the cordial relationship now existing were gradually to degenerate into an atmosphere of retaliation' (*Accountant*, 20 October 1928, 510). He also committed the near heresy of observing that 'CA' has 'now become almost a dictionary word' (ibid., 526).

57. Thompson to ICAEW, 2 September 1927 (emphasis added). See also his reply to Cash of same date (both letters in 28435/2). Plender, concerned that the Canadian opposition may have arced across to South Africa, asked Deloittes (Johannesburg) to investigate Thompson's claims (see letter dated 14 October 1927 in 28435/2).

and recommend that 'nothing further be done in this connection' (*CCA*, 17:187). The DACA president had also received advice from the dominion Ministry of Justice 'that our rights are fully protected and there is no object in taking the matter further' (ibid., 133).[58] In particular, that ministry had advised 'no action could be taken by the English Society that would be effective in over-riding the privileges and rights conferred upon the Canadian Chartered Accountants by the various Provincial Legislatures', and that he considered it unnecessary for the protest to go further.[59]

The Canadian legal opinion obtained on the ICAEW's behalf was mixed. On one hand, it supported Thompson's view that Canadian accountancy legislation effectively prohibited ICAEW members from using 'CA' unless they were members of Canadian CA bodies; also that they could not, in Canada, add 'England and Wales' after 'CA'. While theoretically the imperial Parliament could override that legislation it was unlikely to do so now. Nor were provincial legislatures likely to amend legislation that had been 'in force for so many years'. On the other hand, so long as ICAEW members did not practise using *English* 'CA', the Canadians had no reasonable ground for objecting to the provisions of the supplemental charter as such. Then again, the ICAEW could not reasonably insist *in Canada* that only members of associations incorporated under a royal charter were properly 'chartered' (Blake Lash Anglin & Cassels [Toronto] to Markbys, 24 October 1927, in 28435/2)—a point that Canadian accountants (not to mention lawyers and state agents) had been intermittently been making to the ICAEW for over 20 years (Chua and Poullaos 2002; Poullaos 2008). In December 1927 the ICAEW supplemental charter committee, having reviewed this opinion along with the prospect of opposition from South Africa and Canada, recommended that the extension of service and examinations to the British Empire be dropped from the supplemental charter.[60] In

58. The *CCA* (ibid., 132–33) refers to an ICAEW meeting which proposed and carried amendments to the proposed supplemental charter 'which to a large extent, removed the objectionable features'. I have found no evidence that the examination or service under articles abroad clauses were altered in any material way in September 1927; although a movement in that direction was in motion by December 1927.

59. Drennan to Freeman, 25 November 1927 (28435/2). Although Thompson had acted of his own volition his views were, according to Drennan, supported by 'many' Canadian CAs, and Whinney's remarks 'did not help the situation very much'. Significantly, Drennan added: 'It may be unnecessary to remind you that there are still a number of people in the Old Country (I am a member of the Edinburgh Society myself, and I well remember the attitude of mind many years ago), who have the "Colonial mind complex" very strongly developed. This lack of appreciation of the change in thought that has taken place in recent year [sic—probably a reference to the 1926 imperial conference] is, I think, responsible for a great deal of misunderstanding, and any attempt . . . looking to a perpetuation of such inferiority complex, can only lead to trouble'.

60. Committee report, 6 December 1927 (ICAEWC10). The committee noted that such an amendment would have to be approved by members; also 'that the

Plender's view, however, the ICAEW could desist from actioning this opinion until well into 1928. In the meantime, the Canadian and South African waters could be tested with the action regarding the latter being 'guided by what we heard from Canada' (Plender to Colville, 7 December 1927, in 28435/2). The ICAEW Council must have agreed to this suggestion, for in early February 1928 the DACA president, Percy Edwards, was replying to the ICAEW that the only serious concern in Canada was the holding of ICAEW examinations there. Not for the first time, a dominion association sensing that it had some bargaining power pressed for reciprocity.

> The right of your Institute to hold such examinations is not questioned, but it should not be overlooked that the passing of such examination does not carry any right or privilege to such person to designate himself a Chartered Accountant in Canada such right and privilege accruing from membership in one of the Provincial Societies, and an application from such a person for admission to one of our Provincial Societies would certainly cause a misunderstanding so long as the privilege extended to your members is not accorded equally to ours.
>
> May I suggest that, to extend to our members the facilities we now extend to yours, would remove the ground for any such misunderstanding and constitute a long step toward cementing the happy relations existing between your Institute and ours. (DACA to ICAEW, 7 February 1928, in 28435/2)

Plender was not impressed by the reciprocity proposal. ICAEW members in Canada could not, he noted, use 'England and Wales' after 'CA' whereas Canadian accountants could come to England and add 'Ontario' (etc.) after 'CA' (Plender to Colville, 22 February 1928, in 28435/2). While there was a certain symmetry to this argument, it made no sense at all (from a Canadian perspective) in terms of the signification of relative status; indeed, it represented the ICAEW's own form of retaliation. ICAEW members using English 'CA' in Canada would be highlighting their superior symbolic capital whereas Canadian accountants using Canadian 'CA' in England would be parading their inferiority: heads I win, tails you lose! What the Canadian CAs wanted was to have the *same* CA in Canada so that any advantage attaching to English 'CA' would be muted.[61]

The ICAEW cabled the DACA on 16 March, ignoring the reciprocity issue altogether and asking whether the other aspects of the supplemental charter would be acceptable to the Canadian CA bodies should 'the power of examination in Canada' be abandoned. Edwards cabled back on behalf

---

Opinion of English Counsel on the questions involved has not been taken, as the matter appears to have developed into a question of policy'.

61. Having the same 'CA' in England would also have been advantageous but there wasn't a great exodus of Canadian accountants to the imperial centre during the 1920s.

of the DACA on the same day to say that they would.[62] Plender was pleased (Deloittes [London] to ICAEW, 19 March 1928, in 28435/2). Yet another dominion bluff about reciprocity had been called. More to the point: the ICAEW could now focus on the South Africans.

### *Negotiating with the South Africans*

News of the supplemental charter proposal reached South Africa in June 1927. It was not well received by the Union societies, there having been no prior consultation on the matter.[63] Allegedly, a protest had been lodged with the South African government by September 1927; by early December the threat of South African opposition was a factor in the ICAEW supplemental charter committee's recommendation that the service and examinations abroad provisions be expunged from the supplemental charter. By January 1928 more detailed news was coming through from Fairbridges and Deloittes (Cape Town and Johannesburg). N.S. Wood, a key promoter of the 1924 and 1927 bills, was aggressively campaigning against the supplemental charter as CSAA president. The TSA Council was supporting Wood, at least as far as opposing the holding of local examinations were concerned, and (probably) so would the general membership of the South African bodies, in the Transvaal in particular. They had been unhappy for some time with locals sitting for the SIAA exams instead of their own and to have the ICAEW come in and do the same was anathema to them. Indeed, they were putting pressure on the SIAA to stop examining in South Africa. It should be noted also that the South African bodies could retaliate by removing recognition of ICAEW members from their bye-laws. Apparently the South African government had forwarded the CSAA's protest to the South African High Commission in London but what had happened to it subsequently was unclear.[64] Fairbridges's contribution was to advise that 'the Union Societies' had complained to the Union government that the supplemental charter constituted an 'undue interference' in 'domestic affairs'. The ICAEW had also engaged in 'unfair dealing' in negotiating recognition of its members in South Africa under the designation bill while simultaneously working towards setting up operations there under the supplemental charter. (The

62. Cable and letter ICAEW to DACA, 16 March 1928; cable DACA to ICAEW, 16 March 1928, letter DACA to ICAEW, 29 March 1928 (all in 28435/2).

63. Markbys to ICAEW, 27 February 1928 (28435/2). A major limitation of this section is that the coverage of South Africa is based on primary sources collected in Britain; thus the nuances of the South African arena are not captured.

64. Deloittes (Cape Town) to Deloittes (Johannesburg), 13 January 1928; Deloittes (Johannesburg) to Deloittes (Cape Town), 20 January 1928; see also Deloittes (Johannesburg) to Deloittes (London), 1 February 1928, all in 28435/2. As it turns out the High Commission was waiting for the supplemental charter to be lodged with the PCO before protesting (NSA annual report for 1927–1928 in 28435/2).

implication was that the former had opened the way for the latter, which, in turn, would be used to attract locals away from the examinations of the Union Societies and to deprive South African–born CAs of accounting labour.) Fairbridges vehemently denied any 'double-dealing'. Neither they nor (allegedly) Hooper were aware of the latter while undertaking the former. The Union societies objected both to ICAEW examinations and articles being sat/served locally. By the way: *Thompson of Montreal is in communication with* Wood *of Cape Town* and both are making much of Whinney's speech of October 1926 (emphasis added).[65]

Fairbridges (ibid.) also suggested the first of a series of compromises aimed at defusing the South African opposition. These were:

1. South Africans articled with ICAEW members would sit locally for both ICAEW and South African examinations, the former only upon completion of the latter. In addition, articles would be deemed to be served under the auspices of both the ICAEW and a Union society. The effect of this would be to stop someone from taking on two apprentices as an ICAEW member plus another two as a member of a local society—a dubious practice that should be forbidden to SIAA members as well.[66]
2. The ICAEW would abandon local examinations (with or without the provision regarding apprentices as per 1). If this occurred, it would be helpful to its members in South Africa if one or more South African exams could be taken as equivalent to the ICAEW's (so that their South African clerks would not need to sit two full sets of examinations). A variant of this proposal that might appeal to the Union societies was that a South African clerk could not proceed to England until completion of the South African final examination. Another required that the clerk go to England for the intermediate and final examinations.[67]

In May 1928 the ICAEW stated publicly that the supplemental charter had not been lodged with PCO as negotiations with the Canadians and South Africans were still in the preliminary stages (*Accountant*, 5 May

65. Markbys to ICAEW, 11 February 1928, enclosing cable from Fairbridges, 12 January 1928 (in 28435/2). See also Markbys to ICAEW, 27 February 1928; NSA annual report for 1927–1928; Deloittes (London) to ICAEW, 5 March 1928, in 28435/2.

66. Markbys to ICAEW, 11 February 1928, enclosing cable from Fairbridges, 12 January 1928; Markbys to ICAEW, 27 February and 16 March 1928; Fairbridges to Markbys, 23 March 1928 (in 28435/2).

67. Fairbridges to Markbys, 23 March 1928 and 14 June 1929; Markbys to ICAEW, 26 March, 16 and 30 April, 18 June, 5 July, 3 and 23 October 1928, 4 and 29 July and 6 December 1929; Deloittes (London) to ICAEW, 1 May 1928; Fairbridges to Walkers, 4 July 1929, and 21 February 1930; ICAEW to Markbys, 17 January 1930 (all in 28435/2).

1928, 643–46) and a similar statement was made a year later (*Accountant*, 4 May 1929, 571). In June 1928 the ICAEW council decided to further defer actioning the proposal of the supplemental charter committee that the examination and service abroad provisions be dropped (28411/9). Negotiations dragged on and the Union societies procrastinated. In July 1929 the ICAEW recommenced deliberations as to whether the examinations abroad provision in the supplemental charter should be dropped.[68] In the council meeting of 4 December 1929 opinion was divided as to whether to abandon the supplemental charter altogether or to just chop out the examinations abroad proposal, and at Plender's suggestion (he was now president) the matter was adjourned.[69] Just a few weeks earlier Markbys had advised the ICAEW that three out of four of the Union societies were 'strongly opposed' to the ICAEW proposals and the fourth was still making up its mind (Markbys to ICAEW, 14 November 1929, in 28435/2). Oblivious to the signals from South Africa, the ICAEW persisted into 1930. In February representatives of the Union societies met and sent an even stronger signal: accountants qualifying in South Africa could so only by doing the South African examinations. Members of approved overseas bodies, furthermore, could only join a local society without passing South African examinations if they 'had wholly served their articles of clerkship and passed the examination of such Society or Institute in the Country in which the Head Office of the relative Society is situated' (Fairbridges to Markbys, 13 March 1930, in 28435/2). As far as the ICAEW was concerned, this was exactly the present situation. In effect the jig was up.[70] Its 1927 supplemental charter never made it to the PC (Cash to ICAEW, 10 August 1938 in 28435/2).

## DISCUSSION AND CONCLUSION

In 1930 local accountants in South Africa, Canada and Australia were in a stronger situation *vis-à-vis* their British counterparts than was the case in either 1907 or 1920. The Australians finally had 'CA', from Britain no less. The Canadians, having long had 'CA' under local legislation and having fought off a concerted challenge from the British chartered bodies in 1908–1912 and again during the 1920s (through their resistance to the supplemental charter) had further solidified their control over their own turf. So had the South African 'Union Societies', in part by getting 'CA'

68. Unsigned background memorandum, 18 July 1929 (28435/2); ICAEW to Kemp, 1 November 1929 (28435/2); 28420/3 (8, 10, 12).

69. 'Notes on the discussion which took place at the [ICAEW Council Meeting of 4/12/29]', in 28435/2.

70. The SIAA was also under pressure, albeit it had the advantage of incumbency, having been in South Africa virtually since the turn of the century. See, for example, *IAJ* (1 May 1930, 296–97), *Cape Times* (27 September 1930, in 28435/2), CSAA to ICAEW, 6 July 1932 (ICAEWC13).

(notwithstanding the 'SA') and in part through their own robust defiance of the supplemental charter. While the Australian mode of attaining 'CA' was clearly preferred by the British CA bodies, the Canadians and South Africans had found another, more 'autonomous' way of entrenching or establishing their own versions of 'CA'—with help from members of a seriously divided immigrant British CA community. Clearly, the broader movement towards formal colonial autonomy (as highlighted by the 1926 Balfour declaration) had assisted all three dominions. In the Canadian and South African cases it got the CO/DO 'off their backs', so to speak, allowing local politicians and bureaucrats to be more forthright in refusing official British representations (although the Canadians had had prior experience). For its part Australia was aided by the (counter)-reaction of its Anglophile prime minister to the 1926 imperial conference (Poullaos 1994), while the ICAEW was encouraged to support the Australian charter application as a counterpoint to Canada and South Africa.

Nevertheless, accountants in all three dominions, being all 'CA'-seekers, were to that degree still (or increasingly) British in their mode of professionalization. The struggle to get or keep 'CA' involved activity over long periods of time to set up higher standards of training and examinations than might otherwise have been the case. Variations from the strict British CA model (in particular in terms of years of service under articles and the entry of accountants not in public practice) needed to be justified in public fora, adding further to the integration of the imperial accountancy arena, in part by the enhancement of the curious blend of 'competition and cooperation, mimesis as well as differentiation' (Chua and Poullaos 2002, 439) evident earlier in the twentieth century. The role of the Canadian precedent in the South African debates, the sharing of attitudes and arguments across the dominions and the treatment of them by the ICAEW as a group (in its representations to the PCO and DO) are further illustrations or aspects of the evolution of imperial accountancy arena during the 1920s.[71]

The work of getting and keeping 'CA' within that arena, motivated in part by the desire to compete for 'English audits', helped to resolve the tension noted in the introduction of this chapter between formal equality/autonomy and informal dependence. Dominion accountants had to (at least appear to) be 'good' so as to appeal to British (and other) capitalists. In order to, furthermore, get the 'right' credentials to be (seen as) good enough to compete in the accountancy market place, dominion accountants needed the support of state agencies (local ones in particular). Thus

71. Limitations of space preclude the enumeration of the growing communications between the dominion associations inter se and with British bodies during the 1920s about, for example: reciprocity, sharing of information about training and governance, exchange of year-books/annual reports, invitations to conferences and ceremonial occasions.

the 'formal' (the profession–state relationship) was a crucial element of success in the 'informal' world of markets and capital flows—there was no hard and fast division between them. The arguments put by British CAs early in the twentieth century that British capitalists would react negatively to colonies that did not allow British CAs to work locally (see Johnson and Caygill 1971; Chua and Poullaos 2002) are markedly absent from the primary sources. Furthermore, the concern, vigilance, vigour and persistence displayed by accountants around designations suggest an acute sensitivity on their part to the relationship between (the signification of) professional status honor and opportunities in the marketplace for accounting services.

While the ICAEW may well have been concerned about its members abroad it only sought to 'move offshore' when it could no longer rely on formal diplomatic channels (or the protests of British capitalists) to protect its interests. It was a case of if you can't beat them join them (Poullaos 2009a, 450). Following the failure of the supplemental charter attempt, its prospects of competing abroad (in the short term) with the SIAA and in the longer term with the ACCA were thus diminished. As far as I am aware, the demise of the 1927 supplemental charter spelled the end of the ICAEW's efforts to offer examinations and articles offshore. While this chapter certainly has not explained why the ICAEW did not do so subsequently, it is noticeable that the trend evident in South Africa and Canada during the 1920s (viz., the tightening of the grip of local accountants over their local professional jurisdictions as local state agents became more assertive vis-à-vis their British counterparts) was a longish-term one and, to the extent that the ICAEW was dissuaded from expanding offshore, this chapter provides part of the explanation of why local accountants throughout the empire had to travel to England to get *English* 'CA'.

Finally, and in contrast to Johnson and Caygill (1971, 160), this chapter suggests that the Union societies gained 'CA' in 1927 rather than 1946. As to the suggestion (ibid., 168) that the failure of the supplemental charter was 'due to the protests of the Canadian and South African professions' it might be pointed out first, that the Canadians were prepared to let the supplemental charter proceed with only the examination power removed; second, that the relations between state agents in the centre and periphery playing out amidst an undercurrent of increasing formal dominion autonomy was just as important; and third, the integrative tendencies in the emergent imperial accountancy arena, coupled with the ongoing maintenance of the capacity of British accountants and British-based firms to provide accountancy services locally, had to some degree diminished the 'informal' fear that the poor state of accountancy in the self-governing colonies would hinder the flow of British capital (compare Johnson and Caygill 1971, 169–70).

## APPENDIX A

# Acronyms and Dates of Incorporation of Associations Mentioned in Chapter 2 (Chronological Order)

1854 Society of Accountants in Edinburgh (SAE)[a]
1855 Institute of Accountants and Actuaries in Glasgow (IAAG)[a]
1867 Society of Accountants in Aberdeen (SAA)[a]
1880 Institute of Chartered Accountants in England and Wales (ICAEW)[a]
Association of Accountants in Montreal (AAM)[b]—name changed to Society of Chartered Accountants of the Province of Quebec (SCAPQ) in English and La Société des Comptables Agréés de la Province de Québec in French in 1927
1883 Institute of Chartered Accountants of Ontario (ICAO)[b]
1885 Society of Accountants and Auditors; name changed to Society of Incorporated Accountants and Auditors in 1908 (SIAA)
1886 Institute of Chartered Accountant of Manitoba (ICAM)[b]
1887 Institute of Chartered Accountants in Ireland (ICAI)[a]
1900 Institute of Chartered Accountants of Nova Scotia (ICANS)[b]
1902 Dominion Association of Chartered Accountants (DACA)[b]
1904 Transvaal Society of Accountants (TSA)
London Association of Accountants (LAA)
1905 Institute of Chartered Accountants in British Columbia (ICABC)[b]
1907 Cape Society of Accountants and Auditors (CSAA)
Society of Accountants and Auditors in the Orange Free State (SAAOFS)
1908 Australasian Corporation of Public Accountants (ACPA)
Institute of Chartered Accountants of Saskatchewan (ICAS)[b]
1909 Natal Society of Accountants (NSA)
1910 Association of Chartered Accountants of Alberta (AACA)[b]
1919 Institute of Chartered Accountants (California)
1926 Society of Chartered Accountants in the Province of the Cape of Good Hope (SCAPGH)

a Incorporated by royal charter

b Incorporated by legislation authorizing use of 'CA' designation

## APPENDIX B

# Acronyms—Other*

CA/CAs chartered accountant/chartered accountants
'CA" chartered accountant' as *designation* (used generically, not necessarily reflecting the designations of particular associations)
'CASA' 'Chartered Accountant (South Africa)' as designation
CO Colonial Office
DO Dominions Office
PCO/PC Privy Council Office/Privy Council

*Acronyms used in the main text for primary sources are listed in the References.

## REFERENCES

### Primary Sources (and acronyms as used for them in the main text)

Anonymous. (1924) *Memorandum in re Accountants Registration Bill*, 9 January, available in (ICAEW) 28457.

Colonial Office National Archives, Kew, Surrey, UK

CO532/284, Dominions Original Correspondence, Offices: Council, Department of Overseas Trade 1924, File 14862, National Archives, Kew, Surrey, UK (CO532/284:14862).

Dominions Office, National Archives, Kew, Surrey, UK

DO35/6, Despatches, PCO, 1926, File D6358
UK (DO35/6:D6358).

DO35/6, Despatches, PCO, 1926, File D12527UK (DO35/6:D12527).

Institute of Chartered Accountants in England and Wales, Guildhall Library, London, UK

14–3-3, Correspondence, New South Wales, 1906–1915, Milton Keynes when viewed (ICAEW 14–3-3).

28411, Council Minute Books 1840–1949, vol. 9, November 1924 to August 1929 (28411/9).

28416, General Purposes Committee Minute Books 1883–1950, vol. 5, March 1921 to November 1928 (28416/5).

28420, Parliamentary and Law Committee Minute Books 1891–1951, vol. 2, book B, October 1905 to December 1928 (28420/2).

28420, Parliamentary and Law Committee Minute Books 1891–1951, vol. 3, book C, April 1929 to May 1945 (28420/3).

28432, ICAEW Circulars 1881–1948, vol. 10, 1923 to 1927 (ICAEWC10).

28432, ICAEW Circulars 1881–1948, vol. 13, July 1932 to June 1924 (ICAEWC13).

28435, ICAEW, Filing, 1899–1973, Item 2, revision of charter and bye-laws (C18), 1927–1948 (28435/2).

28456, ICAEW correspondence and papers relating to accountancy bodies overseas, 1881 to 1939 (28456).

28457, Correspondence and papers relating to legislation for the accounting profession in South Africa and Rhodesia 1905–1929 (28457).

Institute of Chartered Accountants in Ireland, Dublin, Ireland.

Minute Book 1916–1930 (ICAIMB2).

Joint Committee of the Councils of the Chartered Accountants Societies of Scotland

Item 13/1, Minute Book 1, 1915–1924, Scottish Records Office, Edinburgh (JCSMB1).

Item 13/2, Minute Book 2, 1924–1927, Scottish Records Office, Edinburgh (JCSMB2).

Item 13/3, Minute Book 2, 1927–1943, Scottish Records Office, Edinburgh (JCSMB3).

Newspapers and Journals

*Accountant*
*Canadian Chartered Accountant* (CCA)
*Cape Times*
*Incorporated Accountants' Journal* (*IAJ*)
*Public Accountant*

Society of Accountants in Aberdeen, Scottish Records Office, Edinburgh, Scotland

Item 11/2, Council Minute Book 2, 1911–1933 (SAACMB2).

Society of Accountants in Edinburgh, Scottish Records Office, Edinburgh, Scotland.

Item 2/4, Council Minute Book 4, 1921–1928 (SAECMB4).

Union of South Africa House of Assembly. (1924) *House of Assembly Debates 24 July to 1 August:* 147–59. Cape Town: Cape Times Ltd. Government Printers.

———. (1924) *House of Assembly Debates 5 August to 8 August:* 310–54. Cape Town: Cape Times Ltd. Government Printers.

———. (1924) *Report of the Select Committee on the South African Society of Accountants (Private) Bill.* Cape Town: Cape Times Ltd. Government Printers (*RSC1924*).

———. (1927) *Report of the Select Committee on the Chartered Accountants Designation (Private) Bill.* Cape Town: Cape Times Ltd Government Printers (*RSC1927*).

## Secondary Sources

Briston, R.J., and Kedslie, M.J.M. (1997) 'The internationalization of British professional accounting: The role of the examination exporting bodies'. *Accounting, Business & Financial History* 7:175–94.

Cain, P.J., and Hopkins, A.G. (2002) *British Imperialism, 1688–2000.* 2nd ed. Harlow, UK: Pearson Education.

Chua, W.F., and Poullaos, C. (1993) 'Rethinking the profession–state dynamic: The case of the Victorian charter attempt, 1885–1906'. *Accounting, Organizations and Society* 18:691–728.

———. (2002) 'The empire strikes back? An exploration of centre–periphery interaction between the ICAEW and accounting associations in the self-governing colonies of Australia, Canada and South Africa, 1880–1907'. *Accounting, Organizations and Society* 27:409–45.

Costigliola, F.C. (1977) 'Anglo-American financial rivalry in the 1920s'. *Journal of Economic History* 37:911–34.

Creighton, P. (1984) *A Sum of Yesterdays. Being a History of the First One Hundred Years of the Institute of Chartered Accountants in Ontario.* Toronto: ICAO.

Darwin, J. (1980) 'Imperialism in decline? Tendencies in British imperial policy between the wars'. *Historical Journal* 23:657–79.

Dawson, R.M. (1965) *The Development of Dominion Status 1900–1936.* London: Frank Cass.

Feis, H. (1950) *The Diplomacy of the Dollar: 1919–1932.* New York: The John Hopkins University Press.

Ferris, J.R. (1991) '"The greatest power on earth": Great Britain in the 1920s'. *International History Review* 13:726–50.

Goldberg, M.D. (1973) 'Anglo-American economic competition, 1920–1930'. *Economy and History* 16:15–36.

Jeffries, C. (1956) *The Colonial Office.* London: George Allen and Unwin.

Johnson, T.J. (1982) 'The state and the professions: Peculiarities of the British'. In *Social Class and the Division of Labour*, ed. A. Giddens and G. McKenzie. Cambridge: Cambridge University Press.

Johnson, T.J., and Caygill, M. (1971) 'The development of accountancy links in the commonwealth'. *Accountancy and Business Research* (Spring): 155–73.

Marshall, P. (2001) 'The Balfour formula and the evolution of the commonwealth'. *Round Table* 90:541–53.

McKercher, B. (1988) 'Wealth, power and the new international order: Britain and the American challenge in the 1920s'. *Diplomatic History* 12:411–41.

Parker, R.H. (1989) 'Importing and exporting accounting: The British experience'. In *International Pressures for Accounting Change*, ed. A. Hopwood. Hertfordshire: Prentice Hall International and ICAEW.

———. (2005) 'Naming and branding: Accountants and accountancy bodies in the British Empire and commonwealth, 1853–2003'. *Accounting History* 10:7–46.

Parrini, C. (1978) 'Anglo-American corporatism and the economic diplomacy of stabilization in the 1920s'. *Review in American History* 6:379–87.

Poullaos, C. (1994) *Making the Australian Chartered Accountant*. New York and London: Garland.

———. (2008) '"Independence with a vengeance!"—maintaining Canadian accountants' symbolic capital, 1908–1912'. Paper presented at the Critical Perspectives on Accounting Conference, New York, 24–26 April.

———. (2009a) 'Profession, race and empire: Keeping the centre pure, 1921–1927'. *Accounting, Auditing & Accountability Journal* 22:429–68.

———. (2009b) 'Professionalisation'. In *Routledge Companion to Accounting History*, ed. R. Edwards and S. Walker. London and New York: Routledge.

Schulzinger, R.D. (2002) *U.S. Diplomacy since 1900*. 5th ed. New York and Oxford: Oxford University Press.

Watt, D.C. (1984) *Succeeding John Bull: America in Britain's Place, 1900–1975; A Study of the Anglo-American Relationship and World Politics in the Context of British and American Foreign-Policy Making in the Twentieth Century*. Cambridge and New York: Cambridge University Press.

Xu, X., and Xu, X. (2003) 'Becoming professional: Chinese accountants in early 20th century China'. *Accounting Historians Journal* 30:129–53.

# 3 Canada Between Empires

*Alan J. Richardson*

## INTRODUCTION

The current Canadian Constitution[1] recognizes that Canada emerged from three founding cultures/nations—the First Nations[2] (Indian, Inuit and Métis), France and England—but in accounting, the true founding nations, i.e., those nations that have had the most significant influence on the current organization of the profession and accounting practice, have been France, England and the United States. These countries have exerted an imperial influence over Canada but none have achieved complete dominance. Rather, the structure of the Canadian accounting profession and practice reflects Canada's position at the interstices of these empires.

Canada's institutional heritage, including a Westminster[3] parliamentary system and the regulation of business through Companies Acts, was taken from the United Kingdom (UK); however, accommodation to French influence is reflected in the division of powers between the federal government and provinces and in the continued use of code law within the Province of Quebec. The institutionalization of French customs within Canada occurred because of the relationship between the UK and the American colonies during a crucial time in Canadian history. The UK accommodated French interests in Canada as a tactic to limit the spread of rebellion from the American colonies. In addition, after the American Revolution, Britain's 'Second Empire' excluded North America and Canada was subject to greater American influence particularly with respect to trade and investment. US imperialism has

---

1. Constitution Act, 1867 (as revised 1982). Canada is a federation of 10 provinces and three territories. The federal government is responsible for national security and other trans-provincial issues but the provinces retain authority over property and civil matters.

2. The constitution recognizes 'aboriginal peoples' and defines this group as consisting of Indian, Inuit and Métis peoples. The term 'First Nations' was adopted in 1982 when the 'Assembly of First Nations' was formed from the former National Indian Brotherhood to represent the Indian, Inuit and Métis groups in negotiations with the Canadian government (see http://www.afn.ca/article.asp?id=59).

3. This term follows from the Statute of Westminster, 1931 (22 Geo. V, c.4 [UK]) by which the UK formally gave all its dominions equal legislative authority to the UK

been reinforced since the end of the Cold War by the US vision of a 'new world order' based on economic globalization. Accounting in Canada is thus a reflection of British imperialism both directly and through the interaction between the British Empire and the emerging US Empire.

This chapter considers the ebb and flow of imperial influences on the Canadian accounting profession and professional practice beginning with the UK, gradually shifting to the US and, most recently, looking back to the UK as a buffer from US influence. The UK and the US exerted their influence in distinctive ways reflecting the historical context in which they operated (Porter 2006; Maier 2006). The first British Empire was a territorial expansion of UK-governed institutions and markets with settler colony and non-settler colony variants. The American Empire[4] has been built on the conceptual foundation of market liberalism reinforced by military might. The chapter identifies the impacts of these forms of imperialism, and their interaction, on the accounting profession in Canada. It concludes by considering Canada's role as a 'middle power' and how this is reflected in Canada's participation in international, multilateral accounting standard-setting activities.

## IMPERIALISM CONSIDERED

Imperialism is a multifaceted concept that at heart refers to 'the practice, the theory, and the attitudes of a dominating metropolitan centre ruling a distant territory' (Said 1993, 8). Each aspect of this characterization of imperialism has been subject to debate. In particular, the means by which a distant power 'rules' another territory and what constraints this 'rule' places on local activities varies widely. Galtung (1971, 91) identified five forms of imperialism based on the nature of the interaction between the

---

Parliament. It also reflects the devolution of authority to independent colonies beginning with the provinces of Canada in the mid-1800s. Canada created a Department of External Affairs in 1909 and established its first delegation (embassy) in Washington in 1927 (Thomson and Swanson 1971). At Canada's insistence, a clause was added to the Statute of Westminster (1931) stating: 'Nothing in this Act shall be deemed to apply to the repeal, amendment or alteration of the British North America Acts, 1867 to 1930, or any order, rule or regulation made thereunder' (s.7). This meant that Canada would not have the power to reform its own constitution. This was done because of the weak federal government created by the British North America Act and the lack of a formula by which the votes of the provinces for amending the constitution could be weighted and combined. The BNA Act was finally repatriated by Canada in 1982 as the Canada Constitution Act.

4. The term 'American Empire' is disputed since it rests more on ideas than occupation and administration. The political science literature uses the concept of hegemony to reflect this difference. Ignatieff (2003) has referred to this as 'empire lite': 'The 21st century imperium is a new invention in the annals of political science, an empire lite, a global hegemony whose grace notes are free markets, human rights and democracy, enforced by the most awesome military power the world has ever known' (2003, 1).

centre and periphery: (a) economic, (b) political, (c) military, (d) communicative and (e) cultural. These forms of imperialism are not mutually exclusive nor do they represent a series of stages of imperialism (leading critics to assert that it is merely a typology of imperialism rather than a theory of imperialism as Galtung claimed). Each type of imperialism reflects different means of influence and different objectives from the perspective of the ruling state.

Accounting is intertwined with each of these forms of imperialism, and in various studies accounting has appeared as either the explanandum or the explanans. This gives rise to two main approaches to understanding the relationship between imperialism and accounting, both of which have been used to understand accounting phenomenon in Canada.

The first approach focuses on accountants and accounting as the means by which imperialism is implemented. Accounting technologies, for example, may be used to allow distant rulers/managers to monetize and control unseen operations. Spraakman's (1999; Spraakman and Davidson 1998; Spraakman and Wilkie 2000) histories of the Hudson's Bay Company, for example, provide detailed examples of how accounting allowed the Company, headquartered in London, England, to control and motivate distant traders throughout the North American wilderness. Bujaki (2007) examines the use of accounting rhetoric in the decision by the UK treasury and military to build the Rideau Canal from the Ottawa River to Lake Ontario, by-passing the St. Lawrence River that borders on the US. The original decision was made for security concerns during the War of 1812 between Britain and the US, but over the 24 years it took to build the canal, these reasons dissipated and a commercial logic was introduced to justify continuing with the project. As the objectives of the canal changed, there were changes in design and a concerted effort to reapportion the costs from the UK to the local population. In both the Hudson's Bay Company case and the Rideau Canal case, accountants and accounting technologies were exported from the UK to Canada to ensure the attainment of economic and military benefits for the UK. In these studies accounting is the explanans with imperialism as the explanandum.

A second approach to understanding the relationship between imperialism and accounting is to focus on the impact of imperialism on the organization of accounting and accountants at the periphery (cf. Chua and Poullaos 1998, 2002). Classifications of national accounting systems have frequently used colonial/imperialist influence as a discriminating variable. American Accounting Association (1977, 106), for example, recognizes 'British, Franco-Spanish-Portugese [*sic*], Germanic-Dutch, U.S. and Communistic [*sic*]' zones of influence. This approach to understanding the development of the Canadian accounting profession has not been used explicitly in the existing literature but is reflected in studies of the institutional origins of the profession (e.g., Richardson 1989a, 1989b) and in studies of the evolution of Canadian corporate reporting practices (e.g., Murphy 1988). In these studies imperialism is the explanans with the form of accounting practice and institutions as the explanandum.

The chapter will highlight the contributions of existing work to our understanding of imperial influences on the development of Canadian accounting institutions and practices. It will address only in passing the use of accounting as a means of implementing imperialism in Canada. The principle focus will be on the interplay between British and US influences on Canadian accounting practice; however, the impact of French tradition within the Canadian state will also be considered. In addition, the chapter will explore how Canada's role as a 'middle power' has been reflected in its contribution to international accounting organizations and to the present balancing of American and British influences. I begin by considering the contributions of the three founding nations to the structure of Canadian accounting practice.

## THE IMPACT OF CANADA'S FOUNDING NATIONS

The Dominion of Canada was formed in 1867, combining peoples from at least three distinct cultures within a single political jurisdiction. Two of these cultures—the French and English—were settler colonies of imperial powers. The third group, the aboriginal population, was actually composed of many cultures but is now referred to collectively as Canada's First Nations. Each of these groups has been affected by and/or affected the development of accounting in Canada.

### First Nations and Accounting

Canada's First Nations do not figure prominently in the history of the accounting profession[5] although the same cannot be said of the impact of accounting on First Nations peoples. In a series of articles and a monograph, Dean Neu and colleagues (e.g., Neu 1999, 2000; Neu and Therrien 2003; Neu and Graham 2006) have demonstrated the ways that accounting technologies have been used to control, assimilate and manage aboriginal populations in Canada. They argue that accounting facilitated the distant management of these populations and that the economic and cultural assimilation of these groups was explicitly part of the strategy of nation-building. These studies are outside the scope of this chapter but do provide important insights into the role of accounting as a technology of imperialism.

5. There is no literature on whether or not First Nations people were historically excluded from accounting practice. The Aboriginals Financial Management Association of Canada was formed in 1999 to provide training and guidance in financial accounting and financial management specific to the needs of aboriginal communities and organizations. This group examines for and grants the Certified Aboriginal Financial Manager (CAFM) designation.

## The French Connexion

France founded the first permanent European settlements in Canada beginning with Port Royal in 1605 (now part of Nova Scotia) and spread inland along the St. Lawrence River founding Quebec City (1608) and Montreal (1611). These settlements and forts supported the export of resources such as fish from the Grand Banks and furs from the hinterland. Montreal was the centre of contact between France and the First Nations, resulting in a treaty signed between France and 39 First Nations in 1701 (primarily the Iroquois, Huron and Algonquian) that allowed 'New France' to develop settlements and trade routes. In spite of these efforts, the French did not succeed in establishing a significant settler population in North America compared with the British colonies. As a result, France was unable to maintain control of the claimed lands during colonial wars with Britain that erupted sporadically between 1689 and 1763 (sometimes referred to as the Second Hundred Years War). The Treaty of Paris (1763) at the end of the fourth intercolonial war (a.k.a. the Seven Years' War) formally gave control of French territory in Canada to Britain.

The British takeover of French lands and populations did not result in the assimilation of the Francophone population. Instead the region was divided into the provinces of Upper and Lower Canada, representing the Anglophone and Francophone populations respectively. Further, because of fear that the Francophone population of Lower Canada might support those expressing discontent with British rule in the 13 colonies to the south, the British Parliament passed the Quebec Act in 1774, guaranteeing freedom of religion in Quebec[6] and restoring their own legal system. This precedent would have significant effects on the structure of Canadian politics and government. It established the basis for regional autonomy within Canada and gave to all provinces the powers normally covered by Code law.

When Canada was created as a separate country in 1867, the existing French (Lower Canada) and English (Upper Canada, Nova Scotia and New Brunswick) settlements were combined into one political unit at a federal level and organized according to Westminster principles. However, the Province of Quebec within Canada retained its French cultural heritage, including a legal system based on the *Code Napoleon*, the predominant Catholic religion and the tradition of craft production through small-scale enterprises. As Mancke (1999, 20) suggests: 'the challenge that Canadians inherited from the empire was not how to create a single organic state, but how to domesticate a composite state system'. The Canadian Constitution (originally the UK British North America Act [BNA]) fostered the development and maintenance of regional variation within Canada by creating a weak central government and

6. Previously any politician or government employee would have to swear allegiance to the British Crown and the Protestant faith. This excluded the majority Catholic population in Quebec from public office.

a division of powers that gave the provinces control over property and civil rights including education and the regulation of the professions. This meant that the organization and regulation of accounting was a provincial responsibility and could develop according to local norms.

Many Quebec provincial leaders, most notably Henri Bourassa (1868–1956), member of Parliament and publisher of the newspaper *Le Devoir*, argued against the imperial connexion between Canada and the UK after Confederation. In particular, Bourassa pushed the federal government to make independent decisions about entering wars in which the UK was involved. During the Boer Wars (1880–1881, 1899–1902) and World War I, for example, Canada gave control of its navy to Britain and entered the war without debate in Parliament. This reflected the legality that Canada's external affairs were handled by the UK Colonial Office until 1931. In 1939 Canada remained neutral for seven days after the UK declared war on Germany as a symbolic gesture of Canadian independence.

Bourassa championed the independence of Canada from both UK and US influence but his philosophy has also been used to support the concept of the independence of Quebec within or from Canada. In more recent years, the possibility of Quebec separating from the rest of Canada has been a source of recurrent political uncertainty. This possibility was at times openly supported by the French government, notably with President Charles De Gaulle's use of the phrase 'Vive le Québec libre' (Thomson 1988) during a speech in Montreal in 1967 (after which he was asked to leave Canada). In the intervening years the Liberal Party endorsed a 'One Canada' policy, arguing that all provinces within Canada were equal and no special recognition of regional diversity was needed, while the Conservative Party attempted to formally recognize Quebec as a 'distinct society' within the Canadian Constitution. On 22 November 2007 the federal Parliament, voting on a motion of the Conservative government, officially recognized that 'the Québécois form a nation within a united Canada'.

The difference in culture and legal traditions between Quebec and the rest of Canada created some difficulties of integration that have affected the accounting profession. Because of the tradition of small-scale business and large families among Québécois, capital formation was restricted among the Francophone population, resulting in the dominance of an Anglophone business elite within Quebec (Porter 1957). This was also reflected in the demographic composition of the accounting profession in the province where UK-born, Anglican accountants were over-represented in elite positions compared with the characteristics of the population as a whole (Richardson 1989a). The leading accounting firm in the Province was P.S. Ross and Sons founded in 1858 (Richardson 2001a). Ross was a Scot but had no formal training in accounting. He went on to champion the first accounting association in the Province,[7] the Accountants Association of Montreal

7. For a chronology of the formation and development of accounting associations in Canada, see Richardson (1993).

(AAM),[8] which was organized following the Scottish model of professional association. A number of the founding members had ties to the Society of Accountants in Edinburgh (SAE) (Thompson 1939, 172).

This body gradually grew in size but primarily attracted Anglophone accountants (since examinations were written in English). In 1912 the Institute of Accountants and Auditors of the Province of Quebec (IAAPQ) was incorporated to represent Francophone accountants explicitly because of the dominance of Anglophones within the AAM (Editorial *Canadian Chartered Accountant* 1913, 119). The existence of separate Francophone and Anglophone associations within Quebec, however, was not stable. The AAM and IAAPQ sought legislation allowing their merger and closure of the profession in 1916 and 1918, but these efforts were rejected by the Quebec legislature, in part because of opposition from the recently formed Certified General Accountants Association, which was centred in the Montreal business community (Mann 1976). The AAM and IAAPQ finally 'merged' in 1946 when the provincial government closed the profession by unilaterally declaring all existing public accountants to be 'Chartered Accountants' ('CA') and requiring that audits of public companies be conducted by the newly constituted Institute of Chartered Accountants of Quebec.

The French tradition of statism[9] implemented in Quebec set the stage for the development of accounting regulation across Canada (the regulation of the professions is a provincial responsibility under the Canadian Constitution, thus allowing for variation across the country). The Ontario profession, on learning of the 1946 changes in the profession in Quebec, began negotiating with other provincial accounting bodies and the Ontario government for a form of regulation of auditing that would be less 'statist' and more 'associational' in character (Richardson 1989b; cf. Puxty et al. 1987). Specifically, they sought regulation that would allow them to retain their elite status and avoid the enforced acceptance of others into membership. This issue will be discussed further later.

The intervention of the state in the organization of the profession in Quebec continued in 1973 when accountancy, along with 38 other occupational groups including medicine and law, were brought under the supervision of the Office of the Professions (*Office des professions du Québec*) and the Professional Code.[10] These acts established a consistent organizational structure and procedural requirements for all of the self-governing professions. The act also gave/reaffirmed monopoly rights to 21 of the 38 occupations affected, including the audit rights of the Order of Chartered Accountants of Quebec. The key changes to existing arrangements were

8. The AAM was later renamed the Institute of Chartered Accountants of Quebec and is currently known as the Order of Chartered Accountants of Quebec/Ordre des comptables agréés du Québec (in order to allow consistent acronyms of the French and English names for the association).

9. Statism refers to the existence of a strong central authority. France, until very recently, was regarded as the epitome of a statist regime (Hall 1986).

10. R.S.Q., chapter C-26 Professional Code 1973.

the requirement to add lay members to the governing boards of each group, the creation of a government oversight board that could review decisions and hear complaints against any profession and the removal of prerequisite educational standards from the purview of the professions.

The last point regarding education is important. Under the Professional Code the professional associations retain responsibility for setting standards for entry to the profession but the state can declare particular students as eligible to write the entrance exams. In accounting, this meant that graduates of certain university accounting programmes were immediately eligible to write professional accounting exams without the experience/articling requirement that existed in other provinces. The result was that the pass rate of Quebec students tended to be consistently below that of other provinces. This system loosened the connexion between the profession and post-secondary education in Quebec.

The unique situation within Quebec, reflecting the lasting influence of French imperialism and the creation of Canadian institutions during the declining years of the British Empire's hold of North America, creates problems for the accounting profession across Canada because of the desire to maintain reciprocal recognition among provincial associations. This means that the tension between French and English, and between common law and code law, has been institutionalized within the fabric of Canadian society. However, with the exception of these French influences on the internal organization of the profession in Canada,[11] the main colonial influence was from the UK.

## The UK Wellspring

The UK became the dominant colonial power in North America following nine years of conflict (1754–1763) between Britain and France. Under the Treaty of Paris (1763), France ceded control of all of Canada and the US east of the Mississippi to Britain. This provided the basis for a period of rapid development of British settlements in Canada and the 13 US colonies. The early population growth of Canada was based primarily on immigration from the UK as people escaped famine in Ireland, religious intolerance and poverty. Among the immigrants at this time were some with business connexions and/or training in UK accountancy. The accounting profession in Canada emerged during the 1840s, drawing largely on the skills of UK immigrants (Richardson 1989a; Edwards and Walker, forthcoming).

Chua and Poullaos (2002) note the 'strength of weak ties' between the UK and its colonies. The model of professionalism in accounting that developed in the UK travelled with immigrants to the colonies and was implemented, with local variations, as accountancy gained a critical mass

11. There was no apparent influence of the French 'Plan Comptable' on accounting practice in Quebec or Canada as a whole.

in these settings. The initial use of the title 'CA', for example, mimicked the emerging UK practice even though the Canadian professional associations were not 'chartered' (Parker 2005).

The two first accounting associations in Canada each mimicked UK associations in their design. The AAM was explicitly based on the SAE, while the Institute of Chartered Accountants of Ontario (ICAO—initially the Institute of Accountants and Adjusters of Canada) was modeled after the 'Institute of Chartered Accountants of Great Britain [*sic*]' (Edwards 1954, 356). At least one of the founders of the Ontario Institute had received their accounting training in the UK (Little 1964, 15), but most moved into accounting from a variety of commercial pursuits. The two early Canadian associations differed significantly in their philosophies concerning the purpose of a professional association. The AAM was restricted to members who had passed examinations and remained full-time practising public accountants while the ICAO was a training and credentialing institution whose members might be employed in any setting. This clash of views continued when the AAM backed the creation of the Dominion Association of Chartered Accountants (DACA) in 1901, but was resolved in 1909 when the DACA was reformed as a federation of provincial associations mirroring the structure of the Canadian confederation (see Richardson 2000 for a discussion of these events). The DACA was renamed the Canadian Institute of Chartered Accountants (CICA) in 1951. This resolution restricted the right to grant designations to provincial accounting associations and established the norm that accounting associations would play a role in training and certifying accountants who would remain members of the association regardless of their ultimate careers.

The importance of UK immigration to the development of the accounting profession in Canada was reflected in the composition of the leadership of the profession. Richardson (1989a) examined the demographic characteristics of the Canadian business elite and accounting elite during the early years of the development of the organized profession in Canada (1880–1930). While both groups had a large proportion of immigrants, the accounting elite were more likely to have a UK heritage than their clients. This skewed distribution of ethnicity is not evident among people classified as 'book-keepers' rather than accountants. It is evident that accounting attracted UK immigrants and these immigrants achieved positions of leadership well out of proportion to their numbers in the general population.

Unlike the situation in the US (e.g., Miranti 1988), there is no evidence that UK accountants and native-born accountants competed for control of the profession in Canada. In several cases, UK-trained accountants were founding members of Canadian associations alongside native-born accountants and as new provincial institutes opened in other provinces it became the norm to have an initial examination for membership set by chartered accountants (CAs) from the UK and existing Canadian institutes (Edwards 1915, 336–37). This is consistent with the largely pro-imperialist views within Canada during its early years as opposed to the 'revolutionary spirit' in the US that would emphasize local qualifications.

As Chua and Poullaos (2002) note, the development of an indigenous CA profession in Canada occurred largely without notice from the organized UK profession and certainly without asking 'permission' from the UK accounting associations. The few brief contacts between the two groups had no noticeable effect. This is in stark contrast to the relationship between the UK profession and the Newfoundland profession (Newfoundland remained a British protectorate until 1949 when it joined the Canadian Confederation). In Newfoundland, the organization of the profession and the designations that an accountant could use were greatly affected by lobbying of the Colonial Office (CO) by the Institute of Chartered Accountants in England and Wales (ICAEW). In part the difference in treatment reflected a difference in timing, with Canadian CA associations becoming established prior to the ICAEW developing its imperial monitoring capabilities and a difference in the status of the governments of the two colonies, with Canada being an independent nation while Newfoundland was still directly administered from London.

The first notable intervention of the UK in Canadian professional affairs was in 1911 by the UK CO in discussions of reserve title legislation in Ontario seeking to ensure that UK CAs could continue to use their designations in Canada.[12] The existence of national and provincial legislation controlling the CA designation could result in the UK CA designation being legally banned in Canada. The response of the Canadian CAs over the following five years, however, was to create lists of accounting societies whose members would be automatically granted membership in the provincial institutes (Creighton 1984, 67–69). This response served to remove any objections to the legislative protection of the CA designation in Canada and also, somewhat incidentally, provided a basis for mutual recognition among provincial institutes. Note, however, that these policies were implemented without reciprocity by the UK associations. This imbalance would become an issue for Canadian accountants as they began to move abroad.

After this initial skirmish, the Canadian CA profession and UK profession found a common interest in ensuring that their reputational capital was protected by acting against new entrants to the profession. In 1920, for example, a group attempted to incorporate as the Society of Incorporated Accountants and Auditors of Edmonton. John Hyde, representing the DACA, intervened in this case; pointing out that the name was too similar to a UK association. As a result, the group renamed itself the United Accountants and Auditors in Canada and Hyde received an honorary membership in the Incorporated Society of Accountants and Auditors of England for his

12. Chua and Poullaos (2002) describe correspondence between the CO and the ICAEW regarding the emergence of the DACA, but this was not reflected in Canadian sources.

service (Richardson 1993). In 1927 a round of articles in UK accounting journals claimed that the CA designation was being debased in Canada. This was quickly resolved (see Chapter 2 of this volume) and, in general, the UK profession and Canadian profession exhibited a high regard for each other.

In spite of the limited direct influence of the UK on Canadian professional development, there is no question that the UK profession remained as a point of reference for Canada on issues of professional ethics and examination procedures (Edwards 1915). For example, on issues such as the entry of women into the profession, the Canadian profession used the policies of the UK profession as a guide (McKeen and Richardson 1988). The Ontario Institute of Chartered Accountants in 1896 (quoted in Creighton 1984, 47), for example, stated:

> that, while not denying to women the right to practice as accountants or their ability in accountancy in certain special businesses, and there being no precedent of their being admitted as members in the older institutions of Great Britain upon which this Institute has been modeled and with which it would seem expedient to act in harmony—it is the opinion of the Institute that women should not be admitted to membership.

As auditing emerged as a regulated activity in Canada after the Second World War, there were renewed concerns about the accessibility of Canadian markets to UK qualified practitioners. Murphy (1958, 616), for example, observes:

> Sir John Somerville, President of The Institute of Chartered Accountants of Scotland, warned at that body's Centenary Celebration (1954), 'in many countries overseas the doors are shutting and the traditional outlets for Scottish Chartered Accountants are tending to become fewer.' Sir John stressed that, while recognition must be given to the problems of these countries, 'good relations with accountancy bodies overseas cannot only help the cause of international understanding, but will be of very direct benefit to many of our members in the future.' Today about one-half of the membership of the Scottish Institute is in practice overseas; of all those qualifying, 11 per cent migrate to Canada.

In general, however, there is no evidence that UK accountants holding designations from recognized associations ever had difficulty in entering the Canadian market (e.g., Chua and Poullaos 2002, 431, quoting a letter from the DACA to the ICAEW). In recent years, Canada as a signatory to the General Agreement on Trade in Services has taken further steps to ensure that citizenship and nationality are not used as barriers to entry to professional markets (WTO, Working Party of Professional Services 1997).

In addition to the importance of the UK models for the creation of professional associations, the UK Companies Acts were the models for Canadian regulation of financial accounting prior to 1900 (Murphy 1986). The Ontario Companies Act of 1907, however, introduced requirements that went beyond the UK, largely based on recommendations of the Ontario Institute of Chartered Accountants and the lobbying of its president, George Edwards (Richardson 2000). From this point forward Canada would pursue an independent role in developing its financial accounting model; however, it was increasingly influenced by the US and the integration of North American product and capital markets.

## FROM BRITISH IMPERIALISM TO AMERICAN IMPERIALISM

The US War of Independence (1775–1782), or the American Revolution as it is referred to in the UK, was a formative event for Canada as well as the US (Lipset 1965). After the war, those residents of the 13 US colonies who preferred to remain within the British Empire emigrated to the Canadian colonies (the so-called 'United Empire Loyalists'). It is estimated that between 40,000 and 70,000 people relocated at this time. This migration reinforced Canada's attachment to, and identity as part of, the British Empire. This heritage is reflected in the motto on the Provincial coat-of-arms for Ontario, *Ut incepit sic permanet fidelis*, adopted in 1868, which may be interpreted as: 'As she began, so she remains: loyal'. Penlington (1965), drawing on a wide variety of sources, has argued that Canadian (pro-British) imperialism and anti-Americanism were two sides of the same coin struck during the War of Independence.

The early acceptance of UK imperialism within Canada ensured that legislators would look to the UK for guidance on business legislation. However, the UK's trade policies weakened the imperial link with Canada and opened the door to the US. Prior to 1846, the UK had a policy of 'imperial preference' that encouraged trade with its colonies. The adoption of the Corn Laws in 1846 opened UK agricultural markets to competition, allowing the US to cut into Canada's trade with the UK. This market liberalism was widely implemented in the UK by 1860. Canada's response was the 'National Policy' adopted by the government of Sir John A. MacDonald in 1879. The policy established high tariffs to ensure the development of Canadian industry and to prevent a flood of cheap US imports. The federal elections of 1891 and 1911 resulted in defeat for the party advocating reciprocity of trade with the US, effectively institutionalizing the National Policy in the platforms of all political parties. This policy remained in force until 1989 when the free trade agreement with the US was enacted (initially it was an agreement to allow the cross-border transport of automotive components without tariff, the Canada–United States Automotive Agreement, 1965; in 1994 the agreement was expanded to include Mexico as the North American Free Trade Agreement [NAFTA]).

The National Policy had the effect of encouraging US investment in Canada. US companies wishing to serve the Canadian market established branch plants, licensed their products to Canadian companies or bought Canadian competitors to provide comparable products and services. These events resulted in the United States replacing the UK as the major source of foreign investment in Canada by the 1920s. Innis (1956, 405) suggests the effect was that 'Canada moved from colony to nation to colony'. By the 1950s the economic influence of America on Canada was a subject of widespread discussion but, in general, the conclusion was that this influence was incidental rather than an overt act of imperialism by the US (Scheinberg 1973). Canadian nationalism had simply created a protected market in which US capital could earn higher returns than in the US.

The growing influence of the US was felt on both the organization of the profession (Richardson 1993) and on financial disclosure practices (Murphy 1986). Given the timing of the development of professional structures versus standard-setting processes, the US would ultimately have more effect on the latter than the former. Initially there was confusion about the appropriate treatment of US accountants in Canada. The first joint meeting of the DACA and American Association of Certified Public Accountants (AACPA) was held in 1915 in Seattle. In the years that followed however, the provincial institutes came to different conclusions about the appropriate relationship between the Canadian and US professions. In 1916, on the creation of the Institute of Chartered Accountants of New Brunswick, members of American CPA associations practising in New Brunswick were automatically admitted to membership (Hudson 1966, 13–17). In the midst of the First World War, however, a motion was passed by the AAM and Institute of Chartered Accountants of Alberta limiting membership in CA institutes to British subjects, effectively excluding most US accountants. The Institute of Chartered Accountants of Manitoba (ICAM), on the other hand, admitted an American CPA to membership in 1922 without examination and the DACA negotiated a mutual recognition agreement with the American Institute of Certified Public Accountants (AICPA) in 1924 (Hoole 1963, 28). This agreement lasted until 1939 when the AICPA introduced a citizenship requirement for their members. The current policy of the CICA is to negotiate reciprocal agreements where a partner meets their standards.

After the First World War, a new specialty of cost accounting was recognized and professional associations supporting this specialty were created in both the UK and US. In Canada, the CAs created the Canadian Society of Cost Accountants (CSCA) as a vehicle for improving the practice of cost accounting, but this group was not intended to conduct examinations or offer a designation. The CSCA signed an affiliation agreement with the US National Association of Cost Accountants (NACA) in 1922 (Allan 1982,

9). The NACA proposed a merger between the two in 1926 but this was rejected and the CSCA ended their relationship and began publishing its own materials (Allan 1982, 13). Perhaps not surprisingly, however, when the Society of Cost Accountants began offering a designation and examinations in 1927 they adopted the curriculum of the NACA rather than the UK Chartered Institute of Management Accountants (CIMA). In part this reflects the greater similarity of practices between the two countries but also a growing cultural and communicative imperialism between the US and Canada. In 1972 the Society of Management Accountants of Canada (SMAC) and the NACA in the US negotiated a joint research programme (Allan 1982, 113). This co-operative relationship continues to the present.

In 1940 the CSCA decided to offer a designation to members as a public signal of their competence. The first attempt to gain legislative approval in Ontario using the name 'Certified Industrial Accountant' was unsuccessful (Allan 1982, 31). A second attempt using the 'Registered Industrial Accountant' (RIA) designation and supported by the CAs was successful. In Quebec the name approved was 'Licentiate of the Cost and Management Institute'. In 1947 the name of the society and the RIA designation was standardized across Canada. The name of members was changed to the present Certified Management Accountant (CMA) in 1977 (Allan 1982, 119). The CMA designation was initiated by the US NACA (renamed the Institute of Management Accountants) in 1972. The designation was designed explicitly to mirror the CPA designation. The decision by the Canadian society to follow this example was based on three considerations: (a) the term 'management accounting' better reflected the changing role of members; (b) the CMA designation could be translated into both English and French equivalent terms; and (c) the CMA designation allowed international recognition of the competency of members while the RIA had purely domestic recognition. Again Canada followed the US example in choosing a name rather than imitating the UK Institute of Cost and Management.

The growing salience of US practices in Canada meant that the US CPA designation was gaining recognition as a 'brand' in Canada (Richardson and Jones 2007). While the CPA is a state-granted designation for public accountants in the US, Canada follows the UK tradition and allows 'reserved titles' granted by provincial legislation for use by professional associations: there is no state-sanctioned title for accountants or auditors in Canada. This institutional inconsistency provided an opportunity for unaffiliated Canadian accountants. In 1936 a group incorporated in Ontario as the Certified Public Accountants Association of Ontario with the right to use the CPA designation (S.O. 1936 c.68). They gradually spread across Canada. In 1952 an attempt by this group to incorporate in Saskatchewan was opposed by existing Canadian associations and by US CPAs, but ultimately the group succeeded in all provinces. The CPAs merged with the CAs in 1960, with the CAs retaining control of the CPA designation (Richardson and Jones 2007).

The evolution of the CMA and CPA designations in Canada provide evidence of the importance of US cultural capital within Canada. There is no evidence, however, that the US attempted to block the use of these symbols within Canada. There is a qualitative difference between the influence of the US and the UK. Unlike UK imperialism that focused on keeping colonial markets open for UK-trained accountants, US imperialism focused on the flow of capital and the reverse flow of information needed to monitor those investments. The issue for the US was the financial reporting and auditing standards applied rather than the citizenship of the professional implementing those standards. This was accomplished initially through the export of intellectual capital in books, articles and practice guidelines; later the emphasis shifted to control of the production of international standards.

Murphy (1988, 92) finds that between 1920 and 1939 the percentage of UK articles in the *Canadian Chartered Accountant* (published by the DACA since 1910; now known as *CA Magazine*) declined from 53 to 36 per cent while the percentage of US articles increased from 44 to 60 per cent. In addition, 11 of 16 text-books in common use in Canada during this period were from the US. So in spite of a desire to remain politically independent of the US, there is evidence that the US was influencing the development of accounting thought and practice in Canada. Murphy (1988, 93–94) speculates that the change may have had three causes: (a) the availability of educational materials; (b) the rise of the 'branch-plant' economy where US companies were establishing operations in Canada to avoid protectionist tariffs; and (c) the development of ties between many of the major Canadian accounting firms and US accounting firms. An additional causal factor may have been that many academics in Canada had received their training in the US (Richardson 2001b). By 1960 Murphy (1988, 120) finds that none of the text-books in use at Canadian universities were from the UK. At this point the reliance of Canada on US accounting thought was virtually complete. The only exception to this was the development of depreciation practices as a result of developments in Canadian tax law.

In 1946 the CICA released its first accounting 'standard': Bulletin #1 of the Accounting and Auditing Research Committee. These bulletins mirrored the creation of the US Securities and Exchange Commission (SEC) Accounting Series Releases beginning in 1937 and the American Institute of Accountants (AIA) research bulletins beginning in 1939. Some commentators began to question whether or not Canadian accounting thought and practice could be independent:

> there is an important question whether Canadian thinking can afford to develop along lines different from the American. If not, we must either be prepared to accept whatever conclusions the American Institute arrives at is its present studies . . . or else we should move to participate with the American Institute in these studies. (Skinner 1961, 468)

Skinner's concern presaged the increasing movement of Canada towards an American style of financial market regulation and, along with it, the increasing influence of US standards on Canadian accounting practice. More formally, the trend towards US-style financial regulation continued with the creation of the Ontario Securities Commission (OSC) in 1966,[13] the creation of the CICA Handbook in 1968 and its adoption as GAAP by the National Securities Commissions (National Policy #27) in 1972 and in the Canada Business Corporations Act in 1975. This series of events created a US-style reliance on formal accounting standards but created by a private sector body without any legislative oversight more reminiscent of UK-style standard-setting.

Murphy (1988, 157–58) captures the dilemma of the change in focus from the UK to the US:

> [US] influence has grown to such proportions that it poses an enormous problem for the Canadian accounting profession. If their [Canadian] research activities go beyond what are uniquely Canadian problems, their efforts can be considered to be redundant, or at least inefficient, in relation to the economies of scale achievable in these matters in America. On the other hand, dealing with peculiarly Canadian problems is a constraint which both acknowledges and aggravates the dependence on America for more general accounting theory.

Since the 1960s there has been increasing co-operation between the US and Canada on the development of standards. In addition, the CICA and AICPA co-operated in a number of 'value-added' assurance products that were jointly branded, including 'Eldercare', an online privacy framework, and 'WebTrust' (Melanson 1998). At the same time, however, a significant international accounting harmonization movement and institutional structure were emerging. Canada's relationship to imperial powers would have to be recast within this context.

## CANADA AS A MIDDLE POWER

At the end of the Second World War it was recognized that many of the economic and social problems facing nations could only be solved through multilateral agreements and action. The 'superpowers' might divide the world into economic blocs and military protectorates, but there was a need to broker agreements on specific issues and to resolve conflicts in ways that allowed mutual gains to all parties. This was part of the rationale for the creation of institutions—such as the World Bank, the International Monetary Fund (IMF), the General Agreement on Tariffs and Trade (GATT) and

13. Ontario Statutes, 1966, chap. 142, sec. 139.

the World Trade Organization (WTO)—to implement the 'Bretton Woods' agreement (1944). Within this framework, countries such as Canada, Australia and France developed a 'middle power' approach to international relations (Chapnick 1999).

Jordaan (2003, 165) captures the essence of what it means to be a middle power:

> All middle powers display foreign policy behaviour that stabilises and legitimises the global order, typically through multilateral and cooperative initiatives. However, emerging and traditional middle powers can be distinguished in terms of their mutually-influencing constitutive and behavioural differences. Constitutively, traditional middle powers are wealthy, stable, egalitarian, social democratic and not regionally influential. Behaviourally, they exhibit a weak and ambivalent regional orientation, constructing identities distinct from powerful states in their regions and offer appeasing concessions to pressures for global reform. Emerging middle powers by contrast are semi-peripheral, materially inegalitarian and recently democratised states that demonstrate much regional influence and self-association. Behaviourally, they opt for reformist and not radical global change, exhibit a strong regional orientation favouring regional integration but seek also to construct identities distinct from those of the weak states in their region.

There are numerous recent examples of Jordaan's (2003) prediction that Canada, as a traditional middle power, would construct an identity distinct from the US. Canada adopted the Kyoto Accord on Environmental Change, sponsored the treaty to ban landmines[14] and championed (with France) the UNESCO Convention on the Promotion and Protection of the Diversity of Cultural Expression—all initiatives that the US opposed (Tiberghien and Dierkes 2006 provide further examples).

In accounting, too, Canada began to develop a middle power approach characterized by the development of a distinct Canadian identity but also supporting institutional arrangements that facilitated global integration. Skinner (1961) was one of the first to recognize that Canada was too dependent on the US to develop independent accounting standards and practices; he advocated that rather than simply accepting the influence of the US that Canada participate jointly with them in standard-setting processes. While, as noted earlier, this was partly accomplished through joint ventures with the US by both CAs and CMAs, Canada also became involved in multilateral ventures. This began in 1966 when Canada joined the UK and the US in the Accountant's International Study Group (AISG),

14. 1997 Convention on the Prohibition of the Use, Stockpiling, Production and Transfer of Anti-Personal Mines and on their Destruction.

organized by Henry Benson (Camfferman and Zeff 2007). The intent of this group was to examine issues of common concern and to encourage members to develop consistent standards across countries. In spite of these efforts, however, Drury (1979) noted the divergence of Canadian accounting standards from the US during the 1960s and early 1970s. This was in part due to the rapid rate of production of standards in the US and the relatively slow reaction to these issues in Canada. But, in addition, Canada, in spite of its desire to harmonize with the US, retained the UK principles-based approach to accounting and hence did not favour the development of detailed accounting rules.

The AISG disbanded in 1976 after the formation of the International Accounting Standards Committee (IASC). The IASC began to expand its membership and the agenda and focus of the group moved away from the needs of capital markets. Initially the IASC simply documented the variety of procedures used and identified clearly unacceptable methods (1973–1982). It then began to narrow the range of acceptable alternatives by specifying a benchmark approach (1983–1989). Finally, the IASC began to create standards which attempted to direct practice (1989–2001; cf. Camfferman and Zeff 2007).

In 1994 the CICA released the *Inter-Institute Vision Task Force Report*, which considered a wide range of issues affecting the future of the profession. With regard to accounting standards it concluded that it was important to 'harmonize accounting and auditing standards globally with a particular focus on developing common standards on an integrated basis (including developing new standards and responding to emerging issues), first in North America and then internationally'. This position was reinforced in the CICA 2004 Strategic Review:

> For the Canadian CA profession, globalization and Canada/U.S. economic integration highlight the importance of CA/CPA reciprocity and the potential for cross-border services. These factors also underscore why it is essential that the Canadian CA profession play an active role in the international governance of the profession, particularly in the areas of accounting, auditing, ethics and education. This requires effective management of our relationships with accounting and other bodies around the world, including the International Federation of Accountants (IFAC), the Financial Accounting Standards Board (FASB), the International Accounting Standards Board (IASB), the National Association of State Boards of Accountancy (NASBA), the Securities and Exchange Commission (SEC), the Canadian Public Accountability Board (CPAB) and the Public Company Accounting Oversight Board (PCAOB). (CICA 2004, 25)

The CICA thus maintained a policy in which it participated in international, regional and bilateral harmonization projects. For example, during the final years of the IASC, the CICA participated in a group, known as the G4, that looked remarkably like the AISG and consisted of the UK, US and developed Commonwealth countries (Canada, Australia and New Zealand) (Street and Shaughnessy 1998). The G4 met four times a year between 1993 and 2001. It provided an alternative to the IASC's generalist orientation towards accounting standards and was instrumental in providing pressure to focus standards on the needs of capital markets and to reform the IASC as the International Accounting Standards Board (IASB). The G4 was composed of accounting standard-setters from each country (notably including the Financial Accounting Standards Board [FASB], which was not represented in the IASC while the AICPA was, reflecting the formation of the IASC by professional associations). The reformation of the IASC into the IASB disenfranchised the professional associations in favour of the standard-setting bodies. The fact that the G4 disbanded when the IASB was formed indicates that its function had been taken over by the IASB.

Canada was also working with the US as part of a group concerned with harmonizing financial reporting among NAFTA countries (Moore 2000). This group first met in 1992 and published a report in 1995 entitled *Financial Reporting in North America* which advocated further harmonization and the creation of the 'American Free Trade Agreement Committee for Cooperation on Financial Reporting Matters'. This committee was formed consisting of the US, Canada, Mexico and Chile[15] and produces a biennial comparison of financial reporting practices entitled *Significant Differences in GAAP in Canada, Chile, Mexico and the United States*. The intent of the group is to provide information that will assist in harmonization efforts but it has explicitly steered clear of setting standards.

Even though Canada continued to work closely with the US, both directly through joint projects with FASB and indirectly through the G4, it also was the most active country in promoting the use of IAS (Hillier and Smith 1996; Camfferman and Zeff 2007). The fact that Canada was, regardless of these multilateral overtures, still focused on the US can be seen in the decision in 1998 to harmonize Canadian GAAP with FASB standards. This statement coincided with FASB's vision statement, which suggested that either it or the G4 could play the role of international standard-setter. Once the IASC was reformed as the IASB, Canada then made a formal commitment to adopt International Financial Reporting Standards (IFRS) as Canadian GAAP.

Canadian accountants have been playing a delicate game in their relationship with the US. Unable to directly influence the US, they have used multilateral organizations as a platform for discussion of key issues:

> Paul Cherry, chairman of the CASB [Canadian Accounting Standards Board] in Toronto, points to Canada's historic interest in the resolving

15. Chile has expressed an interest in joining NAFTA.

> of international issues through multilateral agencies as part of the reason for its strong backing of both the IASC and IASB. 'I think we're kindred spirits in terms of our approach internationally as a culture,' says Cherry. 'In addition, we've never been quite as rules-driven or as oriented to precision as they are in the US, so working internationally has been a more comfortable fit for us. We've always seen the international arena and its forums as giving us considerable influence in the US because they've been at the same table. It has been very fruitful for us over the years rather than working only through bilateral negotiations. Being part of the IASB gives us an excellent arena to build consensus and more influence than our size alone would suggest.' And O'Malley [Canadian liaison on the IASB] agrees. 'I think Canada has always had strong ties to the UK tradition of doing things,' she says. 'At the same time, because we've always had a huge economic pull to the US, working with multilateral groups has been one way to distance ourselves and maintain independence. We don't have a lot of direct influence with the United States but, historically, we have tended to punch above our weight in international forums'. (Quinn 2003, 16)

This view of Canada's multilateralism must be balanced with the US view of their role in international organizations:

> The aim of American foreign policy is to work with other like-minded actors to 'improve' the market place, to increase compliance with basic norms, by choice if possible, by necessity—i.e., coercion—if need be. At the core, regulation [of the international system] is an imperial doctrine in that it seeks to promote a set of standards we endorse—something not to be confused with imperialism, which is a foreign policy of exploitation. (Haass 1997, 70)

## CONCLUSION

The British Empire did not exist in isolation. It developed in conflict with other imperial powers and was reformed by rebellions among its colonies. The influence of the British Empire on Canada and the development of the Canadian accounting profession can thus only be understood in relationship to other imperial influences. Specifically, I have argued that the Canadian accounting profession emerged in the interstices of the French, British and American Empires. Each empire left an institutional legacy that shaped how subsequent imperial influences would be manifest within Canada. The Canadian Constitution, which creates the division of labour amongst the levels of government and provides the legal framework under which professional associations and standard-setting activities occurs, for example, includes aspects of French and British traditions but this amalgam only occurred because of the threat of the American Revolution. The regulation of businesses and financial disclosure in Canada is a combination of American market liberalism and Westminster institutions reflecting the commitment of Canadian law-makers to the British Empire within the context of the North American integration of capital and product markets. The Canadian accounting profession continues to develop within the context of competing influences from America and Europe, exhibiting the diplomatic skill and sensitivities to empires of a middle power. Throughout Canada's development, imperial influence, regardless of its source, was incomplete and inconsistent, allowing Canada to develop a unique voice in the international arena (Berger 1970).

## REFERENCES


Allan, J.N. (1982) *History of the Society of Management Accountants of Canada*. Hamilton: SMAC.

American Accounting Association. (1977) '1975–1976 Committee on International Accounting Operations and Education'. *Accounting Review* 52 (Committee Reports: Supplement): 65–67, 69–75, 77–101, 103–15, 117–32.

Berger, C. (1970) *The Sense of Power: Studies in the Ideas of Canadian Imperialism, 1867–1914*. Toronto: University of Toronto Press.

Bujaki, M. (2007) 'Cost-benefit considerations in communications relating to the construction of the Rideau Canal'. Paper presented at the Fifth Accounting History International Conference, Banff, Canada, May.

Camfferman, K., and Zeff, S.A. (2007) *Financial Reporting and Global Capital Markets: A History of the International Accounting Standards Committee, 1973–2000*. Oxford: Oxford University Press.

Canadian Institute of Chartered Accountants. (2004) *Strategic Crossroads for the CA Profession*. Toronto: CICA.

———. (1996) *Inter-institute Vision Task Force Report*. Toronto: CICA.

———. Instituto Mexicano De Contardores Publicos, Financial Accounting Standards Board. (1995) *Financial Reporting in North America*. Stamford: FASB.

Chapnick, A. (1999) 'The middle power'. *Canadian Foreign Policy* 7 (Winter): 73–82

Chua, W.F., and Poullaos, C. (1998) 'The dynamics of "closure" amidst the construction of market, profession, empire and nationhood: An historical analysis of an Australian accounting association, 1886–1903'. *Accounting, Organizations and Society* 23:155–87.

———. (2002) 'The empire strikes back? An exploration of centre–periphery interaction between the ICAEW and accounting associations in the self-governing colonies of Australia, Canada and South Africa, 1880–1907'. *Accounting, Organizations and Society* 27:409–45.

Creighton, P. (1984) *A Sum Of Yesterdays—Being a History of the First One Hundred Years of The Institute of Chartered Accountants of Ontario*. Toronto: Institute of Chartered Accountants of Ontario.

Drury, D.H. (1979) 'Effects of accounting practice divergence: Canada and the United States'. *Journal of International Business Studies* 10:75–87.

Editorial. (1913) *Canadian Chartered Accountant* 3:119.

Edwards, G. (1915) 'Accountancy in Canada'. *Journal of Accountancy* 20 (November): 334–48.

Edwards, H.P. (1954) 'After three score years and ten'. *Canadian Chartered Accountant* 64:356–63.

Edwards, J.R., and Walker, S.P. (Forthcoming) 'Occupational differentiation and exclusion in early Canadian accountancy'. *Accounting and Business Research.*

Galtung, J. (1971) 'A structural theory of imperialism'. *Journal of Peace Research* 8:81–117.

Haass, R.N. (1997) *The Reluctant Sheriff.* New York: Council of Foreign Relations.

Hall, P.A. (1986) *Governing the Economy: The Politics of State Intervention in Britain and France.* Oxford: Oxford University Press.

Hillier, D., and Smith, S. (1996) 'Global standards bearers'. *CA Magazine* (October): 50–54.

Hoole, A.H. (1963) *A Brief History of the Institute of Chartered Accountants of Manitoba 1886–1961.* Winnipeg: ICAM.

Hudson, G.W. (1966) *A History of the New Brunswick Institute of Chartered Accountants.* Saint John: ICANB.

Ignatieff, M. (2003) 'The burden'. *New York Times Magazine.* http://www.nytimes.com/2003/01/05/magazine/05EMPIRE.html?pagewanted=1. Accessed Dec. 17, 2009.

Innis, H. (1956) 'Great Britain, the United States and Canada'. In *Essays in Canadian Economic History*, ed. H. Innis. Toronto: University of Toronto Press.

Jordaan, E. (2003) 'The concept of a middle power in international relations: Distinguishing between emerging and traditional middle powers'. *Politikon* 30:165–81.

Lipset, S.M. (1965) 'Revolution and counter revolution: The United States and Canada'. In *The Revolutionary Theme in Contemporary America*, ed. L T.R. Ford. Lexington: University of Kentucky.

Little, A.J. (1964) *The Story of the Firm (Clarkson Gordon).* Toronto: Clarkson Gordon.

Maier, C.S. (2006) *Among Empires: American Ascendancy and its Predecessors.* Cambridge, MA: Harvard University Press.

Mancke, E. (1999) 'Early modern imperial governance and the origins of Canadian political culture'. *Canadian Journal of Political Science/Revue Canadienne de Science Politique* 32:3–20.

Mann, H. (1976) *The Evolution of Accounting in Canada.* Montreal: Touche Ross.

McKeen, C.A., and Richardson, A.J. (1988) 'Education, employment and certification: An oral history of the entry of women into the Canadian accounting profession'. *Business and Economic History* 27:500–521.

Melanson, L. (1998) 'Be assured'. *CA Magazine* (January/February): 17–21.

Miranti, P., Jr. (1988) 'Professionalism and nativism: The competition in securing public accountancy legislation in New York during the 1890s'. *Social Science Quarterly* 60:361–82.

Murphy, G.J. (1986) 'A chronology of the development of corporate financial reporting in Canada: 1850 to 1983'. *Accounting Historians Journal* 13:31–62.

———. (1988) *The Evolution of Selected Annual Corporate Financial Reporting Practices in Canada, 1900–1970.* New York: Garland Press.

Murphy, M.E. (1958) 'Comparative professional accountancy'. *Accounting Review* 33:615–21.

Neu, D. (1999) 'Discovering indigenous peoples: Accounting and the machinery of empire'. *Accounting Historians Journal* 26:53–82.

———. (2000) 'Presents for the "Indians": Land, colonialism and accounting in Canada'. *Accounting, Organizations and Society* 25:163–84.

Neu, D., and Graham, C. (2006) 'The birth of a nation: Accounting and Canada's First Nations, 1860–1900'. *Accounting, Organizations and Society* 31:47–76.

Neu, D., and Therrien, R. (2003) *Accounting for Genocide. Canada's Bureaucratic Assault on Aboriginal People.* Black Point, NS: Fernwood Publishing.

Parker, R.H. (2005) 'Naming and branding: Accountants and accountancy bodies in the British Empire and commonwealth, 1853–2003'. *Accounting History* 10:7–46.

Penlington, N. (1965) *Canada and Imperialism, 1896–1899.* Toronto: University of Toronto Press.

Porter, B. (2006) *Empire and Superempire: Britain, America, and the World.* New Haven, CT: Yale University Press.

Porter, J. (1957) 'The economic elite and the social structure in Canada'. *Canadian Journal of Economics and Political Science* 23:376–94.

Puxty, A.G., Willmott, H.C., Cooper, D.J., and Lowe, T. (1987) 'Modes of regulation in advanced capitalism: Locating accountancy in four countries'. *Accounting, Organizations and Society* 12:273–91.

Quinn, L.S. (2003) 'Closing the GAAP'. *CA Magazine* (August). http://www.camagazine.com/index.cfm/ci_id/16030/la_id/1.htm (accessed November 2007).

Richardson, A.J. (1989a) 'Canada's accounting elite: 1880–1930'. *Accounting Historians Journal* 16:1–21.

———. (1989b) 'Corporatism and intraprofessional hegemony: A study of regulation and social order'. *Accounting, Organizations and Society* 14:415–31.

———. (1993) 'An interpretative chronology of the development of accounting associations in Canada: 1879–1979'. In *A History of Canadian Accounting Thought and Practice*, ed. G. Murphy. New York: Garland Press.

———. (2000) 'Building the Canadian CA profession: A biography of George Edwards FCA CBE LLD, 1861–1947'. *Accounting Historians Journal* 27:87–116.

———. (2001a) 'The Canadian audit market in the first half of the twentieth century'. *Accounting Historians Journal* 28:109–40.

———. (2001b) 'Origins of the Canadian Academic Accounting Association'. In *Canadian Academic Accounting Association: 25 Years of Progress*, ed. E. Boritz. Toronto: CAAA.

Richardson, A.J., and Jones, D.G.B. (2007) 'Professional "brand", personal identity and resistance to change in the Canadian accounting profession: A comparative history of two accounting association merger negotiations'. *Accounting History* 12:135–64.

Said, E. (1993) *Culture and Imperialism.* London: Vintage Books.

Scheinberg, S. (1973) 'Invitation to empire: Tariffs and American economic expansion in Canada'. *Business History Review* 47:218–38.

Skinner, R. (1961) 'Generally accepted accounting principles'. *Canadian Chartered Accountant* 78:463–68.

Spraakman, G. (1999) 'Management accounting at the historical Hudson's Bay Company: A comparison to twentieth century practices'. *Accounting Historians Journal* 26:35–64.

Spraakman, G., and Davidson, R. (1998) 'Transaction cost economics as a predictor for management accounting practices at the Hudson's Bay Company, 1860 to 1914'. *Accounting History* 3:69–101.

Spraakman, G., and Wilkie, A. (2000) 'The development of management accounting at the Hudson's Bay Company, 1670 to 1820'. *Accounting History* 5:59–84.

Street, D.L., and Shaughnessy, K.A. (1998) 'The evolution of the G4 + 1 and its impact on international harmonization of accounting standards'. *Journal of International Accounting, Auditing and Taxation* 7:131–61.

Thompson, R.R. (1939) 'The development of accounting in Canada'. *Canadian Chartered Accountant* 34:171–86.

Thomson, D.C. (1988) *Vive le Québec Libre.* Quebec: Deneau Publishers.

Thomson, D.C., and Swanson, R.F. (1971) *Canadian Foreign Policy: Options and Perspectives.* Toronto: McGraw-Hill Ryerson.

Tiberghien, Y., and Dierkes, J. (2006) 'Minerva's moment: Japan, Canada and the EU in global institution-building'. Paper presented at the Minerva's Moment Conference, August. http://www.iar.ubc.ca/centres/cjr/seminars/minerva/intro.html (accessed November 2007).

WTO, Working Party of Professional Services. (1997) *Elements to Be Addressed in Developing Disciplines for Professional Services: Accountancy Sector.* 20 June, WTO document S/WPPS/W/15.

# 4 Colonial Heritage and the Accounting Profession in Nigeria

*Chibuike U. Uche*

## INTRODUCTION

The focus of the accounting profession in any country is shaped by the various social, political and economic pressures that impact on the accounting needs of the jurisdiction (Wallace 1989, 1). An appreciation of the state of development of the accounting profession in a country is therefore enhanced by trying to understand the dynamics of these pressures and how they impact on the country's accounting needs and by extension, the accounting profession. In the case of Nigeria, for instance, the various forces that have often competed for influence in shaping the focus of the accounting profession include: the country's colonial history, its level of economic development and the accounting needs of the multinational business enterprises and the interests of government and local businesses.

The essence of this chapter is to explore the challenges to the accounting profession in Nigeria in the context of the aforementioned trajectory. Emphasis is placed on identifying the influence of the country's colonial past in the current challenges being faced by the Nigerian accounting profession. It shows how colonial economic, legal and accounting structures have extensively influenced the focus of the Nigerian accounting profession. The structures have also worked in tandem with the interests of multinational businesses. The subsequent outcomes have, in the main, been to the detriment of the majority of the indigenous economic interests represented by the numerous small-scale businesses and, by extension, the economic development of Nigeria. Even the state, which gives authority to professions and whose indigenization policies helped promote the rapid growth of the main indigenous accounting association—the Institute of Chartered Accountants of Nigeria (ICAN)—and the interests of its members in the 1970s and 1980s, has been unable to effectively get the accounting profession to focus on the needs of small businesses.

To achieve its aim, the remainder of this chapter is divided into four main sections. The one immediately following explores the economic origins of colonization and the emergence of the accounting profession in Nigeria. The next traces the colonial origins of ICAN and shows how they have impacted on its ability to provide for the accounting needs of the various economic interests in the country. It also examines the impact of this on the proliferation of accounting bodies in Nigeria. A critique of the resurgence of the British-based Association of Chartered Certified Accountants (ACCA) in Nigeria and its implications for the future of ICAN follows. The final section summarizes the key elements of the colonial legacy of the accounting profession in Nigeria.

## COLONIZATION AND THE EMERGENCE OF THE ACCOUNTING PROFESSION IN NIGERIA

The origin of the accounting profession in Nigeria is without doubt linked to the colonization of the country by the British. The whole idea of colonization was in the main driven by British economic interests.[1] Prior to 1861, Africa, dubbed the 'dark continent' by European adventurers and traders, was a 'no man's land' and an 'everyman's land' (Onoh 1982, 25). In those days, there was no uniform method of trading or accepted means of exchange even within territories (Departmental Committee Appointed to Inquire into Matters Affecting the Currency of British West African Colonies and Protectorates 1912, 2). In 1861, the territory of Lagos was formally ceded to the British government and it became known as the Lagos Colony. It thus became the first part of present-day Nigeria to come under British rule. In 1885, the British government proclaimed the Oil Rivers Protectorate over some parts of present-day Southern Nigeria. In 1893, its name was changed to the Niger Coast Protectorate with the new Protectorate incorporating a larger area (Niven 1946, 166–67).

In 1896, a number of British companies then operating around the Niger amalgamated into the Royal Niger Company. The charter of the new company gave it powers to 'administer and make treaties, levy customs duties and trade in all territories in the basin of the Niger and its affluents [*sic*]' (Ekundare 1973, 12). This brought the northern territories of Nigeria under the influence of British traders. In 1900, the British government took over the administration of the northern territories from the Royal Niger Company, proclaiming the area as the Protectorate of Northern Nigeria. Also in the same year, the administration of all parts of Southern Nigeria, with the

1. 'The raw materials of Africa and the market which the continent offered to manufactured goods, became increasingly important in the growing industries of Europe . . . The mania for colonization in Africa with which a number of the European nations were seized proceeded largely from a desire to provide outlets for surplus home products . . . Nigeria did provide a market for some European manufactures, but its real source of profit lay in its own products: there was a much greater contribution to economic growth to be made in the purchase of Nigerian rubber, palm oil and palm kernels than by the sale of gin and cotton goods to the people of Africa' (Ekundare 1973, 62–63).

exception of Lagos, was unified under the Protectorate of Southern Nigeria. In 1906, Lagos was made part of the Protectorate of Southern Nigeria and, in 1914, the Protectorates of Southern and Northern Nigeria were amalgamated to become the Colony and Protectorate of Nigeria (Niven 1946, 244).

Given the economic origins of colonization, the British colonial administration soon began to put in place the necessary structures to ensure the smooth functioning of administration and commerce. The ideological foundation for such structures was the belief that colonial territories were primitive and uncivilized. There was thus the need to help enhance their economic practices in a manner which could be mutually beneficial to both the interest of the British and the colonies. In reality, however, this ideology failed and the structure mainly helped promote the interest of British businesses to the detriment of their indigenous counterparts. Along these lines, it has been asserted that:

> Just as the Colonial rule altered traditional political institutions in the name of civilization, so too did it transform the economy of Nigeria. Ideally, the British believed that they could bring Nigerian societies into 'civilization' through the development of a 'modern' economy. By expanding the commercial infrastructure and promoting increased trade throughout Nigeria, British colonial administrators believed that they were fulfilling the dictates of the Dual Mandate, making the colonial endeavor profitable for European merchants and Nigerian producers . . . Over time [however] colonial economic policy resulted in the growing dependence of Nigerians on an export economy dominated by European firms with which indigenous Nigerian enterprises could not compete and which conducted business primarily with a view towards European profitability at the expense of Nigerian producers. (Falola and Heaton 2008, 118–19)

The preceding broad principles also mirrored the British approach to the development of the accounting profession in Nigeria. Here, the colonial government, in pursuit of civilizing and modernizing the Nigerian business environment, promulgated the Companies Ordinance of 1922. Not surprisingly, this followed closely the UK Companies Act of 1908 (Parker 1958, 693). The impact of the 1922 Companies Ordinance on the practice and development of the accounting profession in Nigeria has been explained thus:

> It required from 1922 each company operating in Nigeria to be registered there and to prepare a balance sheet, and file the same with the Registrar of Companies . . . the Ordinance required auditors to report whether the balance sheet exhibited a 'true and correct' view but gave no legal guidance as to the contents of the balance sheet. The Ordinance did not mandate that auditors be trained or that they belong to

> any professional body. Only those approved by the minister supervising the implementation of the Ordinance could be appointed by registered companies as auditors. Before 1960, such approved status was granted to those who possessed the certificates to practice as auditors issued by the UK accountancy bodies and those who had worked in the audit department of government for a minimum of fifteen years and had passed the intermediate examinations of the UK accountancy bodies. Only fifteen Nigerians obtained the 'approved status' of the Minister before 1960. (Wallace 1992, 27–28)

Aside from creating a structured framework for the advent of more British businesses into the Nigerian colony, the 1922 Companies Ordinance also created the need for professional accountants to service such companies both for internal and external reporting purposes. The ordinance was therefore a major policy push in the development of the accounting profession in Nigeria. It did not, however, effectively apply to most of the African businesses which were not incorporated as companies. Even the incorporated businesses were too small to comprehend the accounting requirements of an ordinance that did not recognize that the needs of small companies were different from those of medium and large enterprises (Wallace 1989, 23).

This, at least in part, was responsible for the fact that by 1939, seven European firms controlled over 67 per cent of all Nigeria's export trade. Even areas where African businesses initially had locational advantages like textiles, brewery and blacksmithing also faced stiff competition from the cheaper European imports that flooded the markets (Falola and Heaton 2008, 121–22). Rather than grow African businesses, the colonial structures contributed to their shrinking. The emergence of a British-style Companies Ordinance in 1922 which did not contextualize the peculiar circumstances of the majority of African businesses simply complicated matters for such businesses.

As foreign businesses grew, so too did their accounting needs and requirements. Interest in providing for their accounting needs facilitated the emergence of foreign accounting firms and accounting professionals in Nigeria. The first professional accounting firm to be established in Nigeria was the British firm of Cassleton Elliot in 1927 (Wallace 1989, 29). It was not until 1948, however, with the enactment of a new Companies Act in the United Kingdom which increased the responsibility of auditors with respect to returns from overseas branches of British registered companies, that the Nigerian accounting market became more attractive to other British firms. This has been explained thus:

> The UK Companies Act 1948 produced the need for accounting services to be provided locally at the overseas branches of British registered companies. This was the result of the requirement for auditors to state expressly in their reports: 'Whether in their opinion . . . proper

> returns adequate for the purposes of their audit have been received from branches not visited by them' . . . The most satisfactory kind of return for the purposes of audit would be one provided by local, independent professional auditors. The outcome was that between 1948 and 1953, three other UK firms of professional accountants developed a substantial clientele in Nigeria and opened offices in the country: Pannell Crewdson & Hardy (now Pannell Kerr Forster) in 1949, Midgley, Snelling and Barnes and Cooper Brothers and Co. . . . [each now part of PricewaterhouseCoopers] in 1949 and 1953 respectively. (Wallace 1992, 32–33)

Given that the source of this change originated from the UK and applied mainly to UK businesses, it was not surprising that UK accounting firms and accountants were also the main beneficiaries of the growth it engendered in the provision of accounting services in Nigeria at the time. Most of the UK firms that set up practice in Nigeria were also staffed, at least at the top, by expatriate accountants. In fact, at the time of Nigeria's independence in 1960, there was no Nigerian partner in any of the UK firms operating in the country.[2]

The establishment of an indigenous professional accounting body in Nigeria became feasible only with the movement towards political independence in the country. Prior to that time, the handful of accountants in the country were all foreigners and it was not until 1950 that Mr. Akintola Williams became the first Nigerian to qualify as a chartered accountant (CA) when he was admitted into the Institute of Chartered Accountants in England and Wales (ICAEW). By 1960 there were 40 Nigerian members of the recognized accounting professional bodies in the UK. Out of this number, 24 were members of the Association of Certified and Corporate Accountants (now the ACCA) (Anibaba 1990, 175–77).

The popularity of the ACCA qualification among Nigerians was no doubt linked to the structure of the association's accounting training at the time. Unlike some professional bodies in the UK at the time, there was little restriction with respect to articleship training. The ICAEW, for example, restricted admission to articled clerks of practising accountants in the UK. In other words, to become student members of the ICAEW, Nigerians needed to secure an appropriate articleship posting in the UK. Widespread racism in the UK accounting profession made articleship appointments for Africans at the time very difficult. Pioneer Nigerian ICAEW member Akintola Williams (quoted in Inanga 1992, 14) documented his experience in this regard thus:

---

2. It was not until 1966 that Mr. C.O.O. Oyediran became the first Nigerian to be appointed as a partner in an international firm of chartered accountants (CAs) (Cooper Brothers and Co.). The next year (1967), another Nigerian, Mr. Anthony Ani, was appointed a partner in Peat Marwick, Cassleton and Elliot and Co.

> Upon arrival in London, I was pacing the pavements of that city looking for a firm of chartered accountants that would take me. I could not find one . . . I reported my frustration to Mr. Bankes, who was then the Secretary of the Institute of Chartered Accountants of England and Wales . . . After saying something about not understanding his people (the English) who would gather together at the LORDS to watch cricket . . . and would applaud a man like Constantine (later Lord Constantine) the great West Indian Cricketer who was a black man, the same English people were not prepared to admit black people in their offices for training as accountants. Mr. Bankes then sent me to speak to a friend of his . . . Ralph Hamlyn who was the next senior partner in the firm of Binder, Hamlyn and Co. . . . [who] offered to give me the opportunity of serving my articleship with his firm. He did, however, explain that my auditing assignments might be limited because some of his clients might actually object to having a black articled clerk look through their books.

Corroborating this view, a former president of the ICAEW suggested that the reluctance of accounting firms to employ overseas students as articled clerks sometimes emanated from the reluctance of their clients to allow such persons carry out audit work in their offices (*Accountant*, 1956, 330).

Given the relatively large number of ACCA members in Nigeria, it was not surprising that it was they who first moved to set up a professional accountancy body by applying in 1957 to form a local branch of the ACCA. By 1959, however, this plan had been overtaken by the idea of forming a local accountancy body that would bring all Nigerians with overseas accountancy qualifications of equivalent standards together (Coker 1990). This culminated in the setting up of the Association of Accountants in Nigeria (AAN), with the main objective of advancing the interest of the accounting profession in Nigeria, in 1960 (ICAN 1985b). This was also the year that Nigeria gained her independence. The qualification for membership of the association was membership in any of the recognized accounting bodies then existing in the UK.[3]

As will be seen in the next section of this chapter, the attainment of political independence and the establishment of a local accounting association fundamentally altered the terrain of professional accounting practice in Nigeria by giving a greater voice to Nigerian accountants. The linkage of the local accounting body with UK accounting bodies also became a major source of both strength and conflict in the development of the Nigerian accounting profession.

3. These were the ICAEW, ACCA, the Institute of Chartered Accountants of Scotland (ICAS), the Institute of Chartered Accountants of Ireland (ICAI), the Institute of Municipal Treasurers and Accountants ([IMTA]—now the Chartered Institute of Public Finance and Accountancy [CIPFA]) and the Institute of Cost and Works Accountants ([ICWA]—now the Chartered Institute of Management Accountants [CIMA]).

## THE COLONIAL ORIGINS OF ICAN AND THE EMERGENCE OF RIVAL PROFESSIONAL BODIES

From the very beginning, disagreements with respect to the relationship of the new body with the various UK professional accounting bodies dominated the debate surrounding the formation of the AAN. Very little thought was given to the need to contextualize the emergent professional body by taking into consideration the economic and social realities of the Nigerian environment. In 1963, for instance, the council of the association decided to explore the possibility of obtaining a government charter for the association with the aim of achieving monopoly over the regulation of the accounting profession in Nigeria. This in itself caused serious rancour among the members of the association. Some people found it difficult to comprehend how members of the various UK professional bodies, with all their differences, could possess similar rights and privileges in an indigenous accounting body (Anibaba 1990). Also, some members of the ICAEW felt that the acronym 'ACA' should be reserved for ICAEW members only (Ogutuga 1990, 43). Apparently angered by the discrimination against Nigerians in the accounting profession at the time, another group of members also proposed, unsuccessfully, that the association should be established purely on racial basis. At its 1963 annual general meeting, the then president of AAN, Mr. F.C.O. Coker (quoted in Anibaba 1990, 47), asserted that:

> I cannot touch on the subject of membership without saying something about the activities of a group of Nigerian accountants who are seeking to establish a professional association on racial basis. All members of the Association should take this matter seriously because it is a great mistake for any group of persons at the present time to imagine that it is a good thing to form a professional association on [a] racial basis. I should have thought that professional qualification is a matter of ability and that men who possess that ability should be deemed to have a level of abstraction which makes the hollowness of such idea quite apparent. We must make it plain to these friends of ours that it is not nationalism but bigotry to seek to form a professional association on [a] racial basis.

The failure of this move, at least in part, was because of the strong presence of expatriate accountants in the AAN. In fact, only five of the 14 pioneer members of the AAN as listed in Clause 6 of its Articles of Association were Nigerians (cf. Anibaba 1990, 46). Despite the various contentions stated earlier, the wider interest of obtaining a charter which would help the body to have monopoly over the regulation of the accounting profession prevailed. This culminated in the enactment of the ICAN Act of 1965. All AAN members subsequently became ICAN members.

Aside from the interests of the accounting profession, there were also other interests at play. A sticking-point during the formation process of ICAN was the genuine concern over the fate of persons who were providing useful service as accountants to various government agencies and businesses despite the fact they were not members of any of the recognized accounting bodies in the UK. This was especially so given the fact that the proposed ICAN Act had the potential of outlawing persons not affiliated to any of the recognized accounting bodies in the UK from the practice of accounting in Nigeria. Such concerns forced ICAN to compromise by providing a category of membership known as 'registered accountants' for such persons (cf. Sections 8 and 19 of the ICAN Act of 1965). This concession was made because the number of such registered accountants 'was small and certain to reduce over the years' (Coker 1990, 24).[4] The fact that there was demand for the services of such persons was of little consequence in the calculations of ICAN.

Internal disagreements among ICAN members again surfaced shortly after the body was formed and authorized by the Nigerian Parliament to use the 'chartered' title. Again, as with the pre-charter disagreements, it revolved around the structure of the British accounting bodies. At the first annual general meeting of ICAN in 1966, the controversial issue of uniform recognition of divergent accountancy bodies came up, culminating in the exclusion of members of CIMA and CIPFA on the ground that they were not entitled to practice as public accountants in the UK (Anibaba 1985). This decision was, however, reversed in 1973. This was because the Nigerian Society of International Accountants (SIA) had at the time become a major threat to the monopoly status of ICAN (Uche 2002). Again, the entire argument surrounding the SIA challenge was based on the structure of the accounting profession in the United Kingdom.

The SIA consisted mainly of Nigerian members of the Association of International Accountants (AIA), a British body whose members were not recognized to audit in the UK at the time. In 1972, they petitioned the federal government of Nigeria, requesting that its members be admitted into ICAN. The leadership of ICAN objected, pointing out that the AIA qualification was not recognized in the UK as the 'body is not listed as one of the recognized bodies of Accountants whose members could be appointed as company auditors under the Companies Act 1948 and 1967 of the United Kingdom' (quoted in Anibaba 1990, 149). The federal military government subsequently decided against the petition (Ani 1977). Since the main reason for ICAN's opposition of recognition for SIA was the body's nonrecognition under UK laws, it soon became clear to ICAN that continued exclusion of CIMA and CIPFA-qualified accountants from its membership could only lead to proliferation of accounting bodies in Nigeria. Since both

4. By the end of 2004, for instance, there were only 22 registered accountants of the institute's total membership of 17,199 (ICAN 2004, 12).

bodies were recognized in the UK, their members were in a strong position to successfully set up recognized rival professional bodies in Nigeria. The result was the readmission of CIMA and CIPFA members into ICAN. This strengthened the ability of the institute to maintain its monopoly to regulate the accounting profession in Nigeria.

Despite this, the SIA did not give up its struggle for recognition. In 1975, under a new military government, the SIA again launched a massive campaign to get the government to reopen the issue. This bid again failed (Uche 2007). ICAN nevertheless realized that the battle was far from over. Questions about its ability to produce enough accountants to support the country's economic development would increasingly become a major source of attack by aspiring rival bodies and a concern for government. This led to the introduction of the accelerated training scheme which was approved by the ICAN council in 1977. The main objective of the programme was to increase the number of CAs trained annually to 500, effective from 1985.[5] The main strategy for achieving this objective was the reduction of the training period for graduates through collaboration with universities (Ani 1990; Olukoya 1990). The approval of the scheme was timely as the government was, not surprisingly, getting worried about the slow pace of the production of accountants in the country (Ani 1990, 22).

The introduction of the programme, however, did little to prevent agitation for the recognition of another professional accounting body in Nigeria. In October 1979, when the military government of General Olusegun Obasanjo handed over power to a new civilian government led by Alhaji Shehu Shagari, the agitation of SIA, which had now metamorphosed into the Association of National Accountants of Nigeria (ANAN), was again resurrected (Anibaba 2005). This culminated in the introduction of an ANAN bill in the National Assembly in 1980. The promoters of the ANAN bill did not hesitate to highlight the poor qualification record of ICAN and its inability to train enough accountants to meet the requirements of the Nigerian economy (cf. National House of Representatives Debates, 2 September 1981). Despite ICAN's opposition, the House of Representatives passed the bill (cf. National House of Representatives Debate, 3 September 1981; Njoku 1981).[6] The battle then shifted to the

5. The ICAN pass rate at the time was relatively low. In 1979, for instance, of the 139 persons that enrolled for the final qualifying exams of ICAN, only 25 passed. In 1980, 54 out of 227 registered candidates qualified. In 1986, of the 2,911 students that took the qualifying exams of the institute, only 396 passed, while 1,123 of 8,232 students qualified in 1991. Perhaps because the poor pass rate of ICAN examinations has become a major rallying point for its opponents, the body, for some time now, has been publishing only the total number of students taking its examinations in its annual reports (cf. various issues of ICAN's Annual Report and Financial Statements).

6. According to the then ICAN president, 'the only language the so called honourable members understood or cared to understand was that of Naira and Kobo [money]' (Adebayo 1990, 38).

Senate, where after the second reading of the bill, in September 1983, it was buried in committee hearings (Odumeru 1997). The military coup of 31 December 1983 brought an abrupt end to the parliamentary debate of this matter.

Despite this setback, ANAN continued its struggle for recognition under the new military government headed by Major General Muhammadu Buhari. During the short life of the Buhari government, the efforts of ANAN led to the issuance of a letter by the Federal Ministry of Education equating the ICAN qualification to the Higher National Diploma (HND) and the AIA qualification (ICAN 1984, 3). Perhaps tired by the perennial conflict with ANAN, the ICAN council proposed a political solution which would allow AIA members automatic membership of ICAN (cf. ICAN 1985, 1). This resolution was, however, defeated at the 21st Annual General Meeting held on 30 May 1986.[7] In 1987 the federal military government, then headed by General Ibrahim Babangida, deemed it necessary to review the 1968 Companies Act and set up a consultative committee on the issue. ANAN members immediately saw this as an opportunity to resuscitate their demand for the recognition of a second accountancy body in Nigeria. Again, their argument was partly based on the fact that ICAN was incapable of producing enough accountants to service the needs of a developing country like Nigeria. ICAN again produced a counter memorandum, hinged mainly on international affiliation, advising against proliferation (Williams 1990, 47).

Despite this, the provisions of the resultant Companies and Allied Matters Decree of 1990 laid the foundation for the recognition of a second professional body of accountants in Nigeria (cf. sections 2 [c] and 358 [1]).[8] An ICAN delegation that included 16 past presidents of the institute subsequently, in April 1990, visited the then Nigerian military leader, General Ibrahim Babangida, to protest the offensive sections of the new decree and make a case for non-proliferation of professional accounting bodies in Nigeria (cf. Kuforiji-Olubi 1990). What the ICAN delegation did not mention was that at that time the AIA, which some of the foundation ANAN

7. According to the then president of ICAN, who championed the failed initiative:

> I strongly believed and still believe that the Institute could not for much longer behave like the proverbial ostrich with its head and neck buried in the sand whilst the rest of the body is exposed to the glare of the scorching sun and predators. I sincerely believed and still believe that the Institute should not for ever be on the defensive. It should take the initiative and put most of the problems behind it so it can concentrate all its resources for the pursuance and achievements of its statutory and moral obligations to Nigeria. (Ogunde 1990, 43–44)

8. There were other contentious issues, at least from the ICAN perspective, that were contained in the decree. These included the issue of countersigning of audit reports by lawyers and the separation of audit from other business services. These are, however, beyond the scope of the current chapter. For a more detailed analysis of these issues please see Uche (2002).

members belonged to, had already been recognized as a qualifying body for company auditors under the British Companies Act of 1989 (cf. Association of International Accountants 2007).

Based on this, it was perhaps not surprising that President Babangida, shortly before stepping down in August 1993, signed a decree recognizing the ANAN. Like ICAN, ANAN was also empowered with the general duty of advancing and regulating the accountancy profession (Section 1 of the 1993 ANAN Decree). The implication is that ANAN members are now allowed to undertake company audits in Nigeria. So far, ICAN has tried without success to persuade the government to abrogate this law (ICAN 2003). Based on the recognition of AIA under British laws, the ICAN council has again tried without success to list AIA as one of the bodies whose members qualify for automatic membership of ICAN. According to the minutes of the 31st Annual General Meeting of ICAN held on 31 May 1996 (6–7):

> At the request of the President, the Vice President . . . presented and moved the Resolution. The Resolution, which was in two parts sought the recognition of the Association of International Accountants (AIA) for the purposes of admission into the membership of the Institute under Section 8b (b) of the Institute's Act . . . The Resolution was rejected on the grounds that: (a) Members of AIA were substantially members of ANAN and if the resolution was passed, it would amount to bringing in members of ANAN into ICAN's fold through the back door . . . (b) The members of AIA who supervised the Association's 1991 examination and beyond were still the same whose qualifications were not recognised by the Institute. And that being the case, it was not possible for them to produce professionals with higher knowledge and skill.

ANAN is not, however, the only threat to the jurisdiction of ICAN. As of 2005, ICAN had identified about 15 accounting bodies aspiring for government recognition to participate in and regulate some aspects of accounting in Nigeria (Anibaba 2005). This led two past presidents of the institute to conclude that the proliferation of professional associations within the accountancy profession had assumed frightening proportions (cf. ICAN 2004, 7; Babington-Ashaye 2007, 8). In most of these cases, the basis for seeking recognition has been hinged either on the need to produce more accountants for the nation or to claims of relationships with internationally recognized accounting bodies. Perhaps the best known of the aspiring entrants is the Institute of Certified Public Accountants of Nigeria (ICPAN), which 'deceptively claimed to be affiliated to the Association of Certified Public Accountants of America (AICPA)' (ICAN 2004, 8). This claim was rebutted by AICPA at ICAN's request (ibid.).

Despite this, the House of Representatives and the Senate unanimously passed the ICPAN bill before the expiration of the last legislative year in

May 2007.[9] From this, it is clear that the major influences in the struggle for recognition of professional bodies in Nigeria have been the claim of acceptability or affiliation abroad and the inability of ICAN to produce enough accountants for the country. Not surprisingly, as the next section will show, the threat to ICAN could be far greater when an internationally recognized professional accounting body like the ACCA decides to take its membership expansionist programme directly to a former British colony like Nigeria.

## THE ACCA THREAT

As already stated, the origin of ICAN in Nigeria is entwined with the history of the ACCA. At formation, ACCA members comprised the majority in the emergent ICAN. Although ICAN started its examinations in 1968 they did not become popular among Nigerians, arguably because an ICAN qualification was considered inferior to British accounting qualifications, like the ACCA's. This was so despite the fact that from the inception of its examinations until 1973, ICAN had a technical agreement with the Overseas Accountancy Examinations Advisory Board. This was a subcommittee of the Joint Standing Committee of the three Institutes of Chartered Accountants (Ireland, England and Wales and Scotland) for the development and conduct of professional examination and certification schemes.[10] While members of the ACCA were automatically admitted as ICAN members, members of ICAN did not enjoy the same reciprocal treatment. The result was that the ACCA remained the body of choice for most Nigerians. This was not surprising given the continued dominance of foreign businesses in Nigeria even after independence (cf. Hoogvelt 1980, 56). The natural preferences for such foreign businesses were British-trained accountants. By 1973, ICAN had realized this fact and decided to reverse the trend. In a 1973 public notice, it notified the general public that from 1 January 1980, admission to membership would only be by passing the institute's examinations and completing the prescribed period of approved training. This decision was premised on the 'growing local peculiarities in the practice of accounting, especially with regards to taxation law and company law and practice [and] the need to build a truly Nigerian Institute capable of meeting the demands of the Nigerian economy' (Akinyemi 1973, 57).

---

9. The bill was not assented to before President Olusegun Obasanjo handed over power to President Umaru Yar'Adua.

10. The Overseas Accountancy Examinations Advisory Board advised interested overseas countries on the conduct of professional accounting examinations. It also sometimes assisted with the implementation of such examinations. The general understanding was that over a period of time, generally within six or seven years, the local institute should be able to take charge of such examinations (Wallace 1989, 43–44).

Some political and economic developments in Nigeria at the time made such pronouncements easy. After independence, the Nigerian government became increasingly interested in discouraging foreign control of its economy. The Companies Act of 1968, for instance, required that all companies operating in Nigeria be registered as Nigerian companies (s.369). Furthermore, such companies were also required to have their accounts audited by members of ICAN. This law, therefore, made it necessary for many Nigerians who held British accounting qualifications to register with ICAN in order to be able to conduct audit in Nigeria. Foreign accountants with auditing interests in Nigeria also had to register with ICAN. In 1972, the federal government promulgated the Indigenisation Decree, which specifically listed 22 enterprises under its schedule one as reserved exclusively for Nigerians. Schedule two of the decree also listed 33 enterprises as reserved partially for Nigerians. In 1977, a more comprehensive Indigenisation Decree was promulgated by the federal government to replace the 1972 decree. The 1977 decree listed business services as one of the enterprises in which Nigerians must have majority shareholding. This enhanced the opportunities for local accounting firms to operate in Nigeria. Some local accounting firms certainly appreciated this and did their best to block all possible loopholes in order to prevent foreign firms using Nigerians as fronts. At the 13th Annual General Meeting of ICAN held on 19 May 1978, for instance, Mr. D.O. Dafinone, senior partner of D.O. Dafinone and Co., a local accounting firm, proposed that:

> (1) The Nigerian Nationals in practicing firms in Nigeria composed of both Nigerian and non-Nigerian Partners should be prohibited from registering another firm with Nigerian nationals only as members with a view to 'Fronting' for the non-Nigerian controlled firms, and thereby defeating the purpose and object of the Nigerian Enterprises Promotion Decree Number 3 of 1977. (2) That all Partners in Practicing Firms in Nigeria should be resident in Nigeria as from the 1st of January 1979. (ICAN 1979, 3)

This proposition failed. This was not surprising especially given the fact that the Nigerian audit market at the time was dominated by foreign firms, some of which subsequently set up parallel indigenous local firms in order to circumvent the relevant provisions of the 1977 Indigenisation Decree.[11] Although the number of foreign accountants practising in Nigeria

---

11. According to a past president of the institute:
 As a result of the favorable economy of the early 1970s, and the indigenization policy of the Nigerian government, many Nigerian chartered accountants went into public practice, some as partners of the big international firms such as Peat Marwick, Cassleton Elliot & Co (with its subsidiary [the] fully indigenous firm of Ani Ogunde Sotinwa & Co.), Coopers and Lybrand (with its subsidiary firm of Oyediran Faleye Oke & Co.), Deloite Haskins & Sells (with its subsidiary firm of Anibaba, Adetona Isichei & Co.). (Anibaba 2005, 9)

was continuously decreasing, especially as a consequence of the various post-independence government policies aimed at encouraging increased participation of Nigerians in the economy, international accounting firms, increasingly under the control of Nigerian accountants, continued to thrive. In fact, even the leading indigenous accounting firms had to seek international affiliation in order to remain visible.[12] Given this structure, it was not surprising that some of the Nigerian partners of the foreign accounting firms were also influential members of ICAN. This no doubt contributed to the defeat of the aforementioned motion moved by Mr. Dafinone.[13] It is clear that the interest of ICAN members were not always homogenous. Such divergence of interests might explain the internal tensions and disagreements that have occurred from time to time, especially with respect to ICAN's relationships with colonial accounting structures, in the history of the institute. In the preceding case, for instance, while the Nigerian accountants who were linked to international accounting firms benefited immensely from the entwinement of such firms with foreign businesses, the same could not be said of their counterparts who had no foreign links.

By 1983, following the review of its syllabus, ICAN approved an exemption scheme for UK professional bodies seeking membership of ICAN. Specifically, all those who had passed the qualifying examination of ICAEW, ACCA, CIMA, ICAS or CIPFA were exempted from all subjects except Taxation and Law. In addition, CIMA qualified candidates were also required to write the Auditing and Investigations paper if they desired to practise as auditors in Nigeria (ICAN 1982, 7). Despite the prominence of the claim by ICAN that it was essentially motivated by the peculiarities of the Nigerian business environment, the institute had other objectives. Specifically, it was keenly interested in using such threats as a tool to achieve reciprocity in qualification recognition with the internationally recognized accounting bodies. Arguably, because of the colonial heritage, any independent local accounting body like ICAN would naturally be considered as inferior to the international accounting bodies and treated with some degree of trepidation. The consequence is that to date, no international accounting body has been willing to equate its qualification to that of ICAN through mutual recognition. ICAN's frustration was made explicit in its 1983 *Annual Report* which asserted that:

12. 'An analysis of the structure of the market for auditing services . . . reveals that over 80 percent of the market is concentrated in the hands of those firms with effective linkage with international accounting firms. The two largest and most successful of the locally founded accounting practices—Akintola Williams and Co. and Z O Ososanya and Co. had to link up with Touche Ross and Klynveld Main Goerdeler (KMG) . . . respectively to share effectively in the market for the audits of multinational enterprises resident in the country' (Wallace 1989, 30).

13. For instance, at the time the motion was moved in 1978, the then ICAN President (Anthony Ani) and his predecessor (Cecil Oyediran) were both senior partners in the big international accounting firms of Peat Marwick, Cassleton Elliot & Co. and Coopers and Lybrand, respectively. Both firms also set up subsidiary indigenous firms.

> After due deliberations on the matter, Council resolved that the partial exemption granted in ICAN PE II to holders of foreign professional certificates . . . without reciprocal recognition . . . should be terminated with effect from 1987 and that holders of the . . . certificates would have to write and pass ICAN PE II to be eligible for admission to the Institute's register of members. (ICAN 1983, 2)

In practice, however, it has not been possible for ICAN to live up to this threat. This is arguably because the legitimacy and recognition of ICAN was built on the fact that most of its founders were qualified members of recognized professional accounting bodies in the United Kingdom.

By 1984, ICAN had reversed its earlier decision not to grant automatic membership to members of internationally recognized accounting bodies who qualified before 1980 and who failed to take advantage of its seven-year grace period to register with ICAN (ICAN 1984, 2). In 1996, ICAN went ahead to further ease the requirements for all members of recognized international professional bodies aspiring to join it. Such persons are now simply required to undergo an orientation seminar during which Government Accounting, Taxation, Nigerian Law, Auditing and Investigations and Public Finance (whichever is applicable) are the main subjects of intense discourse. Candidates are also required to make an oral presentation before admission (ICAN 1996, 6).

This move no doubt made sense in the context of discouraging members of UK-recognized accountancy bodies from joining rival accountancy bodies in Nigeria or setting up new ones. Unfortunately, it has also further weakened the position of ICAN and its members, especially when compared with members of recognized international accounting bodies like the ACCA. This is especially so given the fact that anyone attaining the international qualification is almost automatically awarded the ICAN certificate in Nigeria. Perhaps more worrying is the fact that the quest for international recognition and reciprocity has made ICAN downplay the peculiarities of the Nigerian economy as the following statement suggests:

> The Institute during the year initiated a move to secure reciprocal recognition from our peers in other parts of the world. It is a well known fact that the basis for reciprocal recognition of professional certificates is the training programme. Where there are similarities in their training programmes, and examination syllabi, the process will be simple. A committee has been set up to this end. (ICAN 2001, 6)

The implication of this is that ICAN is willing to downplay its role in training accountants suited for the peculiarities of the Nigerian economy in its quest to gain international reciprocal recognition. The ICAN problem has been complicated by the recent drive by the ACCA to increase its global membership in most parts of the world, including Africa.[14] In fact, at the end of 2007, 5.2 per cent of the 122,426 ACCA members and 19.1 per cent of its 325,606 students were resident in Africa (ACCA 2007, 15). Arguably because of the international nature of its qualification, ACCA members usually have enhanced employment prospects both in their home countries and overseas.[15]

Perhaps because of the widespread consensus that the accounting needs of a particular country depend on the level of its social and economic development, the ACCA now tries to adapt its examinations to specific local conditions in a bid to ensure that its qualifications are both local and global (cf. Lyall 1996). Remarkably, African laws and tax are considered too backward to be examined by the ACCA. This is the case in Sierra Leone where the local institute is partnering with the ACCA to conduct professional accounting examinations. The ACCA requires that the country's 'tax and laws must be of equivalent complexity to that in the UK'. This is a precondition for allowing the setting of local tax and law examinations (ACCA 1992, 14). The fact that the accounting needs of businesses in Sierra Leone are totally different from those in the United Kingdom is of little consequence.

Based on this, the strategy of the ACCA in its recent resurgence in Nigeria cannot be expected to be different.[16] Despite this, ICAN will be less concerned by the ACCA's lack of interest in establishing an accounting system that takes cognizance of the local terrain as ICAN is also guilty of this. ICAN instead realizes that the re-emergence of the ACCA in Nigeria could have implications for its dominance of the accounting market in the country. The fact that the Nigerian government, under pressure from the International Monetary Fund (IMF) and the World Bank, has since adopted market-based reforms (which in part have lifted restrictions on foreign capital) does not help matters. This is so because the Nigerian government is now unlikely to provide the kind of indigenization policy support of the 1970s that enabled ICAN and its members to grow rapidly at the expense of foreign accounting bodies. ICAN is therefore left to fight the battle with the ACCA without much support from the Nigerian government.

In 2002, the ACCA informed ICAN of its plans to open an office in Nigeria that would co-ordinate the planned expansion of its examination activities in Nigeria. The ACCA also sought ICAN's co-operation on the

14. 'We continue to pursue a strategy of focused growth . . . Our member growth in 2007, at 6.1% and with a total increase of 7,081, was our strongest to date'. Not surprisingly, the body 'was presented with its fourth Queens Award for Enterprise this time in the category of International Trade' (ACCA 2007, 13).

15. Historically, the international focus of ACCA has been driven by the fact that its growth potential in the UK was restricted due to the predominance of the ICAEW (Briston and Kedslie 1997).

16. In response to my question as to whether ACCA has plans of incorporating Nigerian laws and tax into its syllabus, the body responded thus: 'This is a matter that is reviewed from time to time. [T]here are no immediate plans to do this' (email from Toyin Ademola, ACCA Nigeria, to author, 22 April 2008).

development of the accounting profession in Nigeria (ICAN 2002, 9). By 2004, the Strategic Committee of ICAN had identified the entry of the ACCA into the Nigerian market as a major issue that was bound to influence the development of the accounting profession in Nigeria. At the time, ICAN was also considering the possibility of signing a Memorandum of Understanding (MoU) with the ACCA (ICAN 2004, 22). By 2005, ICAN's suspicion and mistrust of the ACCA had come to the surface. This was triggered by visits by an ACCA monitoring team to some accounting firms in Nigeria. According to the 2005 ICAN president's report:

> During the year, we strove to redefine our relationship with the ACCA and I was privileged, in the company of the Chairman, Body of Past Presidents, to play host to the International Development Director of the ACCA, Ms. Jane Biggs on November 3, 2005. Since the meeting and following our protestation about the attempt by ACCA to monitor accounting firms in Nigeria, I have received a letter from the Chief Executive of ACCA, Mr. Allen Blewitt inviting ICAN for discussions of all issues in the UK by a Joint Task Force of ICAN and the ACCA. Council however felt that such a meeting should be held in Nigeria and accordingly has set up a Task Force to examine the whole issues comprehensively preparatory to such meeting. I am convinced that the ACCA like kindred professional bodies abroad, has commenced according more respect to our Institute than hitherto and I believe we can improve on the existing relationships to our Institute's advantage. (ICAN 2005, 7)

As a consequence of these talks, ICAN has now signed a co-operation agreement with the ACCA. In this direction, the Nigerian newspaper *Guardian* reported on 14 February 2008 that:

> The agreement, which forms the basis of a general . . . MoU . . . between the two bodies, covers such areas as continuing professional education programme by harmonizing CPD policies and arranging joint seminars; financial reporting issues confronting Small and Medium Enterprises (SMEs) in Nigeria; sustainability reporting and conducting joint research into business issues ranging from pensions, retirement planning, corporate governance, health management to financing options. The MoU will see both bodies cooperating in the field of education standards, enhanced recognition and areas of capacity building . . . After the meeting, [Ms. Gill] Ball [ACCA president, 2007–2008] welcomed the landmark agreement reached by the two bodies . . . 'Our future work together in a number of key areas will deepen the relationship between ACCA and ICAN and bring real benefits to our respective members. We look forward to developing the work programmes, which will enable the two bodies to collaborate, but still retain their

> separate identities and roles,' Ball said. Ball emphasized that ACCA and ICAN are not competitors, but would rather work together in a complementary fashion, with ACCA providing an international qualification alongside the national qualification. (Ojo 2008, 31)

How this co-operation will work in practice remains to be seen. Given the international acceptability of ACCA certificates, the non-reciprocal recognition of its qualifications by ICAN and the fact the Nigerian government is unlikely to offer ICAN any meaningful local industry protection, it is safe to predict that ICAN will be the underdog in this wary partnership. If the preceding prediction holds, then we are likely to see more Nigerian accountants and aspiring accountants courting the ACCA.[17] This clearly will be a safer route in their bid to participate in the lucrative accounting and audit market in an increasingly global world. Unfortunately, the majority of the Nigerian businesses, which also need accounting services, operate outside this global world. This fact, however, also creates a unique opportunity for ICAN to reinvent itself.

Although the need to train accountants for small businesses has never been the priority of ICAN, there is now need for the body to pay increased attention to this sector. At the very least, improved accounting structures for such businesses would engender their growth and development. This will no doubt translate to more accounting jobs for ICAN members. While ICAN members affiliated with international accounting firms may not be excited by such prospects, the same cannot be said of ICAN members affiliated with local accounting firms. The growth and development of small businesses will also positively impact on the nation's economic development. As already mentioned, the need for such businesses was a major concern of government in the formative stages of ICAN. While ICAN compromised by allowing for registered accountants, its focus remained on big businesses. Earlier suggestions that ICAN rethink its training strategy in the interest of economic development were rebuffed (Ezejelue 1976; Dev and Inanga 1978; Kear 1981). It was not until 1989, after the adoption of the IMF- and World Bank–induced market reforms in Nigeria that ICAN introduced the Accounting Technicians Scheme (ATS), which is aimed at producing a second tier of accounting professionals.[18] Thus far the scheme has produced over 10,000 accounting technicians (cf. ICAN 2004).

The ATS scheme, however, has serious structural problems. Solutions to some of these problems however lie outside the jurisdiction of ICAN.

17. Statistics on the number of Nigerians currently taking the ACCA examinations or the number of Nigerians qualified as ACCA members are unavailable. This is because ACCA consider such statistics as 'commercially sensitive information' (email from Toyin Ademola, ACCA Nigeria, to author, 22 April 2008).

18. An accounting technician has been defined as a person who has the capabilities at a technical level in specific spheres of accounting, without necessarily the sum of knowledge and ability to handle problems of a more complex nature at a professional level (Obe 1989, 6; see also Olukoya 1990).

The major problem is that under the Nigerian Company Law, there is no recognition for holders of ATS certificates. There is therefore little avenue for holders of the certificate to set up practising firms irrespective of their target market. Specifically, section 152 (1) of the 1968 Companies Decree, promulgated three years after the ICAN Act was enacted, made it mandatory for all limited liability companies to have audited accounts. Section 357 (1) of the Companies and Allied Matters Act of 1990, which repealed the Companies Decree of 1968, also contains a similar provision. The implication is that all companies, irrespective of size, are expected to require the services of auditors. Regrettably, holders of the ATS certificate are not eligible for appointment as auditors irrespective of the size of the company involved. Surely, the current membership of ICAN, numbering about 20,000, cannot be able to effectively provide this service to all registered Nigerian companies satisfactorily.[19]

Furthermore, it is also doubtful whether all companies can realistically afford to pay for the services of CAs. Interestingly, even in the United Kingdom with its multiplicity of recognized accounting bodies, not all limited liability companies are expected to have their accounts audited. In that jurisdiction, companies with a turnover of less than £5.6 million (N1.4 billion) and a balance-sheet size of less than £2.8 million (N700 million) are exempted from audit. This essentially prevents recognized auditors that are unable to provide economically viable services to small businesses from becoming an impediment to such businesses. Perhaps more important is the fact that this has created a thriving market for cheap accounting services for such small businesses. Such services are provided by persons who possess some basic accounting skills without necessarily being members of any of the recognized professional accounting bodies in the UK. The adoption of such a scheme in Nigeria will no doubt create a desirable market for ATS certificate holders. Until this is done, ATS certification will continue to be used mainly as a stop-gap in the attempt to obtain the main ICAN qualification. This builds on the foundation laid by the country's colonial heritage, impeding the idea of training second- tier accounting professionals to provide for the accounting needs of the small businesses that dominate the Nigerian economic landscape.

## CONCLUSION

This chapter has attempted to trace the various pressures that have impacted on the development of the accounting profession in Nigeria. Specifically, it has shown how the country's colonial heritage influenced the development

19. As at May 2008, only 1,663 practising accounting firms were registered by ICAN. These are the ICAN-certified firms able to sign the audit of the 691,668 limited liability companies registered by the Nigerian Corporate Affairs Commission (CAC) as of 27 November 2008. This translates to an average of one accounting firm to 416 limited liability companies (I am grateful to ICAN and CAC for providing this information).

of company law in Nigeria along the lines of British law. Nigeria's colonial heritage also includes the emergence and dominance of British businesses in the country's economic landscape. This also influenced the influx of British accounting firms and accountants and the structure of the emergent accounting profession in Nigeria. These influences have been to the detriment of training accountants to provide for the needs of smaller indigenous businesses. Rival accounting bodies that have emerged to challenge the dominance of ICAN have in the main relied on linkages to international accounting bodies in their bid to gain recognition. The recent resurgence of the ACCA in Nigeria and the preference for its qualifications by local aspiring accountants and international businesses are also obvious traces of the continued colonial influence in the development of the accounting profession in Nigeria.

## REFERENCES

*Accountant.* (1956) 'The South Wales and Monmouthshire Society of Chartered Accountants'. (24 March): 330–31.

Adebayo, J.A. (1990) 'My reminiscences'. *Nigerian Accountant* (July/September): 37–39.

Akinyemi, D.K. (1973) 'Public notice: Direct admission to Membership'. *Nigerian Accountant* 6(4): 57.

Ani, A.A. (1977) 'Control of the accountancy profession: A rejoinder by the Institute of Chartered Accountants of Nigeria'. *Daily Times*, June 13.

———. (1985) 'My reminiscences as a past president of the institute'. *Nigerian Accountant* (July/September): 33–36.

———. (1990) 'My reminiscences'. *Nigerian Accountant* (October/December): 21–24.

Anibaba, M.O. (1985) 'My year of office'. *Nigerian Accountant* (October/ December): 18–20.

———. (1990) *A Short History of the Accounting Profession in Nigeria.* Lagos: West African Book Publishers Limited.

———. (2005) '40 years of excellent accounting services to the nation'. Presented at the ICAN 40th Anniversary Public Lecture/Symposium, Lagos, 21 June.

Association of Certified Corporate Accountants. (1992) *Consultants Report: Accountancy Development in Sierra Leone.* London: ACCA.

Association of Chartered Certified Accountants. (2007) *Annual Review.* London: ACCA.

Association of International Accountants. (2007) *Proposed Revised and Redrafted International Standard on Auditing: ISA 200, Overall Objective of the Independent Auditor, and the Conduct of an Audit in Accordance with International Standards on Auditing (Submitted 14 September).* Newcastle Upon Tyne: AIA.

Babington-Ashaye, A.A. (2007) Acceptance speech on his election and investiture as the 43rd president of the Institute of Chartered Accountants of Nigeria, Lagos, 31 May.

Briston, R., and Kedslie, M. (1997) 'The internationalization of British professional accounting: The role of the examination exporting bodies'. *Accounting, Business & Financial History* 7:175–94.

Coker, F.C.O. (1990) 'How it all started'. *Nigerian Accountant* 23:23–24.

Departmental Committee Appointed to Inquire into Matters Affecting the Currency of British West African Colonies and Protectorates. (1912) *Emmott Report (Parliamentary Papers 1912, XLVIII).* London: His Majesty's Stationery Office.

Dev, S., and Inanga, E. (1978) 'Educating accountants in Nigeria'. *Accountancy* (April): 127–29.

Ekundare, R.O. (1973) *An Economic History of Nigeria, 1860–1960*. London: Methuen and Co. Limited.

Ezejelue, A. (1976) 'The developing profession in Nigeria'. *Accountant* (15 January): 71–73.

Falola, T., and Heaton, M.M. (2008) *A History of Nigeria*. Cambridge: Cambridge University Press.

Government of Nigeria. (1981) *National Assembly Debates (House of Representatives)*. Lagos: Government Printer.

Hoogvelt, A. (1980) 'Indigenization and foreign capital: Industrialization in Nigeria'. *Review of African Political Economy* 14:56–68.

Inanga, E.I. (1992) *A History of Akintola Williams and Co*. Lagos: West African Book Publishers.

Institute of Chartered Accountants of Nigeria. (1979) *Annual Report and Financial Statements*. Lagos: ICAN.

———. (1982) *Annual Report and Financial Statements*. Lagos: ICAN.

———. (1983) *Annual Report and Financial Statements*. Lagos: ICAN.

———. (1984) *Annual Report and Financial Statements*. Lagos: ICAN.

———. (1985a) *Annual Report and Financial Statements*. Lagos: ICAN.

———. (1985b) 'The first two decades'. *Nigerian Accountant* (October/December): 10–12. Lagos: ICAN.

———. (1996) *Minutes of Annual General Meeting*. Lagos: ICAN.

———. (2001) *Annual Report and Financial Statements*. Lagos: ICAN.

———. (2002) *Annual Report and Financial Statements*. Lagos: ICAN.

———. (2003) *Annual Report and Financial Statements*. Lagos: ICAN.

———. (2004) *Annual Report and Financial Statements*. Lagos: ICAN.

———. (2005) *Annual Report and Financial Statements*. Lagos: ICAN.

Kear, S (1981) 'Nigerian accountancy's growing pains?' *Accountancy* (December): 11.

Kuforiji-Olubi, D.B. (1990) 'Address by Chief (Mrs.) D.B.A Kuforiji-Olubi, President of the Institute of Chartered Accountants of Nigeria during a courtesy call on the President and Commander in Chief of the Armed Forces of Nigeria, Ibrahim Badamasi Babangida on April 6, 1990'. *Nigerian Accountant* (April/June): 27–29.

Lyall, H. (1996) 'Qualification goes global'. *Certified Accountant* (March): 1.

Niven, C. R. (1946) *A Short History of Nigeria*. London: Longman.

Njoku, C.E. (1981) 'Rationale for incorporating ANAN'. *National Accountant* (September): 12–16.

Obe, F. (1989) 'Accounting technicians' scheme comes alive'. *Nigerian Accountant* (April/June): 6–7.

Odumeru, J.K. (1997) *Getting to Know ANAN*. Lagos: Association of National Accountants.

Ogunde, A.O. (1990) 'My reminiscences'. *Nigerian Accountant* (July/September): 43–44.

Ogutuga, D.B. (1990) 'My reminiscences'. *Nigerian Accountant* (July/ September): 43.

Ojo, O. (2008) 'ICAN, ACCA sign pact to improve accountancy profession'.*Guardian* (14 February): 31.

Olukoya, S.M. (1990) '25 years of ICAN'. *Nigerian Accountant* (July/September): 18–22.

Onoh, J.K. (1982) *Money and Banking in Africa*. New York: Longman.

Parker, R.H. (1958) 'Company law in Nigeria'. *Accountant* (6 December): 693–94.

Uche, C.U. (2002) 'Professional accounting development in Nigeria: Threats from the inside and outside'. *Accounting, Organizations and Society* 27:471–96.

———. (2007) *The Accounting Profession in British West Africa*. Edinburgh: Institute of Chartered Accountants of Scotland.

Wallace, R.S.O. (1989) *Accounting and Financial Reporting in Nigeria*. London: Institute of Chartered Accountants in England and Wales.

———. (1992) 'Growing pains of an indigenous accountancy profession: The Nigerian experience'. *Accounting, Business & Financial History* 2:25–53.

Williams, S.A. (1990) 'My reminiscences'. *Nigerian Accountant* (July/September): 44–48.

# 5 The Malaysian Accountancy Profession and its Imperial Legacy (1957–1995)

*Devi S. Susela*

## INTRODUCTION

The British presence began in Malaya in the eighteenth century, when the East India Company started to extend its influence beyond India, seeking a route to China. The Malaysian economy has since transformed significantly. After independence from the British in 1957, the Malaysian state pursued an active policy of economic development (including aspirations to economic growth plus structural, social and economic changes). In tandem, the accountancy profession's transformation was shaped by the nation's political economy as well as the forces of internationalization. This chapter argues that the nature and course of professional transformation has been affected by Malaysia's colonial legacy. That legacy is identified by an analysis of the formation of the Malaysian Association of Certified Public Accountants (MACPA)[1] in 1958 and the Malaysian Institute of Accountants (MIA) in 1967; and the relationship between them, complicated as it was, and continues to be, by the activities of 'foreign' professional bodies with their own (British) imperial legacies, against the backdrop of a modernizing Malaysian[2] society and its international relations.

In particular, British colonial rule in Malaya resulted indirectly in an economic divide between the various races that necessitated concerted efforts by the post-colonial government to rectify racial economic disequilibrium whilst actively promoting economic development. This chapter will argue that the development of the profession has been indirectly impacted by these efforts.

A political economy perspective guides the exploration of the profession's history in the post-colonial era covering four decades, from the 1960s to the 1990s. This framework acknowledges the interconnectedness and interdependencies between accounting and the wider contexts in which it operates (see Susela 1996, 1999 for detailed discussion of the political economy perspective). This chapter is written largely based on primary

1. MACPA later changed its name to Malaysian Institute of Certified Public Accountants (MICPA) in 2001. See http://www.micpa.com.my.

2. The discussion in this chapter covers only West Malaysia, which was the official designation given to the Federation of Malaya after it was incorporated into Malaysia. East Malaysia officially covers Sabah and Sarawak.

research through 65 in-depth interviews with selected individuals closely connected with the profession (Susela 1996).[3]

## THE POWER STRUGGLE

The existence of two professional accounting bodies, one set up as a statutory body (the MIA) and another set up as a private body (the MACPA), provides an interesting case study of the complex dynamics of the development of the profession in a rapidly developing economy. It is clear that external actors and structures, largely the British influence and the Commonwealth connexion, do have important implications for the profession's development when they interact with powerful internal factors.

As seen in Figure 5.1, several routes are currently available for persons aspiring to practise accountancy in Malaysia.[4] The MACPA, set up following the British model, and the only local non-government body incorporated in Malaysia (the MIA is a government body), struggles to maintain its premier national accountancy body status in the face of stiff competition from foreign (mainly British and Australian) professional bodies that have become

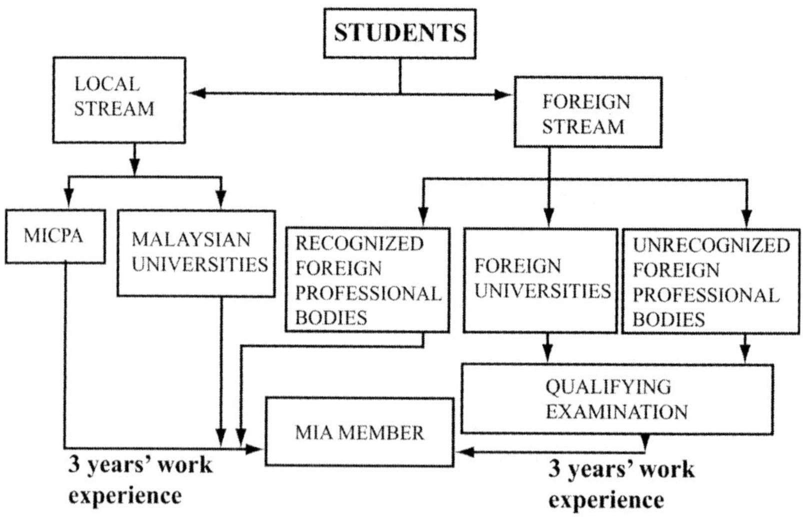


*Figure 5.1* Routes to becoming an MIA member.

3. The anonymous interviewees are subsequently identified using the format 'I-no-#'.

4. Under the Accountants Act 1967 and subsequent amendments, holders of seven local universities' accounting degrees and members of 11 professional bodies are eligible to directly become members of MIA. The bodies are: MACPA, Institute of Chartered Accountants in England and Wales (ICAEW), Institute of Chartered Accountants of Scotland (ICAS), Institute of Chartered Accountants in Ireland (ICAI), Institute of Chartered Accountants in Australia, CPA Australia (successor

established in Malaysia as a result of their qualifications being recognized in the Accountants Act 1967 (Susela, Hooper and Davey 2004); and the MIA itself. The framework in Figure 5.1 was in place in 1967 with minor tweaking to allow recognition of local university degrees taking place in the 1970s. With the 1967 act the word 'accountant' became protected. Only those registered with the MIA were allowed to hold themselves out as 'accountants'. The subsequent analysis shows that the empire legacy is found throughout Figure 5.1 and the critical elements in the Malaysian profession's development cannot be explained in the absence of this legacy. Furthermore, the analysis helps to explain historically how the settings in Figure 5.1 came about. The discussion in this chapter focuses principally on developments during the period 1957–1995, wherein the key features of Figure 5.1 were institutionalized.

Interestingly, unlike most of the other British Commonwealth countries around the world, Malaysia was not allowed to use the 'chartered accountant' ('CA') designation for professionally qualified accountants even though it was at one time a British colony (Susela 1996). Instead the local association was called the Malayan Association of Certified Public Accountants. To become a member of MACPA, graduates of local universities are required to undergo further professional examinations in contrast to the MIA where they are admitted upon completing three years' work experience with no further examination.

The discussion that follows is organized thus: the next section discusses the colonial impact and its implications for the profession. The two sections following discuss the establishment of MACPA and MIA and developments in the 1960s; and the MACPA–MIA power struggle from the 1970s to 1995, respectively. The final section summarizes the various ways in which the empire connexion has influenced the organization of the profession in Malaysia.

## BRITISH LEGACY IN MALAYSIA—THE RACIAL DIVIDE

Malaysian society is characterized by three main races, namely, Malays,[5] Chinese and Indians—and a myriad of other ethnic and sub-ethnic groups such as Kadazans, Ibans and Dayaks. The British colonial conquest was not only a matter of superior weapons, political and diplomatic shrewdness and economic energy—it was also a cultural invasion in the form of a conquest of the native 'epistemological space' (Stenson 1976; Shamsul 2001).

---

to the Australian Society of Accountants), Chartered Institute of Management Accountants (CIMA), Association of Chartered Certified Accountants (ACCA), Canadian Institute of Chartered Accountants (CICA), New Zealand Institute of Chartered Accountants (successor to the New Zealand Society of Accountants) and Institute of Chartered Accountants of India (ICAI). Since 2001 members of foreign professional bodies and graduates with degrees not recognized in the act have been required to undergo the qualifying examination. The inclusion of holders of local accounting graduates dates back to the 1970s.

5. The Malays and the other indigenous races such as the Kadazans and Ibans were also collectively referred to as *Bumiputras*, literally meaning 'sons of the soil'.

An appreciation of the separate and unequal development of Malay, Chinese and Indian societies is central to an understanding of the evolution of the Malaysian socio-political and economic environment (Stenson 1976). During the colonial period a plural society based on ethnic division was created under a policy of divide and rule (Jesudason 1990, 40).

Indirect rule through theoretically sovereign Malay sultans in the late nineteenth and early twentieth centuries necessitated the retention of the traditional structure of Malay society. Non-elite Malays were therefore encouraged to maintain their subsistence agricultural economy while the British encouraged the large-scale importation of Chinese and Indian labour for road and rail building and tin and rubber production. The Indian and Chinese labour soon became more permanently settled in West Malaysia. By 1970 the population comprised 51.8 per cent Malays, 37.1 per cent Chinese and 11.1 per cent Indians (Snodgrass 1980, 24). The resultant social structure was marked by ethnic pluralism, while the export economy was distinguished by segmentation along ethnic lines. The Malays were marginalized in an economy dominated by Europeans (mainly British) and, to a lesser extent, the large Chinese migrant group. These economic and ethnic structures were influential in shaping Malaysia's post-colonial development.

The changes wrought by colonialism had a major imprint on the psyche of the Malays. The experience of external domination weakened their collective self-confidence, and drove them, particularly, the second-generation post-independence Malay elite and intelligentsia, to recover this loss in the symbolic, political and economic spheres (Jesudason 1990). However, colonialism brought much economic dynamism to Malaya too. It installed a competitive economy in place of a quasi-feudalistic economy and introduced the abstract notion of economic development as an end for the government to pursue (Jesudason 1990, 36). Nevertheless, Malays were concentrated in agriculture and poorly represented in commerce. In the 1960s only 3.1 per cent of the economically active Malays were involved in commerce compared to 16.5 per cent Chinese and 10.3 per cent Indians (Means 1976, 16). Organizationally, the Malays lacked institutions that could mobilize capital and pool economic resources effectively. In contrast, the Europeans (mainly British) had international financial networks whilst the Chinese had clan-based organizations (Lim Teck Ghee 1977). For the elite Malays, there was an alternative source of prestige and income in bureaucracy. Possibly this diluted whatever inclination they might have shown towards commerce (Jesudason 1990; Means 1976).

The aristocratic Malays were carefully groomed as reliable allies of British officialdom. The children of aristocratic and upper-class Malay families were sent to an elite college—Malay College, Kuala Kangsar (founded in 1905) and trained there as junior administrators and civil servants in the Malay Administrative Service. However, during the early 1950s, the government was keen to get more Malays involved in business and commerce. A recommendation was made in the *Progress Report on the Development Plan 1950–1952* (Government of Malaya 1953) that the Rural and Industrial Development Authority (RIDA, established in 1950) carry out the dual function of promoting economic development and assisting the country's rural population to improve its living conditions. As there was a severe shortage of trained staff, intensive efforts at recruiting suitable candidates from the UK and elsewhere were carried out and facilities for the training of local personnel were improved (Government of Malaya 1953, 8).

The need for qualified accountants was stressed in the report which argued that, in order to strengthen the co-operative movement, it was desirable that a co-operative college be set up to carry out audits of the co-operatives and further recommended that two or more of the senior audit clerks should be sent to the UK to be articled as chartered accountants (CAs) (Government of Malaya 1953, 52, 76). Many of these privileged Malays returned to play a major role in the development of accounting in Malaysia as seen later in this chapter.

Despite the steps taken, the British legacy of ethnic economic disparity remained critical and post-colonial economic development called for efforts to restructure the imbalance in favour of the Malays/*Bumiputras* who were the most economically disadvantaged group. The development of the profession is further entwined in these efforts as discussed in the next section.

## POST-INDEPENDENCE: FORMATION OF MACPA AND MIA—1950s AND 1960s

Malaysia's economy in the post-colonial era underwent significant transformation and the accounting profession developed in tandem with it (Susela, Hooper and Davey 2004). During the 1960s there were persistent calls for improving corporate financial reporting and legislation was introduced subsequently to regulate the profession.[6] The focus of the government was on rural development and building up rural infrastructure, leaving the rest of the economy to grow at its own pace without much government intervention. Compromises between the top ethnic leaders encouraged this relatively *lasissez-faire* economic framework between 1957 and 1969. The state was responsive to and supportive of both foreign and (predominantly Chinese) domestic private sector interests.[7]

### 1956–1960: Private Sector Initiative—Formation of the Malaysian Association of Certified Public Accountants

During the period of colonial rule many locals (including non-Malays) went to the UK to gain professional accounting qualifications. A number of those

6. The regulation of reporting is discussed further in Susela (1996, 1999). The remainder of this chapter highlights the organization of the profession per se.

7. This is also evident in the appointments of the presidents of the MACPA and MIA in the early years as discussed in the following sections. This also accounts for the significant dominance of the non-Malays in the accounting profession as membership statistics reveal in later years (see Tables 5.4 and 5.5).

who returned formed the Malayan branch of the Association of Certified and Corporate Accountants (ACCA) in 1936 (Azham 2006). It was only after independence, on 26 July 1958, however, that a specifically local body was formed. Twenty local professionals, mostly members of the Institute of Chartered Accountants in England and Wales (ICAEW) and Institute of Chartered Accountants in Australia (ICAA) incorporated the Malayan (later Malaysian) Association of Certified Public Accountants in Singapore under the Straits Settlement Companies Ordinance 1940 (Azham 2006).

MACPA's first three presidents were British (see Appendix C) and the ICAEW model significantly influenced the structure and organization of the local professional body (Megat Abdul Rahman 1980; MACPA 1981). A senior practitioner from the Big Six recounted that:

> in 1958, a group of overseas qualified foreign professional accountants got together; there [needed] to be a body where they [could] share experiences, common understanding . . . and [which] at the same time, [could be] a focal point for the government and other users . . . and [through which the citizens of] . . . a young nation gain professional qualification. This was when MACPA was formed. (I-no-10)

MACPA had strong state support as acknowledged by a founding member who notes that the then Minister of Finance had told him in 1963 that he 'was most anxious to see MACPA grow to meet the demand of the country' (I-no-25).

The state was then pursuing policies to better shape development in response to internal political priorities. The orientation switched to raising rural incomes so that the domestic market could be enlarged and hence assist in industrial development (Jesudason 1990). In support, MACPA instituted an examination and articleship system in February 1961 and registered its first batch of students (MACPA 1988, 10). The first MACPA examination—'Intermediate'—was held in December 1963 and the other two—'Final Part I and II'—in December 1965. This was done with the assistance of the Overseas Accountancy Examination Advisory Board (OAEAB) established by the Chartered Accountants Joint Standing Committee of the CA institutes of Scotland, England and Wales and Ireland. This support by the OAEAB was extended until 1969 (Enthoven 1977, 323) by which time the local examiners had gained sufficient exposure and expertise to take over from their UK counterparts.

In 1980, the then MACPA president Dr. Nawawi Mat Awin described why the MACPA needed assistance from OAEAB (Nawawi Mat Awin 1981, 45):

> We consider that help [from OAEAB] important because we wanted to be sure that right from the start our professional examinations were of the highest standards. That was of the utmost import[ance]; we wanted to ensure that our professional qualifications would be recognized and respected by the government, the private sector and the community generally.

### *Respondents' View: MACPA Dominating*

During the 1960s MACPA developed into a very strong professional body with its own examinations and trained a number of qualified professional accountants (I-no-10). In an attempt to preserve the quality of its members, members of the Australian Society of Accountants (ASA) were not admitted into MACPA.[8] One respondent recalled that the members of MACPA trained as CAs (both British and Australian) did not welcome the ASAs because 'they were not comfortable with the level of qualification that in those days the ASA was doing; they [entrants to the ASA] just get an accounting degree and they become members' (I-no-3). The respondent felt that since its formation, MACPA had done a good job 'of at least holding on and maintaining some form of standard [for example, through] . . . setting examinations' (I-no-3).

Another respondent observed that MACPA was spawned by those trained in the UK 'because the economy here will grow and they need accountants and all that and they started it' (I-no-18). The respondent felt that MACPA had grown 'rather steadily, serving the needs of the market and the economy'. This practitioner from the then Big Six added that if it had been just MACPA (meaning without interference from MIA and other bodies), 'it would have done its job with much credit'. Another practitioner supported this notion:

> Even . . . after MIA was born, it was inactive for a long period of time. So, the vacuum was filled by the initiatives of the members of MACPA . . . the MACPA has got the history of setting standards. (I-no-19)

### *1960–1965: Establishment of Accounting Firms*

Major international accounting firms had already established their offices in Malaya during the colonial period. They were complemented by several local *Bumiputra* accounting firms set up in the 1960s. For example, Hanafiah, Raslan and Mohamed, a firm of mainly Malaysians (with mostly *Bumiputra* partners) who obtained CA qualifications from the UK, was set up in 1964 (Azham 2006).

## 1966–1970: Establishment of the MIA

During this period the state became directly engaged in commercial and industrial activities in contrast to the earlier periods (Jesudason 1990). Jesudason attributes this to urban Malay pressures for greater Malay progress in business.[9] Whilst leaving the responsibility for manufacturing operations to the private sector, the government continued to focus on maintaining a favourable

8. ASA members were not then required to spend a period of time in public practice before gaining membership.

9. As a result, several projects were set up, including a Malay bank (Bank Bumiputra), a Council of Trust for the Indigenous People (Majlis Amanah Rakyat, com-

investment climate by providing industrial estates and transport, power and communication facilities, and granting tax and other incentives.[10] It was in this context that the MIA was established under the Accountants Act 1967.

One long-serving member of the profession observed that the establishment of the Accountants Act was a political issue coupled with professional jealousy. He recalled that the act was based on the New Zealand Society of Accountants Act. The latter was also the genesis of the Singapore Society of Accountants Act, the main difference being that the Malaysian act was 'much briefer' and thus 'less explicit' than the Singaporean act (Goh 1970, 27–28). This is noteworthy because the ASA was the main body invited by the Singapore government to draft the said Singaporean Act. According to one respondent:

> Even though they themselves [i.e., the Australians] did not have an SSA Act, they were in fact influenced by development in New Zealand. The original SSA Act is almost word for word taken from the NZ Act. (I-no-8)

The real reason for establishing the MIA, he claimed, was professional jealousy. I-no-8 added that:

> for a long time, the accountancy profession here was indirectly controlled by the UK base [a reference to the control of MACPA by locals trained as CAs in the UK]. Of course, the war in UK has been transferred here also. There the CAs looked down on the ACCAs and the ACCAs say I am better than you etc.

He recalled that, at that time, there were two major groups, namely, CAs from the UK and Australia and the ACCAs from the UK. Those in practice were largely CAs in the Big Eight (as they were in those days) and that 'there were a large number of ACCAs in [small practices]'. The CAs dominated the big audits. This respondent perceived the formation of MACPA as an attempt by the CAs (British and Australian) to form a 'trade union in order to protect members' interests'. He recalled in the early years 'there was [a] closed door policy' (I-no-8).[11] He recalled that at that time there was a (Chinese) member of Parliament who 'sponsored' the MIA Bill through Tun Tan Siew Sin (the then Finance Minister). However, 'the said Member of Parliament did not have the clout or power to administer it so it was left at that' (I-no-8). This helps to explain the inactivity of the MIA after the passing of the bill into law.

---

monly known as MARA). MARA provides commercial loans to existing and aspiring Malay entrepreneurs and engages in commercial and industrial projects on its own.

10. During this period several acts of Parliament were passed pertaining to the regulation of the corporate sector, amongst which the most prominent was the Income Tax Act 1967. This act covered some aspects of accounting policies to be adopted and reflected in the accounts, for example, in the valuation of stock. That had an indirect impact on the development of accounting.

11. Entry requirements for ASAs and ACCAs became more stringent in the 1970s.

The then Assistant Minister of Finance, Dr. Ng Kam Poh (cited in Azham 2006) remarked:

> The position of the accountancy profession in Malaysia at present is not entirely satisfactory in that although many accountants are members of long established and reputable associations and have within the last few years between them formed the Malaysian Association of Certified Public Accountants for the purpose of maintaining adequate standards of competence and ethics in this country, there are many who wish to be considered as accountants but who belong to accountancy associations imposing lower standards or whose members could be considered . . . qualified except for a measure of practical experience [the concern being lack of adequate practical experience].

The initiation of MIA appeared to be related to dissatisfaction with MACPA's stringent requirements for membership. The rejection of ASA members seemed to have displeased a lot of people. One respondent noted 'a lot of it is personal, perhaps [reflecting] parochial interests' (I-no-9).

The existence of several accountancy bodies, wherein membership was based primarily on regional ties of academic and professional training, posed a major obstacle to the formulation of uniform policies in accounting regulation and a suggestion for an integration of all these bodies into one body was raised (Chin 1964). The government was aware that such a body was essential since many individuals calling themselves accountants or in public practice in the years following independence had a variety of educational backgrounds and qualifications.[12] It was in this context that the Accountants Act 1967 was enacted. The empire connectedness is visible through the adoption of the New Zealand Act, which was the latest available at that point of time (Susela 1996). The first head of the MIA, D. Mortimer (a British CA), was elected on 22 November 1967[13] (MIA 1987, 14). However, in the following year, on 31 May 1968, a local, Dato' Shamsir Omar, the then accountant-general, was appointed as the MIA president.[14] He held the post of accountant-general for 21 years until July 1989 and also acted as the MIA president until 9 April 1987, at which time Haji Hanifah Noordin took over the post. For the two decades whilst the accountant-general served as MIA's president, no annual general meeting was held. The MIA under his leadership performed the role of a 'registering body' as noted in its first annual report in 1987:

> [The MIA] has confined itself to playing the regulatory role to complement the functions of the MACPA, which has, since its incorporation in

12. Chin (1964) notes that among the more important bodies representing the profession in Malaysia were MACPA, the ICAEW, the ASA and the Singapore Society of Accountants.

13. Initially, the members of the institute elected the president showing the most dominant pro-British sentiments.

14. He was among the first few *Bumiputra* sent to Australia under the Colombo Plan to do accounting (*Business Times*, 17 August 1989). He qualified as a CA in

> 1958, been actively involved in promulgating and developing standards of accounting practice, training of students and conduct of professional accountancy examination. It was the intention of the Council then not to undertake a parallel line of activities as that of the MACPA to avoid duplication of efforts and resources and confusion as to which set of standards that members of the profession should follow. (MIA 1987, 15)

But even the role of maintaining the register was delegated to the audit firm Price Waterhouse and ironically, in 1982, to the MACPA (Azham 2006). Only in 1987 did MIA begin to play its intended role.

## Exploring the Empire Dimension in the 1960s: A Summary

Interestingly, the first three MACPA presidents as well as the first MIA president were British. Though this contrasts with more aggressive localization in other parts of the empire around the time of independence, it illustrates Malaysia's unique relationship with its former master. Two reasons are noteworthy. Firstly, after independence, the Malaysian leaders in pursuing wider geopolitical and economic goals did not opt for nationalization (i.e., taking over the plantation and mining concerns from the British owners) as Malaysia depended heavily on British military defence (Jesudason 1990, 52). Hence, it was not in a position to risk upsetting local British commercial interests (Jesudason 1990, 53). Secondly, in the economic sphere, Malaysia was trying to diversify its economic base away from over-reliance on primary commodities, and since it possessed only a rudimentary industrial capital, it welcomed any foreign (mainly British and Chinese) investment; hence the leeway granted to the foreign sector (Morais 1972).

The 'independence pact' of 1957, over which the United Malays National Organization (UMNO)[15] and the Malayan Chinese Association (MCA) had bargained, allowed for Malay cultural and political dominance in return for safeguarding of the Chinese economic position. Its purpose was to lay the basis for political stability in a potentially divisive multi-ethnic society. The independence pact facilitated the MCA's influence in preserving free enterprise and its control of the important ministries such as finance, commerce and industry, and housing and development. This placed MCA ministers in a powerful position to influence the relative balance between the public and private sectors (Jesudason 1990).

---

1960 after five years with Price Waterhouse in Melbourne. Upon his retirement in 1989, he took over the business of the audit firm Baharom-Jasani (*Business Times*, 17 August 1989). In 1991, The *Star* (10 July 1991) reported that Shamsir Jasani & Co., the seventh largest accounting firm in the country, had 130 staff and was backed by Grant Thornton International.

15. UMNO is a political party which primarily protects Malay interests. MCA is a parallel political organization safeguarding Chinese interests; while the Malayan Indian Congress (MIC) looks after the Indian interests. In the UMNO–MCA electoral pact, the Alliance Party was formed, comprising the three political parties,

## MACPA–MIA POWER STRUGGLE 1970–1995

### MACPA Still Dominating—1970s

The MACPA secretariat moved from Singapore to Kuala Lumpur in March 1970, and the following years saw MACPA playing an active role as a professional accountancy body (MACPA 1989). Reflecting the nationalistic sentiment of the 1970s, MACPA's connexions with the OAEAB on examinations were severed. Since 1970 MACPA examinations have been conducted with the assistance of senior members of the profession and professionally qualified academics from the local institutions of higher learning (Enthoven 1977).

An ACCA member and managing director of a firm of consultants recalled that in the 1970s the practitioners in the big firms were all CAs and that most (but not all) supported MACPA by only hiring people who had passed its examinations:

> Some of us who were there at that time will remember . . . certain firms . . . the partners gave full support, certain partners just lip-service . . . they were not interested. Basically, these things were thrust upon them and they carry on. (I-no-29)

Another medium firm consultant observed the rivalry between the different professional bodies and commented that:

> there should be complete trust of each other over their own aims . . . the key players in both camps should trust each other. I think there are a lot of bitter accountants who blame their bitterness on the Big Six. Of course, the Big Six will say everybody has the right to grow. (I-no-49)

The zeal of the big firms dominated by CAs to support MACPA explains the preceding remarks. I-no-29 noted that in the late 1970s and early 1980s, the Tunku Abdul Rahman (TAR) College (exclusively Chinese) and MARA Institute (exclusively Malay) were beginning to promote the ACCA 'in a big way'. They produced a large number of 'paper ACCAs' who were excluded from the large accounting firms that supported MACPA. The 'paper ACCAs' were on the losing end for a long time as the Malaysian accounting profession in the seventies was dominated by CAs (both British and Australian) and MACPAs. He opined that the big firms did not recruit the ACCAs because they would only sign on with the firms for two years whereas students from A-levels or university graduates would sign on for four years or three years, respectively. Indeed, the paper ACCAs might only stay for six or nine months and were not bound to the big firms.[16] He perceived that the big firms wanted

---

and this party won the general election and attained government power in an independent Malaya in 1957.

16. The term 'paper ACCAs' refers to those who had completed ACCA examinations but not yet gained the required work experience. They were usually full-time students who joined the Big Six for experience upon completion of their studies but

articled students basically so that the four-year articleship 'can bind them, thereby providing cheap labour' for four years.

A rift was developing between the CAs and the other MACPAs in the big firms on one hand, and the ACCAs in the smaller firms and in industry on the other. One practitioner and MACPA council member recalled having arguments in MACPA council during the early 1980s in order to give recognition to the ACCAs so that this could 'give them greater numbers'. He noted that MACPA did not recognize the ACCAs because 'the emphasis on audit was not the same' within the ACCA and the ACCA's examinations were not recognized by MACPA (I-no-34). He was, however, the sole dissenting voice among the Big Six practitioners on the MACPA council. As a result, MACPA's membership numbers remained low and a large number of ACCAs remained outside MACPA. Naturally, they joined the MIA because they were recognized and so they became the driving force behind it.

> When you exclude people from your club, they will form a rival club . . . that is what I kept telling them [meaning the MACPA]. They did not recognize that at that time. Even now [in 1995], I think they refuse to recognize that. (I-no-34)

The view that MACPA was an elitist organization was growing, as I-no-33 from the Big Six observed:

> [Perhaps] the problem lies, maybe it is a failing on the part of the profession . . . because you had CPA [referring to MACPA] . . . which was very good in its standard setting, but it was construed, or there was a perception, or people saw it in the market place as an elite group which only defended the interest of [a] certain small grouping. The majority of the people, especially, the ACCA block, they came up with the revival of MIA.

A practitioner from another Big Six firm explained that some big accounting firms were biased towards MACPA and he noted that 'if you are not CPA you can't be a partner . . . [and] that [it] was partly [because of] their zeal to promote the local CPA exams that they had done that and raised this sentiment against CPA' (I-no-28).

It may also be argued that an 'elitist status' might work favourably for MACPA members as they could command a higher market price. Several respondents noted that the market differentiates between MACPA and other bodies (I-no-33, I-no-34, I-no-29, I-no-57). Relatedly, there was concern raised about the low number of qualified *Bumiputra* accountants. The then Deputy Prime Minister observed in 1979 that the *Bumiputra* participation in accountancy was still unsatisfactory and that greater efforts were

---

who, in contrast to MACPA-articled students, left to complete the ACCA experience requirement in the corporate sector.

required to promote their entry to the profession (Mahathir Bin Mohamad 1979, 6). There was also growing concern about the shortage of qualified accountants during this period. As I-no-34 noted, in such circumstances the government could recognize local accounting graduates as accountants through the MIA to fill vacancies in the government sector and also to increase the supply of accountants generally.

Although the local accounting undergraduate degrees had been recognized through the amendments to the Accountants Act since 1972, graduates were still required to undertake further examinations prior to attaining membership in MACPA/MICPA. This resulted in a low number of local graduates (especially Malays) becoming members of MACPA (see Table 5.1).

As noted in Table 5.2, a significant number of local graduates become MIA members without further professional examinations. This further enshrined the elitist perception of MACPA.

The graduate issue was elaborated on by one Big Six practitioner who explained that the act was amended without much dialogue with the

*Table 5.1* Composition of MICPA Membership by Race for the Year 1999

| Race | In practice | | Not in practice | | Total | |
|---|---|---|---|---|---|---|
| | No | % | No | % | No | % |
| Chinese | 338 | 80.5 | 2008 | 87.1 | 2346 | 86.1 |
| Indian & others | 38 | 9.0 | 155 | 6.7 | 193 | 7.1 |
| Malay | 44 | 10.5 | 142 | 6.26 | 186 | 6.8 |
| **Total** | 420 | 100 | 2305 | 100.0 | 2725 | 100.0 |

*Source:* MICPA Membership Report 1999

*Table 5.2* MIA Membership as of 1 July 2004—Professional versus Local Graduates

| | Bumiputra | | Non-Bumiputra | | Total | |
|---|---|---|---|---|---|---|
| | No | % | No | % | No | % |
| Professional | 857 | 4.2 | 13,844 | 68.5 | 14,701 | 72.8 |
| Local Graduates | 3,194 | 15.8 | 2,312 | 11.5 | 5,506 | 27.2 |
| **Total** | 4,051 | 20.0 | 16,156 | 80.0 | 20,207 | 100.0 |

*Source*: Susela (2005)
*Note*: the percentages are computed based on grand total 20,207.

profession. It was felt that it was easier to increase the supply of accountants by establishing accounting programmes in local universities as the number of accountants qualifying from MACPA was dismally low. He accepted that MACPA was perceived to be elitist and to be reducing pass rates to keep numbers low but denied allegations that there was a quota for successful candidates (I-no-57).

Table 5.3 shows local CPA graduates increasing compared to other qualification holders in the membership of MACPA.

## Competition Ensues and Professional Jealousy Intensifies

The MIA was set up to unite the profession. Instead, rivalry with MACPA resulted, especially when the MIA was 'activated' in the late 1980s. A senior civil servant also commented on the rivalry among accountants from different professional bodies within the accountant-general's office. There were CAs who felt that they were better than the others there; allegedly they looked down on all other qualifications (I-no-22). In short, the existence of different professional bodies seemed to be a contributing factor to the perception of disunity in the profession:

*Table 5.3* MACPA Membership Statistics by Parent Bodies

| | 1977 | 1980 | 1985 | 1989 | 1993 |
|---|---|---|---|---|---|
| ICAEW | 378 | 348 | 316 | 262 | 252 |
| ICA (Australia) | 181 | 172 | 159 | 137 | 122 |
| ICA Ireland | 13 | 12 | 12 | 11 | 7 |
| ICA (India) | 11 | 8 | 7 | 4 | 3 |
| ICA (Canada) | 7 | 5 | 3 | 2 | 2 |
| ACCA | 83 | 90 | 101 | 123 | 137 |
| ASA/ASCPA | 384 | 371 | 356 | 307 | 328 |
| CA (Scotland) | 5 | 4 | 3 | 3 | 3 |
| CA (NZ) | 26 | 26 | 25 | 21 | 23 |
| CPA graduates | 81 | 169 | 477 | 721 | 1091 |
| **Total** | 1169 | 1205 | 1459 | 1591 | 1968 |
| **% CPA graduates** | 6.9 | 14.0 | 32.7 | 45.3 | 55.4 |

*Source*: Susela (2006)

> [All] the professional bodies have this professional jealousy. Even in the UK there is. One way [to resolve this problem] is to have one national body—MICA (Malaysian Institute of Chartered Accountants). (I-no-28)

He noted that when people take different examinations, although the subjects are the same, they are trained differently, some overseas, some locally, so that by the time they qualified they had acquired a feeling of differential achievement which persisted subsequently:

> [Perhaps] they don't want to let go of this feeling. 'I have achieved something which I want to protect'. It is a natural feeling of being human anyway. (I-no-28)

In his view such feelings could only be eliminated 'if [we] had [only] one professional examination which they [i.e., everyone, has] to sit' (I-no-28). Although the MIA had been set up, and included the ASA and ACCA on its list of recognized professional bodies, MACPA was still dominant. MACPA was perceived to be elitist but well connected and carrying out important functions like standard-setting and running examinations, unlike the MIA, which was (until 1987) merely performing a registering role. The MIA annual general meeting in that year represented a turning-point in Malaysian accounting professional development wherein MIA was activated, as discussed next.

## 1981–1990: MACPA–MIA Merger Attempts Fail and MIA is Reactivated

Up to the 1980s the accounting profession was seen to be solely represented by MACPA. Apart from the activities noted earlier, it was actively organizing seminars and talks, and there was general support from top government leaders (Abdul Aziz 1980; Megat Abdul Rahman 1980). The MACPA president, in an interview upon taking office in June 1981, suggested that priority be given to creating closer rapport with government and its agencies. The accounting profession was advised to assist the government agencies, especially those involved with trade and industry and finance.

### *Respondents' Account: Merger Proposals Rejected by Cabinet in 1985*

During this time there were attempts by MACPA to merge with the MIA. In 1979, the deputy prime minister in his speech at the twenty-first anniversary of MACPA noted:

> The MACPA has over the last 21 years developed into an active professional body, with the organization to look after professional education,

> training and examinations, professional standards and discipline and development of the profession in Malaysia. It would make sense if the actively functioning organization of the MACPA rather than be dismantled, could simply be converted into the new single national body, with, of course, whatever amendments to its constitutions, by-laws and regulations as are considered necessary for the purpose. (Mahathir bin Mohamad 1979, 8)

There was, thus, strong state support for the merger of the two professional bodies. However, when the proposal was finally submitted in 1985 for approval by cabinet in order to amend the Accountants Act 1967, it was rejected. The reasons for rejection are not clear but the common understanding from all accounts is that the Institute of Cooperative Auditors (ICA), with approximately 50 members at that time, was not included by the MIA although it was claimed that MACPA was agreeable to 'accepting them and then controlling them'. The ICA members and Licensed Accountants (LAs)[17] whose qualifications were not recognized for membership in MIA felt left out and lobbied to stop the merger (I-no-3, I-no-8).

## *Activation of the MIA*

When proposals for a merger fell through in 1985, the MIA was activated in 1987, at which time its first annual general meeting was held. Its priority upon activation was to track down 'bogus' accountants, i.e., accountants who were providing accounting services without being registered (MIA 1987).

One respondent recounted that 'at that time feelings were running high as to who would control MIA. XXXX[18] (a former member of MACPA and a practitioner from [the] Big Six) wanted MIA to takeover MACPA' (I-no-3). There was also rising discontent within the ACCA group (as noted previously), which provided strong support for the activation of the MIA. A practitioner from a small firm (I-no-24) explained the involvement of ACCA members. He noted the dominance of MACPA (in 1987) and the inactivity of the MIA: 'no AGM [annual general meeting] was held since inception which was wrong'. In his view, however, it was not really a case of MACPA dominating MIA; rather it was 'just that nobody really wanted to bother about MIA'. He expressed concern also about the subsequent position of the ACCA group within the MIA: 'it now looks like MIA is dominated by ACCA members and that is not good for the country because [they] . . . belong to a foreign body' (I-no-24). Another Big Six practitioner supported this view (I-no-33). He noted that the ACCAs were 'actually running the MIA council through their block votes'. Yet another respondent (an ACCA member) corroborated: 'those who got into MIA from ACCA, then had a bit of "missionary zeal"'. He reasoned that when MIA was revived, the ACCAs feared that if they:

17. See note 25 for an explanation of the 'Licensed Accountant' designation.
18. It was requested by the respondent that the name be not disclosed.

> did not take a very active role in trying to chart the agenda of MIA, to influence MIA, then MIA would become another MACPA-controlled body . . .
>
> That is why the paper ACCAs fought very hard . . . to try and swing MIA and they succeeded. (I-no-29)

A corporate executive observed that the activators of the MIA were those unhappy with the practices of MACPA. He admitted that 'there is a fair amount of professional jealousy among the big firms and small firms'. He claimed that as a non-practitioner 'outsider' he had observed that the ACCAs 'fight very hard to get business . . . [Their] complaints are very real and some are very angry' (I-no-9).

A respondent who served in the first council of MIA noted that:

> it took a few years [for the MIA to be activated. Either] the people do not want to give up their positions . . . or there is some political manipulation at that time . . . I don't know. . . . [The country is fortunate to have an] . . . Accountants Act—that is supposed to tell them, according to an Act of Parliament to look after the accountancy profession but [it is also unfortunate] in that there is a lot of jealousy—those who are CAs or CPAs, felt they are one step higher than the others . . . I must say they [the MACPA] were better organized . . . they have more interest in the profession, they have lectures . . . [It] took quite some time, until this new president, Dato' Hanifah, stepped in and most of us old-timers stepped down at the AGM in 1987. They came in and now they are far more active. (I-no-1)

It was noticeable that once the MIA was revived, one of its first actions seemed to be directed at MACPA. One practitioner offered the following insight:

> [The merger issue] actually started aggressively after [the MIA] passed the bye-law 6.[19] Suddenly MACPA realized they cannot use the [CPA or CA] qualification. I believe YYY[20] went to see the Minister of Finance and they told MIA to stop it because they [i.e., the Ministry of Finance, represented on the MIA council by the accountant-general] were not consulted. So the accountant-general was asked to talk to MIA. But they enforced it vigorously. All the firms have now ceased to practise as CPAs. (I-no-7)

The passing of bye-law 6 is seen as an attempt by the MIA to reduce the 'prominence' of MACPA. An MIA council member identified a further consequence:

> [Because] of MIA's insistence [that] all accounting firms must describe themselves as public accountants, there was no restriction as to who can become partners now [in 1995]. (I-no-28)

19. Bye-law 6 required that members indicate only whether they are Public Accoun-

He clarified that 'previously when you say AB and Co., Chartered Accountants, that itself describes that the firm is a CA firm, meaning all partners are CAs'.

## 1991–1995—MACPA Tries to Take Over MIA

Some respondents recounted MACPA's crusade to get MACPA members into the MIA Council during the 1990s. This was not possible as 'the [MACPA] numbers are too small' (I-no-34, I-no-56, I-no-24). I-no-56 observed that the intense lobbying by MACPA members to get their representatives into the MIA council contributed to the rift between ACCAs (in the MIA) and the CAs and CPAs (in MACPA). Thus, whilst the MIA and MACPA worked together briefly on standard-setting (Susela 1996) the rivalry between them was intensifying.

Another former MIA council member agreed that there was an element of truth in the claim that MIA was dominated by the ACCA group at that time (I-no-35). Another ACCA member concurred, adding that the success of ACCA members in gaining control of the MIA Council led to the result that the 'CPA people [i.e., MACPA members and council] are jealous now [and] at the end of the day the rift is still there' (I-no-29).

## State–Profession Relationship

In the 1970s the Malaysian state played a highly interventionist role in the economy under the banner of the New Economic Policy (NEP).[21] To increase its control over the private sector, the government instituted many new regulations on the terms of economic participation of non-Malay firms; creating new bodies to monitor and influence the behaviour of the private sector, such as the Foreign Investment Committee (FIC), whose brief initially was to monitor foreign acquisitions of Malaysian companies. It integrated Malaysia into the world capitalist economy, albeit on different terms, in the context of the new international division of labour (Jomo 1987). The 1980s witnessed the call from the government for the private sector to play a more positive role in commerce and industry and at the same time, the government was also involved in setting up businesses to complement the role of the private sector (Megat Abdul Rahman 1980, 7). Many government agencies were privatized in this period (Jesudason 1990). The 1990s marked the development of the capital market with the establishment of the Securities Commission and greater focus on internationalization of trade (Susela 1996). Through all these changes the state has been intimately linked to the 'war' between

tants (PAs) or Registered Accountants (RAs). Prior to this, MACPA members (who had to be members of MIA to practise) included the designation 'CPA' or 'CA'. However this issue was resolved with the Accountants Act amendment in 2001.

20. Name withheld at the request of respondent.

21. This resulted from the racial tensions in 1969 which manifested in a change in the state's role. The NEP sought to counter foreign and Chinese dominance in

MACPA and the MIA. The respondents expressed a range of views as to the relationship between state and profession and associated (regulatory) issues.

One practitioner felt that the state was not unduly concerned about tensions within the profession:

> [The] state is aware but they have left it to the profession to sort out its affairs . . . [For] example, at the last annual dinner [in 1994], the deputy prime minister . . . put it quite strongly . . . 'we are not here to teach you your business but if the situation warrants it, we would do so'. (I-no-56)

However, another practitioner felt that the state should be concerned about issues relating to the accounting profession:

> The profession is also not really progressive [enough] to think through [the issues on hand and look at the bigger picture] . . . [At] one time they were trying to keep the number [of accountants] down . . . MACPA would not want to increase the numbers so that their value will go up.[22] But that is not right, my view . . . we need to consider the needs of the country . . . [The] state could have a role here. (I-no-7)

A very senior accountant thought the problem should be sorted out by the profession itself: the state appreciates 'that accountants are very essential . . . [They] gave us self-regulation . . . it is up to us to do so' (I-no-61). Also relatively sanguine was a retired senior government official who opined that 'the government is quite happy with the development in the profession . . . they were not worried about getting enough accountants' (I-no-16).[23]

There is a general acceptance that the profession needs to self-regulate in the wider interest of the nation. However, a respondent from the academic community opined that the state had only intervened in the profession on account of ethnic redistributive purposes, to meet its socio-economic goals under the NEP:

> [What] little I know . . . about the profession is that the only intervention that has taken place which has been pursued by the government has been mainly to try to, for ethnic redistributive purposes . . . so you have, for instance, you have one body which is officially recognized and one body which is not officially recognized . . . I think, the government intervention should be more broad and much more oriented towards

---

the economy (Jesudason 1990, 74). The government's view was that to achieve national unity in the context of the *Rukunegara* (the National Ideology), it was crucial to develop a socio-economic foundation that would provide for a viable and equitable participation of all races in the development process (Government of Malaysia 1971).

22. That is, keeping the numbers down will make their value go up.

23. This is because they have the graduate direct entry route to the MIA without further examination (see Figure 5.1).

> developing the profession as a whole rather than simply in terms of ethnic ratios and typical NEP type of initiatives. (I-no-54)

Further, the rivalry between the two professional bodies is seen as a 'natural occurrence' since it occurs in other countries too. Several respondents mentioned similar developments in the UK and Australia. Almost all respondents agreed, furthermore, that personality differences were involved. The suggestion to integrate the profession by unifying MIA and MACPA did not make many happy, especially within the MIA (I-no-8).

Possibly the state's reluctance to get involved may be due to MACPA's strong rapport with the state and other regulatory bodies. On the whole, the consensus is that it has served the state well. For example, a former senior state official remarked:

> [Personally], I think the MACPA has more public image, the accountants in MACPA are more professional compared to [those in the] MIA. I say this because I know a lot of them personally . . . [They] are more professional about it because they have been in the business longer but whatever it is, they should come together. (I-no-16)

Similar accounts were provided by a respondent who was formerly in a regulatory authority (I-no-47) and a non-accountant from the civil service (I-no-21).

Another practitioner remarked:

> [People] are using the accounting body as a political platform to get political mileage for themselves. That is sad . . . [Even regarding] this issue of entering the profession through the university only . . . I have got no clear preference either way. . . . I have got one worry . . . where the universities are controlled by government [a reference to the accreditation of local universities' accounting degrees introduced in the 1970s] . . . that is, where quality control [becomes a problem—the concern being that the curriculum in the universities may not adequately prepare graduates to enter the profession, especially as they are allowed to enter the profession without further examination] . . . *Bumiputra* accountants who want favour from the government will tell the government that if you make it a graduate qualification, you, the government can make sure there are more *Bumiputra* accountants because you can control the inflow . . . that is my fear. A lot of *Bumiputra* accountants in MACPA have their reservations but [in] MIA . . . there are people with political aspirations . . . [who] play their card 'we are short of *Bumiputra* accountants' . . . [Their] interest is politics . . . they are not worried about whether we have quality accountants or not. (I-no-5)

There is a contention here that university degrees were accredited to ensure ample supply of Malay accountants as the availability of university places to various ethnic groups is determined by the government. Whilst I-no-16 was content with the quantity of accountants, I-no-5 was concerned with the quality.

The issue of shortage of *Bumiputra* accountants seems to clearly emerge as an argument against the MACPA and has given an advantage to the MIA from the perspective, at least, of the politicians.[24] For one MIA council member this was the key issue: 'MACPA doesn't produce that many accountants . . . that is the problem . . . [I] can't see any immediate solution' (I-no-26). As Tables 5.1 and 5.2 indicate, the predominance of the Chinese in both MACPA and MIA is clear even though the Malays represent the majority in Malaysian society, the MIA presidents have all been Malays (apart from the first) and the MACPA presidents since 1967 have been Malays, except in 1977–1979, 1986–1989, 1994–1996 and 2002–2004 (see Appendix).

On one hand, the rate of growth in MACPA's membership has decreased significantly, as noted in Table 5.4. On the other hand, the membership of MIA[25] has grown tremendously, as shown in Table 5.5.

As summarized in the following, these ongoing conundrums have imperial roots.

*Table 5.4* Membership Statistics for MICPA (2000–2006)

| | 2000 | 2001 | 2002 | 2003 | 2004 | 2005 | 2006 |
|---|---|---|---|---|---|---|---|
| Total Membership | 2822 | 2902 | 2951 | 3009 | 3034 | 3082 | 3088 |
| CPA Graduate members | 2028 | 2110 | 2205 | 2312 | 2395 | 2463 | 2519 |
| **% increase** | | 2.8 | 1.7 | 2.0 | 0.8 | 1.6 | 0.2 |

*Source*: MICPA Annual Reports

24. It has caused particular concern even in present times. See Table 5.2 and Susela (2005).

25. Prior to amendments to the Accountants Act 1967 in 2001, there were three categories of membership, namely, PA, RA and LA. PAs referred to those in public practice who had obtained the licence (approved by the Ministry of Finance) to perform public practice services, and had relevant years of work in a public practice. RAs were generally employed in the corporate sector or the public sector. They were not required to have work experience relating to public practice. The LAs were a small number of accountants who were admitted into the profession in the early years and allowed to practise although they did not possess the required professional qualifications. After the 2001 amendments, the

*Table 5.5* MIA: Total Membership—1987–1997

| Year | Number of members |
|---|---|
| 1987 | 4,301 |
| 1988 | 5,314 |
| 1989 | 5,496 |
| 1990 | 5,492 |
| 1991 | 5,693 |
| 1992 | 6,205 |
| 1993 | 6,932 |
| 1994 | 7,431 |
| 1995 | 8,464 |
| 1996 | 9,640 |
| 1997 | 10,843 |

*Source*: MIA Annual Reports 1987–1997

## DISCUSSION AND CONCLUSION

The formation and subsequent activities of MACPA—a largely British-influenced local body set up by overseas-qualified accountants who returned from the UK and Australia—evidences the empire connectivity. In addition, the first three MACPA presidents were British and the ICAEW was a key influence on MACPA examinations in its early years. Furthermore, the establishment of the MIA by the state, propelled as it was by different factions of the empire connexion (the ACCA from UK and ASA from Australia) and its complex relationship with MACPA, provides a rich context for examining the British Empire interconnectedness in the development of the Malaysian accountancy profession. The Accountants Act 1967 was based on the Singapore Act devised by an Australian borrowing from a New Zealand act. It clearly evidences the importation into Malaysia of the professional struggles in UK and elsewhere. On a broader level, the importation of Chinese labour into Malaysia and the subsequent ethnic tensions that have permeated the profession as well as Malaysian society generally are also, arguably, the product of empire. One result of the combined effect of all these factors has been that the contribution of the Malaysian accounting

categories are: Chartered Accountant in Practice, Chartered Accountant not in Practice, Licensed Accountants and Associate Members. See http://www.mia.org.my.

profession to the post-colonial state's domestic policies and priorities has been contentious, and (arguably) muted.

The common theme that arises from the MACPA–MIA relations is that of post-colonial politics and the struggle to attain control over the profession, with different factions fuelling the feud at different occasions. Given the state's obsession with ethnic relations, the MIA appealed to the state by drawing upon the *Bumiputra* issue whilst MACPA tried hard to show that it was not anti-Malay. Table 5.2 shows that *Bumiputra* accountants only represent 20 per cent of the total registered members of MIA and of this only 4.2 per cent are professionally qualified. The 'disproportionate' role of Chinese accountants versus Malays is an outcome of the ethnic division legacy of the British.

Interestingly, the Accountants Act 1967 was amended further in 2001 in a manner which highlighted the significance of designations as 'brands' or forms of symbolic capital. The amendments allowed all MIA numbers to be designated as CAs. The CA brand has both a sentimental and a market impact, given that many of the high-ranking officials in the accountant-general's office also recognize the CA brand. The idea that MIA members use the CA title was mooted and supported by the accountant-general's office. In effect, it cancels out the advantage of the local CAs (who are members of the ICAEW or ICAA in addition to being MACPA members and who thus previously followed the rules of the UK and Australian CA bodies). Alternatively, there is a strong sense that this as an attempt to get back at UK CA bodies for not allowing MACPA to use the 'CA' designation in the first place when MACPA was formed (Susela 1996). The 2001 amendments further compound the challenges for MACPA. Its membership growth has decreased significantly whilst the membership of MIA has grown tremendously. The MACPA–MIA power struggle saga continues to this day. All the foreign professional bodies accredited by the MIA, furthermore, have an empire/Commonwealth connexion.

The increased globalization and internationalization of the accounting profession has also brought further challenges for MACPA and the MIA. In line with the nation's aspirations to become a developed economy by 2020, much focus is directed to human capital development in the Ninth Malaysia Plan. Compounded with this is the development in the international regulation of the profession by the International Federation of Accountants (IFAC). Presently, much discussion is directed to charting a new competency framework for the education and training of professional accountants in Malaysia. IFAC has issued International Education Standards and Statement of Members Obligations, among other things, which need to be complied with by member bodies. The MIA issued a consultative document entitled *A New Framework for the Accountancy Profession: Enhancing Effectiveness of the Malaysian Institute of Accountants in meeting Stakeholders Expectations* in July 2007 (MIA, 2007); an initiative that may well have significant implications for MACPA. The document essentially reveals a plan to introduce a competency assessment to be conducted by MIA prior to admission of its members, in line with IFAC's International Education Standard 6: *Competency Assessment.* That might make MACPA redundant, an outcome broadly consistent with the claim that the power struggle is likely to continue until some definitive action is taken by the Malaysian state or external players (Poullaos 1999, 282).

It may be too early, however, to claim that the power struggle will cease. The MACPA has recently undertaken a branding exercise, having earlier changed its name from an association to an institute. These moves suggest that MACPA is aware that it has to re-engineer itself if it is to survive in the face of IFAC initiatives and global competition. Interestingly, it has also drawn on post-independence empire connectivity by signing (in early 2009) a Memorandum of Understanding (MoU) with the ICAA for recognition, examination and membership arrangements as between the two institutes. This indirect empire connexion has provided an added twist to the fascinating power struggle that continues within the Malaysian profession to this day.

## APPENDIX

**PAST PRESIDENTS OF MICPA [1958–2009]**

| | |
|---|---|
| 1958–1959 | En R.D. Stewart |
| 1959–1961 | En W.M. Piercy |
| 1961–1962 | En H.R. Villiers |
| 1962–1963 | En Chan Kum Chee |
| 1963–1964 | En Frederick Weatherly |
| 1964–1965 | En Y.C. Kang |
| 1965–1966 | En C.H. Yong |
| 1966–1967 | En Cheah Pee Aik |
| 1967–1969 | YBhg Datuk Abdul Razak Yusof |
| 1969–1971 | YBhg Tan Sri Dato' Jaffar Hussein |
| 1973–1975 | YBhg Tan Sri Dato' Jaffar Hussein |
| 1971–1973 | YBhg Dato' Mohd Salleh Yusof |
| 1975–1977 | En Abdul Rahman Abdul Hamid |
| 1977–1979 | YBhg Datuk Peter Yew Min-Sang |
| 1979–1981 | Dr. Nawawi Mat Awin |
| 1981–1984 | YBhg Dato' Hj Megat Abdul Rahman |
| 1984–1986 | YBhg Dato' Abu Hassan Kendut |
| 1986–1987 | En Subimal Sen Gupta |
| 1987–1989 | En Larry Seow Thiam Fatt |
| 1989–1991 | YBhg Dato' Hj Zainal Abidin Putih |
| 1991–1994 | Y.M. Raja Datuk Arshad Raja Tun Uda |
| 1994–1996 | YBhg Datuk Oh Chong Peng |
| 1996–1998 | En Abdul Jabbar Abdul Majid |
| 1998–1999 | YBhg Datuk Ali bin Tan Sri Abdul Kadir |
| 1999–2002 | YBhg Datuk Dr Abdul Samad Hj Alias |
| 2002–2004 | En Beh Tok Koay |
| 2004–2007 | YBhg Dato' Abdul Halim Mohyiddin |
| 2007–2009 | YBhg Dato' Nordin Baharuddin |

*Source*: Malaysian Institute of Certified Public Accountants. (2008) *Golden Jubilee Handbook*. Kuala Lumpur: MICPA.

## REFERENCES

Abdul Aziz, H.T. (1980) 'Opening address: International accounting standards seminar'. *Malaysian Accountant* (July): 40.

Azham, M.A. (2006) 'Phantasmagoric accounting in Malaysia: A case study of the triumph of hope over experience?' Paper presented at the 18th Asian Pacific Conference on International Accounting Issues, Hawaii, 15–18 October.

Chin, T. (1964) 'Standards of financial reporting in Malaysia: A sequel'. *Kajian Ekonomi Malaysia* 1:30–36.

Enthoven, A.J.H. (1977) *Accountancy Systems in Third World Economies.* Amsterdam: North Holland.

Goh, Joon Hai. (1970) 'Recent legislation on the profession of accountancy in Malaysia and Singapore'. *Accounting Journal* 1:25–36.

Government of Malaya. (1953) *Progress Report on the Development Plan 1950–1952.* Kuala Lumpur: Government Printers.

Government of Malaysia. (1971) *Second Malaysia Plan (1971–1975).* Kuala Lumpur: Government Printers.

Jesudason, J.Y. (1990) *Ethnicity and the Economy: The State, Chinese Business and Multinationals in Malaysia.* Singapore: Oxford University Press.

Jomo, K.S. (1987). 'Economic crisis and policy responses in Malaysia'. In *Southeast Asia in the 1980s*, ed. R. Robinson, K. Hewison and R. Riggot. Sydney: Allen and Unwin.

Lim Teck Ghee. (1977) *Peasants and Their Agricultural Economy in Colonial Malaya 1874–1941.* Kuala Lumpur: Oxford University Press.

Mahathir bin Mohamad. (1979) 'Future of the accountancy profession in Malaysia'. Seminar speech by the Deputy Prime Minister who was also Minister of Trade and Industry, Kuala Lumpur, 29 September.

Malaysian Association of Certified Public Accountants. (1981). 'Interview with the president of the MACPA'. *Malaysian Accountant* (2 July): 6–7.

———. (1989) *MACPA Annual Report 1988.* Kuala Lumpur: MACPA.

Malaysian Institute of Accountants. (1987) *Malaysian Institute of Accountants: 1987 Report and Accounts.* Kuala Lumpur: MIA.

———. (2007). *A New Framework for the Accountancy Profession: Enhancing Effectiveness of the Malaysian Institute of Accountants in meeting Stakeholders Expectations.* Available at http://www.mia.org.my/enews/25-2007.htm.

Malaysian Institute of Certified Public Accountants. (2008) *Golden Jubilee Handbook.* Kuala Lumpur: MICPA.

Means, G.P. (1976) *Malaysian Politics.* 2nd ed. London: Hodder and Stoughton.

Megat Abdul Rahman. (1979) 'Future of the accountancy profession in Malaysia'. Speech at the seminar organized in conjunction with MACPA's 21st anniversary, September.

———. (1980) 'The accountancy profession in Malaysia—some current issues'. *Malaysian Accountant* (1 July): 1–6.

Morais, V.J. (1972). *Blueprint for Unity: Selected Speeches.* Kuala Lumpur: Malaysian Chinese Association.

Nawawi Mat Awin. (1980) 'Seminar on IAS: Opening address'. *Malaysian Accountant* (1 January): 5–7.

Poullaos, C. (1999) 'Introduction: From the East—stories about accountants in Asia'. *Accounting, Auditing & Accountability Journal* 12:274–85.

Shamsul, A.B. (2001) 'A history of an identity: The idea and practice of "Malayness" in Malaysia reconsidered'. *Journal of Southeast Asian Studies* 32:355–66.

Snodgrass, D.R (1980) *Inequality and Economic Development in Malaysia.* Kuala Lumpur: Oxford University Press.

Stenson, M. (1976) 'Class and race in West Malaysia'. *Bulletin of Concerned Asian Scholars* (March/April): 45–54.

Susela, D.S. (1996) 'Accounting standard setting in Malaysia'. Unpublished PhD thesis, University of Waikato, New Zealand.

———. (1999) '"Interests" and accounting standard setting in Malaysia'. *Accounting, Auditing & Accountability Journal* 12:358–87.

———. (2005) 'Overview and implementation of international education standards and challenges for the accounting profession'. Seminar on accounting education organized by the Indonesian Institute of Accountants, Jakarta, 9 September.

Susela, D.S., Hooper, K., and Davey H. (2004) *Accounting Theory and Practice: A Malaysian Perspective.* Kuala Lumpur: Pearson Education (Malaysia).

# 6 The Imperial Roots of Accounting Closure

## The Case of Sri Lanka

*P.W. Senarath Yapa*

## INTRODUCTION

British colonial rule commenced in Sri Lanka in 1796 and came to an end with independence in 1948.[1] At the time of political independence, Sri Lanka provided a classic example of an export-oriented modern plantation economy financed by British capital. The British had introduced coffee, tea, rubber and coconut, and the plantation sector had become the backbone of the Sri Lankan economy, accounting for 88 per cent of export earnings, 37 per cent of GDP and 27 per cent of employment at the time of independence (Snodgrass 1966). The country also had a system of commercial banking and other financial facilities, including accounting, introduced by the British to serve trade and commerce. A capitalist form of management had been instituted in the plantations. The rise of accountancy in this colony is closely linked to the changing economic climate and originated with the need to provide investors in Britain with financial information pertaining to their investments in Sri Lanka.

The purpose of this chapter is to chart the rise of accountancy in Sri Lanka and to examine the influence of the British Empire on its organization. Highlighting the influence of British accountants practising in Sri Lanka and British models of education and training for accountants of Sri Lankan origin, the chapter will focus on the tussles between competing groups within the profession. There were two main groups: the 'elite accountants' with British accountancy qualifications who founded the Institute of Chartered Accountants of Sri Lanka (ICASL); and the 'non-elite' Registered Accountants (RAs) who took the examinations of the local accountancy board, graduated from local universities and formed the lower tier of the profession. The former group, being members of the elite stratum of Sri Lankan society with access to British-style education and local political connexions, crafted an elite accountancy tradition that

1. Sri Lanka is a tropical island in the Indian Ocean, 25,483 square miles in area. The population is 19.9 million and highly educated; the literacy rate of 96 per cent being attributable to the free education system. Colonial rule began in Ceylon with the arrival of the Portuguese in 1506 and the subsequent arrival of the Dutch in the seventeenth century.

formed the linch-pin of a strategy to effect market closure by excluding the non-elites from public practice. It was the elite group that pioneered the institutional arrangements for professional accountancy in post-independence Sri Lanka. Its members were generally wealthy, of relatively high status in terms of family background and lifestyle and they were motivated by ambitions to preserve imperial connexions in post-independence Sri Lanka.

The Institute of Chartered Accountants of Ceylon (ICAC) was established under the Institute of Chartered Accountants Act No. 23 in 1959, 11 years after the achievement of political independence. Subsequently, in 1972, under new constitutional arrangements, the name of the country was changed from Ceylon to Sri Lanka and the institute was eventually renamed the ICASL. The 1959 act institutionalized the distinction between the 'elite' and 'non-elite' accountants and determined the type of work that could be conducted by both. The elite accountants monopolized public practice and dominated the ICASL council, which in turn sanctioned UK-moderated examinations and training under articles.

The period covered in this chapter ranges from the Institute of Chartered Accountants Act of 1959 to 1977. Reference has also been made to the period pre-1959 to identify factors at play when the ICAC was formed. The pre-1977 period was one of relatively 'high closure' at the institute. The specific argument of this chapter is that closure had imperial roots. In contrast, following a transformation of the institute's scheme of education and training in 1977 the accounting profession (which had been the preserve of a few hundred privileged members) was opened to thousands of students from all over the country who were able to sit their examinations in Sinhala,[2] Tamil and English.

This chapter is based on unstructured interviews conducted by the author with nine individuals, including two past presidents of the ICASL and a civil servant involved in various government committees associated with the ICASL. These interviewees are retired or semi-retired and played key roles within the institute, in accounting practice and in the reform process during the period under study.[3]

The next section charts the arrival of British capital in the colony and the subsequent rise of accounting professionals and institutions prior to independence in 1948. The hiatus between independence and the ICA Act of 1959 is discussed subsequently. The following section examines the strategies utilized by the ICASL from 1959 to 1977 to effect closure and the

2. Sinhala is the official language in Sri Lanka and the majority of Sri Lankans work in this language.

3. In the interviews, the author raised issues relating to the professionalization process of the ICASL, the rationale for the behaviour of particular groups involved in that process and several other key issues relating to university accounting graduates during the period 1959–1977. In doing so, every effort was made to triangulate the interviewee responses with secondary and archival records on major events.

ensuing debate surrounding the closure process. The final section provides a summary of the imperial roots of professional closure in Sri Lanka by way of conclusion.

## PRE-INDEPENDENCE

The arrival of British capital and new company legislation were the catalysts for the development of the accounting profession in Sri Lanka. Generally, statutory changes in England led to amendments from time to time to the law applicable to Sri Lanka, although the changes did not always keep pace with British law. After the enactment of the UK Companies Act of 1929, steps were taken to revise company law in Sri Lanka and to follow closely the principles and provisions of the English Act (Perera 1975), culminating in the passage of the Companies Ordinance No. 51 of 1938. The ordinance required that persons appointed to audit company accounts should first be registered under regulations made for the purpose and drew attention to the need for establishing a controlling body called the 'Accountancy Board' and an avenue for formal admission into the accounting profession in Sri Lanka. In 1938, there was a small group of 28 accountants, mainly of British origin and holding British qualifications, in public practice in Sri Lanka (G: retired practising accountant).

### British Capital in Sri Lanka

British capital played a significant role in Sri Lanka both before and after independence. According to De Silva (1982), British capital took one of two forms: 'productive' and 'mercantile'. Productive capital came in the form of direct investment in plantations provided by the scattered mass of absentee stockholders of British plantation companies, commonly known as 'Starling Companies'. 'Fixed' productive capital was mainly for factory buildings and infrastructure development. Labour was the largest portion of the 'variable' capital and, generally, it represented around 60 per cent of the total operating capital of the estate. 'Mercantile' capital included various fees, commissions on sales proceeds and margins on various services such as insurance and freight. Mercantile capital utilized a greater portion of the plantation surplus compared to productive capital (De Silva 1982; Wickramasinghe and Cameron 2004).

The 'agency house system' was the operational mode of mercantile capital in the plantation economy. It was wholly British-run during the colonial period, although some Sri Lankans entered into the agency business late in the 1930s. Nevertheless, even after independence in 1948 and as late as the 1960s, the operation of agency houses was still largely in the hands of British investors and executives (Government of Sri Lanka 1974, 16–17). The operational framework of agency control consisted of an agency house in London, another agency house in the capital city of the colony (Colombo) and plantation managers. The control responsibilities were shared amongst the managers responsible for managing the labour process: the Colombo agency, which managed the plantation and the London agency, which managed the company. This separation of duties necessitated the production of reliable independent financial information and the Colombo agency houses were entrusted with a series of managerial, accounting, secretarial and other related functions (ibid.).

The British influenced every aspect of the lives of Sri Lankans, keeping them bound to the empire with a strong sense of loyalty (Wickramasinghe and Cameron 2004). The economic and social transformation that took place during colonial rule and post-colonial rule provided some individuals and families with the opportunity of social advancement through educational accomplishments in the medium of English and economic enterprise in the plantation of cash crops. These two avenues of advancement were closely interwoven. The hard-earned wealth of the pioneer entrepreneurs enabled them to educate their children in the best schools and even to send them overseas for education and professional training at higher levels. The second and third generations employed their education and social contacts to further consolidate their elevated social positions and elite status. In other instances, the professions provided a ladder to the ramparts occupied by the national elite (Gamage 1991). The links with Britain were perpetuated through the introduction of British businesses, educational, political and social institutions through which a long-lasting relationship and fraternal friendship could be maintained between the two countries (Gamage 1991). The influence of empire has perhaps been the greatest external influence on the country and has had a significant impact upon many spheres of the post-independence period, as argued in the following.

## The Operation of the Accountancy Board

In 1941 an accountancy board was set up under the Companies (Auditors) Regulations 1941, which functioned under the aegis of the Ministry of Commerce and Trade. The board consisted entirely of persons nominated by government, but of these, officials or public officers were in a minority. The only public officer was the permanent secretary to the Ministry of Commerce who was the chairman of the board (Ceylon Sessional Paper 1950). Other members were leading businessmen involved in the plantation sector in Ceylon in the 1940s, some of whom were also members of the Chamber of Commerce. Under the regulations of the board, registration for the purposes of the audit of company accounts was open to members of the established professional societies in Britain and to persons registered under company legislation in India.[4] Registration had also been granted to persons who, though not professionally qualified, had been in practice as accountants for a sufficient period to satisfy the board as to their knowledge and experience. These accountants predominantly worked in the government audit department and were not in public practice.

The authority of the board was limited to the approval and control of accountants only for the purpose of the audit of companies as per the Companies Ordinance 1941. Other than this restriction, any individual, qualified or otherwise, was free to offer his or her services to the public as an accountant (Ceylon Sessional Paper 1950; Nesaratnam 1999). Anyone registered by the board was referred to as an RA whether he or she was (say) a chartered accountant (CA) or not.

## Accounting Practice

Prior to the establishment of the ICASL, accountancy in Sri Lanka was practised mostly by members of the Institute of Chartered Accountants in England and Wales (ICAEW) and by RAs who had qualified through examinations conducted by the accountancy board. Members of the government audit department aside, it was not possible to become a RA/auditor solely on the grounds of having been in practice for a given number of years. There were various other groups that could become RAs in Sri Lanka prior to the ICA Act of 1959: those who had been provisionally registered under the Companies (Auditors) Regulations 1941; holders of book-keeping and accountancy certificates of Ceylon Technical College; or holders of certificates of membership of an accountancy institute of the UK. However, in practice, the RAs who did not have British qualifications only provided audit/accounting services to small businesses (sole proprietors, co-operative societies and some partnerships) (G: retired practising accountant).

The non-elite RAs were either graduates of new universities such as Vidyodaya and Vidyalankara[5] or non-graduates. Many of the graduates came from poor economic backgrounds and had faced disillusionment and frustration on entry to higher education. Their grievances related to a wide range of issues, including a lack of educational facilities in accounting in the universities, a lack of facilities in the universities, shortages of reading material in the national languages, inability to read books available only in English and scant prospects of employment in public practice on graduation (De Silva 1977). Many non-graduates, on the other hand, came to practise with accounting experience gained through working in industry as junior clerical assistants.

---

4. The Indian accountants were not members of the accountancy elite but their numbers in Ceylon during this period were limited. During the post-independence period the Indian accountants left Ceylon and thus did not pose any threat to CAs in Ceylon. This is an area for further research on the Sri Lankan accounting profession.

5. These were new universities, established in support of a 'national-local ethos' promoting the social elevation of local indigenous people in the early 1960s.

## FROM 1948 TO 1959

Although moves towards independence begun in the 1930s did not result in independence till 1948, the transition was mainly peaceful and this shaped much of what followed in the new nation's economic, political and social spheres. In particular, the peaceful transition to freedom ensured that Sri Lanka embraced British precedent in many areas, including accountancy. The authorities promoted the establishment of a new local institute in Sri Lanka to regulate the profession and the standards applicable to its practice. The Commission on Company Law was established by the government under the chairmanship of Mr. L.M.D. De Silva in the early 1950s, and its report recommended the establishment of the Institute of Chartered Accountants (Commission on Company Law, Banking, Insurance and Accountants and Auditors 1950). Despite this, the plans remained shelved for a number of years due to political turmoil[6] and it was only in late 1959 that an act of Parliament was enacted that paved the way for its establishment (Yapa and Perera 2005; Yapa 2006).

It is interesting to note that at the initial stage of the parliamentary bill for the establishment of the ICASL there had been some concerns aired by the Ceylonese with regard to the creation of an accounting profession that would accommodate two classes of accountants, namely 'Chartered Accountants' ('CAs') and 'Registered Accountants'. This was quite different to the situation in other countries. For instance, the ICAEW did not make any such distinction and in India under the Indian Institute of Chartered Accountants Act, all registered certificate holders whether permanent or temporary were eligible for membership (*Ceylon Daily News*, 1959). In this respect the following comments are relevant:

> [The] majority of the practising accountants in 1959 in Ceylon who were registered under the Companies (Auditors) regulations, 1941, are non-Ceylonese. The request that the Ceylonese should be given an opportunity to gain admission for membership in this indigenous organization is a fair and just demand. The Ceylonese practitioners have a claim to form the nucleus of this national organization. We informed the authorities that it is unfair to recommend legislation to consolidate the position of a particular class of practitioners which may aim ultimately at monopoly. (B: retired practising accountant, RA)

6. From 1950 to 1959 the political situation in Sri Lanka was highly volatile and three successive governments ruled the country. Prime Minister S.W.R.D. Bandaranayake was assassinated during this period. Due to conflicting views among different groups of politicians in the ruling party, a number crossed over to the opposition party. Hence the passing of the ICAC act was postponed and not given any priority until 1959.

In addition to such opposition, there were those that supported the bifurcation of the profession, as proposed in the ICASL bill. At the drafting stage of the bill, the founding members, the elite accountants, championed the superiority of CAs. As one participant in the debate put it:

> An accountant is as useful to the community as a doctor or lawyer. In the case of a person who has his own private business, the accountant comes in as an outsider, surveys the management of the business over a period of a year and submits a report which has a good effect on the owner of the business because he knows the defects of the management of it. When it comes to the general public, an auditor's report would serve as a guide to investors, and therefore in the field of investment the auditor plays a very important part. Most business investments are based on British interests. So an auditor or an accountant must be a person of high integrity; such as Chartered Accountants, [on] whose reports people can rely. For that reason we must have reputed people in the accounting profession. (E: founder of a local accounting firm and past ICASL president)

The elite accountants further argued that there might not be the same degree of confidence in the RAs and hence their right to audit accounts ought to be restricted to small private companies (Ceylon Sessional Paper 1950). Although aware of the disadvantage at which they would be placed if the bill progressed, the RAs (the non-elite local practitioners) were unable to mobilize strong opposition to the ICA bill. It may be speculated that this was the result of the fact that many of them came from disadvantaged family backgrounds and lacked the social connexions of the 'chartered' group and therefore political power (*Ceylon Daily News*, 1960). The elite group influenced decisions through their personal connexions with government members (Perera 1975) and consequently the ICA bill was passed by the Parliament in May 1959. Significantly, the proposed clause 13 of the act, whose effect was summarized as follows, was not passed and RAs were not allowed to undertake audit and accounting work for bigger businesses and government entities:

> Existing regulations under the Companies Ordinance permit the registration of persons who have actually been in practice in Ceylon as public auditors for a specified period. Persons who have been registered for the purposes of Company Law should be permitted to continue to practise as accountants. These accountants should be registered as: Registered Accountant and Auditor, Ceylon. Apart from this distinction in designation, there will be no fetter on their right to practise. (Ceylon Sessional Paper 1950, 5, 6)

Several months after passing the bill, the relevant minister invited Mr. Lionel Weerasinghe, F.C.A. (England and Wales), the then auditor-general, to serve as the institute's first president from December 1959. Under the law, the responsibility for nominating members of the first council rested with the minister, but he left the selection in the hands of the ICASL's president. It was a clear opportunity, therefore, for the elitists to secure their dominant position and appoint members to the council. The president selected 10 persons—all ICAEW members[7]—with educational, professional and business roles (Nesaratnam 1999), prominent in the profession already and coming from high-status family backgrounds. Thus professional practice in independent Sri Lanka retained a strong British influence, as this elite group sought to defend its status and adopt the British model of professionalization (Gamage 1991).

However, the post-independence period also witnessed the rise of another group of accountants who espoused more nationalist sentiments and did not support the adoption of the British model for accounting in Sri Lanka. Most members of this group were RAs who had opposed the ICA bill on the issue of creation of a high-status group within the profession. This group was of the view that the local resources such as universities and technical colleges ought to be utilized to meet local needs for the production of accountants (Ministry of Planning and Implementation 1980). In order to address this issue, this group pressured the government to act. The process and outcome of this action is explored next.

## THE ICASL FROM 1959 TO 1977

### The Early Days of the ICASL

Whilst the ICASL council was being constituted the president had set up a secretariat headed by the ICASL secretary, with the assistance of the auditor-general's private secretary. In the total absence of local guidelines on membership and examinations, the task involved a considerable volume of initial work including consultation with various accounting bodies in the UK (Nesaratnam 1999).

7. They were: Mr. L.L. Attygalle, Municipal Treasurer, Colombo Municipal Council; Mr. T.H. Burah, Senior Partner, Burah Hathy & Company, Chartered Accountants; Mr. S. Cumaraswamy, Director, Whittall Bousteads Ltd; Mr. D.S. de Silva, Deputy Auditor-General; Mr. B.L.W. Fernando, Chief Accountant, Marketing Department; Mr. R.J. Gilmour, Chairman, George Steuart & Co. Ltd; Mr. E. Turner Green, Senior Partner, Turquand, Youngs & Co., Chartered Accountants; Mr. A.I. Macan Marker, Senior Partner, A.I. Macan Marker & Co., Chartered Accountants; Mr. Y.A.D.S. Samaratunga, Lecturer, Ceylon Technical College; Mr. K. Satchithananda, Senior Partner, Satchithananda Schokman, Wijeratne & Co., Chartered Accountants (Nesaratnam 1999).

### *Examinations*

As the institute was to conduct its own examinations, the assistance of the ICAEW secretary was sought for the appointment of experienced examiners to serve as moderators for all the papers in the intermediate and final examinations. The locally-set question papers were referred to the British moderators and on completion of examinations the marked answer scripts were also moderated in the UK. The moderators' comments were taken into account in the final evaluation of the scripts (Nesaratnam 1999). This system was instigated by the elite group, who had long supported the continuation of British input:

> As far as I know the comments of the British moderators gave the institute . . . valuable guidelines to prepare examination papers and in the conduct of examinations. As a result the institute developed the capacity to maintain British standards. (D: retired accountant, member of the Future Training of Accountants Committee)

The council had resolved that a full-time director of studies should co-ordinate the tutorial programmes, lectures and other services that would help to enhance the quality of the students sitting the institute's examinations. The ICASL president invited E. Cockson-Jones, an ICAEW Fellow, to take on this role in January 1964, and Foulks Lynch, a British private firm, was asked to design and transport the teaching materials. The process was funded through the Colombo Plan[8] (Nesaratnam 1999) and, in addition, a significant amount of foreign exchange was allocated for this purpose by the Central Bank of Sri Lanka (Yapa 2006).

### *The ICASL's Relationship with the University Sector*

Although university accounting programmes were not recognized as the primary basis for a professional accounting career in Sri Lanka, several universities had been offering accounting and related subjects in their programmes of studies since the 1960s. The institute accepted those with a General Certificate of Education (GCE)[9] advanced level (English medium)

---

8. The Colombo Plan, Australia's first major foreign aid programme, was established at a meeting of Commonwealth foreign ministers in Colombo in January 1950. At this meeting a consultative committee was established to provide a framework within which international co-operation efforts could be promoted to raise the living standards of people in the region. Originally conceived as lasting for a period of six years, the Colombo Plan was extended several times until 1980, when it was extended indefinitely. This was a first step towards economic co-operation and development in South and South-East Asia. The primary focus of all Colombo Plan activities is on human resources development. The initial membership of the consultative committee was: Australia, Canada, Ceylon, India, Pakistan, NZ and the UK (Dawson 1990).

9. The GCE, advanced level, is the university entrance examination conducted by the Department of Examinations annually in Sri Lanka. Based on the results of

who could not attend university degree programmes due to low marks, and this opened the way for them to follow a professional course of study in accounting through the ICASL, whose examinations were conducted only in English up to 1977. This route required the trainee to secure an articled clerkship, pay a premium to the principal and successfully complete five years of study without a salary for non-graduates (three years for graduates). Therefore, those from privileged backgrounds with an English-language education, namely the children of the British-educated elite with plantation and business interests, could afford this route for professional accounting throughout the 1960s (Yapa and Perera 2005; Yapa 2006; Balachandran 2007). This opportunity was not available to those who did GCE (advanced levels) in Sinhala and Tamil, and who came from the poorer, rural areas of the country.

University graduates were generally not encouraged to enter the profession during this period as the dominant elite group believed graduates to be less proficient in English language and lacking the family background and social connexions necessary for acceptance to and progression within the profession (Wijewardena and Yapa 1998). Thus, as indicated by one of the interviewees, the ICASL seemingly intended to attract the children[10] of the Sri Lankan elite who had working relations with former colonial administrators and capitalists; sharing their essentially British outlook, politics and lifestyles (F: retired accountant and ICASL member). Over almost two decades, the ICASL pursued a strategy of occupational closure, that is, of restricting the supply of qualified public accounting practitioners, as examined in the following.

## The Closure Strategies Pursued by the ICASL

The importance of class, status and social standing in the emergence of the profession has been highlighted in the case of Britain (Walker 1991, 1995) and her colonies (Richardson 1997; Chua and Poullaos 1998, 2002; Annisette 1999; Yapa 1999; Sian 2006, 2007a, 2007b). In Sri Lanka, the ICA Act of 1959 empowered the ICASL to determine the standards for persons wishing to become members of the accounting profession and to maintain the register of persons entitled to practise as accountants and auditors. Accordingly, having completed the required professional examinations and practical training, trainees were eligible to apply for admission as associate members of the institute and entitled to use the title of 'CA' and/or the letters 'ACA'. Once an associate member had completed two years of practical training in a firm of public practising accountants

---

this examination, students seek entrance to various degree programmes, including accounting, in the university. Up until 1962 the examinations were conducted in English; subsequently they were conducted in Sinhalese, Tamil and English.

10. Those who qualified from the ICASL were mostly old students of Royal College, St. Thomas and other elite schools in Colombo that maintained the tradition of English education.

and fulfilled the other professional development requirements, the member would be admitted as a Fellow with the entitlement of using the 'FCA' designation. The ICASL was thus authorized to create a monopoly over public practice for its members.

Section 24 of the act also specifically stated the kind of work that accountants could perform as public practitioners:

> (1) For the purpose of this Act, a person shall be deemed to practise as an accountant if, in consideration of remuneration received or to be received, and whether by himself or in partnership with any other person, he: (a). engages himself in the practice of accountancy or holds himself out to the public as an accountant; or (b). offers to perform or performs service involving the auditing or verification of financial transactions books, accounts of records, or the preparation, verification or certification of financial accounting and related statements; or (c). renders professional service or assistance in or about matters of principle or detail relating to accounting procedure or certification of financial facts or data; or renders any other service which may be declared by the Council by regulation to be service constituting practice as an accountant. (Government of Sri Lanka 1959)

The 1959 act also conferred upon the institute the power to determine entry rules. It is interesting to note that the recommendations of both the National Education Commission (NEC) report (1961) and the Future Training of Accountants (FTA) report (1972) clearly articulated the expectation that the ICASL should get involved in training accountants generally to meet the accountancy needs of the country rather than just producing accountants for public practice. To this end, section 24 provided an opportunity for the ICASL to take on such a role but the institute declined to do so.

At the time of the establishment of the institute there were 121 original members in Sri Lanka, consisting of 91 British qualified CAs and 30 RAs (Ministry of Planning and Implementation 1980). As noted earlier, tensions between the chartered (elite) group and the registered (non-elite nationalist) group were running high:

> The accounting profession in Sri Lanka mainly assisted chartered accountants who enjoyed better facilities including practice in public companies and much better opportunities to safeguard their businesses, thus creating a privileged class which in turn led to undesirable repercussions within the institute. (B: retired practising accountant, RA)

> The ICASL provided the necessary support, with the help of British accounting bodies, for those who wished to become chartered accountants. All such facilities [were] provided by the English-educated elite group at the institute. It was this English-educated elite group with

> plantation-associated business interests who were in the forefront of the campaign for setting up of a certain status within the institute. Chartered accountants also were concerned more with personal gain than with the growth of the national economy. (E: founder of a local accountancy firm)

The total population of the island being relatively small and the socio-economic structure being geared to meet the interests of British capital, the whole gamut of business and the plantation sector worked with predictable efficiency. By 1962–1963, a significant number of RAs (about 23) had left public practice, given their secondary status, to become company accountants in the private sector or accountants in government departments (G: retired practising accountant). This exodus and the pressure from the registered group encouraged the institute to act and by 1964 the ICASL administrators had made all the necessary arrangements to amend the 1959 act to eliminate the category of 'RA'. A past president of the ICASL was of the opinion that the elimination of RAs was an important step to strengthen the accounting profession and ultimately this was an important recognition of the accounting profession by the government (*Ceylon Daily News*, 1964). There were, however, other later episodes in which the elite group again sought to exert dominance by employing exclusionary tactics. It is to these that we now turn.

### *Exclusion of Local University Graduates, 1959–1977*

The Sri Lankan university system was established in 1942 under the Ceylon University Ordinance No. 20 of 1942. However, it did not include accountancy as a separate area of specialization in its programmes of studies until 1960. As pointed out in the *Report of the Commission of Inquiry on Technical Education* (Commission of Inquiry on Technical Education 1963), before 1960 accountancy education at the University of Ceylon was confined to only a few subjects offered in the Bachelor of Arts special degree in Economics. The reason for exclusion of accounting in the degree programmes is that the local university followed the British system of university education.[11] The elite British universities had been reluctant to develop accounting programmes and, as a result, the ICAEW stands out as an empirical anomaly in that it has not developed its training, education or certification within the university sector (Annisette and Kirkham 2007). In Sri Lanka, the offering of a Bachelor of Commerce degree programme by the University of Ceylon in the mid-1960s was a significant development; however, the university accounting qualifications were disregarded by the institute.

The ICASL and the accounting profession received adverse comments in local newspapers during this period. As cited in the editorial of the

---

11. See Abbott (1988) and Annisette and Kirkham (2007) for further discussion of how the oldest British universities opposed professional education.

ICASL's quarterly journal the *Accountant*, 'poor financial administration in the public sector is apparently due to the inaction of the institute for the past 27 years'; 'the rate of output of chartered accountants over the past 27 years has been considered to be negligible'; 'the Institute does not have national programmes to turn out accountants to serve the indigenous sectors'. Several other articles cited asked: 'Has the Accountants' Institute failed to deliver the goods?' and 'Are accountants putting their price up?' (Editorial 1988). Another charge levelled against the institute was that:

> In the normal course of events one would expect the Institute to have contributed to the nation much more than the value for money it had drawn from the Government Coffers. (*Ceylon Daily News*, 1960, cited in Editorial 1988)

In order to investigate these criticisms and other educational issues in the country, the government appointed a National Education Commission (NEC) in early 1961. The commission made the following recommendation:

> The present rules and regulations of the Ceylon Institute of Chartered Accountants are so rigorous that it is unlikely to train accountants numerically adequate to meet the existing demand for them in this country. It is, therefore, suggested that there should be a joint scheme between the universities and the Institute. Graduates of universities who have obtained a degree which has been approved by the Institute, for example, the Bachelor of Commerce degree of the University of Ceylon should be exempted from the Intermediate examination of the Institute. . . . [This] scheme will undoubtedly increase the supply of professional accountants. (NEC 1961, 45)

In response to such recommendations and many other issues raised through the media, the ICASL decided in 1970 to allow graduates with a full-time degree in accounting to claim exemption from its intermediate examination. Only a few B.Com graduates (about 45) were accepted by the ICASL under this new arrangement (G: retired practising accountant). As revealed by some interviewees, there was a feeling that the ICASL did not encourage graduates to enter to the profession. For example:

> It seems that the ICASL is under the impression that university graduates do not have any practical orientation towards business. Moreover, they are of the opinion that most graduates are not properly prepared to become an accountant . . . Another issue is the proficiency in English language . . . [University] graduates are lacking the required English-language proficiency to perform in the accounting profession. Some ICASL members are of the opinion that Chartered Accountancy is for the elite class . . . Hence graduates are not included in this group. (C: retired civil servant)

Given the lack of practical exposure in accounting degrees, proficiency in the English language and the generally growing unemployment faced by graduates in the country, there was much concern in different echelons of society. Many employers in commerce and the public sector were reluctant to recruit graduates. Moreover, the broadening of secondary education brought into the university sector large numbers of students from rural areas and lower income groups. As a result of their simmering frustration, a radical group of youths, including graduates and undergraduates from poorer backgrounds, joined forces to lead an unsuccessful insurrection against the ruling United Front government in April 1971 (De Silva 1977). Consequently, it became necessary for the government to take steps to rectify the situation and be seen to meet the new social and employment needs. A Committee on Higher Education[12] was appointed by the government in 1971 to investigate the requirements for higher education in the country. It recommended that the universities introduce job-oriented degree programmes to satisfy the needs of the national economy (Jayaratne Committee on Higher Education 1971).

In addition, the government sought remedies with respect to emerging unemployment in the area of higher education, particularly in the areas of business and accounting. In 1972 government appointed a further committee (the Future Training of Accountants (FTA) Committee) to investigate the affairs of the accounting profession and to bring about a major revision of the training scheme in the institute (Sub-Committee of the Forum of Practising Chartered Accountants on the Future Training Scheme 1972). The main functions of the FTA were to identify difficulties in the existing system of training provided under the Articles of Agreement (or Articled Clerk system) of the ICASL and to make recommendations for improving the system. On the basis of its investigation, the FTA committee submitted a comprehensive report, which included several important recommendations:

> The committee found that the articled clerk system of training based on the old British model was inadequate and proposed instead a more flexible scheme of training. Experience under articles is heavily biased towards the legal and statutory audit. This approach does not give adequate recognition to accounting as a control function. Experience is centred generally on the techniques of book-keeping and preparation of accounts which is no doubt important. But this concentration could result in a warped attitude to the subject on the part of the student. The committee was of the opinion that the new scheme of training, apart from increasing the number of accountants, must also satisfy the special needs of the economy. (Sub-Committee of the Forum of Practising Chartered Accountants on the Future Training Scheme 1972, 34)

---

12. A seven-member committee was appointed to draft proposals for this purpose (see Jayaratne Committee on Higher Education 1971).

The report highlighted that the existing British model of producing accountants was not suitable for the emerging economic needs in the country. Sri Lanka had pursued socialist policies in the early 1970s and had a strong tendency for economic planning and state capitalism. Active state participation in industry was promoted and a number of large-scale industrial enterprises were set up as state ventures. Priorities in the allocation of resources between industry and other sectors were to be determined by the state, taking into consideration factors such as export prospects, development of underdeveloped areas and labour intensity of production. A heavy emphasis was placed on the ICASL members as competent and responsible experts in analysis, measurement and reporting of business activities, profits, assets, liabilities and equity. It was intended that their professional opinions on, and interpretations and justifications of, financial statements and reports would also be used to allocate resources of the country (Sub-Committee of the Forum of Practising Chartered Accountants on the Future Training Scheme; Lakshman et al. 1991). Thus, the committee recommended a new scheme of training of accountants that would take into account the local needs and circumstances. As a member of the FTA committee noted:

> [The] elite tradition, status quo, vested interests and the class system were partly contributory for the tensions among the university graduates. There was no logical reason as to why university graduates should do all the exams of the institute. Certain members of the institute were reluctant to recruit university graduates as they did not have a proper background. (D: retired accountant and member of the FTA committee)

The FTA report recommended that the ICASL should co-operate more with local universities for further development of the accounting profession and, consequentially, that:

> An attempt should be made to evaluate accounting syllabuses adopted by universities and technical colleges on the lines proposed for the professional examinations so that graduates and diploma holders of the universities and technical colleges could become eligible to sit or [be] exempt from certain papers at [the] Institute's examinations. (Sub-Committee of the Forum of Practising Chartered Accountants on the Future Training Scheme, 7)

This proposal was approved by the council of the ICASL in March 1972. It included a period of planned training[13] as opposed to the previous articled clerk system. Based on these recommendations, the ICASL

---

13. Under the new scheme, firms of CAs rather than individual CAs were authorized to train students. Accordingly, students became employees under contract to a firm of CAs rather than articled to an individual accountant practising within a firm.

introduced a new examination structure in 1976 (Yapa 2000, 2006). However, graduates wanting to become professionally qualified accountants had no option other than to continue taking all the examinations (i.e., Intermediate, Final 1 and 2) of the institute. This might suggest that between 1960 and 1977 the ICASL pursued an agenda of 'occupational closure' in order to restrict graduate entry to the profession. It is the opinion of the author that the restrictions to graduate entry were attributable to the increased influence and status of the elite accountants who have dominated and maintained the control of the profession over time (see also Yapa 2006). The next section investigates the elite group's attempts to create a rigorous training regime in order to limit the number of accounting practitioners.

### *Rigorous Training Arrangements, 1959–1977*

The professional accounting education, training and examination framework in Sri Lanka up to 1977 followed the British system, although there were some variations. Under the old system of 'Articles of Clerkship' five articled clerks were allowed in Sri Lanka for each practising ICASL member, or principal, unlike the four permitted in the UK. An apprentice was selected by a principal and the terms of the articles imposed certain responsibilities on each party. The principal was to allow study time and provide on-the-job training to the apprentice and the apprentice was expected to pay a premium to the principal and prepare himself or herself for two examinations held by the institute (Perera 1975).

Following the British model (Freear 1982), the ICASL also utilized examinations as entry barriers: only those who passed those examinations and successfully completed the specified period of apprenticeship were admitted to the membership of the institute as CAs. As a result of this stringent recruitment process fewer accountants were produced (NEC 1961, 45; Larson 1977).

The articled clerk system attracted much criticism and met strong resistance not only in the community but also from state authorities from the early 1960s (Perera 1980). These criticisms came mainly from the locally qualified graduates, who were often unable to afford the payment of a premium to the principal, and other professionally qualified people in the accounting discipline. Supporting this viewpoint, the NEC recommended that:

> [the] present quota of 5 articled clerks allowed for each practising accountant be increased and the premium payable for articleship reduced. Furthermore, the students who intend to take to Accounting as a profession must be allowed, if they so desire, to serve the three year period of articleship in broken periods before entering the university, provided that they serve a continuous period of more than one year after graduation. (NEC 1961, 45)

The specific objective of the preceding recommendation was to increase the supply of ICASL qualified accountants. Nevertheless, the ICASL was able to maintain the articled clerk system for many years. An interviewee suggested that this was partly due to political connexions, personal friendships and lobbying; and partly to a lack of government follow-up (G: retired practising accountant).

The average failure rate in the ICASL examinations from 1959 to 1977 was around 80 per cent, meaning that of the large number of students enrolling for these examinations each year, very few eventually qualified as professional accountants (Yapa 2006). A similar situation existed in the case of the ICAEW throughout the 1960s and 1970s (Freear 1982). In the author's view, the dominant elite group actively sought such restrictions as a means of closing off opportunities for those from less privileged backgrounds. According to one interviewee:

> This is a manoeuvring . . . the high failure rate is a strategy to curtail the number of accounting professionals. (A: ACCA qualified member in the public service)

However, this could also be attributed to the poor quality of education available to the aspiring entrants and the consequent low level of academic achievement. It is the case that students obtaining the highest marks, mainly in Sinhala and Tamil,[14] in the GCE advanced level examination preferred to opt for university degree programmes while those sitting for ICASL examinations tended to be the ones that could not secure a place at university. Perhaps a reason for this choice was the fact the ICASL was not a full-time educational institution, and the amount of time devoted to lectures, tutorials and assignments and the subject matter covered through its different modes of instruction were not as extensive as those of the full-time educational institutions (Wijewardena and Yapa 1998).

## CONCLUSION

This chapter set out to examine the enduring influence of empire on the organization of Sri Lankan accountancy and the attempts by the elite Sri Lankan British-qualified accountants to close off opportunities for entry to the market to local RAs and later to the graduates of local universities in the period 1959–1977. It has argued that Sri Lanka's imperial history and continuing British investment in the post-independence period significantly impacted upon the business, social, political and educational spheres. Those families and individuals with connexions were able to take advantage of

14. A small number of students who did GCE advanced levels in English medium also entered the university programmes.

the opportunity of an English education to consolidate their elite status. This group was instrumental in fostering the elite status of the accountancy profession both before and after independence. That is, the ICASL chiefs entrusted to establish the professional body in Sri Lanka did so willingly in the shadow of a strong imperial influence and were keen to maintain the British traditions with which they (and their clients) were familiar. Their interests and actions were thus aligned with those of British capital before and after independence.

The closure strategy developed by pioneers of the ICASL, the elite group, focused on three interconnected and overlapping key areas. Firstly, the adoption of British training models familiar to British capitalists with features that discouraged the entry of Sri Lankans from the lower strata of society. Secondly, local university graduates were discouraged from joining the ICASL (e.g., by having to sit for all ICASL examinations in English). Third, those that did sit for ICASL examinations modeled on those of the ICAEW were subjected to high failure rates and arduous practice requirements. All three areas have imperial roots.

Eventually, the elite accountants were successful in excluding the second tier of accountants (i.e., RAs) and the graduates who sought to voice and enact a nationalist-local ethos in the early 1960s while simultaneously promoting social elevation of the lower strata of Sri Lankan society. Significantly, during the period covered by this chapter, they were able to resist all pressures to expand the number of Sri Lankan 'qualified' accountants, train accountants for arenas other than public practice and provide a professional career path and social mobility for poorer Sri Lankans.

## REFERENCES


Abbott, A. (1988) *The System of Professions*. Chicago: University of Chicago Press.

Annisette, M. (1999) 'Importing accounting: The case of Trinidad and Tobago'. *Accounting, Business & Financial History* 9:103–33.

Annisette, M., and Kirkham, L.M. (2007) 'The advantages of separateness explaining the unusual profession–university link in English chartered accountancy'. *Critical Perspectives on Accounting* 18:1–30.

Balachandran, B. (2007) 'Western imperialism and Eastern accounting—the story of CIMA in Sri Lanka'. Paper presented at APIRA conference, Auckland, New Zealand, 7–10 July.

Ceylon Sessional Paper. (1950) *V*. Colombo: Government Press.

Chua, W.F., and Poullaos, C. (1998) 'The dynamics of "closure" amidst the construction of market, profession, empire and nationhood: An historical analysis of an Australian accounting association, 1886–1903'. *Accounting, Organizations and Society* 23:155–87.

———. (2002) 'The empire strikes back? An exploration of centre-periphery interaction between the ICAEW and accounting associations in the self-governing colonies of Australia, Canada and South Africa, 1880–1907'. *Accounting, Organizations and Society* 27:409–45.

Commission on Company Law, Banking, Insurance and Accountants and Auditors. (1950) *Report of the Commission on Company Law, Banking Insurance and Accountants and Auditors, Ceylon, Sessional Paper V.* Colombo: Government Press.

Commission of Inquiry on Technical Education. (1963) *Report of the Commission of Inquiry on Technical Education—Sessional Paper X.* Colombo: Government Press.

Dawson, S. (ed.) (1990) *The Penguin Australian Encyclopaedia.* Ringwood, AU: Viking.

De Silva, S.B.D. (1982) *The Political Economy of Underdevelopment.* London and Boston: Routledge and Kegan Paul.

De Silva, Wimala. (1977) 'The current scene and emerging trends in Sri Lanka: The universities'. In The Sri Lanka Foundation Institute (ed.) *Education and Socio Economic Development of Sri Lanka.* Colombo: Sri Lanka Foundation Institute.

Editorial. (1988) *Accountant (Journal of the Chartered Accountants of Sri Lanka)* 3: 3.

Freear, J. (1982) 'The final examinations of the Institute of Chartered Accountants in England and Wales, 1882–1981'. *Accounting Historians Journal* 9:53–89.

Gamage, D.T. (1991) 'How did the British colonial policy influence the contemporary system of Sri Lankan education?' *Asian Profile* 19:473–83.

Government of Sri Lanka. (1959) *Institute of Chartered Accountants of Ceylon Act.* Colombo: Government Press.

———. (1974) *Sessional Paper No. XII, Report on the Commission of Inquiry on Agency Houses and Brokering Firms.* Colombo: Government of Sri Lanka.

Jayaratne Committee on Higher Education. (1971) *Report of the O.W. Jayaratne Committee on Higher Education.* Colombo: Government Press.

Lakshman, W.D., Vidanagama, S.S., Senanayake, K.S.M.P., and Wettasinghe, A. (1991) 'Small and medium scale industry in Sri Lanka'. Working paper, Department of Economics, University of Colombo.

Larson, M.S. (1977) *The Rise of Professionalism.* Berkeley: University of California Press.

Ministry of Planning and Implementation. (1980) *Manpower Planning Review Report.* Colombo: Government Press.

National Education Commission. (1961) *Interim Report, Ceylon Sessional Paper.* Colombo: Government Publication Bureau.

Nesaratnam, A.K. (1999) 'The early years of the institute—the Institute of Chartered Accountants of Sri Lanka'. Fortieth Anniversary Supplement. *Accountant* 34:2–6.

Perera, M.H.B. (1975) 'Accounting and its environment in Sri Lanka'. *Abacus* 2:86–96.

———. (1980) *Accounting for State Industrial and Commercial Enterprises in a Developing Country.* New York: Arno Press.

Richardson, A. J. (1997) 'Social closure in dynamic markets: The incomplete professional project in accountancy'. *Critical Perspectives on Accounting* 8:635–53.

Sian, S. (2006) 'Inclusion, exclusion and control: the case of the Kenyan accounting professionalization project', *Accounting, Organizations and Society,* 31: 295–322.

———. (2007a) 'Patterns of prejudice: Social exclusion and racial demarcation in professional accountancy in Kenya'. *Accounting Historians Journal* 34: 1–42.

———. (2007b) 'Reversing exclusion: The Africanisation of accountancy in Kenya, 1963–1970'. *Critical Perspectives on Accounting* 18:831–72.

Snodgrass, D.R. (1966) *Ceylon: An Export Economy in Transition.* Homewood, Illinois: Richard D. Irwin, Inc.

Sub-Committee of the Forum of Practising Chartered Accountants on the Future Training Scheme. (1972) *Report of the Future Training of Accountants Sub-Committee of the Forum of Practising Chartered Accountants of Sri Lanka on the Future Training Scheme*. Colombo: ICASL

Walker, S.P. (1991) 'The defence of professional monopoly: Scottish chartered accountants and "satellites in the accountancy firmament" 1854–1914'. *Accounting, Organizations and Society* 16: 257–83.

———. (1995) 'The genesis of professional organisation in Scotland: A contextual analysis'. *Accounting, Organizations and Society* 16:285–310.

Wickramasinghe, D.W.A., and Cameron D.C. (2004) 'British capital, Ceylonese land, Indian labour: The imperialism and colonialism of evolution of tea plantations in Sri Lanka'. Working paper, Department of Business Administration, University of Sri Jayewardenepura, Sri Lanka.

Wijewardena H., and Yapa, P.W.S. (1998) 'Colonialism and accounting education in developing countries: The experience of Singapore and Sri Lanka'. *The International Journal of Accounting* 33:269–81.

Yapa, P.W.S. (1999) 'Professional accounting environment in Brunei Darussalam'. *Accounting, Auditing & Accountability Journal* 13:328–39.

———. (2000) 'University–profession partnership in accounting education: The case of Sri Lanka'. *Accounting Education: An International Journal* 9:297–307.

———. (2006) 'Cross-border competition and the professionalization of accounting: The case of Sri Lanka'. *Accounting History* 13:328–39.

Yapa, P.W.S., and Perera, M.H.B. (2005) 'Sri Lanka'. In *Asian Accounting Handbook—A User's Guide to the Accounting Environment in 16 Countries*, ed. S.M. Saudagaran. Singapore: Thomson.

# 7 Imperialism and Professionalization
## The Case of Accountancy in Jamaica

*Owolabi M. Bakre*

## INTRODUCTION

Jamaica first became a colony under Spanish rule between 1495 and 1655 before falling under British rule from 1655 to August 1962. This chapter focuses on this latter period of colonization as Jamaica became one of the oldest colonies of the British Empire. Under the British, a purely white colonialist regime, the political system and governance in Jamaica were organized around the key principles of self-interest, competition and social stratification; their primary goal being the protection of the sanctity of private property for the colonialists and their capital (Sheridan 2000). Jamaica was initially of commercial interest to the British as a primary source of sugar. African slaves and Indian and Chinese indentured labour were brought, often by force, to work on the plantations operated by the British and financed by British capital (Mintz 1961).

Although some basic book-keeping was utilized as an aid to governance by the Spanish during their term of rule (Mepham 1977), it was under British rule that a more formal mode of accounting was introduced, initially for the purpose of allowing non-resident investors to monitor their capital investments and measure their returns. The arrival of British accountants and accounting firms in the colony heralded the introduction of British accounting practices, many of which remain in place today.

As in other racially-diverse colonies, for example Trinidad and Tobago (T&T) (Annisette 2003) and Kenya (Sian 2006), the British introduced into Jamaica a system of race-based social stratification (Williams 1973). A key consequence of this was the creation of an exclusionary education policy (Norris 1966), which meant that in colonial Jamaica it was extremely difficult to find indigenous[1] educated Jamaicans (Miller 1989), and therefore qualified indigenous Jamaican accountants, too, were rare (Ogle 1961; Thurborn 2000). On achieving political independence from the British in 1962, the new indigenous Jamaican–dominated government and the

1. The term indigenous here refers to black African, Chinese and Indian people even though all were imported into the country. However, in this chapter the focus is on the exclusion from accountancy of those of African origin.

handful of indigenous accountants who existed at the time set out to incorporate a degree of 'nationalism' into the accountancy profession. In practice, this meant ensuring that the post-independence professionalization of accountancy was led by mostly indigenous Jamaican accountants and influenced by the socio-economic requirements of an independent Jamaica (see Bakre 2006).

However, as this chapter will show, this ideal was under threat from the continuing rise of foreign professional bodies, particularly the United Kingdom–based Association of Certified Corporate Accountants (ACCA) acting in unison with local powerful and influential indigenous Jamaican accountants.[2] Such action continued to jeopardize the stability of the accounting profession in Jamaica even after the formation in 1965 of the local professional body, the Institute of Chartered Accountants of Jamaica (ICAJ).

It is within this context that this chapter examines the impact of empire, British accountants and professional bodies on the professionalization of accountancy in Jamaica. In particular, it will draw attention to the assertion that the relative failure of localization cannot be understood without reference to the conflict of identity experienced by indigenous Jamaican accountants and their allegiance to the UK professional bodies, which remained strong even when Jamaican accountancy was ostensibly under the control of Jamaicans.

The analysis proceeds by examining the socio-economic structure that emerged under both British rule and in the post-independence period. It traces the impact on Jamaican accountancy of British capital and institutions that were brought to the colony, and reflects on how the continued conflict of identity amongst the indigenous Jamaican accountants became a factor in their support of foreign professional bodies, namely the ACCA.

## COLONIAL JAMAICA AND THE DEVELOPMENT OF ACCOUNTANCY

### The Motives for Early Colonization

Jamaica is one of the oldest British colonies outside Europe. Throughout the period under examination the essential character of the Jamaican plantation-based economy remained unchanged. The British-owned and British-run plantations utilized mainly African slave labour, although indentured labour was also mobilized from other parts of the formal and informal empire, such as India and China.

2. The ACCA had cornered the lucrative accountancy market through its colonial relationship with Jamaica (see *ACCA Newsletter* 1999a). The powerful, indigenous accountants had a preference for the 'prestigious' British accounting qualifications for international accreditation and recognition, rather than a local qualification.

The requirements of British-expanded capitalism necessitated conquest, settlement, profiteering and eventually colonialism, leaving an indelible imprint on Jamaica (Black 1993). Economic returns from the colony were plentiful but spasmodic. The mercantile plan that Jamaica would provide ready markets for a high volume of British exports at high prices in exchange for Jamaican staples imported at low prices needed two things in order to be realized (Sheridan 2000). These were: (a) a crop that was cheap and easy to produce and (b) a large labour force that could work effectively in a tropical climate. Sugar became the crop (Williams 1973) and Africans provided the labour in the form of slavery (Beckford 1972), ushering in an era of capitalism and stable settlement for Jamaica (Alleyne 1988).

The preceding analysis suggests that British mercantilism in Jamaica was successful only as the result of the employment of British capital, which was procured from many sources in England (Bakre 2008), including the Colonial Development and Welfare Fund (Hoogvelt and Tinker 1978). British capital was brought to Jamaica to invest in plantations that would produce a return on capital, which would then be remitted back to England (Bakre 2008). As Mills (1864, 100) observed:

> Our West Indian colonies (including Jamaica), for example, cannot be regarded as countries with a productive capital of their own . . . (but are rather) the place where England finds it convenient to carry on the production of sugar, coffee and a few other tropical commodities. All the capital employed is English capital; almost all the industry is carried on for English uses; there is little production of anything except for staple commodities, and these are sent to England, not to be exchanged for things exported to the colony and consumed by its inhabitants, but to be sold in England for the benefit of the proprietors there. The trade with the West Indies is hardly to be considered an external trade, but more resembles the traffic between town and country.

Within this context, it was suggested that, 'for colonialism to become a success, the colonialists require empire technology of calculation, appropriation and legitimization' (Hendricks 1981, 56). Thus, accounting techniques and practices became part and parcel of the empire's tools of calculation, appropriation and legitimization (Bakre 2008), and there is some evidence to show that accounting techniques and practices were critically employed in the colonization of Canada (Neu 1999), Belize (Bolland 1988) and Jamaica (Black 1993; Bakre 2008).

The demand for adequate financial information by the plantation and other business owners resulted in the importation of essentially the British legal framework for accounting and British accountants (Mepham 1977). Indeed, as Macbeath (1982, 132) observed: 'the colonial economic development ushered in by the British expanded capitalism created a legal framework that gave impetus for the emergence of the accountancy profession in Jamaica'.

## The Importation of British Accountancy

Although 'early accounting in Jamaica dates back to the emergence of pirates, the slave trade, sugar plantations and other elements of its diverse and stormy history' (Mepham 1977, 469), the formal history of accounting regulation in the colony can be traced back to the nineteenth century. Two years after the passing the Companies Act of 1862[3] in the UK, the Jamaican legislature subsequently passed its own first Companies Act in 1864, based on the UK act. Mendes and McLean (1987, 26) described the Jamaican Act of 1864 as a 'selection and modification of the mother country's Act of 1862'. The adoption of the UK 1862 Act in Jamaica was intended to be temporarily operative (Mendes and McLean 1987), as it was originally evolved specifically to find solutions to British economic problems (Thurborn 2000), implying that it was not necessarily relevant to the Jamaican economic problems of the time. Despite such concerns, the Jamaican Act of 1864 remained in operation in the country until 1923. By the time it was finally considered necessary in 1923 to change the act, 157 companies had already been registered under it. As a direct result, it was the case that 'limited liability became the vehicle for big business in Jamaica' (Rattray 1963). Between 1923 and 1965[4] a surge occurred in the economic activities of Jamaica, as evidenced by the significant increase in the number of registered companies (Registrar of Companies 2000). In order for the accounts of this increasing number of Jamaican public and private businesses to be appropriately serviced, there was a corresponding major increase in the demand for qualified accountants, external auditors and accounting regulation.

Prior to independence in 1962, the majority of the businesses on the island were either British or employed purely British capital (Mintz 1961), and many practised racial discrimination by not allowing non-white Jamaicans to work as accountants in their businesses, let alone audit their accounts as external auditors (Rattray 1962). Macbeath[5] (1982) suggests that the colonial administration had enacted ordinances stipulating that the accounts of companies operating in Jamaica were to be audited by auditors who had qualified through one of the professional bodies in the UK. However, since non-white Jamaicans had long been denied any formal education by the colonial administration (Norris 1966; Miller 1989), very few indigenous Jamaicans had been able to train and qualify as accountants through one of the UK professional bodies (Ogle 1961). As a result, during the period from World War II to the late 1950s Jamaica opened its doors to transnational accountants and accounting firms, mostly from the UK.

3. Macdonald (1985) claimed that this was critical in the development of the accountancy profession in the UK.

4. In 1965 a new post-independence Companies Act came into effect.

5. Macbeath was with the firm of Pannell Fitzpatrick and came to Jamaica on secondment from his firm in London in the early 1960s.

As will be shown, it was not until 1965, after Jamaica's independence, that the independent Jamaican government had the opportunity and power to pass new legislation that could more effectively serve the independent Jamaican economy. Despite such opportunity, Jamaica remained in the shadow of its colonial past and Jamaica's new Companies Act of 1965 was also drawn from similar legislation in the UK (the UK Companies Act 1948).

## The Rising Demand for British Accountants

The first British accounting firm to open an office in Jamaica in the 1920s was Pannell Fitzpatrick (Macbeath 1982). After its arrival, Peat Marwick, Mitchell and Co. established an office in Kingston, Jamaica, closely followed by Price Waterhouse and Touche Ross (now known as Deloitte & Touche).

By the 1950s and the early 1960s momentum towards independence was building in Jamaica. Bauxite had been discovered and a general increase in economic activity required the services of professional accountants in greater numbers in order to service the increase in trade. Consequent upon the shortage of indigenous qualified accountants, this period witnessed a major inflow of British firms and of accountants to staff them. Touche Ross, for instance, first opened an office in the Jamaican second city of Montego Bay in 1954 and during the 1960s, some other UK accounting firms, such as Coopers and Lybrand, opened offices in Jamaica.

Within this context, during the period of colonial occupation, no less than three different professional bodies were formed in Jamaica. The Association of Accountants of Jamaica (AAJ) was founded in 1946 by resident members of the Institute of Chartered Accountants in England and Wales (ICAEW). This was closely followed by the Jamaican branch of the ACCA, which was formed in 1947. By 1962, indigenous accountants had led the formation of the Society of Chartered Accountants in Jamaica (SCAJ).[6]

However, the number of indigenous Jamaican accountants remained small. Some had managed to qualify through either scholarships or self-funding, involving travel to the UK to undertake training and articleship with one of the chartered bodies. At the same time, others were pursuing professional examinations from Jamaica through correspondence courses. The first Jamaican to qualify as an articled student in the UK was Mr. Nosworthy Harold George Dundas, who qualified in 1936 as an articled student in the London office of Pannell Fitzpatrick. The first Jamaican to complete all the professional examinations, while studying wholly in Jamaica with full practising office experience, was Mr. Caroll Thorburn in 1955, an articled student with Touche Ross.

Macbeath had been brought from Britain to the island to join Pannell Fitzpatrick in the early 1960s and was well placed to comment on the state of accounting and auditing at the time. According to him, before

6. Members were holders of foreign accounting qualifications (such as those of Australia and Canada) other than those of the ICAEW and ACCA.

the arrival of British accounting firms in Jamaica, the accounting and auditing system was not up to the standard demanded by the Jamaican Companies Act 1923: 'audit procedures and financial reporting were of a Neanderthal quality' (1982, 133). He observed that audit planning consisted of determining that the audit programme book had not been 'mislaid since the previous audit' and 'obtaining the best junior staff possible'. This was irrespective of the scope or nature of the engagement or whether the staff had any previous experience of a particular job. Additionally, in his opinion, some of the accounting and audit staff did not possess the basic skills required of a trained accountant and his general impression of the state of accounting and auditing at the time was that it was 'chaotic'. The presence of large British accounting firms proved to be key to improving the country's reporting system as they provided technical support to the Jamaican firms and they were exclusively partnered by qualified UK accountants. Perhaps as a result of lobbying, the British colonial authorities also allowed any authorized UK accounting firms operating in Jamaica which were lacking a partner 'in residence' to send an employee out from their London office to Jamaica. Such transfers allowed innovations and new techniques to be introduced into the financial system of the country. It has been suggested that the 'leading role' the Jamaican accounting profession played in national and regional accounting development was the result of the arrival of the UK firms in the country in the early 1960s. As Macbeath (1982, 132) put it:

> In our case, an audit practice partner was seconded to Kingston for a year. The results were most dramatic and beneficial. By the end of twelve months from the day of the engagement letter, standard working papers and reporting formats and the representation letter had arrived.

However, the fact that firms operating in Jamaica continued to accord preference to UK accounting qualifications was criticized by both the Jamaican public and private sectors (see Mendes 1990; Jackson 1990), some practising accountants (see Preston 1990; Thurborn 2000) and accounting academics (see Bakre 2005, 2006; Chaderton and Taylor 1993; Mendes 1990). The main criticism was that, where it was actually available, the training received by Jamaican accountants in the areas of taxation, law and financial systems was often irrelevant to their own local situation (see the Institute of Chartered Accountants of the Caribbean [ICAC] 1998). Another criticism was that the accountancy training available for indigenous Jamaicans lacked focus and a professional emphasis (Ali 1998).

However, in the period leading up to independence, the virtual exclusion of indigenous Jamaican accountants by the foreign firms became a cause for concern. In response, the small number of indigenous Jamaican accountants grouped together to consider ways of professionalizing and indigenizing accountancy in Jamaica, ultimately proposing the establishment of a national professional body, the ICAJ. Paradoxically, when some of the local accountants began to assert themselves, they were doing so as members of UK professional bodies. Such actions were to some extent, therefore, constrained as these local accountants sought to achieve independence from the predominantly British foreign accountancy professional bodies operating in Jamaica. The division within the ranks of the Jamaican accountants presented an opportunity for the ICAEW and ACCA, who competed to exert influence over the proposed creation of a national professional body (the ICAJ) just before independence. The next section examines in greater detail this element of competition.

## Impending Independence

The period leading to independence was witness to a key struggle for the control of Jamaican accountancy as observed by Johnson and Caygill (1971, 160):

> It was not until after the Second World War that, in line with its general spread to the developing areas, the influence of the British accountancy bodies was fully experienced in the West Indies, channeled in large part through the membership of the [London] Association [predecessor to the ACCA].

Whilst there were 25 indigenous accountants who had managed to qualify, mostly through the professional examinations of ICAEW, the actual struggle for the control of accountancy education and training began with the arrival of the ACCA in Jamaica after World War II. In a concerted attempt to influence and control the professionalization of accountancy in the Commonwealth Caribbean through Jamaica, in December 1961 the ACCA's secretary wrote to its branch in Jamaica as follows:

> I am sure that *the Council is extremely anxious that in Jamaica, an acceptable pattern is laid down for the rest of the West Indies. It is moreover, the one place where we are most likely to be able to enforce our wishes because it is only here, from the whole of the Caribbean, that we actually outnumber the members of the various Institutes.* The Council has therefore been giving some consideration to the desirability of an official visit from the Association's officers. Such a visit I may say would not be in any way with the intention of interfering with your own legislative activities, but rather with the intention of giving such assistance as we can if you desire it. (Letter from the ACCA secretary to Jamaica branch, 12 December 1961; emphasis added)

Although the ICAEW did not conduct examinations locally, it enjoyed popular support through its Jamaican members, who had strong influence through their contacts within the colonial government and the British business community in Jamaica. By the early 1960s the ACCA was conducting examinations locally and, in trying to establish itself in the colony, was competing with the already well-established ICAEW. In the midst of this, the indigenous Jamaican accountants (who were mostly ICAEW and ACCA members) sought the support of the Jamaican government to put in place a Public Accountancy Law, which could guarantee professional 'nationalism' in Jamaica, the objective being to free themselves from foreign influence after independence. The constrained nature of the response of the new government is examined in the next section.

## POST-INDEPENDENCE: PROFESSIONAL DEVELOPMENT

This part of the analysis is divided into four sections. The first section draws attention to the contradictory stance of the post-independence government with regard to issues of nationalism within the profession. The second section examines in greater depth the acute crisis in cultural identity exhibited in post-colonial society in Jamaica and how this was reflected in the development of the accountancy profession. In light of this, the third section details the struggle for professional independence from the UK professional bodies, and the final section highlights the struggle amongst indigenous Jamaican accountants for control of the profession, post-independence.

### The New Nationalism

Having on the one hand promised to pass laws to support professional 'nationalism', the new government was still according priority to British accountants and British accounting firms when it came to hiring accountants and auditors for companies established in Jamaica. As Rattray (1963; emphasis added) noted:

> As regards the attitude of business and indeed, of government, the combination of prejudice and ignorance has operated to deprive Jamaicans of their fair share of accountancy practice and experience. *It would be interesting to examine the occasions on which the government over the past few years have employed the services of accountants, to note the firms that they have employed and to try to determine why these firms have been employed.*

He further argued:

> *Another profitable exercise would be to try and find out just who has been assigned by these firms to do the work.* I believe that it would

> become apparent that the main effect of this policy (dictated by ignorance and prejudice) is to deprive Jamaicans of their opportunities in the heart of their own land.

Others entered the debate, and a council member of the AAJ, Smith (1962; emphasis added), argued:

> It would, I think, be difficult to justify taking any drastic action against the Institute of Chartered Accountants of England and Wales, as a body, in the matter of colour discrimination, *when it appears that individual members of government and the business community have in the past been guilty of the same practice.*

The post-independence Jamaican government seemed to be outwardly supporting a nationalist agenda, whilst somewhat contradictorily protecting the interests of the British accountants. This contradiction arose, perhaps, because the post-independence government wanted professional independence for national accountancy whilst at the same time coveting the economic certainty of international aid and the 'prestigious' British accounting qualifications. Such action meant that some Jamaican accounting professionals hesitated to launch out on their own to establish practices, thereby providing further opportunities for British accountants, accounting firms and professional bodies to control and influence accountancy education, training and examinations (Salmon 1998).[7]

In an attempt to address the issues raised, the Ministry of Trade and Industry in Jamaica established a committee to investigate the foreign domination of national accountancy in Jamaica in 1963. In its report, the committee resolved that 'nationalism' should be promoted in the profession, and proposed the enactment of a new Public Accountancy Law (PAL) to protect the interests of Jamaican accountants (see Report of the Committee on Public Accountancy Law 1963). It was also resolved that the new PAL should encourage the Jamaican accountancy profession to respond positively to the post-independence socio-economic and cultural problems of Jamaica. Moreover, the new PAL should encourage the Jamaican accountancy profession to be independent of the UK-based professional bodies which had historically controlled Jamaican accountancy. In order to accomplish these goals, the PAL would empower the newly proposed local professional body, the ICAJ, to determine which qualified accountants would be eligible to practise accountancy in Jamaica (Report of the Committee on Public Accountancy Law 1963).

These events would be the starting-point of a struggle for the control of the independence of the Jamaican profession. The proposed PAL also sought to exclude foreign qualified accountants, a proposal that would

7. Uriel Salmon was one of the founding fathers and a past president of the Institute of Chartered Accountants of Jamaica (ICAJ).

not be welcomed by the large numbers of foreign (mainly British) qualified accountants present in Jamaica, and it is to this post-independence professional struggle that we now turn.

## The Crisis in Cultural Identity Post-Independence

The stratified colonial society established by the British resulted in the differential treatment of individuals depending upon their race. Thus an exclusionary education system generally discriminated against the non-white sector of the population, thereby preventing them from pursuing educational qualifications (see Norris 1966; Miller 1989). The few Jamaicans who had the opportunity of being educated were moulded at an early age by their education into a state of mind that sought to re-create Britain in Jamaica (Norris 1966) and it was these educated Jamaicans who formed the elite class that occupied positions of power after independence. As national identity is to a large extent a by-product of education, the only identity with which a Jamaican child could empathize was British (Norris 1966).

Thus, exposure to the British education system created within Jamaica, as with other ex-colonies, a crisis of cultural identity that impacted upon the post independence socio-political and economic development of the country. On one hand, there was the 'local' capitalist elite class, who attempted to change the names of almost everything from streets to crockery in the determined pledge to break with the colonial past (Nettleford 1989). Although this class wished to align themselves with the people and their country, they did not wish to entirely sever their colonial and transnational capitalist ties, in order to continue to protect private local capital interests (Birds 1994). On the other hand, the 'global/international' capitalist class tended to place their 'nationalism' in the confidence that Jamaica could successfully build a miniature Britain, America or a European-type state (Norris 1966). The global/international capitalist wanted both local independence and the economic certainty of international aid (see Madden 2000).

This identity conflict extended to and included the professionalization of accountancy, as will be highlighted later. In the pre-independence period it was apparent in the conflict between the 'chartered accountants' ('CAs') and 'certified' accountants. Post-independence, it was again discernible in the battle that saw the emergence of 'local' and 'global/international' capitalists in the profession. In accountancy, the local capitalists wished to change the form of accountancy education, training and professional organization inherited from the UK professional bodies at independence (Bakre 2001), whilst the global capitalists wished to retain the 'prestigious' British accounting qualifications. The Jamaicans were greatly affected by this cultural identity crisis, which continued to have consequences for the post-independence socio-political and economic development of Jamaica. It also had significant implications for the development of accountancy, as will be illustrated in the next section.

## The Struggle for Independence from the UK Professional Bodies

In order to boost the production of qualified indigenous accountants after independence, scholarship programmes were initiated by the independent Jamaican government for indigenous Jamaicans to qualify through professional bodies in the UK. Private sector organizations were also encouraged to offer scholarships to encourage prospective Jamaican accountants to receive training and to qualify through any of the UK professional bodies. These and other indigenous Jamaicans, who had qualified through correspondence courses, became partners in the UK accounting firms in Jamaica. The British influence, therefore, remained strong even post-independence. In fact, two migrant Scottish CAs, Macbeath and Adam, who both became naturalized Jamaicans, served as presidents of the ICAJ. As Mendes (1990, 120) observed:

> A proper examination of the history of accountancy in Jamaica would, all things being equal, reveal that the British and the Scottish influences have, from the colonial era, had a great impact on the emergence and subsequent development of the accountancy profession in Jamaica.

The PAL had set out to 'protect' future prospective indigenous Jamaican accountants and the accounting profession (see Ministry of Trade and Industry 1963). Part A section C of subsection 3 of PAL, which was subsequently passed in 1970 with the main objective of building 'nationalism' into the Jamaican accountancy, states:

> All persons ordinarily resident in Jamaica at the time the law came into effect, who at the commencement of the law are members of any professional accountancy body, recognized by the Minister for the purpose of this sub-clause, and who do not qualify for membership in the Public Accountancy Professional body incorporated under this law could be recognized for the purpose of practising as an accountant in the island.

It was further contemplated that the PAL would complement the Work Permit Act (WPA), which was passed in 1964. In this context, section 3(1) of the WPA 1964, which relates to the control of employment of foreign nationals or Commonwealth citizens, became an additional tool to control the influx of accountants to Jamaica. It stated that subject to the provisions of this act, a foreign national or a Commonwealth citizen shall not:

> (a) Engage in any occupation in Jamaica for reward or profit, or (b) be employed in Jamaica, unless there is in force in relation to him a valid work permit and he is so engaged or he is so employed in accordance with the terms and conditions which may be specified in the permit.

> In pursuance of section 3 (2) subject to the provisions of this Act, no person shall have in his employment in Jamaica a foreign national or a Commonwealth citizen without there being in force a valid work permit in relation to that employment.

This section of the WPA 1964 effectively curtailed the employment of foreign accountants by companies in Jamaica.

In brief, foreign accountants and accounting firms wishing to work in Jamaica would have to satisfy the conditions of the proposed PAL and the WPA. The intention was that this would ultimately prevent the newly independent Jamaica from being dominated by foreign accountants and would also make it easier for newly qualified indigenous Jamaican accountants either to obtain employment or to establish their own practices. During this period, newly qualified Jamaican accountants were qualifying either through the ACCA or ICAEW. Whilst the former route became more popular, given that examinations could be taken locally, the latter route to qualification was in decline mainly due to the difference in regulations of the professional examinations and articleship requirements of the two bodies.[8] This turn of events proved to be a point of conflict in the struggle for the control of Jamaican accountancy between the local supporters of the two UK professional bodies (Rattray 1962).

This struggle for control was a remnant of the way in which the accountancy profession was organized in colonial times. Three 'local' professional bodies (the AAJ, the Jamaican branch of the ACCA and SCAJ)[9] had formed before independence and each had had a joint scheme arrangement with their respective foreign parent bodies for the examination and credentialing of accountants in Jamaica. Various discussions by the indigenous Jamaicans who formed the three 'local' professional bodies towards setting and marking their own examinations in Jamaica before the formation of the unified institute (ICAJ) at independence failed (see Bakre 2006). This failure led to the decision to identify one of the UK professional bodies as the temporary 'parent body' of the proposed Jamaican

---

8. With the ACCA students could study either by correspondence or at a local educational institution and sit their examinations in Jamaica. It also allowed articles to be served after passing the professional examinations. In comparison, the ICAEW route became unpopular because it inviolved traveling to the UK to sit the examinations. This was in addition to the strict condition of articleship before examinations, which was considered unsuitable for most Jamaicans because it involved serving articles in Britain.

9. The Association of Accountants of Jamaica (AAJ) was founded in 1946, representing the interests of the ICAEW members in Jamaica. The Jamaican branch of the Association of Certified Coporate Accountants (now the Association of Chartered Certified Accountants, ACCA) was formed in 1947, representing the interests of the ACCA. The Society of Chartered Accountants in Jamaica (SCAJ) was founded at independence in 1962. Although it claimed to be an indigenous professional body, all its members were holders of Australian and Canadian professional qualifications.

institute, ICAJ. As a result, two main groups of 'certified' accountants and 'CAs' from the original three emerged. The former supported the ACCA to become the parent body of ICAJ while the latter supported the ICAEW to become the parent body despite the government's agreement to establish the new institute and to produce accounting qualifications independent of any foreign influences.

The District Society of 'Certified' Accountants drafted a bill from the prototypes of similar legislation in other jurisdictions (namely, Australia, Canada and New Zealand) and set about lobbying for a consensus among the members of the other professional accounting bodies. However, the draft bill met with strong opposition from the 'chartered' group, who resolutely held that the proposed local institute, the ICAJ, should be incorporated under the proposed Companies Act and not under the proposed PAL, as suggested by the 'certified' accountants. The chartered group felt that, if it was incorporated under the proposed Companies Act, which would be a general law, this could make the internationalization of the profession possible, which might not be the case under the PAL, which was a law specifically implemented to nationalize the profession in Jamaica.

By way of a compromise, the District Society of 'Certified' Accountants revised the draft bill by incorporating some agreed amendments, such as allowing either the ACCA or the ICAEW to set the Jamaican professional examinations for two to three years before handing it over to a professional body formed in Jamaica. The revised bill was then submitted for consideration to the Ministry of Trade and Industry on the eve of Jamaica's independence in 1962. The then assistant under-secretary in the Ministry of Trade and Industry, the Honourable Alfred Rattray, reviewed the draft bill, along with similar submissions from the other accounting bodies, in his capacity both as a certified accountant and an attorney-at-law. His opinion was as follows:

> The Draft submitted by the 'Certified' Accountants group best addressed the Jamaican situation, and in concept, it accorded with the direction being taken by the Ministry. Certain changes were deemed necessary, however, to ensure the livelihood of persons with years of practising experience, who might not have been eligible for membership of a qualifying body. (Gordon 2000, 13)

The 'livelihood of persons' referred to those Jamaicans who had been working in the public service as accountants in the country long before independence, but without any accounting qualifications either academic or professional.

Much remained to be discussed and in the interim between the submission of the draft bill at independence in 1962 and the establishment of the ICAJ in 1965, a committee was formed with members from the two main groups of 'certified' and 'chartered' associations. The purpose of the committee was to encourage the two parties to agree on an operational framework for the unification of the profession, tailored to the needs of the post-independence Jamaican socio-economic problems. As Gordon (2000, 12) observed:

> Denis Goldson of Paul Goldson and Company, who laboured over the minutes during the protracted three-year period, concluded that the amount of dialogue was equal only to the paper work, as they drafted the Constitution and Rules twice. The second draft, which was more tailored to the needs of the Jamaican situation, was finally accepted. This formed the basis of the Incorporation & Bye-Law of the ICAJ, found in Volume 1, Section 1 of the Members' Handbook.

In addition to the formal exchange at committee level, there was also an ongoing dialogue between the two principal professional bodies represented in Jamaica and the major audit firms of the day. Whereas there was now a consensus on the need to form a local institute, the ICAJ, many within the 'chartered' group were still not entirely convinced that it should fall under the proposed PAL 1970. However, as the lobbying intensified, people like William Thwaites of the 'chartered' association (the ICAJ's first president) and Philmore Ogle of the 'certified' association (the ICAJ's first vice- president) acted to enlist the support of the members of the 'big three' firms, Tapley Bowman & Company (now KPMG Peat Marwick), Carman & Bruce (now Price Waterhouse) and Coopers and Lybrand. Thus, in 1965 the unincorporated 'unifying' ICAJ was formed. While the Companies Act was finally enacted in 1965, the PAL was enacted in 1970 to specifically guide the professional activities of the ICAJ formed in 1965.

After further proactive dialogue between the two groups (the certified and the chartered associations), it was agreed between the representatives of the two groups that the professional examinations of the proposed ICAJ be temporarily managed by the ACCA, after which the ACCA would grant professional independence to the ICAJ. However, this agreement failed to materialize. The reasons for this failure and the related critical consequences are now examined in greater depth.

## The Internal Struggle for the Control of Accountancy

As the foreign parent body of the Jamaican Institute, it had been agreed that the ACCA would continue to conduct the ICAJ examinations for two to three years. It was further agreed that the ACCA would hand over the conduct of the ICAJ examinations to the Mona Campus of the University of the West Indies (UWI, Mona) or any subsequent institution formed by the ICAJ to undertake the task. As the first vice-president of the ICAJ, Ogle (2000, 2) observed:

> In 1962 (before the formation of the ICAJ) the ACCA agreed to allow accountants in Jamaica to mark examination papers in anticipation of and in preparation for a Jamaican Body eventually taking over completely. In May 1965 the ICAJ Council contemplated that the ACCA examinations would be phased out after 3 years! In hindsight, the objective was far beyond the resources. The ICAJ/ACCA joint examination scheme remains in place today.

Available evidence suggests that, apart from a lack of resources, the failure of this arrangement was mainly due to further disagreements within the ICAJ membership (see Bakre 2001). While some ICAJ members (the localization group) were of the opinion that such an agreement should be strictly adhered to, other members (the internationalization group) were of the view that the ACCA should continue to be the parent body of the proposed ICAJ beyond the two to three years agreed. The internal wrangling within ICAJ's membership permitted the ACCA to take advantage of the instability of the new institute and it continued to control the ICAJ professional examinations beyond the two to three years laid down in the original agreement (see ACCA 1999a).[10]

In 1969, the ACCA wrote to the ICAJ urging it to consider the development of a local professional qualification, as in the event of unification of the British profession it would no longer be in a position to assist the ICAJ. In response, the Jamaican institute immediately took steps to form an alliance with UWI, Mona, to develop an MSc degree in accounting. The programme closely mirrored the ACCA's qualification with a view to replacing it should the ACCA withdraw its assistance. The next section examines the development of the UWI, Mona, MSc accounting degree and its adoption as the entry qualification of the ICAJ.

## UWI, MONA, MSC ACCOUNTING DEGREE AS AN ICAJ ENTRY QUALIFICATION

One of the conditions of the unification of British accountancy was that participating UK professional bodies would not be able to peddle their accounting qualifications outside the UK. With this in mind, the ACCA dispatched the following letter to all its empire branches in 1969 (including ICAJ):

> If the proposed British national bodies' integration materializes, the ACCA may no longer be in a position to continue the same relationship

10. When it was first formed the ICAJ admitted holders of professional qualifications from any of the UK-based professional bodies. Holders of professional qualifications outside the UK were also entitled to automatic entry to the ICAJ, as long as they were allowed to audit the accounts of public companies in the country of qualifications (see Public Accountancy Act 1970, section 3(b) (ii)).

> regarding examination and credentialing of the non-UK resident accountants as it has at present. (ACCA letter to ICAJ, 1969, ICAJ Archival Records)

Consequently, with the support of the ACCA, by 1975 the ICAJ had allied itself with the Department of Management Studies, UWI, Mona, and put in place an MSc accounting degree programme. The main objective was to develop a programme equivalent to the ACCA qualification in Jamaica with a view to eventually replacing it. Holders of the MSc were to be directly admitted to the membership of the ICAJ after completing two years of practical experience under an ICAJ member.

Ultimately, the unification of the British profession failed to materialize. In Jamaica, a small but powerful group of influential ACCA loyalist members of the ICAJ lobbied for the ACCA to retain control of Jamaican professional examinations (see Madden 2000). The ACCA itself was also posturing to regain its interest in the lucrative accountancy market in Jamaica (see ACCA 1999b). The outcome was that the ACCA was again installed as the key provider of professional qualifications in Jamaica and the recognition of the UWI, Mona, MSc degree in accounting by the ICAJ was eventually withdrawn in 1986. In an interesting and disputed twist of events, the withdrawal of recognition of the UWI, Mona, programme was consequent upon a controversial assessment[11] carried out by the ACCA on the standard and quality of the MSc.

The ICAC was formed in October 1988 by the professional accountancy bodies of the Commonwealth Caribbean in an attempt to integrate accountancy throughout the region. In 1989, the ICAC appointed a panel of international assessors[12] to advise the ICAC council on a suitable programme of professional training and examinations for its accountants throughout the region. The panel was asked to look into the possibility of using the MSc accounting degree programme offered at the UWI, Mona, as a suitable professional qualification for candidates being considered for ICAC membership (Terms of Reference for the Panel of Assessors 1989).

Between 1989 and 1990, the panel met several times in Jamaica and two recommendations emerged from its assessment. The first was that a School of Accountancy should be established by the ICAC to train future accountants in the Caribbean. A second recommendation was for the ICAC to introduce a single professional examination as an entry requirement for the institutes throughout the Caribbean (Recommendation of the Panel of

11. The assessment of the UWI, Mona, MSc degree in Accounting by the ACCA became controversial because the UWI complained that the ACCA did not involve the UWI or obtain any information or explanation from the UWI before arriving at its conclusion. However, it was on the basis of the controversial conclusion by the ACCA that the ICAJ had based its decision to withdraw the recognition of the UWI, Mona, MSc degree in accounting as an entry qualification in 1986.

12. The international panel of assessors comprised representatives of the UK-based ACCA, the American-based AICPA and the Canadian-based CGA.

Assessors 1990). Regarding the second recommendation, the panel assessed the suitability of the MSc accounting degree programme of UWI, Mona, and suggested that:

> A revised syllabus and examinations of the MSc Accounting, UWI, Mona, would provide an adequate match to the recommended exempting requirements. The panel therefore, recommended full exemption status on the understanding that a Joint Advisory Committee (JAC) and Joint Examination Board (JEB) comprising representatives of UWI, Mona, and the profession be established to conduct regular periodic reviews to ensure that the current standard of programme, content and examinations are maintained.[13]

On the basis of the recommendation by the panel of assessors, a revision subcommittee comprising the UWI and ICAC members met over an 18-month period (September 1996 to March 1998) and made revisions to the UWI, Mona, MSc degree as recommended by the panel. On satisfying the revision, the council of the ICAJ reversed its previous decision by lifting the suspension of admission of MSc accounting graduates of UWI, Mona, to membership of the ICAJ (Minutes of the Meeting of the Council of ICAJ 1998).

Despite the lifting of the ban by the ICAJ council, some transnational audit firms in Jamaica, such as Deloitte & Touche, still required holders of the UWI, Mona, MSc degree in accounting to pass the ACCA professional examinations before being recognized as CAs within these firms:

> They [the MSc degree holders] must, in addition to their MSc degrees, pass the ACCA's examinations, before they can be permanently employed in the firm as chartered accountants. (Condition in a letter of employment from Deloitte & Touche, Jamaica 2000)

This episode brings to the fore, yet again, the continuing conflict within the Jamaican profession between the 'local' and 'internationalization' elites. The latter still supported the notion that the PAL 1970 should continue to defend the freedom of practice of accountancy for both Jamaicans and other foreign accountants. The former wanted the PAL to guarantee professional independence in Jamaica through the continued adoption of the UWI, Mona, MSc degree in accounting as an ICAJ entry qualification. The first president of the ICAJ, William Thwaites (1990, 20), recalled his experience of this struggle as follows:

> Well, as you know, we have had changes in the Constitution from time to time since then, but I think that even from those days, we had obtained consensus of what we wanted. We have had a certain amount

13. Outcome of the assessment of the UWI, Mona, MSc Accounting programme by the special panel appointed by the ICAC, Feb 1989, ICAC Archival Records.

> of trouble with getting the Law in the fashion we wanted, and that delayed the thing for quite a while. But certainly, our first Council and 'Shadow Council', if I may put it that way, prior to the actual formation had one consensus and that was that there should be no rift or divisions between the two sides that were to form and be The Institute of Chartered Accountants of Jamaica.

The continued conflicts of interest and the tension were reaffirmed by Thwaites (1990, 21): 'there has never been a time in the last twenty-five years that you haven't had some problem or another to solve, but good sense has always prevailed and that's it'.

In addition to paving the way for the ACCA to continue to take control of Jamaican accountancy, in more recent times the conflict has also encouraged the entry of other foreign professional bodies, such as the American Institute of Certified Public Accountants (AICPA), to the Jamaican accountancy market.

## THE ARRIVAL OF THE AMERICAN-BASED AICPA

In August 1965, the three extant 'local' professional bodies amalgamated to form the national professional institute, the ICAJ.[14] It was originally intended that the ICAJ would conduct its own examinations and provide a qualification process for prospective Jamaican accountants (ICAJ Act 1965). In order for this nationalistic imperative to become legally binding, in 1970, the PAL was enacted to give 'nationalistic' backing to the ICAJ. This was to enable the ICAJ to set its own examinations relevant to the socio-economic problems of Jamaica and to protect the professional interest of indigenous Jamaican accountants. For instance, the PAL further restricted persons eligible to practise as accountants in Jamaica to:

> Members of the body incorporated under the Jamaican law, or to other persons recognized for this purpose as specified by the regulatory body to that effect. (Jamaican Public Accountancy Law 1970, part A section 22[3])

Although British influence remained strong after independence, the cultural reorientation brought about by the socio-economic relationship between Jamaica and its economically stronger neighbours, America and Canada, impacted upon the dominant position of the ACCA in

14. On the formation of the ICAJ and recognition of the UWI, Mona, MSc degree in accounting in 1975, there were two main routes to the membership of the ICAJ. These were either through any of the colonial or global professional qualifications (ACCA, ICAEW, AICPA, CCA, etc.) or the UWI, Mona, MSc degree in accounting. The ACCA's qualification was the most common route to ICAJ entry overall.

accountancy. In particular, the discovery of bauxite in the 1950s, which was mined exclusively by multinational corporations mainly from the US and Canada, had provided an opportunity for some states in America to establish centres for the preparation of the AICPA final examinations in Jamaica. The AICPA final examinations were to be held in centres in America. Moreover, after independence, the migration of people from Jamaica, particularly of professionals such as accountants, had mostly been to America and Canada rather than Europe, in contrast to the situation before independence. As a result, the adoption of the ACCA's syllabus and professional examinations in Jamaica came in for greater scrutiny and questioning. As the former president of ICAJ, Garth Kidoe (2000), observed:

> I would not suggest that the ICAJ adopt the entire syllabus of the ACCA. My information is that the ACCA syllabus, while it is very widely acceptable worldwide, is not recognized in this region of the world—in the Americas. Most of our traffic after the independence is with North America and not with Europe.

The proximity of the US, the belief that it was 'easier' to pass the American CPA examinations and also the non-recognition of the ACCA in America all combined to reduce the number of Jamaicans qualifying through the ACCA route.

Notwithstanding the cultural reorientation of Jamaica, however, the ACCA qualification remained the key mode of entry to the Jamaican profession, mainly because the ICAJ council continued to embrace the ACCA's examinations. However, prospective Jamaican accountants were able to qualify as AICPA members by: preparing for the AICPA examinations in Jamaica or sitting the AICPA examinations in an examination centre in the US and then applying for ICAJ membership as AICPA members. As of 2008, whilst about 10 per cent of the total of 878 ICAJ members became registered through the AICPA route, less than 2 per cent were registered through the Canadian-based Certified General Accountants route (CGA). Such data indicate that the ACCA continues to be the greatest foreign influence on the ICAJ and, as will be shown next, this influence extends beyond professional examinations.

## THE WIDER ACCA INFLUENCE

The strong influence of the ACCA on the ICAJ is not restricted to the sphere of professional examinations. Its administrative structures, too, have formed a blueprint for the ICAJ. For example, as in the case of the ACCA, each ICAJ president is automatically succeeded by his/her vice-president without any elections or due democratic process.

All ICAJ members use the designation ACA and ICAJ members who are also ACCA members use the designation of both bodies and refer to themselves as ACA and ACCA. The designation ACA indicates their membership in the non-examination-setting local body, the ICAJ, and ACCA indicates their membership of the examination-setting body, the UK-based ACCA.

The links between the ACCA, the UK and the Jamaican institute remain strong. In attempts to legitimize its activities in former colonial outposts, such as Jamaica, the ACCA appoints a core loyalist member of the ICAJ (representing the entire Commonwealth Caribbean) to be a council member. The ACCA pays for the flight ticket of this member to come to London each year to attend the council meeting, where he/she becomes a nominal member/spectator, having no vote or power to alter the status quo. Petras (1981, 15) asserts that:

> In fact, the strength of the imperial system in large part rests on the influence and control exercised by the collaborative classes and strata within imperialist society. The collaborator classes are oriented towards capital accumulation by continuing to defend the status quo, through the use of their influence to repress class conflict.

In this context, it is the Caribbean regional representative who is given the task of persuading the entire council and members of the ICAJ and the regional institute, the ICAC to defend the status quo[15] and to continue to support the activities of the ACCA, in order to facilitate the growth and development of accountancy. This strategy has enabled the ACCA to continue to protect its lucrative accountancy market in Jamaica and some other Caribbean countries (see ACCA 1999a, 1999b). It has also enabled the local loyalists of the ACCA in Jamaica and other Caribbean countries to continue to protect their individual capital in Jamaica and the Commonwealth Caribbean.

## DISCUSSION AND CONCLUSION

This chapter has provided evidence highlighting the strong links between the British Empire and the development of accountancy in both colonial and post-colonial Jamaica. It suggests that British accountants and practices followed British capital to colonial Jamaica in the late seventeenth

15. The Institute of Chartered Accountants of the Caribbean (ICAC) was also established by the Chartered Institutes in the Commonwealth Caribbean in 1988 with the main objective of putting in place purely Caribbean professional examinations devoid of any foreign influence and positively responding to the socio-economic problems of the region. This regional institute has also failed to achieve its main objective, due to the conflict of identity facing regional accountants and the imperial interest of certain colonial and global professional bodies, particularly the UK-based ACCA.

century and that this continues to influence the professionalization of accountancy in Jamaica. The social stratification which characterized the British colonization of Jamaica and the consequent exclusionary education policy combined to impede the production of qualified indigenous Jamaican accountants in the colony. The indigenous Jamaican government joined forces with the indigenous Jamaican accountants to draw up plans to localize the accountancy profession once the country became independent. The prime objective was to encourage the profession to respond positively to the socio-economic requirements of post-independence Jamaica.

However, as the wider literature indicates, post-colonialism is often afflicted by conflicts of cultural identity. Thus Williams (1973, 56) notes: 'in each former colonial society, the question of psychological independence and dependence may become a matter of conflict of identity between the defender and challenger of the colonial system in any matters of post-independence socio-economic development'. Although one might expect that 'where groups of people have secured political independence with a single voice, their psychological socio-economic independence would be assured with a unity of purpose' (Nettleford 1978, 25), this is not always the case—for instance, in the absence of a single voice (Norris 1966) or where political independence has subsequently produced a spectrum of cultural identities (Hall and Du Gay 1996).

Such issues are reflected in the story of accountancy in post-colonial Jamaica. Despite displaying unity in the struggle for independence and, at the same time, supporting the assertion that accountancy in Jamaica should be relevant to the socio-economic problems of the country and free from foreign influence, some ACCA members of the ICAJ formed a class alliance with the ACCA (Bakre 2001). Petras (1981, 18) observed that the 'post-independence national capitalist forms a strategy of class alliance with imperial firms in intensifying surplus extraction from the labour force through a variety of post-independence working relationships under the rubric of dependent neo-colonialism for capital accumulation'. This, perhaps, can help to explain the conflict of identity afflicting those members that continued to support the ACCA's appropriation of the Jamaican professional examinations. Perhaps their education and upbringing in a system that was so closely aligned to British culture left an indelible mark, a conflict of allegiance that could not be eradicated in the short space of time since independence. Those that lead the profession in the future may be better placed to dispense with the marriage of convenience with the ACCA and actualize the vision of their founding fathers to create a profession that is responsive to the changing and very specific socio-economic climate of Jamaica.

## REFERENCES

Ali, R. (1998) 'Presidential report'. In *1998 ICAC Annual Report.* Kingston, Jamaica: ICAC.

Alleyne, M. (1988) *Roots of the Jamaican Culture*. London: Pluto Press.

Annisette, M. (2003) 'The colour of accountancy: Examining the salience of race in a professionalisation project'. *Accounting, Organizations and Society* 28:639–74.

Association of Certified Chartered Accountants (ACCA) (1961) Letter to Jamaica Branch, 12 December. ICAJ Archival Records, Kingston, Jamaica.

———. (1969) Letter to ICAJ. ICAJ Archival Records, Kingston, Jamaica.

———. (1999a) 'ACCA announces massive increase in student numbers worldwide'. In *ACCA Newsletter* (February 23). London: ACCA.

———. (1999b) 'ACCA membership figures worldwide exceed 66,000'. In *ACCA Newsletter* (February 10). London: ACCA.

Bakre, O.M. (2001) 'An examination of the emergence of the accountancy profession in developing countries: The case of Jamaica'. Unpublished PhD Dissertation, University of Essex, England.

———. (2005) 'First attempt at localising imperial accountancy: The case of the Institute of Chartered Accountants of Jamaica (ICAJ) (1950s–1970s)'. *Critical Perspectives on Accounting* 16:995–1018.

———. (2006) 'Second attempt at localising imperial accountancy: the case of the Institute of Chartered Accountants of Jamaica (1970s–1980s)'. *Critical Perspectives on Accounting* 17:1–28.

———. (2008) 'Financial reporting as technology that supports and sustains imperial expansion, maintenance and control in the colonial and post-colonial globalisation: The case of the Jamaican economy'. *Critical Perspectives on Accounting* 19:487–522.

Beckford, G. (1972) *Persistent Poverty: Underdevelopment in Plantation Economies of the Third World*. London: Oxford University Press.

Birds, L. (1994) *Address to the Caribbean Heads of Government Meeting Held in Bridgetown, Barbados, from July 4–7*. Kingston: ICAC Archival Records.

Black, C.V. (1993) *History of Jamaica*. Kingston: Carlong Publishers.

Bolland, O.N. (1988) *Colonialism and Resistance in Belize: Essays in Historical Sociology*. Mona: ISER.

Chaderton, R., and Taylor, P.J. (1993) 'Accounting systems of the Caribbean'. *Research in Third World Accounting* 2:45–66.

Gordon, R. (2000) 'The Institute of Chartered Accountants of Jamaica 35th anniversary (1965–2000): An historical perspective'. *Jamaican Financial Gleaner* (4 February): 12–14.

Hall, S., and Du Gay, P. (1996) *Questions of Cultural Identity*. London: Sage Publications.

Hendricks, D. (1981) *The Tools of Empire*. New York: Oxford University Press.

Hoogvelt, M.M., and Tinker, A. (1978) 'The role of colonial and post-colonial states in imperialism—a case study of the Sierra Leone Development Company'. *Journal of Modern African Studies* 16:67–79.

Institute of Chartered Accountants of the Caribbean. (1998) *ICAC Annual Report, 1998*. Kingston: ICAC.

Jackson, J. (1990) 'Interview with Thwaites, W.' In Institute of Chartered Accountants of Jamaica, *25 Years (1965–1990) Anniversary Publication*. Kingston: ICAJ.

Johnson, T.J., and Caygill, M. (1971) 'The development of accountancy links in the commonwealth'. *Accounting and Business Research* 1:155–73.

Kidoe, G. (2000) Interviewed by author, July 15, Kingston, Jamaica.

Macbeath, A. (1982) 'A Scots CA in Jamaica—two decades of development'. *Accountant's Magazine* (April): 131–33.

Macdonald, K.M. (1985) 'Social closure and occupational registration'. *Sociology* 19:541–56.

Madden, A. (2000) Interviewed by author, 10 August, Kingston, Jamaica.

Mendes, M. (1990) 'Innovation in professional accountancy education at the University of the West Indies, Jamaica'. Unpublished MA Dissertation in Education, University of the West Indies, Mona, Jamaica.

———. (1999) Interviewed by author, 20 July, Kingston, Jamaica.

Mendes, M., and McLean, R. (1987) *Regulatory Framework of Accounting in Jamaica*. Mona: CFM Publications.

Mepham, M.J. (1977) 'The accountancy profession in Jamaica'. *Accountant's Magazine* (November): 468–70.

Miller, E. (1989) 'Educational development in independent Jamaica'. In *Jamaica in Independence: Essays on the Early Years*, ed. R. Nettleford. Kingston: Heinmann Caribbean; London: James Currey.

Mills, J.S. (1864) *Disquisition and Discussions, Vol. 3*. London: Longmans, Green Reader and Dyer.

Ministry of Trade and Industry. (1962) *Minute No. 2 of March 29*. Kingston: ICAJ Archival Records.

Mintz, S. (1961) 'The question of Caribbean peasantries, a comment'. *Caribbean Studies* 1:31–34.

Minutes of the Meeting of the Council of ICAJ. (1998) *May 26*. Kingston: ICAJ Archival Records.

Neu, D. (1999) '"Discovering" indigenous peoples: Accounting and the machinery of empire'. *Accounting Historians Journal* 26:53–82.

Nettleford, R.N. (1978) *Caribbean Cultural Identity, the Case of Jamaica*. Kingston: Herald Limited.

———. (1989) 'Fledging years'. In *Jamaica in Independence: Essays on the Early Years*, ed. R. Nettleford. Kingston: Heinmann Caribbean; London: James Currey.

Norris, K. (1966) *Jamaica, the Search for an Identity*. London: Institute of Race Relations, Oxford University Press.

Ogle, P. (1961) *Various Discussions on the Formation of the ICAJ and Training of Jamaican Accountants*. Kingston: ICAJ Archival Records.

———. (2000) 'Development of accountancy in Jamaica'. Paper presented at the ICAJ Conference on Training and Ethical Consideration, ICAJ Archives, Kingston, Jamaica, 26 February.

Petras, F. (1981) *Class, State and Power in the Third World*. London: Zed Books.

Preston, A.Z. (1990) 'The profession in the Third World'. In ICAJ (ed.) *Institute of Chartered Accountants of Jaimaca Twenty-Fifth Anniversary Publication*. Kingston: ICAJ.

*Public Accountancy Act/Law*. (1970) Kingston: Government of Jamaica Press.

Rattray, A (1962) 'Summary of the post independence movements in the accountancy profession in Jamaica'. Unpublished manuscript, ICAJ Archival Records, Kingston, Jamaica.

———. (1963) *Minute No. 21 of the Honourable Minister of Trade and Industry on the Proposal on a Public Accountancy Law, February 11*. Kingston: ICAJ Archival Records.

Recommendation of the Panel of Assessors. (1990) ICAC Archival Records, Kingston, Jamaica.

Registrar of Companies. (2000) *Listing of Companies*. Kingston: Jamaica Government Press.

Report of the Committee on Public Accountancy Law. (1963) ICAJ Archival Records, Kingston, Jamaica.

Salmon, U. (1998) Interviewed by author, 12 August, Kingston, Jamaica.

Sheridan, R.B. (2000) *Sugar and Slavery, An Economic History of the British West Indies, 1623–1775*. Kingston: Canoe Press.

Smith, V.C. (1962) *Minute No. 13 to the Permanent Secretary, Ministry of Trade and Industry: Proposal on Public Accountancy Law, March 29*. Kingston: ICAJ Archival Records.

Sian, S. (2006) 'Inclusion, exclusion and control: The case of the Kenyan accounting professionalisation project'. *Accounting, Organizations and Society* 31:295–322.

Terms of Reference for the Panel of Assessors. (1989) ICAJ Archival Records, Kingston, Jamaica.

Thurborn, E.C. (2000) Interviewed by author, 26 August, Kingston, Jamaica.

Thwaites, W. (1990) 'Interview with John Jackson'. In Institute of Chartered Accountants of Jaimaca (eds.) *Institute of Chartered Accountants of Jamaica Twenty-Fifth Anniversary Publication*. Kingston: ICAJ.

Williams, E. (1973) *Caribbean Economic Integration*. Mona: ISER.

# 8 Maintaining Empire
## The Practice Link in Trinidad and Tobago

*Marcia Annisette*

### INTRODUCTION

Trinidad and Tobago (T&T) is a twin island nation-state and thus does not have a unitary imperial history. The smaller island, Tobago, changed hands over 20 times before it became a British colony in 1814. The larger and more dominant island, Trinidad, experienced over three centuries of Spanish imperialist rule from 1498 until it was incorporated into the British Empire in 1802. It is during the historical period spanning the islands' formal incorporation into the British Empire to their informal incorporation into the US Empire that developments with regards to accountancy took place, for it was the economic transformations of that period which called for a particular configuration of accounting institutions and labour (Annisette 1999, 2000, 2003). In particular in 1907, just over 100 years after being ceded to the British, oil was discovered in Trinidad, and in 1910 when Churchill decided to convert the British navy from coal to oil, Trinidad was transformed from a sugar plantation economy to a petroleum-based plantation economy.[1] During World War I, Trinidad's oil production doubled from one to two million barrels per year (Ministry of Energy and Natural Resources 1984), making the island the largest source of purely British oil (Rothenberg and Wishner 1976; Johnson 1975). By 1946, oil accounted for as much as 75 per cent of the country's export earnings (Carrington 1967). As has been shown elsewhere (Annisette 1999), Trinidad's experience as a plantation economy, dominated first by sugar and later by petroleum, was a critical factor in the way the island's accountancy labour market and practice organizations developed. This chapter focuses on the development of the latter.

In doing so it builds upon the work of Annisette (1999, 2000, 2003). Collectively these articles provide useful insights into the nature and organization of professional accountancy in post-colonial 'Third World' states

1. The economy of a plantation economy is deeply integrated into the economy of another country, and its production and economic life are dominated by a single product. For more on the plantation economic model see Pantin (1980), Beckford (1972) and Best (1968).

of the British Commonwealth. In particular they draw attention to the impact of source, timing and local social structures on the profession in these sites. In Annisette (1999), I show that in contrast to the elite-inspired movements of the UK and the 'Old-Commonwealth', the *source* of professionalization in T&T was the state. In spear-heading the Institute of Chartered Accountants of Trinidad and Tobago (ICATT), the post-independence T&T state sought to open up the practice of accountancy, which until then had been the preserve of British expatriates, to locals. I therefore linked professionalization movements in these sites to nation-building (Annisette 1999), and argued that profession formation in accountancy should be considered part and parcel of the making of the post-colonial 'Third World' state. In Annisette (2000), I show that the *timing* of these accountancy professionalization movements, which took place simultaneously with the construction of a US-dominated global capitalist economy, was less than coincidental and I argue that this timing created the conditions for the establishment of strong links between local accountancy institutions and their foreign counterparts. In the case of T&T this led to the marginalization of the University of the West Indies (UWI) in the education and training of accountants in T&T. Although in Annisette (2000) I argued that political-economy factors created the conditions for external collaboration, in Annisette (2003) I illustrate the role of *social structures* in reinforcing the external link and securing the complete marginalization of the UWI. There I show how the colonial practice of racial and ethnic differentiation so left its imprint on T&T society that, as late as the 1980s, there was a tight coupling of race, accountancy credential and work-site. As a result, the exclusion of the UWI's Master of Science (MSc) accounting graduates from the ICATT, while it might have been based on technical motives, was interpreted by many as a racially motivated act to disenfranchise Afro- and Indo-Trinidadians from elite sectors of accountancy practice.

A major empirical focus of my previous work was the strong education link between the ICATT and the UK-based Chartered Association of Certified Accountants (ACCA). I was particularly concerned to explain the ICATT's strong dependence on the ACCA for the education and certification of the country's accountants. I argued that the power–knowledge relations that characterize this link facilitated the maintenance of imperialistic relations long after the end of formal empire in 1962 (Annisette 2000). This argument was inspired by Gallagher and Robinson's insight in their 1953 classic, which pointed to the role of indigenous actors in determining the nature of the imperial encounter. To recap, they argued that British imperialism proceeded according to the policy of 'trade with informal control if possible, trade with rule where necessary' (1953, 13). Formal rule, they suggested, was only undertaken when the internal politics within an overseas territory or the likelihood of foreign challenge to British supremacy jeopardized the incorporation of that territory's economy into the expanding British capitalist economy. Thus for them the difference between formal empire of rule and informal empire of trade and influence was not one of fundamental nature, but only one of degree, for the latter suggested that 'local collaborative systems were sufficiently developed and in place to facilitate dominion without formal rule' (Annisette 2000, 636). Given that perspective, I conceived of post-colonial professional accountancy qualifying bodies such as the ICATT as agents of informal empire and sought to identify the coincidences of interest between the local professional institute (the ICATT) and its external counterpart (the ACCA) in enacting the imperial enterprise after formal empire. For the ICATT, I argued that collaborating with the UK-based ACCA would confer symbolic capital (Annisette 2000, 655) whereas, as pointed out by Briston and Kedslie (1997), for the ACCA such links have been the organization's source of money, markets and prestige. But as was noted previously, there were other local agents and linkages at play (Annisette 1999, 2000). Another crucial element linking the T&T profession to the imperial centre was the practice link. Indeed as I indicated earlier, the practice link *preceded* the educational link and it was the post-independence transformation of this practice link which gave internal coherence to the ICATT–ACCA education link. Specifically, I argued that:

> The strengthening of the ICATT–ACCA relationship . . . can therefore be considered an outcome of a growing belief in the ICATT that since accounting practice was being increasingly standardised at an international level, so too should professional accountancy training be internationally standardised. (2000, 650)

My aim in this chapter, therefore, is to shift emphasis from previous work and to focus instead on the evolution of the practice link that so connected the T&T profession with the profession at the imperial centre. I focus on the period spanning 1911 to 1995. The beginning of the period signifies the emergence of the overseas practice link, represented by the entry of UK-controlled accountancy practising firms into T&T. The end date of 1995 is the date at which the educational link supporting the practice link appeared permanent and stable (Annisette 2000). Over this period I show how the practice link was transformed, itself reflecting transformations in the nature of the imperialist encounter but nonetheless further intensifying the same power–knowledge relations that obtained under formal colonialism. Specifically, I conceptualize the practice link as the 'parent-subsidiary-like' relationships that exist between T&T professional accountancy practices and overseas professional accountancy firms. I trace their evolution from small satellite branches of British firms during the period of formal empire to their incorporation into large US-based multinational accounting firms (MAFs) by the early 1970s—the era of informal US Empire. I explore the local motives for establishing these links and consider their power–knowledge consequences. In so doing, I give a more comprehensive explanation as to why I argue that there is internal coherence between professional practice links and professional educational links in dependent countries like T&T.

The remainder of the chapter is organized as follows. In the next section I highlight the hegemonic significance of the professional practice link in T&T by illustrating the dominant position of the MAFs in the T&T accounting landscape at the end of the focal period 1995.[2] I give insights into their market position as providers of professional accountancy services and employers of professional accountancy labour, illustrate their dominance in the professional qualifying institute—the ICATT—and give an historical account of how these MAFs came to inhabit the market for accountancy services in T&T. I then give broad details of post–World War II transformations in the global political economy and the overall impact of these transformations on the worldwide organization of accountancy practice. I go on to show how local leading firms interpreted these changes and thereby highlight their incentives for ceding control of critical aspects of their operations to overseas-based practice organizations. Further, I give illustrative examples of the power–knowledge consequences of these dependent practice relationships. Finally, I conclude.

## PRACTISING FIRMS AND CHANGING EMPIRES: FROM UK BRANCHES TO US SATELLITES[3]

The accountancy profession worldwide is known to be dominated by practitioners who operate in powerful accountancy mega-firms which have wide networks of international operations. In 1995 there were about 10 such MAFs in the world and of those, six were considered the global market leaders (the then so-called Big Six).[4] At the end of 1995 five of the Big Six had member offices in T&T. They were:

1. Price Waterhouse (PW)
2. Deloitte & Touche (DT)
3. Ernst & Young (EY)
4. Coopers and Lybrand (CL)
5. KPMG Peat Marwick (KPMG)

2. I refer to these mega-practices as MAFs because of their fit with Fayerweather's (1978) definition of a multinational enterprise as one that: first, is significantly involved in international business having permanent operations in two or more countries; and second, has the capacity for central control of foreign operations.

3. All of the information presented has been obtained from in-depth interviews with the founding members of these firms. In the case of Hunter Smith and Earl, interviews were held with a past senior partner who was then a junior partner at the time of the Price Waterhouse takeover.

4. By the time of writing (2008), due to the merger of Price Waterhouse and Coopers and Lybrand, as well as the spectacular dissolution of Arthur Andersen in 2002 following the Enron debacle, they had dwindled to four.

The last of the then Big Six, Arthur Andersen (AA), had nonetheless by then maintained a covert presence in the country for almost 40 years—a period exceeding that of any of its then Big Six rivals—through a series of correspondence relationships.[5] Collectively in 1995 these five firms employed approximately 200 professional accountants, representing almost one-quarter of the country's then total stock of professional accountants (Annisette 1999, table 3). Additionally, over one-third of the accountants working in industry and commerce had spent an average of four years training in these practices.[6] These firms have, therefore, played a considerable role in socializing professional accountants in T&T.

In 1995 the five MAFs operating in Trinidad and Tobago were owned by 25 partners, all of whom were ICATT members and, though representing a mere 5 per cent of total institute membership, they nonetheless wielded a significant amount of influence in the institute's affairs; maintaining a strong presence on all of the body's standing committees and on its governing council. By 1995 seven of ICATT's 14 past presidents had been partners of MAFs, and MAF partners and employees constituted 43 per cent of the body's governing council and 31 per cent of its standing committees. They were also dominant in terms of their market power. Even though ICATT's 1995 records indicate the existence of 52 registered practising firms operating in the T&T market for professional accounting services, Tables 8.1 and 8.2 highlight the overwhelming dominance of PW and EY. Table 8.1 indicates that the audit market for the largest companies in Trinidad and Tobago is fairly concentrated with these two firms earning between 44 per cent and 57 per cent of the total audit fees in the market, and Table 8.2 indicates an increasingly duopolistic market structure involving these two practices in the listed company market over the 10-year period (1983–1993).[7]

As the following chronological outline of the emergence of these megafirms on the accounting landscape of T&T will show, the market power of this twosome is linked to the close historic ties which they have had with the local comprador class in T&T—a link developed since the colonial era.

## The Establishment of Fitzpatrick Graham and Hunter Smith and Earl 1910–1950

Present-day EY and PW were first established in T&T by UK partnerships Fitzpatrick Graham (FG) and Hunter Smith and Earl (HSE), respectively,

5. Another international player, Pannell Kerr Forster, through its founder firm Fitzpatrick Graham, had been well established in the country for over 80 years. In 1995 it established a correspondent relationship with an indigenous firm, Mark Castillo Toney and Company.

6. Information gained from the results of a questionnaire administered to ICATT members in 1994.

7. Excessive concentration is usually associated with reduced competition, monopolistic pricing practices and supernormal returns to supplier firms (Demstez 1973; Krouse 1990).

*Table 8.1* Auditors of Top 48 Companies in Trinidad and Tobago, 1993

| | TOP COMPANY STATISTICS 1993 | | ESTIMATED MARKET SHARE | |
|---|---|---|---|---|
| **AUDIT FIRM** | **No. of companies audited** | **Net Revenue TT $mill** | **Net Revenue %** | **Square Root of Net Revenue %** |
| Price Waterhouse | 16 | 8,974 | 39% | 26% |
| Ernst & Young | 12 | 4,208 | 18% | 18% |
| KPMG Peat Marwick | 6 | 4,144 | 18% | 18% |
| Auditor General | 6 | 2,731 | 12% | 14% |
| Coopers and Lybrand | 2 | 1,258 | 6% | 10% |
| Deloitte & Touche | 5 | 905 | 4% | 8% |
| Mark Castillo and Toney | 1 | 547 | 2% | 6% |
| **Total** | 48 | 22,767 | 100%* | 100% |

*Source:* Financial Statements ending 1993, HRC Associates (1995).
*Note*: Net revenue and square root of net revenue have been used as proxies for audit fees following Moizer and Turley (1987), who suggest that these two figures mark the upper and lower boundaries for the true concentration statistic.
*Includes minor rounding error.

during the early decades of the twentieth century. FG had already established a presence in Guyana to service its sugar industry client Bookers, and it was this same industry and client which attracted it to Trinidad in 1911 (Smith 1950; Hobday 1995). HSE arrived 13 years later in 1924 to service its prestigious London client the Imperial College of Tropical Agriculture, which had a major college in the country. Although both firms originally went to T&T to service local subsidiaries or branches of UK organizations, by 1950 they both had a portfolio of clients that were substantially local. In the case of FG, its early entry into the country and its association with sugar allowed it to quickly develop strong links with the local 'comprador' plantocracy, which had traditionally engaged in agriculture, import, export and local distribution. But by the 1950s, when the T&T colonial government enacted the Aid to Pioneer Industries Programme to promote the development of a manufacturing sector (Annisette 1999, 109–10, 117–18), most of the plantocracy used the incentives of the programme to move into assembly-type, agro-

*Table 8.2* Audit Market for Public Companies

| | PERCENTAGE MARKET SHARE based on audit fees | | |
|---|---|---|---|
| **Firm** | **1993** | **1989** | **1983** |
| Price Waterhouse | 69.0% | 45.7% | 46.3% |
| Ernst & Young[1] | 21.8% | 40.0% | 42.9% |
| Deloitte & Touche[2] | 5.9% | 4.3% | 0.9% |
| KPMG Peat Marwick | 1.9% | 3.3% | 2.9% |
| Auditor General | 0.6% | 3.0% | 1.0% |
| Coopers and Lybrand | 0.0% | 3.7% | 6.0% |
| Lee Kim | 0.8% | 0.0% | 0.0% |
| Total Percent | 100% | 100% | 100% |
| Total Fees $TT'000 | 8,746 | 7,200 | 7,584 |
| **Total Audit Clients** | 23 | 29 | 31 |

*Source*: Financial Statements ending 1993.
[1]1989: Arthur Young; 1983: Pannell Fitzpatrick
[2]1989: Touche Ross; 1983: Touche Ross Law and Marinez

based industries, construction, insurance and real estate (Craig 1982, 398). By 1950, therefore, FG was well entrenched within this market, being the auditor for 19 of the 27 largest local comprador firms listed in the 1950 publication *Trinidad—Who, What, Why* (Smith 1950). HSE on the other hand, though struggling with only six of the remaining eight top local businesses, set up a successful practice in neighbouring Venezuela as early as 1946.

As Table 8.3 indicates, by 1950 FG dominated the market for professional accountancy services in T&T. It dominated the foreign sector, auditing five of the 11 largest oil and asphalt companies and the largest sugar producers. Its only rival, HSE, held audits for only two of the top 11 firms operating in the oil industry. The remaining large oil companies were audited by non-resident firms.

## From Hunter Smith and Earl to Price Waterhouse—1960

HSE was the first of these two partnerships to localize. It did so in 1957 by buying out the interests of its London-based partners, therefore becoming financially independent of UK-based interests; although up until the early 1970s the

*Table 8.3* Auditors of Top 48 Companies in Trinidad and Tobago, 1950

| NATURE OF ENTERPRISE | FG | HSE | OTHER | TOTAL |
|---|---|---|---|---|
| Trade and Commercial | 11 | 2 | 1 | 14 |
| Oil and Asphalt | 5 | 2 | 4 | 11 |
| Pioneer Industries | 7 | | | 7 |
| Sugar and Agriculture | 3 | | | 3 |
| Auto. Assembly | 1 | 2 | | 3 |
| Finance | 5 | | 2 | 7 |
| Printing and Publishing | | 2 | | 2 |
| Other | | 1 | | 1 |
| **Total** | 32 | 9 | 7 | 48 |

*Source:* Annisette (1999, Table 2, 113)).

majority of its partners were UK-born (Smith 1995). It was also the first firm to become closely involved with the large international practices. The local HSE first became involved with AA after it sold off its Venezuelan practice to AA in 1957. The sale ushered in a period of loose co-operation between HSE and AA, whereby HSE did all AA work in Trinidad and AA represented HSE in the US. In 1960, however, this relationship came to an end when HSE accepted a PW offer to act as its correspondent firm in Trinidad.[8] The PW offer had immediate appeal to HSE, for at this time PW was auditor for two of the largest companies in T&T's petroleum sector—British Petroleum and Shell. Moreover, given that PW's overseas client base was essentially British, there was a greater cultural compatibility between HSE and PW than with the Chicago-based AA, a point not entirely lost to HSE. As one retired HSE partner put it:

> All staff came from the UK, the partners all UK qualified and the major clients—BP and Shell—all reported back to the UK. (David Earl, retired partner PW, 1995)

After a year of acting as correspondent for PW, HSE began to practise as PW. For the sake of some of its older clients who were used to the firm's original name, it also continued to operate under the HSE name for over a decade after formal integration into the PW network.

8. A correspondent relationship is a loose representative relationship set up by one firm with another, the latter operating in a jurisdiction where the former does not have a physical presence. It is very common amongst banking institutions.

## From Law and Martinez to Touche Ross—1967

Law and Martinez was the first truly indigenous firm of practising accountants in T&T. Its founders, David Law and Peter Martinez, both started off their careers in practice in the offices of HSE in 1948. Being of European descent, they were both able to qualify as chartered accountants (CAs) with the firm's London office, returning to the Trinidad firm in 1958. By 1965 Law left the firm—which by then had formally tied the knot with PW—to start his own practice. He was soon to be joined by Martinez, then a partner designate at PW. The firm Law and Martinez rapidly developed, appealing to the local 'French Creole' clientele of FG and attracting some of the latter's smaller more price-sensitive clients. By 1967 the firm had a solid and growing client base, and at that time Touche Ross (TR) was looking to establish its presence in Trinidad, having already done so in Barbados. The Barbados office was used to scout the Trinidad market for an appropriate target and Law and Martinez were approached via this link to consider an association with TR. Law and Martinez's association with TR created the firm Touche Ross Law and Martinez. From an ownership standpoint, the firm remained completely local. It was one of only two firms (the other being in Jamaica) in the entire TR family of firms that was allowed to carry an appendage to the TR name. To the partners of the local firm, this arrangement had distinct advantages. The international name added prestige to the firm, allowing it to attract clients who otherwise would not have wanted to identify with a local firm. At the same time, by retaining the name Law and Martinez, the firm was able to maintain its former identity and appeal to those local clients who patronized the firm because it was indigenous. In the mid-1980s, however, the Law and Martinez appendage was dropped and the firm practised as TR. By 1995 the firm was practising as DT as a result of the international merger of TR with Deloitte, Haskins and Sells.

## From John Hunt to Coopers and Lybrand—1970

John Hunt, the first Afro-Trinidadian to become a CA, qualified with the Institute of Chartered Accountants in Scotland (ICAS) in 1964. Wishing to work in public practice but unable to do so by dint of his race (Annisette 2003), Hunt set up his own firm, John Hunt & Company (JH), in September 1968 after a four-year stint in the petroleum industry. The firm developed a market niche amongst trade unions, credit unions and small unincorporated black businesses which had not been serviced by the larger practices. In 1970 the firm was approached, first by Haskins and Sells and then later that year by CL, to act as a correspondent firm. It chose the latter, and in 1972, JH formally joined the CL international partnership as a member firm. Between 1972 and 1979 the local practice operated under two separate names (John Hunt and Coopers and

Lybrand), signing off its international clients as the latter and its local clients as the former. This dichotomy ceased on January 1980 when the two names were merged to carry on the practice under the name Coopers & Lybrand/John Hunt & Company.[9] Finally in September 1991, the John Hunt appendage was dropped and the firm began operating as Coopers and Lybrand.

## From Fitzpatrick Graham to Arthur Young—1989

In 1966, FG, Trinidad's oldest and largest practising firm of accountants became Pannell Fitzpatrick (PF) as a result of the international merger of Fitzpatrick Graham and Pannell Crewdsen. Within months of that merger, however, the T&T firm entered into a relationship with the international firm Peat Marwick Mitchell (PMM) in which the Canadian office of PMM partially merged with the Trinidad office of PF to establish a PMM presence in Trinidad. The firm operated with two UK-resident PF partners, two Canadian-resident PMM partners and six Trinidad-resident partners. It practised in T&T as two separate firms—PF and PMM—for two years until PMM severed the connexion and set up its own practice in the country. This arrangement with PMM was an early indication that the local firm (PF) had begun to outgrow its international parent, for the local standing of PF's Trinidadian office was in no way matched by the firm's fairly moderate ranking on the international scene.[10] PF's break with PMM was immediately followed by a correspondent relationship with AA. This new alliance facilitated the development of a strong consultancy capability within the firm such that by the early 1980s PF in T&T was not only the largest consultancy practice in the country, it was also the largest in the entire PF international partnership, employing over 200 professionals as consultants. According to the senior partner at the time, however:

> We felt we were getting left behind in terms of training input and all the latest computer and technical developments and so on. We had set up quite a significant Management Consulting practice and we felt that we weren't getting the kind of backup input we really needed. (Hobday 1995)

Moreover, the local firm had suffered a series of audit failures during the 1980s and there was widespread speculation that this had arisen because it had not aligned itself with a higher-quality audit supplier. Even the attempts by the international firm to increase its international clout through merger to produce the firm Pannell Kerr Forster failed to provide the local firm with the kinds of technical inputs it felt that it needed to support its service

9. *Institute of Chartered Accountants Newsletter* vol. 6 (2), June 1980.
10. For instance, in Kubin (1975) PF is not even listed in the top 10 of the international firms, whereas it was the dominant firm of accountants in Trinidad.

delivery. Thus by 1989, PF Trinidad began to scout for a new international partner and, following the lead of its Barbados PF counterpart, it joined the Arthur Young partnership. The firm operated as Arthur Young for some 12 months, later changing its name to EY as a result of the international megamerger between Arthur Young and Ernst and Whinney.

## Two Phases of Internationalization

The preceding historical highlights indicate that expansionism has been a feature of the earliest professional accountancy firms. Indeed as Daniels, Thrift and Leyshon (1989, 85) point out, for London-based firms such as PW, Haskin and Sells and TR, the establishment of overseas offices and branches preceded the opening up of regional UK offices. T&T, as a receiving country, experienced two distinctly different phases of internationalization of professional accountancy practice, the first of which occurred during British colonialism and was consistent with Johnson and Caygill's (1971) observation that British accountants and firms followed British capital into the far reaches of empire. The second phase of internationalization occurred in T&T's immediate post-colonial period of the mid-1960s to the early 1970s (see Figure 8.1).

Whereas the first phase was characterized by what one might call colonization, that is, the establishment in T&T of pioneer British practising firms which subsequently became localized in terms of their ownership; the second phase was characterized by the capture of localized practices and their incorporation into the mega US-based multinational practices in the 1960s and

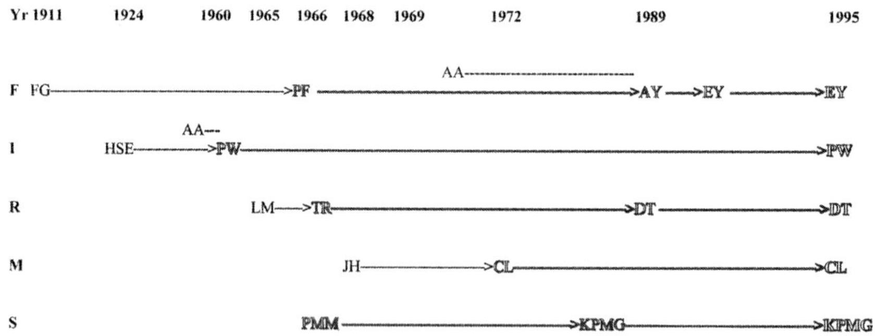


*Figure 8.1* Time-line of MAFs in T&T.
Key: FG: Fitzpatrick Graham; PF: Pannell Fitzpatrick; AY: Arthur Young (became Ernst and Young [EY] by international merger activity in 1990); HSE: Hunter Smith and Earl; PW: Price Waterhouse; LM: Law and Martinez; TR: Touche Ross (became Deloitte & Touche [DT] by international merger activity in 1989); JH: John Hunt and Co.; CL: Coopers and Lybrand; PMM: Peat Marwick Mitchell (became KPMG by international merger activity in 1987); AA--- represents correspondent relationship with Arthur Andersen.
*Sources*: Interviews.

1970s. In the following section, I turn to examining the most critical aspect of this transformation—the shift in the practice link from the UK to the US.

## THE TRANSFORMATION OF THE PRACTICE LINK

The transformation of the T&T accounting practices from UK-controlled to US-controlled firms took place in the context of the political decolonization of the island, a process which was itself part of the wider changes in the global political economy in the post–World War II era. For a number of theorists of imperialism the post–World War II era ushered in a new phase of imperialism in which the US came to dominate the world politically and economically in a way that Britain had never done (Wesseling 1986). As pointed out previously, unlike Britain in the classical phase of imperialism, but in a similar fashion to the mid-Victorian Britain, the US succeeded in establishing imperialism without formal empire (Annisette 2000, 653; Mommsen 1986; Wesseling 1986). Thus although T&T's political independence from Britain in 1962 marked the end of its incorporation into the formal British Empire, it also marked the beginning of its incorporation into the informal US Empire—a phenomenon characterized by a massive inflow of US foreign direct investment (FDI) into the country and a closer incorporation of the T&T economy into the US economy. For instance, whereas during the period 1956 to 1965, the UK and the US equally contributed to the FDI inflow into T&T, by 1966 the UK share had declined to just under 10 per cent (McIntyre and Watson 1970). Export trends showed a similar trend of UK decline and US ascent. Whereas in 1954, the value of T&T's exports to the UK and the US were US$60.3 million and US$16.5 million respectively, by 1962, the year in which T&T gained its political independence from Great Britain, these figures were US$80 million and US$101.6 million respectively (Boodhoo 1972).

The post–World War II rise of the US informal empire had a transforming effect on the nature of accountancy practice. The prime agent for US economic expansion was the US-based multinational corporation (Gilpin 1975). The emergence of this entity in the post-war era in turn gave rise to the creation of the modern-day mega Anglo-American MAFs. These were created through a proliferation of mergers between US and UK accounting practices during the 1950s and 1960s (Daniels, Thrift and Leyshon 1989; Wootton, Wolk and Normand 2003), which created what is often referred to as the Anglo-American firm. Importantly, despite their Anglo-American constitution, these were not necessarily mergers of equals for, based on the composition of the policy committees[11] of the firms so

11. This is the most powerful body within the MAFs. According to Daniels, Thrift and Leyshon (1989), one could find more partners from the US arms than from the UK arms on the MAFs' policy committees.

created, it was the US arm of the practice which usually called the shots. And for many such firms, mergers with UK practices were only the beginning of the type of internationalism that was in store. Daniels, Thrift and Leyshon (1989, 85) note that these early mergers provided the framework that enabled the Anglo-American MAFs to systematically enter previously unserved national markets. And they often did so, as the T&T case illustrates, by the capture of local indigenous firms. Whereas much is known about the motives behind the geographic expansion of these US-dominated MAFs—e.g., client service or merely to establish a market presence—little is known as to why thriving local practices, such as those which were already dominating the T&T supplier market in the late 1960s, would integrate into these large US-dominated networks. In what follows I suggest that the increased complexity of professional accounting practice brought about by the emergence of a new world of accounting knowledge generation, involving amongst other things the burgeoning of standards, guidelines and other technical material, was a prime motive for local firms to integrate into MAFs practices. I first give the background behind the emergence of accounting standardization at this time and indicate how T&T practice leaders viewed this novel world of standards. I argue that the way local practice leaders construed the benefit of the 'international' link and, indeed, its implementation reinforced an already strong predisposition (created during the colonial period when accounting was practised along British lines ) by T&T practice leaders to solve local accounting problems by importing foreign accounting knowledge products. I then give further illustration of this knowledge dependency and its consequences.

## STANDARDIZATION AND INCREASING COMPLEXITY OF ACCOUNTING AS A MOTIVE FOR INTEGRATION

A number of factors conspired to press for radical change in the practice of accountancy in the post–World War II era. Two have been previously identified (see Annisette 2000, 653). The first was the emergence of the MAFs. Citing Benson (1976, 34), I previously suggested that:

> it was the desire to reduce the complexity of their multinational service which placed these Anglo-American practices in the forefront of the movement to reconstitute accountancy as a single world-wide profession with standardised practices and a standardised knowledge base. Unsurprisingly therefore, the products of such standardisation bear a distinct Anglo-American accounting bias (Hove, 1990) and internationalisation in accountancy came to mean the world-wide acceptance of the Anglo-American accounting model. (Annisette 2000, 653)

The second was the shift in the US economy from industrial capital to finance capital which, as Polychroniou and Targ (1992, 65) point out, became particularly pronounced in the 1970s. This shift was characterized by an intensification of the phenomena associated with the expansion of finance capital—foreign investment, foreign assistance, loans, corporate buyouts, mergers and capital flight. As Polychroniou and Targ (1992) posit, a critical outcome of this transformation was increasing concern among US capitalists for the organization of global capital markets and for the need to facilitate transactions between multiple capitals. I therefore argued that this development:

> not only served to catapult accountancy into being an 'international' profession, and one of greater significance, it also served to intensify the drive for global congruence in accounting practice. (Annisette 2000, 653)

There was, however, a third and perhaps more critical factor pressing for radical change. The 1960s and 1970s were also marked by a series of corporate scandals that rocked both sides of the Atlantic, shattering public confidence in the practice of accountancy and audit (Lowe and Tinker 1977). In the US the financial press took issue with the diversity of accounting practice, one influential commentator noting that 'many of the statements of the accounting profession are "authoritative excuses" for misleading accounting' (Spacek 1965, cited in Zeff 1972, 188). Meanwhile, UK critics identified the 'plasticity of accounting practices' (*The Times*, 30 July 1968, 21). There, the Institute of Chartered Accountants in England and Wales (ICAEW) came under growing pressure to reform accounting and audit by defining more clearly what was considered correct practice (Stamp and Marley 1970; Nobes and Parker 1979, 41). In both countries therefore, there were increasing calls for the profession to undertake more research so as to narrow the diversity of acceptable accounting practice (Stamp 1969). These public calls for more research, standards and guidance material were met by a number of matching developments in the US and the UK including the creation of technical directorships within the ICAEW and the American Institute of Certified Public Accountants (AICPA)[12] and the issuing of national accounting standards.

As accounting standardization came to be promoted in the US and the UK as the panacea for all of accounting's ills, it was only a small step to translate the process of standardization from the domestic to the international stage. Thus on 29 June 1973, with a founding membership of eight countries including the US and the UK, the International Accounting

12. In the case of the AICPA this was fulfilled through the creation of a new post of executive vice-president to take charge of the institute's expanding technical activities (Zeff 1972, 190).

Standards Committee (IASC) was formed with a mandate to write accounting standards for international use (Benson 1976, 36).[13] Growth in membership was swift. By 1975 the IASC comprised 44 professional accountancy institutions representing 32 different countries (Benson 1976), one of which was the five-year-old ICATT (Annisette 2000).

The birth of the IASC can be viewed as an important part of the Anglo-American profession's strategy to assuage negative public opinion on accountancy and to reinstate public perception of accountancy as an occupation worthy of being called a profession. According to Henry Benson, the person accredited with its formation, the establishment of the IASC was in response to:

> A spontaneous feeling in the accounting profession that something needed to be done quickly and that it was important to let the public see that some action was being taken. (1976, 36)

The strategy, therefore, was to socially reconstruct accountancy as a single worldwide international profession with an increasingly standardized knowledge base.

It was thus in an atmosphere of increasing calls for accounting research and an increasing proliferation of rules, standards and guidelines that governed practice in their home countries that Anglo-American MAFs made their move into T&T seeking to incorporate leading local practices into their international networks. For well-established T&T firms, the provision of accounting and audit services was now subject to an expectation of adherence to international standards and it was in confronting this new challenge that these firms saw the benefit of integrating with the emerging Anglo-American giant firms. John Hunt, whose firm was captured by CL, put it thus:

> There [was] no way that an individual in practice could . . . keep up with the multitude of standards and publications without the research department of an international firm. [B]eing part of an international firm mean[t] bringing you up to certain international standards. (Hunt 1995)

Dick Hobday, retired senior partner, Pannell Kerr Forster, now EY, noted:

> What is more important [than foreign clients] is the technical competence, the standards the training, the audit, how they do your business, because the business of accounting has developed tremendously over the last 30 years. (Hobday 1995)

And for Geoff Smith (retired senior partner of PW and past partner of HSE) the benefit of the PW nexus was that:

13. The other six member countries were Australia, Canada, France, Japan, Mexico and the Netherlands (Samuels and Piper 1985, 70).

> To the extent that Continuing Education was in its infancy in Trinidad we could get publications and could get entry into courses and all that sort of thing. (Smith 1995)

The move toward internationalization by these local firms was therefore very much linked to the burgeoning of accounting standards, guidelines and other technical material that was being generated at the time. The attraction of these overseas links was that they brought privileged access to the new and growing body of accountancy knowledge; more so since it was these very Anglo-American firms which were in the forefront of the knowledge generation and standardization process. Thus for T&T's practising firms, incorporation into the Anglo-American accounting conglomerates was a means of achieving international standardization.

## Illustrating Power–Knowledge Relationships

Whereas, as pointed out earlier, from the standpoint of the Anglo-American MAFs, standardization reduced the complexity of multinational service provision, from the standpoint of small practising firms in T&T, the ever-increasing proliferation of accounting and auditing standards and other technical guidelines increased the perceived complexity of the auditor's task. One aspect of maintaining high quality and high standards in service delivery, then, became the ability to keep abreast of the newest developments in the field. There was a strong belief amongst partners interviewed that *only* through membership of the international networks could they keep abreast of the growing proliferation of accounting and auditing standards and other technical developments in the profession. Consequently, the MAFs' centralized information collection and dissemination machinery and its centralized research facilities were seen as valuable resources in keeping up to date. This view is epitomized by John Hunt:

> Being part of an international firm means bringing you up to certain international standards . . . They don't just send you work because you are a member of an international group. You have to satisfy the quality control that you are up to the standard; that you adhere to the policy of the firm [and] that you are producing work of a certain level before you are let loose on the client. (John Hunt, founder of John Hunt & Co., now CL)

Peter Martinez, founder of Law and Martinez, now DT, noted further that 'Touche Ross international . . . ensured that we maintained a high standard of work' (1995).

Moreover, the ability to tap into the vast training and continuing education facilities within the MAFs network gave T&T firms the comfort that they were at the cutting edge of the industry. It is useful to note that all of the MAFs partners interviewed mentioned this as an important aspect of the benefit of internationalization. A senior partner of CL noted, for instance: 'We have access to up to date training materials—accounting standards, the literature and so on' (1995).

Unlike the two earliest professional firms in Trinidad, which were structurally bound to their parent firms by the flow of human and financial capital provided by the latter, contemporary international firms are bound to an overseas parent by the flow of intellectual capital which the parent provides in the form of training courses and materials, audit methodologies and technologies, technical publications and other outputs of firm-based accounting research.[14] The relationship can be described as one of dependency because it is the overseas office which produces and supplies all professional accounting knowledge products and the Trinidad member firm simply applies these technologies to the local production site.[15] The technological dependency that characterizes the relationship between local practices and their MAFs parents has two important side effects. One is that it inhibits the emergence of any research or problem-solving capabilities within the Trinidadian firm. The other is that the latter shows an over-reliance on the overseas office for solving domestic matters. For instance one partner, describing his firm's relationship with the Canadian office, stated:

> If we have a problem we call them, if we need to research a problem, we call that office. That's part of the arrangement. (Partner, DT 1995)

This is not a relationship of interdependence, because the converse does not hold true. The local firm is therefore structurally linked to the parent firm by dint of the fact that the only way in which its current menu of services can be delivered is through constant flows of technological inputs from the overseas parent.

The other aspect of technological dependence is the application of inappropriate technologies—a problem which is not unique to manufacturing situations.[16] In the delivery of a professional service such as an audit, differences in size and structures of business organizations, for instance, would demand different approaches to the audit.[17] Thus in a business environment such as T&T's, the import and application of US-based

---

14. A distillation of the seven interviews held with current and past senior partners of four local MAFs suggests that for these firms the singular benefit of membership in these international accounting organizations is the technical support which MAFs offer.

15. In this kind of arrangement it is considered more 'efficient' for all research activity to be centralized in one or a few locations assumed to have a comparative advantage in research and development.

16. For instance, the import of capital intensive technologies by a labour-rich, high-unemployment country may be considered the import of an inappropriate technology.

17. The literature suggests that the demand for audit arises out of four factors: (a) conflict of interest due to separation of ownership and control, (b) complexity,

audit technologies does pose some problems. As a retired senior partner of PW pointed out:

> I think that things [here in Trinidad] got overdone because having worked in New York for a while [I know] that their small clients are organisations like Neal and Massey. So for them [it is impossible] to think about something like Rentokil something as small as that . . . and even that has its own international link. So an independent client of that size does not exist in the thinking of the people who are developing the check-lists. That's where your gap is and it is very difficult to bridge that.[18] (David Earl 1995)

Limited research and problem-solving capabilities of the firm meant that local branches of the MAFs are incapable of devising their own technologies or of making necessary adaptations to imported technologies not necessarily well-suited to local conditions. Even if local firms did have the capability to tailor certain technologies to suit local conditions, to do so would go against the whole philosophy of internationalization. As Lall and Streeteen (1977) point out, the very essence of profiting from international business lies in the ability to apply a given package to different areas with as little costly adaptation as possible. This requirement is even stronger for the MAFs whose selling point is their one-firm image, and the notion that each of their geographically diffuse service outlets will produce a uniform service delivery through strict adherence to set methodologies. Thus tight quality control procedures are exercised by the international office so as to ensure compliance by member firms. In relating his own experience of complying with some of these methodologies and the firm grip exercised from overseas, a retired senior partner of PW noted:

> You've got strings that get pulled from overseas, so you've got to conform to the overseas accounting policies appropriate or not . . . If you accept that the profession developed properly in the metropolitan countries then, yes, Trinidad should follow those rules. If you don't accept that then you have a different story. And if there should be something [midway] that Trinidad should be following, it is more difficult to do it when you've got a big brother pulling your strings. (David Earl 1995)

---

(c) consequence and (d) remoteness. The relative importance of each factor varies from country to country and in turn affects the nature of the audit exercise. Thus in France, where companies have a history of small shareholder membership, separation of ownership and control is minimal and thus conflict of interest does not present as much of a problem as in the UK or US. In Germany, banks have a history of direct investment in industrial enterprises. Thus the problems of remoteness are less important in Germany than they are in the UK.

18. Neal and Massey is the largest conglomerate in T&T and Rentokil T&T is considered a small company.

## The Mutually Supportive Enterprise of Practice and Education in Professional Accountancy

The previous section attempted to reveal the mindset of the individuals who were the undoubted leaders of the T&T profession at a critical juncture in its development. Of particular note are Richard Hobday and John Hunt, two individuals who played formative roles in the development of the early ICATT and who have in different ways left distinctive legacies. At a time when factors of race, colour and ethnicity had a determining influence on an individual's life chances in T&T (Annisette 2003), the career histories of these two leaders could not be further apart. Richard Hobday, white, British and senior partner of the country's oldest, largest and most prestigious practising firm, having qualified in his home country with the ICAEW, at first played no role in the establishment of the ICATT or its predecessor body (Annisette 1999, 2000). As an expatriate British accountant living in T&T he was part of an elite group of practitioners who saw little need for a local professional institute given the built-in market shelter that T&T's caste-based colonial society provided. As I argued earlier, the group of British expatriate accountants resident in colonial T&T could achieve occupational closure without professionalization (Annisette 1999, 112–13). Nonetheless, in 1972 in an attempt to establish some legitimacy for the ICATT amongst the T&T business community, Hobday was approached to take on its leadership and became its president for three years until 1975 (Annisette 2000, 652).[19] John Hunt, on the other hand, was an Afro-Trinidadian who by winning an island scholarship was able to obtain his accountancy qualification with the ICAS at the colonial state's expense. Hunt was the country's first, and for many years only, non-white CA (Annisette 1999, 118). Upon his return to the island in 1964, unable to find employment in any of the established practices by dint of his race and colour (Annisette 2003), Hunt set up a small practising firm whose client base was largely black-owned unincorporated businesses (Annisette 1999, 2003). Hunt—one of the three promoters of the ICATT bill (Annisette 2003, 658) and its vice-president from 1970 to 1973—was a nationalist at heart. Reminiscing about the 1970 establishment of the ICATT, Hunt noted that:

> We did not see ourselves [a]s being a Colonial Institute. In the spirit of independence, what we had intended was an independent institute. (Hunt 1995)

Yet, by the early 1970s, despite their vastly different career trajectories and perspectives, both Hobday and Hunt converged on the view that

19. Unlike the professional accounting institutes in England and her settler colonies, the ICATT was not formed by public accountancy practitioners. It was initiated by government-linked accountants who in one way or the other had been spurned by the white bias of the practising firms and business community (Annisette 1999, 2000, 2003).

surrendering some degree of control of their local practices to US-based MAFs provided them access to what they saw as highly valued accountancy knowledge products centred around standardization. Given that at this time the ICATT was struggling to develop a programme of professional accountancy education and training (Annisette 2000) and had Hobday and Hunt at its helm, the institute's decisions to cede control of this task to the expansionary UK-based ACCA (Annisette 2000) is consistent with the mindset which accepted the idea of accounting standardization around the Anglo-American (private enterprise) accounting model.[20] Thus there was a certain degree of complementarily between the Anglo-American practice-based firm and the ACCA towards this end. As I argued:

> Whereas the Anglo-American firms became the appropriate medium for the world-wide standardisation of accounting practice, the ACCA had an important role in the standardisation of accounting education and training. (Annisette 2000, 650)

As a result the two institutional arms of T&T's accounting constellation were tightly linked to and controlled by overseas institutions. This dual linkage was not perfect. The ACCA as a UK examining body prepared its candidates for the UK regulatory accounting and practice environment. On the other hand the MAFs, though constitutively Anglo-American, had their centre of power located in the US. But, as pointed out elsewhere, there has never been a US accountancy credential comparable to that of the ACCA which could be pursued outside the US (Annisette 2000, 654). In terms of the accounting knowledge products involved (rules, standards and practices) this therefore was not a seamless arrangement. There were some differences between the US and the UK accounting 'worlds'. But this mixed arrangement—a US practice link and a UK educational link—nonetheless bore an uncanny resemblance to T&T's historic and contemporary experience of imperialism in the economic and cultural spheres. Importantly, the fact that these links were created at such a formative stage in the development in the T&T profession guaranteed a path-dependant accounting development consistent with the Anglo-American (private enterprise) accounting model, even though the evolving realities of T&T's economic structure with increasingly widespread state ownership (Annisette 1999, 2000, 2003) might have suggested an alternative accounting model (see, for instance, Hove 1989).

20. Crucially, as indicated in Annisette (1999, 2000), Hunt was one of the founding members of the profession who in the mid-1960s to late 1960s had pioneered the idea of indigenizing professional accountancy training by collaborating with the UWI. Yet by the early 1970s he had bought into the idea of internationalization and no longer seemed to actively push for collaboration with the UWI.

## CONCLUSION

The overall aim of this chapter has been to give a fuller account than previously rendered of the role of the practice link in T&T in the maintenance of empire after formal independence. The chapter has attempted to show how the dependent links established in the colonial period between local practising firms and overseas firms have intensified rather than diminished in the post-colonial period. It has revealed the mindset that has encouraged the intensification of these links and highlighted some of the consequences of that mindset. For a number of thinkers on the subject, colonialism and imperialism are more than economic and political processes. For them it also involves the subjugation of minds (Nandy 1983; Fanon 1967). In other words, it is also a mental/psychological/cognitive process. To the extent that in 1995 T&T was 'as dependent on metropolitan actors for guidance, inspiration and solutions to local accounting matters as it was during the period of formal British colonialism' (Annisette 2000, 654), then from a cognitive standpoint in 1995, some 33 years after the country's independence from Great Britain, very little had changed.

By focusing on the role of the practice link in T&T in the enterprise of maintaining empire, this chapter has additionally pointed to a potentially fruitful way of thinking about the MAFs and theorizing about their increasing dominance in the organization of worldwide accountancy. That professional accounting practice and professional accounting education were mutually supportive in this particular episode in the development of the accounting profession in T&T might be reflective of what was then the beginning of another crucial transformation in the configuration of accountancy. Numerous authors have expressed a concern about the distant relationship between accounting academia and accounting practice which for them manifests itself in a much-lamented the gap between accounting theory and accounting practice (e.g., Hopwood and Bromwich 1984; Zeff 1989; Scapens 1994; Abdel-Khalik 1981; Lee 1989). Indeed, it seems to be the case that with respect to accountancy, the practice arm and the academic arm have increasingly departed in their respective notions of what constitutes accounting knowledge and, in some sites, who is an accountant. Thus what has come to constitute academic accounting research (knowledge) has increasingly moved away from the concerns of accounting practice, and academic accountants are increasingly less likely to have professional accounting experience or qualifications (Annisette and Kirkham 2007, 20). What is at stake here is not just the gap between theory and practice *per se*; also at issue is the manifestation of this gap in distinctive modes of professional education. It would therefore appear that, certainly in terms of knowledge base, the practice arm and the academic arm of accountancy occupy vastly different disciplinary spaces and their respective boundaries have moved further apart rather than narrowed over time. In short, the practice world of accountancy and the academic world of accountancy might well be contemporarily conceived of as two different professions. As the major contributor to the accountancy standardization movement in the late 1960s and early 1970s, MAFs came to usurp the traditional role of the university as producer and diffuser of professionally relevant (practice-based) accountancy knowledge. This is particularly so given accounting academics' increasing interest in abstraction which does not result in forms of knowledge that MAFs can immediately use. Their relative dominance in the highest-status professional education and certification bodies has in turn served to ensure that they retain control over the certification of what constitutes professional accountancy knowledge and who can claim to be a professionally qualified accountant. And thus, professional accountancy educational and certification bodies perhaps quite unlike educational and certification bodies of other occupational groups (e.g., doctors, lawyers—see Geddes 1995) can play a far more direct role in the strategic projects of elite practitioners and their practice-based organizations.

## REFERENCES

Abdel-Khalik, A.R. (1981). 'How academic research should be restructured for impact'. In *The Impact of Accounting Research on Policy and Practice: Proceedings of the Arthur Young Professors' Round Table*, ed. J.W. Buckley. Reston, Virginia: The Council of Arthur Young Professors.

Annisette, M. (1999) 'Importing accounting: The case of Trinidad and Tobago'. *Accounting, Business & Financial History* 9:103–33.

———. (2000) 'Imperialism and the professions: The education and certification of accountants in Trinidad and Tobago'. *Accounting, Organizations and Society* 25:631–59.

———. (2003) 'The colour of accountancy: Examining the salience of race in a professionalisation project'. *Accounting, Organizations and Society* 28:639–74.

Annisette, M., and Kirkham, L. (2007) 'The advantages of separateness explaining the unusual profession–university link in English chartered accountancy'. *Critical Perspectives on Accounting* 18:1–30.

Beckford, G. (1972) *Persistent Poverty: Underdevelopment in Plantation Economies of the Third World*. New York: Oxford University Press.

Benson, H. (1976) 'The story of international accounting standards'. *Accountancy* 87:34–39.

Best, L. (1968) 'Outline of a model of pure plantation economy'. *Social and Economic Studies* 17:35–42.

Boodhoo, K. (1972) 'External influences on the behaviour of a small state: Penetration of the Trinidad political system'. Unpublished PhD thesis, University of the West Indies.

Briston, R. and Kedslie, M. (1997) 'The internationalization of professional accounting: The role of the examination exporting bodies'. *Accounting, Business & Financial History* 7:175–94.

Carrington, E. (1967) 'The post-war political economy of Trinidad and Tobago'. *New World Quarterly* 4:45–66.

Craig, S. (1982) 'Background to the 1970 confrontation in Trinidad and Tobago'. In *Contemporary Caribbean: A Sociological Reader*, ed. S. Craig. Trinidad: College Press.

Daniels, P., Thrift, N., and Leyshon, A. (1989) 'Internationalisation of professional producer services: Accountancy conglomerates'. In *Multinational Service Firms*, ed. P. Enderwick. London: Routledge.

Demsetz, H. (1973) *The Market Concentration Doctrine*. Washington, DC: American Enterprise Institute-Hoover Institute on War, Revolution and Peace.

Fanon, F. (1967) *Black Skin, White Masks*. Trans. C.L. Markmann. New York: Grove Press.

Fayerweather, J. (1978) *International Business Strategy and Administration*. Cambridge, MA: Ballinger.

Gallagher, J., and Robinson, R. (1953) 'The imperialism of free trade'. *Economic History Review* 6:1–15.

Geddes, S.B. (1995) 'The development of accountancy education, training and research in England: A study of the relationships between professional education and training, academic education and research, and professional practice in English chartered accountancy'. Unpublished PhD thesis, University of Manchester.

Gilpin, R. (1975) *US Power and the Multinational Corporation: The Political Economy of Foreign Direct Investment*. New York: Basic Books Inc.

Hobday R. (1995) Interviewed by author, December, Port of Spain, Trinidad.

Hopwood A.G., and Bromwich M. (1984) 'Accounting research in the UK'. In *European Contributions to Accounting Research: The Achievements of the Last Decade*, ed. A.G. Hopwood and H. Schreuder. Amsterdam: V.U. Uitgeverij/Free University Press.

Hove, M. (1989) 'The inappropriateness of international standards in less developed countries: The case of international accounting standard number 24—related parties disclosures concerning transfer prices'. *International Journal of Accounting Education and Research* 24:165–79.

———. (1990) 'The Anglo-American influence on international accounting standards'. In *Research in Third World Accounting*, ed. R.S.O. Wallace, J. Samuels and R. Briston. London: JAI Press.

HRC Associates. (1995) *Top 50 Companies in Trinidad and Tobago*. Port of Spain: HRC Associates.

Hunt J. (1995) Interviewed by author, December, Port of Spain, Trinidad.

Institute of Chartered Accountants of Trinidad and Tobago. (1980) *The ICAN: Newsletter of the Institute of Chartered Accountants of Trinidad and Tobago*. Port of Spain, Trinidad: ICATT.

Johnson, H. (1975) 'Oil, Imperialism and the Trinidad Disturbances, 1937.' *Journal of Imperial and Commonwealth History* 4: 29–54.

Johnson, T.J., and Caygill, M. (1971) 'The development of accounting links in the commonwealth'. *Accounting and Business Research* (Spring): 155–73.

Krouse, C.G. (1990) *Theory of Industrial Economics*. London: Basil Blackwell.

Kubin, K. (1975) 'The international profession of accountancy'. in *Collected Papers of the American Accounting Association, Annual Meeting*, ed. American Accounting Association.

Lall, S., and Streeteen, P. (1977) *Foreign Investment, Transnationals, and Developing Countries*. Boulder, CO: Westview Press.

Lee T. (1989) 'Education, practice and research in accounting: Gaps, closed loops, bridges and magic accounting'. *Accounting and Business Research* 75:237–53.

Lowe, A., and Tinker, T. (1977) 'Siting the accounting problematic: Towards an intellectual emancipation of accounting'. *Journal of Business Finance & Accounting* 4:263–76.

Martinez, P (1995) Interviewed by author, December, Port of Spain, Trinidad.

McIntyre, A., and Watson, B. (1970) *Studies in Foreign Investment in the Commonwealth Caribbean, Vol.1. Trinidad and Tobago*. Mona: Institute of Social and Economics Research.

Ministry of Energy and Natural Resources. (1984) *Information on the Petroleum Industry of Trinidad and Tobago*. Port of Spain: Government Printery.

Moizer, P., and Turley, S. (1987) 'Surrogates for audit fees in concentration studies'. *Auditing: A Journal of Practice & Theory* 7:118–23.

Mommsen, W. (1986) 'The end of empire and the continuity of imperialism'. In *Imperialism and After: Continuities and Discontinuities*, ed. W. Mommsen and J. Osterhammel. London: Allen and Unwin.

Nandy, A. (1983) *The Intimate Enemy: Loss and Recovery of Self under Colonialism*. New Delhi: Oxford University Press.

Nobes, C., and Parker, B. (1979) 'Landmarks in accounting history'. *Accountancy* (June): 37–42.

Pantin, D. (1980) 'The plantation economy model and the Caribbean'. *IDS Bulletin* 12:17–23.

Polychroniou, C., and Targ, H.R. (1992) 'Internationalization of capital and U.S. imperial state policy: A Marxist analysis of U.S. struggles for global hegemony'. In *Perspectives and Issues in International Political Economy*, ed. C. Polychroniou and H.R. Targ. Connecticut: Praeger.

Rothenberg, J., and Wishner, A. (1976) 'A focus on Trinidad'. *NACLA's Latin America and Empire Report*, 14–30.

Samuels, J.M., and Piper, A.G. (1985) *International Accounting: A Survey*. London: Croom Helm.

Scapens, R.W. (1994) 'Never mind the gap: Towards an institutional perspective of management accounting practices'. *Management Accounting Research* 5:302–21.

Smith, G. (1995) Interviewed by author, December, Port of Spain, Trinidad.

Smith, L.S. (ed.) (1950) *Trinidad—Who, What, Why: Public Life, Business, People and Sport*. Port of Spain: Trinidad Publishers.

Stamp, E. (1969) 'Auditing the auditors.' *The Times*, 11 September: 25.

Stamp, E., and Marley, C. (1970) *Accounting Principles and the City Code: The Case for Reform*. London: Butterworths.

Wesseling, H. (1986) 'Imperialism and empire'. In *Imperialism and After: Continuities and Discontinuities*, ed. W. Mommsen and J. Osterhammel. London: Allen and Unwin.

Wootton, C.W., Wolk, C.M., and Normand C. (2003) 'An historical perspective on mergers and acquisitions by major US accounting firms'. *Accounting History* 8:25–60.

Zeff, S. (1972) *Forging Accounting Principles in Five Countries: A History and An Analysis of Trends*. Champaign, IL: Stripes Publishing Company.

———. (1989) 'Recent trends in accounting education and research in the USA: Some implications for UK academics'. *British Accounting Review* 21:159–76.

# 9 The Influence of Empire on the Establishment of the Institute of Chartered Accountants of India After Independence

*Shraddha Verma*

## INTRODUCTION

India was a formal British colony from 1858 to 1947, and during this period British imperial policy significantly impacted upon India and her population.[1] The achievement of political independence in 1947 heralded the implementation of new Indian social, political, legal and economic systems. Although there was little direct involvement by Britain once the transfer of power had been completed, an indirect British influence remained, exemplified by the retention of many British institutions such as the parliamentary system and the legal system, suggesting that British models functioned as templates for India even after the cessation of formal empire.

Nehru, the first Indian prime minister, a Western-educated Fabian socialist influenced by central planning in Russia, introduced a mixed economy to India, in which there was a role for both private and public enterprise and in which socialist ideals operated within a secular democracy. The key elements of the mixed economic system included central planning of the economy, the development of a large public sector, control and licensing of private enterprise, price control within the private sector, the use of import substituting policies, the introduction of a predominantly public financial sector with nationalized banking and insurance, state control of foreign investment, protective tariffs and prohibition of imports. These were implemented using legislation promulgated by Parliament, government resolutions and ordinances and government bodies (Panikkar 1964; Spear 1978; Kumar 1982; Kulke and Rothermund 1990; Rothermund 1993; Brass 1994; Brown 1994).

This early period of independence (1949–1955) was also an important time for the accounting profession in India with the establishment of the Institute of Chartered Accountants of India (ICAI), an institution that is still important in the regulation of accounting today. This chapter sets out to explore the remnant influence of imperialism on the establishment of the ICAI in post-independence India. It will focus on the involvement of the

1. Within this context, imperialism refers to 'the practice, the theory and the attitudes of a dominating metropolitan centre ruling a distant territory' (Said 1993, 8).

state in the development of the profession, credentialism and the importance of the 'chartered accountant' ('CA') designation, mutual recognition and reciprocity. In addition, the enduring impact of imperial links on the policy decisions of both the Indian accounting profession and the new Indian government are highlighted.

In the context of historical studies of accounting professions in post-colonial states, India is important for several reasons. It was hugely important for Britain in trading terms, providing many natural resources to Britain as well as becoming an important market for British goods, for example, cotton, spinning machines, iron and steel (Tomlinson 1978, 1993; Misra 1999). In addition, it was important to Britain in times of crisis; for example, providing military support to Britain during the two world wars. It was also one of the first countries to gain independence from Britain after the Second World War, and the path of professionalization here exhibited some interesting features, falling between the professionalization models commonly found in the settler and non-settler post-colonial states. Today, India is the largest secular democracy in the world and is becoming increasingly important in economic terms.

Kapadia, the first ICAI president, undertook a major historical study of the professionalization of accounting in India in 1972. This chapter extends the work of Kapadia and draws from a more recent comprehensive study (Verma 2000) of the professionalization process in India to identify the factors influencing the establishment of the ICAI. The chapter is organized into three time periods which cover three very different stages in the development of the ICAI: in the pre-1945 period we see the antecedents to the establishment of the ICAI; between 1946 and 1949 we see the establishment of the ICAI; and in the period 1949–1955 we see the early operation of the institute and the involvement of government in the activities of the ICAI post-independence.

## PRE-1945—THE ANTECEDENTS TO THE ESTABLISHMENT OF THE ICAI

The establishment of the ICAI in 1949 can be traced to events in the period before independence. The ideal of an autonomous accounting profession had been inherited from the colonial period and the groundwork for such a profession, based on the UK model, had been put in place with the establishment of the Indian Accountancy Board (IAB) in 1932, under the Companies (Amendment) Bill 1930. The role of the IAB was to advise the governor-general on all matters of administration relating to accountancy and auditing and to assist him in maintaining the standards of qualification and conduct of persons enrolled on the register of accountants (*Company Law Amendment Bill*, 1930), on which all auditors in India had been required to register since 1913. These accountants were known as 'registered accountants'. In addition to Indian accountants, members of the Institute of Chartered Accountants in England and Wales (ICAEW), the Society of Incorporated Accountants and Auditors, the Society of Accountants in Edinburgh (SAE), the Institute of Accountants and Actuaries in Glasgow (IAAG), the Society of Accountants in Aberdeen (SAA) and the Institute of Chartered Accountants of Ireland were recognized to audit company accounts in India (*Gazette of India*, 1914).

The IAB was chaired by a British representative, very much in line with British imperial practices whereby Indians were involved in key institutions but these were led by Britons. The IAB continued in existence until 1949 and was disbanded when the ICAI was formed. The minutes of the IAB are not available; however, summaries provided by Kapadia identify that the issues discussed by the IAB included regional and religious representation, requirements for admission onto a national register of accountants and the introduction of elections for membership of the IAB. Initially the members of the IAB were senior British and Indian accountants nominated by the government but later included both nominated members and members who were elected by those included on the register of accountants, with Indian representation increasing in the 1940s.

In addition to its regulatory role, the IAB was set up to advise the British government on all issues relating to accounting and auditing, including the training and examining of accountants. Before the existence of the IAB, the opportunities that existed for the training of Indian accountants included a Government Diploma in Accounting (GDA) run by the Bombay Government and a specialist accounting course run by Sydenham College, Bombay (Kapadia 1972). The IAB phased these qualifications out and introduced its own accounting examinations for admittance onto the register of accountants as accounting was perceived to be a suitable profession for Indians.

At the IAB's fifth meeting held on 11 December 1936:

> Another important issue discussed was with regard to the devising of ways and means for reducing unemployment amongst the educated middle classes. There was a feeling that something might be done in the way of development of opportunity of employment in accountancy. (Kapadia 1972, 96)

Pre-independence, the Indian members of the IAB had hoped to develop an indigenous accounting profession headed by an autonomous national institute very much along the lines of the CAs' bodies which had emerged in self-governing settler states. This was discussed by the IAB in several meetings. For example, in the second meeting of the IAB on 12 December 1933:

> With regard to the suggestion of elective principle, the Chairman observed that when the board was first constituted, the idea was that after

> some time there would be an autonomous body which would regulate its affairs without the intervention of Government and it would be granted something in the nature of a charter on which it could work. (Kapadia 1972, 90–91)

At the board's seventh meeting, held on 15 December 1938:

> Sir Shapoorji Billimoria recalled that when the accountancy board came into existence, the idea was that in the course of time the board should apply to His Majesty's Government for a charter. (Kapadia 1972, 103–4)

At its eighth meeting, held on 11–12 December 1939:

> Mr Sodhbans . . . added that he wanted Chartered Accountants of India in the same manner as Chartered Accountants of Australia and Chartered Accountants of South Africa. . . .
>
> One of the important issues discussed at this meeting was the designation of accountants and the suggestion for consideration was that they should adopt the designation of Chartered Accountant. (Kapadia 1972, 124)

The emergence of an autonomous national accounting institute was, however, delayed—the time never seemed quite right for such a development. For example, the first chairman, the Honourable Mr. J.A. Woodhead, stated at the first informal IAB meeting on 12–13 May 1931 that 'it had been generally agreed that the formation of an autonomous body for accountants to control its own members was not possible for the time being' (Kapadia 1972, 81).

The issue of designation was also discussed at board's eighth meeting in December 1939:

> Finally the Board decided that the Government should be requested to secure by such means as are lawful and proper the title of Chartered Accountants for Registered Accountants in India. The chairman, however, made it clear that the resolution as passed by the Board was to be recorded as a mere desire of the members and so far as the views of the Government of India were concerned, there was a complete and entire reservation. (Kapadia 1972, 124–25)

Delay was also evident at IAB's 13th meeting, held on 28 February 1946, at which it:

> [gave] consideration to a proposal to the effect that an ad hoc committee be constituted to draft the constitution of the Board as an autonomous body. The chairman suggested that it would not be a proper

> to tie down the hands of the Government by a resolution of this kind. (Kapadia 1972, 140)

No reasons are given for these delays, but it may have been the case that accounting issues were not a priority at this time when British policy was focused on other issues such as the war and India's call for independence. There is some evidence that race may have been a contributing factor in this delay. Other authors have identified the issue of race in professionalization and Poullaos (2009), in particular, explored the reluctance of British accounting institutes to admit non-British members to their institutes in the 1920s. Misra (1999), too, has commented on the reluctance of British managing agencies to involve Indians in their businesses and it may be speculated that British accountants and companies were possibly averse to being regulated by an Indian-led accounting profession. However, Indians were permitted to enter the profession and Kapadia (1972, 110) suggests that race was not an issue within the board at the time as:

> the Board during its whole period of existence had never shown any tendency to divide on racial lines, that the European members had worked on the Board for the good of the profession as a whole and that their absence would inevitably react adversely on the prestige which the Board had built up for itself.

Although the ideal of having a national autonomous accounting institute had been accepted by the Indian accountants on the IAB, one had not been established in India at independence. There is evidence that professional accounting associations were in existence in the colonial period, albeit at the regional level (Kapadia 1972),[2] and many of these local associations were actively involved in forwarding suggestions to the IAB with regard to the establishment and operation of the IAB throughout the 1930s (ibid.). The calls for an autonomous chartered accounting profession in India had been present throughout the life of the IAB and became stronger in the 1940s. By 1946 in-depth discussions were being held more frequently by the IAB (ibid.). The next section examines developments in the period from 1946 to 1949, during which the ICAI was established.

## 1946 TO 1949—THE ESTABLISHMENT OF THE ICAI

In the period from 1946 to 1949, the Indian members of the IAB worked to establish an accounting profession based on the ICAEW model. There

2. For example: The Society of Registered Accountants, Calcutta; The Incorporated Accountants Bengal and Districts Society, Calcutta; The Indian Society of Accountants and Auditors, Bombay; The Society of Registered Accountants in Northern India, Lahore; The Society of Auditors, Madras.

seems to have been little or no direct involvement by the British government in the development of the ICAI, although the evidence shows that the Indian accountants on the IAB did aspire to the British model of professionalization, suggesting perhaps a strong indirect influence (Kapadia 1972).

By 1946, after many years of anti-imperial feeling in the country, there was an acceptance by the British of the end of imperial rule and key issues under negotiation and debate included: how independence was to be achieved, how the newly independent India would be structured and how the concerns and wishes of the leaders of the Hindus and the Muslims could be accommodated (Spear 1978; Kulke and Rothermund 1990; Misra 1999). Once independence from Britain had been achieved, it was not uncommon for British systems, such as the political and legal systems, to be retained and run by Indians. Other systems were retained but modified, for example, in relation to the economy, a mixed economic system developed. This was also seen in the development of the accounting profession with the British model of professionalization being adapted by the Indian government. The Ministry of Commerce representative on the IAB was more cautious than the Indian accountants on the Board about the establishment of a national autonomous accounting institute. He wanted to consider carefully the question of whether to set up an accounting institute and what form this institute should take if established. At the 14th meeting of IAB (7 October 1946), the Minister of Commerce observed that:

> The accountants were destined to play a vital role in the future economic development of the country. As regards the aspirations of the profession to manage its own affairs through an autonomous body, he said that the formation of a body was not an easy task. The matter was under active consideration and any suggestions made by the Board would receive its fullest consideration. (Kapadia 1972, 140–41)

The members of the IAB continued to argue their case to members of parliament, government ministers and government officials, and in 1948 persuaded the Ministry of Commerce to agree to the establishment of an accounting institute to head the Indian accounting profession. The Indian accountants on the IAB were, therefore, instrumental in the formation of the ICAI, but it was clear that they would not be able to proceed without the authorization and approval of the government.

One of the main factors that persuaded the government to support the development of an accounting profession was the perception that accounting was an important tool for economic development (*Company Law Committee Report*, 1952). In particular, the key aims of the government at independence included rapid economic growth and social development leading to a fairer distribution of wealth amongst the population. The perception held at this time was that accounting could help facilitate both of these aims by allowing for the provision of comparable information across the corporate sector which would facilitate decision-making. It was also thought that the provision of information within the accounting system might help encourage the private sector to act in ways congruent to the government's aims, rather than just for private gain, and that a stronger audit framework would help to monitor the actions of directors and perhaps curb abuses within the corporate sector. Finally, it was also assumed that accounting information might prove to be useful for national central economic planning purposes (*Parliamentary Committee Report on the Chartered Accountants Bill*, 1948; *Company Law Committee Report*, 1952; *Company Law [Amendment] Committee Report*, 1957).

The Ministry of Commerce did not, however, necessarily favour the organization of the profession along the lines proposed by the IAB. The ministry proposed instead a quite different institutional framework: that of an accounting institute established under statutory legislation promulgated by Parliament, with government and corporate sector representation on the council set up to head the institute. No mention of other systems of accounting, such as the development of a uniform chart of accounts, seems to have been made despite the perceived importance of accounting to the centrally planned economy, perhaps an indication of the continuing strong links with Britain post-independence and a reflection of India's colonial inheritance.

The British accounting model, in its original format, was not considered to be an appropriate model in the social and political environment of India at this time, although it did provide a starting blueprint. Strong government involvement characterized all areas of political, economic and social life and this was evident in areas such as corporate regulation, economic planning and social affairs in terms of government ordinances, statutes and the involvement of government bodies. The economy was highly planned with the implementation of five-year plans. As a consequence, an autonomous profession was not a possibility at this juncture and the practice of accountants joining together to form a self-regulating professional body and closing off opportunities to non-members was not seen in India. Instead, the ICAI was set up by legislative enactment with direct government involvement in both its formation and subsequent operation. In short, when constituted, the ICAI did not reflect the imperial accountancy ideal promoted by the Indian accountants. Local concerns, structures and processes, as interpreted by the post-independence government, amended the structure of the Indian accounting profession to one more congruent with the social, legal, economic and political context of India. The government's recasting also reflected the anti-imperial feeling in the country: its preference for a highly centralized and planned economy was a response to the imperial experience, for example, the supposedly damaging effect of British importers on the Indian textile industry, land revenue policy and the rupee exchange rate policy (Misra 1999, 136). Nevertheless, the accountants managed to persuade the Indian government of their importance, perhaps reflecting the long tradition of business in India, links between business and the freedom movement and the existence of the IAB, which promoted the possible benefits of accounting to the Indian economy.

In 1948, the state took control of the process for the establishment of the ICAI. The Ministry of Commerce prepared a memorandum on a scheme for an association of accountants in India and requested feedback on its ideas, in particular on what the name of the institute should be and on whether foreign qualifications should be recognised (Kapadia 1972). The ministry also required the IAB to set up an expert committee to review the proposed scheme, devised its terms of reference and required its recommendations to be approved by the ministry. The terms of reference were to examine the tentative scheme for an association of accountants and to indicate whether the institute could be set up by amendments to existing laws or whether new legislation was necessary. The expert committee was set up on 1 May 1948 by the IAB and approved by the Ministry of Commerce on 13 May 1948 (Kapadia 1972).

In carrying out its role the expert committee conducted a detailed study of the constitutions of accounting associations and accountants outside India. In particular, they studied the workings of the ICAEW in the UK and the Society of Certified Public Accountants of New York (Kapadia 1972; Editorials 1952–1960). The influence of empire on the development of the ICAI is seen in this review process with frequent referral back to the British accounting institutes as appropriate and ideal models to follow in India.

The expert committee set up by the IAB submitted their report on the scheme proposed by the Ministry of Commerce together with a draft of legislation in July 1948. The main recommendations were that a professional accounting institute, the ICAI, should be set up by a special act of Parliament—a Chartered Accountants Act. The members of the institute would initially be Indian registered accountants renamed as CAs. The role of the ICAI would be to set entry examinations, regulate the training of its members, regulate the certificates of practice given to its members and exercise disciplinary procedures with respect to members. The affairs of the ICAI would be managed by a council consisting of 15 elected representatives, one nominated representative of the corporate sector and three nominated representatives of central government. The ICAI council and the accounting profession would be completely autonomous, free of the control of the central government, except in a small number of matters which would be agreed and specified in the Chartered Accountants Act.

During this period, the Indian accountants tried to restrict outside involvement in the institute and tried to minimize the perceived adverse effects of the institutional form that had been imposed on them. Their aim was to retain as much control over the admission, educational and disciplinary requirements of accountants as was possible in the socio-economic and political climate of India at this time. For example, they obtained an informal agreement that government involvement in the new institute would be kept to a minimum and that it was not the government's intention to be involved in the day-to-day operation of the new institute. These understandings were informal in that they were not written into statute but discussed between the Indian accountants on the IAB and the Ministry of Commerce and in parliamentary debates. For example, the Honourable Mr. K.C. Neogy (Minister for Finance and Commerce) confirmed in his address to the institute on its inauguration that the ICAI council 'could have the privilege of serving the profession subject to minimum possible control of Government' (Kapadia 1972, 231).

The Ministry of Commerce then prepared a circular on the proposals to set up the ICAI and circulated this to all government departments. At this stage, the Ministry of Finance, in particular the Central Bureau of Direct Taxes (CBDT) within the Ministry of Finance, amended the disciplinary process of the ICAI, making it subject to high court approval. The Chartered Accountants Act 1949 was then promulgated through the parliamentary system and the ICAI was eventually formed.

Interestingly, the path of professionalization in India shows aspects of professionalization in both settler and non-settler colonial states. In common with other non-settler states, an Indian-led national accounting institute was not in existence at independence, but rather developed post-independence. Additionally, the importance of the state and the use of legislation in the development of the accounting profession were seen in the professionalization process in India, alongside other non-settler colonies (Annisette 1999, 2000, 2003; Susela 1999; Yapa 1999; Uche 2002; Bakre 2005, 2006; Sian 2006, 2007; Verma and Gray 2006, 2009). However, professionalization in India also exhibits some commonalities with professionalization in settler states, where accounting professions emerged in the late nineteenth and early twentieth centuries (Lee 1997; Chua and Poullaos 1998, 2002; Carnegie and Parker 1999; Carnegie and Edwards 2001; Neu and Cameron 2006). Some local professional associations did emerge in India in the colonial period, as accounting was seen as a profession suitable for Indians by the British government (*Companies Amendment Act*, 1930). This is in direct contrast to the treatment of indigenous populations in other non-settler states before independence where accountancy was not deemed suitable for the local population and professionalization only commenced post-independence (Annisette 2000, 2003; Sian 2006). The entrance of suitably qualified indigenous accountants to the profession in India is a practice not observed in other non-settler states that perhaps reflected a greater respect for local Indian culture and business traditions. The development of accountancy for Indians may also have arisen as part of the response by the colonial government to the strong opposition to colonization in India and their attempts to pacify the Indian political elite and the population at large as a means of averting rebellion and maintaining its hold over the colony. The British achieved this through constitutional reform to allow Indians some say in the running of their country and by trying to increase the representation of Indians in business, for example, within managing agency firms although this had limited success (Tomlinson 1978, 1993; Misra 1999). Imperialism nevertheless continued to cast a shadow over the development of accountancy in India even after independence had been negotiated and was particularly in evidence in the ensuing debates about credentialism and mutual recognition, to which we now turn.

## Credentialism and the Importance of the 'Chartered' Designation

As is evident in other ex-colonial cases, in India the name of the institute became a critical issue in the formation stage of the ICAI. Although the IAB had suggested that the name of the institute might be 'The Institute of Chartered Accountants of India', the Ministry of Commerce aired concerns about the use of the 'chartered' designation. They argued that this might raise some problems with the British accounting profession, given the reaction of the ICAEW to attempts to appropriate the designation elsewhere in the empire (Chua and Poullaos 2002; see also Chapter 2 of this volume). Further, following consultation with the Ministry of Justice, the Ministry of Commerce also contended that the use of the term 'charter' required royal assent:

> Registered Accountants should not be designated as Chartered Accountants. In that case they would be liable to be sued for injunction and damages for "passing off" by the Society of Chartered Accountants . . . Moreover a Charter can only be granted by the Crown. (Ministry of Law note, cited in Kapadia 1972, 215)

In this case, the Indian government did not wish to act in a way which might adversely affect its relationship with British trade institutions, in particular the UK Board of Trade. The Ministry of Commerce was supported by some CAs who had qualified with the ICAEW (either British accountants or Indians who had qualified in the UK). They raised objections to the use of the term 'CA' by the proposed institute, arguing that this might cause confusion as to which institute accountants had qualified with. The British qualified Indian accountants wished to be distinguished from accountants qualified in India as they expected that they would have higher status and hence gain more work than Indian qualified accountants, indicating that the notion of 'British is best' was still prevalent in India at this time (Kapadia 1972; *Indian Parliamentary Debates on the Chartered Accountants Bill*, 1948). These arguments indicate that at least some of the accounting hierarchies within India were based on membership of British chartered accounting bodies and provided an impetus for the Indian accountants to fight for the title of ICAI for their accounting institute.

The expert committee debated the issue of the name, and reached a consensus that they would prefer the designation 'chartered', although this was not unanimous since some members (those who had qualified with British chartered bodies) were of the view that the use of 'chartered' was not appropriate as it was associated with British chartered institutes. Ultimately, the IAB was able to successfully argue that the name 'Institute of Chartered Accountants of India' was appropriate and that no confusion would arise from its use (Kapadia 1972).

The name was of great importance to the IAB due to the perception of quality, prestige and status that had become associated with the term during the colonial period as well as the preference for audit work to be carried out by CAs in this period. Any other designation, in the IAB's opinion, would signal a lower-status profession and was therefore undesirable:

> Some members of the expert committee pointed out that some Accountants with foreign qualifications practising in India were using the term 'Chartered Accountants' for creating the impression that persons who were chartered accountants were better qualified than Indian Registered Accountants. They felt that in order to counter the impression already created in the public minds about the word chartered, Indian accountants should also be called chartered accountants. (Kapadia 1972, 216)

The importance of the title to the Indian accounting institute is perhaps indicative of the continuing imperial influence over India after independence. It may also have been an attempt by the Indian government to create parity between those qualified in India and those holding British qualifications in order to avoid the creation of a tiered profession.

At the request of the IAB, the Ministry of Commerce obtained further advice from the Ministry of Justice, who advised that the proposed accounting institute could be set up under a parliamentary charter.

> The only, but to my mind final objection to designating all practising accountants in this country as 'chartered accountants' is not that the Dominion Parliament is incompetent to make a law to that effect—it can certainly provide that for the purposes of a particular Act a donkey may be deemed to be a horse—but that the expression 'chartered accountants' is admittedly understood by the public to mean those accountants who are members of one of the three Institutes of Chartered Accountants in Great Britain and Ireland, and it would, therefore be grossly improper to perpetrate a species of deception on the public by giving other accountants the same designation. (Ministry of Law note, cited in Kapadia 1972, 217)

The determined defence of the 'chartered' designation by the ICAEW and the rights to its use elsewhere in the empire have been highlighted already (Chapter 2, this volume). In India, references to the superiority of the British chartered institutes were rife in the debates on the professionalization process. However, it is not clear whether, in India, the defence was promulgated by the ICAEW directly or by the resident British CAs.

Even though the Ministry of Justice was strongly against the use of the term 'CA' for the Indian accounting institute, they confirmed that its use was legal. Thus the Ministry of Commerce authorized the accounting institute in India to use the title 'chartered' on the following grounds:

> 1. I respectfully submit that the use of the term 'chartered' is not so exclusive as stated . . . Institutes of Chartered Accountants exist in other parts of the British Dominions, notably in Canada, and not in all other cases have such Institutes been incorporated by Royal charter . . .
> 2. . . . the question of calling registered accountants in this country by the name chartered accountants was discussed in detail in the late Indian Legislative Assembly on 5th and 6th October 1936 . . . It would be clear from these speeches that even then it was contemplated to create by means of a statute an autonomous body of accountants and that the members of that body should be designated as chartered accountants. It was made clear by several members of the Opposition in the then Legislative assembly that there was no fraud or deception on the public in designation members of the profession by the term Chartered Accountants.
>
> In view of the fact that there is no insuperable legal objection in using the term 'Chartered Accountants', that precedent exist in other parts of her Majesty's Dominions where accountants are designated by this term by statute and not by Royal Charter and that it was contemplated as early as 1936 that when an autonomous body of accountants was brought into existence, such accountants should be designated as Chartered Accountants, I submit, with due deference to the Ministry of Law, that we may adopt the term 'Chartered Accountants' for designating the members of the profession in this country. (Ministry of Commerce note, cited in Kapadia 1972, 219)

It was of great importance to both the expert committee and the Ministry of Commerce that the term had been used by dominions such as Australia, Canada and South Africa and the Ministry of Commerce was finally persuaded to accept the 'Institute of Chartered Accountants of India' as the name of the proposed institute.

## Mutual Recognition and Reciprocity

The issue of mutual recognition and reciprocity was perhaps the most contentious issue faced by the Indian accounting profession in this period. The Indian accountants on the IAB were keen that the proposed ICAI should be recognized by the ICAEW and other foreign professional accounting bodies on a mutual recognition basis. The Ministry of Commerce was keen for the ICAI to continue to recognize foreign professional accounting bodies, in particular the ICAEW, without any conditions attached and put pressure on the expert committee to include provisions to recognize foreign qualified accountants, in particular British CAs, with no reciprocity requirement. Such action was perceived as important for their relationship with the UK trade authorities, in particular with the Board of Trade (Kapadia 1972).

The Indian members of the ICAI rather reluctantly included recognition provisions in their scheme which did not specifically require mutual recognition. However, they also included a provision that stated that the ICAI would recognize accountants qualified with foreign qualifications but that this would usually be on a reciprocal basis. This was acceptable to the Ministry of Commerce at this stage and became part of the Chartered Accountants Act. However, the issue continued to be contentious once the ICAI had been established and the next section examines this in greater depth, in the period from 1949 to 1955.

## 1949–1955—The Operation of the ICAI in its Early Years

The ICAI gained government support in its early years (Editorials 1952–1960; Kapadia 1972) as well as attaining a monopoly over audit work, as the Chartered Accountants Act specified that auditors had to be members of the ICAI. ICAI members were also involved in income tax, cost accounting and government accounting work (*Indian Parliamentary Debates on the Chartered Accountants Bill*, 1948; *Indian Parliamentary Debates on the Chartered Accountants [Amendment] Bill*, 1955). However, the ICAI still needed to persuade the government and the wider community of their expertise and credentials in relation to accounting. In particular, they wanted to demonstrate to the government, and wider interest groups, that the ICAI was indeed the leader of a 'reputable profession' with strong procedures and processes which regulated their members effectively. The reasons for this were twofold: firstly, the ICAI sought to pre-empt any undue interference by the government in their affairs, and secondly, it wanted to prevent the development of rival professional accounting institutes. To some extent, this was achieved externally through close interaction and liaison with the relevant government departments and internally through the development of robust internal controls and procedures. In relation to its own internal operation, the ICAI worked to establish a strong, competent secretariat and established processes to deal with examinations, education, professional ethics and discipline (Editorials 1952–1960; Kapadia 1972). The Chartered Accountants Act identified those accountants who were eligible to become members of the ICAI when it was formed and had conferred upon the ICAI the authority to establish entrance criteria for post-formation membership. At its inception, all registered accountants were eligible to become members of the ICAI along with members of other accounting societies such as the Association of Accountants (whose members held the GDA) and those who held degrees in commerce from Indian universities (subject to fulfilling practical training requirements).

The entrance requirements for new members were similar to those of the ICAEW and included having to pass a series of professional examinations and complete articles with a CA to gain practical experience. Unlike other developing countries (Briston and Kedslie 1997), India did not import foreign qualifications but rather developed local training and examination material. Still subject to the British influence, however, these examinations closely followed the ICAEW model.

On the whole, at this time, there was general support for the ICAI. The corporate sector and other parties interested in accountancy supported the ICAI and the government relied upon it to create a strong, semi-independent and ethical accounting profession. However, there was a departure from the intended low-level government involvement in accounting matters to significant government intervention on the issue of mutual recognition in the 1950s. This post-formation shift in policy is highlighted and analyzed in the next section.

## Mutual Recognition and Reciprocity After the Formation of the ICAI

Soon after its establishment, the ICAI asked the representative of the Ministry of Commerce, Mr C.C. Desai, to contact the UK authorities in relation to the recognition of the ICAI. As a result:

> Mr. C.C. Desai undertook to get official confirmation from the Board of Trade in England through the High Commission and added that in case it was indicated that the Board would be prepared to grant licences to the members of the Indian Institute to practice in the UK, there would be an obligation put on the Indian Institute to extend reciprocity. (Kapadia 1972, 236)

Subsequently, the representative of the Ministry of Commerce updated the council of the ICAI on this issue, stating that practising rights rather than full recognition were likely to be granted to members of the ICAI.

> The matter had been taken up with the Indian High Commission in London and the UK representative in India. The Ministry was hopeful of the UK Board of Trade readily agreeing to grant the necessary recognition to members of the Indian Institute for being appointed by any company in the UK as auditors. (Kapadia 1972, 237)

However, the members of the council of the ICAI, after investigating the position in relation to reciprocity themselves, discovered that mutual recognition had been granted to other non-British chartered accounting institutes. This fell far short of the mutual recognition desired by the ICAI and the majority viewpoint of the ICAI Council was to issue the following resolution:

> That although reciprocity is desirable, the question of reciprocity with the United Kingdom and the colonies should be postponed until the Council decides the terms and conditions on which reciprocity is desirable and request the Government of India to ascertain whether the United Kingdom and the Colonial Governments are prepared to agree to these terms and conditions. (Resolution, cited in Kapadia 1972, 242)

The council's position was that if its conditions could not be met then reciprocity should in turn be denied to British CAs. The government of India was concerned at the stance of the ICAI. Mr. B.K. Kaul, the government representative on the ICAI council, raised several arguments in defence of according foreign institutes recognition in India. These included the claim that the ICAI was afraid of competition from other institutes that might have similar or even higher standards (Kapadia 1972, 246). Kapadia, responding to the government nominee, argued that:

> the Council never knew that while the offer in respect of rights of practice in the UK to the members of the Indian Institute was made, it was made with reservations inasmuch as it now transpired that in respect if at least two bodies reciprocal arrangements on an institute basis with other Dominions in the Commonwealth did exist and this is what the ICAI wanted. (1972, 247)

Even after independence, the council of the ICAI continued to refer to practices in other dominions. The differential treatment of the ICAI compared to chartered accounting bodies in other dominions angered most of the members of the council of the ICAI, prompting them to issue the aforementioned resolution. This differential treatment may be indicative of the relevance of the race issue in the case of India. Poullaos (2009) discusses the reluctance of British accounting institutes to treat those of 'other race or colour' equally in the 1920s, showing, for example, that some British clients were unwilling to accept Indian accountants. Such a negative attitude towards Indian accountants, in particular, was probably still relevant in this later time period, too.

At this stage, the ICAI wished to withdraw their recognition of professional accounting bodies that did not recognize the ICAI. The Ministry of Commerce was concerned that its interests and negotiation position on other issues might be adversely affected if the goodwill of the UK authorities was lost over the issue of reciprocity. It therefore put pressure on the ICAI to continue to recognize British professional accounting bodies and their qualifications both at meetings of the ICAI council and in letters to the council of the ICAI (Kapadia 1972; *Indian Parliamentary Debates on the Chartered Accountants [Amendment] Bill*, 1955).

> It is somewhat surprising that just after most colonies and particularly those with which we are mainly concerned, from the point of our nationals practicing there, have expressed their willingness to follow the lead given by the UK Government, the council should have decided to drop the question altogether. In the opinion of the Government of India, the Resolution of the Council does not give adequate reasons for this step and it will be extremely embarrassing for the Government of India at this stage to withdraw, without very strong justification from the negotiations which they had initiated with the UK Government at the instance of the Council . . . Viewed in that light, the Government hope that the Council will readily concede that the tests and training prescribed for membership of the UK Institutes concerned are in no way inferior to those laid down by the Indian Institute and that they intrinsically deserve to be recognised. Moreover, contacts with members of such institutes who have long traditions of professional competence will be of not inconsiderable benefit, at least in the earlier stages to the Indian Accountancy profession in establishing its own traditions. . . . In the larger interests of the country and of the profession, Government would therefore advise the Council to reconsider the matter at its forthcoming meeting . . . in the light of the views expressed above. (Letter, Indian government to ICAI, cited in Kapadia 1972, 251)

The ICAI did eventually succumb to this pressure but only in part. The ICAI proposed issuing regulations on reciprocity, which allowed the recognition of foreign qualifications, but with conditions. These included a requirement that the foreign qualified accountant must be resident in India, that recognition would be for five years, that the accountant would not allowed to vote in or become a member of the ICAI council, that membership of the ICAI would cease if the accountant ceased to be resident in India and that recognition would usually be given only if there was recognition by the foreign accounting body of the ICAI (Kapadia 1972).

This was a compromise between the ICAI's position and the government's. Many members of the ICAI, including council members, felt that they had given in to the government by allowing foreign accountants to be recognized by the ICAI without a reciprocal arrangement. However, they also recognized that the government did have powers to regulate the ICAI under the Chartered Accountants Act and had indicated that it would override the ICAI if necessary. Hence, the ICAI accepted that they had little choice in bowing to the will of the government, since the ICAI's position might well have been weakened further if the government had insisted on full recognition of UK qualifications with no reciprocal measures at all (Kapadia 1972; *Indian Parliamentary Debates on the Chartered Accountants [Amendment] Bill*, 1955).

In short, the relationship between the Indian and British governments became a crucial issue for the former and directly influenced the ICAI in this phase of its development. Continuing links with Britain and the relationship between the Indian government and British trade agencies post-independence affected key policy decisions of the Indian government with regard to the ICAI, leading to the tightening of the legal framework surrounding the ICAI.

Despite the actions of the ICAI, the government was not happy with the reciprocity provisions and in 1955 amended the Chartered Accountants Act to give itself the right to specify those foreign accounting qualifications which would be accepted in India against the wishes of the ICAI (Kapadia 1972; *Indian Parliamentary Debates on the Chartered Accountants [Amendment] Bill*, 1955). In the debates on the bill, there was a call for a wider review of the accounting profession with some criticism of the profession from some members of Parliament arguing that auditors were not acting honestly, for example, incorrectly giving clean audit reports.

> Shri M.S. Gurupadaswamy:
>
> I have got certain figures to show that the Council of Chartered Accountants has been exercising its powers of monopoly . . . And power has been given to this Council which is not exercising that power in the interests of the country. At present you are favouring a set of people who are unscrupulous, who are corrupt and who are unfit to be chartered accountants.
>
> Shri Jaspat Roy Kapoor:
>
> Many of us feel that the way in which auditors have been conducting themselves in this country leaves much to be desired. (*Indian Parliamentary Debates on the Chartered Accountants [Amendment] Bill*, 1955)

However, the bill was restricted to the issue of mutual recognition with two different viewpoints broadly presented; one being that government needed the power to recognize foreign accountants to protect the national interest, the other supporting the ICAI retaining the right to decide on recognition of foreign accountants. For example, arguments promulgated by the government and support for the amendment in the debates from other members of Parliament suggested that in some ways India's trading relationship with Britain might be affected if recognition of foreign qualifications was withdrawn. For example:

> Shri M.C. Shah (Minister of Revenue and Civil Expenditure):
>
> In relation to recognition of foreign accountancy qualifications . . . This may well involve, in many cases, negotiations between

Governments concerned on a Governmental level. In order to facilitate the implementation of the results of such negotiations, we consider it necessary that the power to recognise foreign qualifications should be concurrently vested in the Central Government as a matter of public policy.

Shri V.P. Nayar:
I am prepared to concede—if their views were not accepted or acted upon by the council as such, there is a risk of Government's interests being put in jeopardy.

Shri A.M. Thomas:
I also raised the fears that have been entertained by the chartered accountants in our country that if this power is vested in the Government, the Government might use that power in a way which will facilitate entry of persons with foreign qualifications who will flood the field of Chartered Accountants, and this the indigenous elements might gradually be ousted . . . I feel that even if Government takes up these powers, it should be very guarded and careful in allowing persons with foreign qualifications to take up the work. (*Indian Parliamentary Debates on the Chartered Accountants [Amendment] Bill*, 1955)

In the debates, several members of Parliament put forward arguments against mutual recognition, including that Indian jobs may be at risk if mutual recognition was granted to foreign institutes and that government interference was unnecessary. For example:

Shri C.R. Narasimhan:
The chartered accountants institute agreed only after protracted negotiations and that itself shows that the institute was not very eager about this.

Shri V.B. Gandhi:
In short, my plea is that whatever we do to recognise foreigners and their qualifications in India should not lead even indirectly or unintentionally to a position where Indians who are holding qualifications which are recognised both in India and England should become disqualified.

Shri Bhupesh Gupta:
I should have thought that the Government would be frank enough to tell us as to why this amendment was called for . . . because a number of foreign concerns have demanded that their auditors should be recognised by the Government of India . . . We want our system of accounting to be entirely in the hands of the Indian Nationals and we want to eliminate the foreigners from the whole system of accounting

> and auditing in our country. (*Indian Parliamentary Debates on the Chartered Accountants [Amendment] Bill*, 1955)

In addition, the number of companies in India were estimated to be around 30,000 (Shri M.S. Gurupadaswamy, cited in *Indian Parliamentary Debates on the Chartered Accountants [Amendment] Bill*, 1955) of which a few hundred were foreign companies, with at least five or six being large concerns. One member of Parliament raised the issue of foreign capital:

> Shri Bhupesh Gupta:
>
> As far as we are aware, they are wanting this power to recognise the training from 'without India'—that is the expression used—as equivalent to the examination and training prescribed for members of the Institute, precisely because a number of foreign concerns have demanded that their auditors should be recognised by the Government of India and allowed to function here as full fledged chartered accountants and placed on the same footing with those qualified in India. It is in order to oblige certain companies, the Standard Vacuum Oil Company and other British concerns, that the Government is assuming this power. (*Indian Parliamentary Debates on the Chartered Accountants [Amendment] Bill*, 1955)

This was refuted by the minister Shri M.C. Shah:

> Now with regard to Mr. Bhupesh Gupta's point, I say that it is absolutely untrue to say that the Bill has been brought forth because of foreign interests. (*Indian Parliamentary Debates on the Chartered Accountants [Amendment] Bill*, 1955)

The identification of foreign capital in India is not unproblematic as discussed by Tomlinson (1978, 1993). Such investment existed and increased during the first 15 years of independence with little evidence of repatriation at independence. In addition, Tomlinson concurs with the view that a structural change occurred between the 1920s and 1960s from portfolio investment to direct investment, probably before rather than after independence. Before independence there existed large, mainly British-run managing agencies, as well as other British companies including accounting firms such as Price Waterhouse and A.F. Ferguson's (Jones 1995; Misra 1999). The existence of foreign capital provided foreign accountants, including British accountants, with an important role and their work included audit, tax, cost accounting and review of accounting systems of railway companies (*Indian Parliamentary Debates on the Chartered Accountants Bill*, 1948; Kapadia 1972; Jones 1995; Misra 1999).

After some debate, the government's amendment bill was accepted, giving it the right to recognize foreign accountants concurrently with the

ICAI. Thus, although the ICAI was given some autonomy to carry out its activities, the government proved itself to be the more influential partner in the relationship. On issues that were of little importance to the government, such as operational structure, the ICAI were permitted to progress with little interference. However, on any issues which had wider implications for the government, in this case relations with the UK, the government acted quickly and unequivocally to force the ICAI to act in accordance with its wishes and were prepared to change legislation in order to achieve this. The Indian government's concerns regarding its relationship with British trade institutions, post-independence, and the comparison of the treatment of the ICAI to chartered accounting bodies in various dominion states provide evidence of the importance of continuing empire-related linkages to the development of the ICAI post-independence.

## CONCLUSION

In this chapter, the influence of imperialism on the establishment of the ICAI has been explored with particular focus on the issues of the state–profession relationship in determining the structure of the ICAI, credentialism and the 'chartered' designation, and mutual recognition and reciprocity. The importance of the state–profession axis in determining the outcome of the professionalization process in India is prominent throughout the formation of the ICAI and also once the ICAI was formed. An interesting contrast is seen in the case of India. The British model of an autonomous profession was accepted as an appropriate model of professionalization by Indian accountants, but it sat oddly with the highly centralized and planned economy instituted by the Indian government in reaction to the imperial experience and the perceived problems caused by British imperial policies in India.

There was little direct involvement on the part of the British government and British accounting institutes in the establishment of the ICAI post-independence in India. However, imperial concerns influenced both the Indian government and the ICAI in several ways.

Firstly, British models and institutions were seen as 'ideals' in India with the view that 'British is best' generally prevalent post-independence, leading many Indian institutions to be based on the British system (for example, the parliamentary and legal systems). Such notions were very much present throughout the establishment of the ICAI and, before that, reflected in the sentiments of the IAB. A more complex picture emerged after independence. Some accountants who had qualified with British chartered accounting institutes argued against allowing an Indian accounting institute to adopt the 'chartered' title as they believed that this might adversely impact upon their perceived competitive advantage. At the same time, some members of the ICAI wanted to exclude British

CAs from working in India when mutual recognition was not on offer to the ICAI. The former points to the stratification of the Indian profession on the basis of a British designation, while the latter signifies a desire for equality with the 'British best'.

Secondly, the operation and structure of the British accounting institutes were reviewed and referred to as appropriate models to follow in setting up the Indian institute. Although many of the practices of the ICAI were drawn from British accounting bodies (such as the ICAEW),[3] local concerns led to a quite different institutional structure for the ICAI, which was ultimately established under statute rendering it vulnerable to government intervention. Even though examinations were set by the ICAI, these were modeled on the examinations of British institutes. In addition, throughout the debates on the ICAI, reference was made to the experience of chartered accounting bodies in Britain's dominion states—yet another means by which empire continued to influence accounting professionalization in India after independence.

Finally, the relationship between the Indian government and British trade institutions (for example, the British Board of Trade) affected the state–profession relationship post-independence in India. This was seen particularly in the debates surrounding the issues of credentialism, the adoption of the 'chartered' designation and mutual recognition and reciprocity. The potential effect of decisions made by the ICAI on the relationship between the Indian and British governments resulted in intervention in the policy decisions of the ICAI by the former government and in legislative amendments to ensure that the Indian government's interests were safeguarded.

As this chapter has shown, the state–profession relationship in the case of Indian accountancy has been strong. This is partly the result of the operationalization of new political ideals in the period after independence and partly the result, paradoxically, of a strong and enduring colonial legacy. Whilst the post-independence government sought to execute a departure from inherited colonial ideals and policy, they struggled in the face of long-established institutional structures and closely held beliefs that 'British is best'. Within this context, the British model became a starting blueprint for the Indian accountancy profession, although ultimately it carved its own unique path as it matured and developed.

## REFERENCES

### Primary Sources

*Chartered Accountants Act.* (1949) New Delhi: Government of India.

*Chartered Accountants (Amendment) Act.* (1955) New Delhi: Government of India.

3. For example, in terms of its administrative structures, training and exams.

*Companies Amendment Act.* (1930) New Delhi, Government of India.
*Company Law Amendment Bill.* (1930) New Delhi: Government of India.
*Company Law (Amendment) Committee Report.* (1957) New Delhi: Government of India.
*Company Law Committee Report.* (1952) New Delhi: Government of India.
Editorials. (1952–1960) *Chartered Accountant, Journal of the Institute of Chartered Accountants of India.*
*Gazette of India.* (1914) 'Notification No. 1626–6', 14 March.
*Indian Parliamentary Debates on the Chartered Accountants Bill.* (1948) New Delhi: Government of India.
*Indian Parliamentary Debates on the Chartered Accountants (Amendment) Bill.* (1955) New Delhi: Government of India.
*Parliamentary Committee Report on the Chartered Accountants Bill.* (1948) New Delhi: Government of India.

## Secondary Sources

Annisette, M. (1999) 'Importing accounting: The case of Trinidad and Tobago'. *Accounting, Business & Financial History* 9:103–33.
———. (2000) 'Imperialism and the professions: The education and certification of accountants in Trinidad and Tobago'. *Accounting, Organizations and Society* 25:631–59.
———. (2003) 'The colour of accountancy: Examining the salience of race in a professionalization project'. *Accounting, Organizations and Society* 28:639–74.
Bakre, O.M. (2005) 'First attempt at localising imperial Accountancy: The case of the Institute of Chartered Accountants of Jamaica (ICAJ) (1950's–1970's)'. *Critical Perspectives on Accounting* 16:995–1018.
———. (2006) 'Second attempt at localising imperial accountancy: The case of the Institute of Chartered Accountants of Jamaica (ICAJ) (1970's–1980's)'. *Critical Perspectives on Accounting* 17:1–28.
Brass, P.R. (1994) *The Politics of India since Independence.* 2nd ed. Cambridge: Cambridge University Press.
Briston, R.J., and Kedslie, M.J.M. (1997) 'The internationalization of British professional accounting: The role of the examining exporting bodies'. *Accounting, Business & Financial History* 2:175–94.
Brown, J. (1994) *Modern India, the Origins of an Asian Economy.* 2nd ed. New York: Oxford University Press.
Carnegie, G.D., and Edwards, J.R. (2001) 'The construction of the professional accountant: The case of the Incorporated Institute of Accountants, Victoria (1886)'. *Accounting, Organizations and Society* 26:301–25.
Carnegie, G.D., and Parker, R.H. (1999), 'Accountants and empire: The case of co-membership of Australian and British accountancy bodies, 1885 to 1914'. *Accounting, Business & Financial History* 9:77–102.
Chua, W.F., and Poullaos, C. (1998) 'The dynamics of "closure" amidst the construction of market, profession, empire and nationhood: An historical analysis of an Australian accounting association, 1886–1903'. *Accounting, Organizations and Society* 23:155–87.
———. (2002) 'The empire strikes back? An exploration of centre–periphery interaction between the ICAEW and accounting associations in the self-governing colonies of Australia, Canada and South Africa, 1880–1907'. *Accounting, Organizations and Society* 27:409–45.
Jones, E. (1995) *True and Fair: A History of Price Waterhouse.* London: Hamish Hamilton.

Kapadia, G.P. (1972) *History of the Accountancy Profession in India, Volume 1*. New Delhi: Institute of Chartered Accountants of India.
Kulke, H., and Rothermund, D. (1990) *A History of India*. London and New York: Routledge.
Kumar, D. (ed.) (1982) *The Cambridge Economic History of India Vol. II*. New Delhi: Cambridge University Press.
Lee, T.A. (1997) 'The influence of Scottish accountants in the United States: The early case of the Society of Accountants in Edinburgh'. *Accounting Historians Journal* 24:117–41.
Misra, M. (1999) *Business, Race and Politics in British India c. 1850–1960*. Oxford: Clarendon Press.
Neu, D., and Cameron, G. (2006) 'The birth of a nation: Accounting and Canada's first nations, 1860–1900'. *Accounting, Organizations and Society* 31:47–76.
Panikkar, K.M. (1964) *A Survey of Indian History*. New Delhi: Asia Publishing House.
Poullaos, C. (2009) 'Profession, race and empire: Keeping the centre pure 1921–1927'. *Accounting, Auditing & Accountability Journal* 22:429–68.
Rothermund, D. (1993) *An Economic History of India from Pre-Colonial Times to 1991*. London: Routledge.
Said E. (1993) *Culture and Imperialism*. London: Vintage Books.
Sian, S. (2006) 'Inclusion, exclusion and control: The case of the Kenyan accounting professionalization project'. *Accounting, Organizations and Society* 31:295–322.
———. (2007) 'Reversing exclusion: The Africanisation of accountancy in Kenya 1963–1970'. *Critical Perspectives on Accounting* 18:831–72.
Spear, P. (1978) *A History of India, Vol. 2*. New Delhi: Penguin Books.
Susela, S.D. (1999) '"Interests" and accounting standard setting in Malaysia'. *Accounting, Auditing & Accountability Journal* 12:328–39.
Tomlinson, B.R. (1978) 'Foreign private investment in India 1920 to 1950'. *Modern Asian Studies* 12:655–77.
———. (1993) *The Economy of Modern India 1860–1970*. Cambridge: Cambridge University Press.
Uche, C.U. (2002) 'Professional accounting development in Nigeria: Threats from the inside and outside'. *Accounting, Organizations and Society* 27:471–96.
Verma S. (2000), 'The influence of culture and politics on accounting change in India from 1947 to 1998'. Unpublished PhD thesis, University of Warwick.
Verma, S., and Gray S.J. (2006) 'The setting up of the Institute of Chartered Accountants of India: A first step in creating an indigenous accounting profession'. *Accounting Historians Journal* 33:131–56.
———. (2009) 'The development of company law in India: The case of the Companies Act 1956'. *Critical Perspectives on Accounting* 20:110–35.
Yapa, P.W.S. (1999) 'Professional accounting environment in Brunei'. *Accounting, Auditing & Accountability Journal* 12:328–39.

# 10 Between the Lines
## The Professionalization of Accountancy in Kenya

*Suki Sian*

## INTRODUCTION

When Kenya was incorporated into the expanding British Empire,[1] it became another nodal point on an international network that encompassed a diverse array of territories across the globe. The network connexions became common routes for the transfer of commodities, goods, services and peoples. Along these routes, trade was undertaken mainly with the mother country (or with other colonies) and peoples were moved either voluntarily to administer/settle the colonial outposts or by force to provide cheap and reliable labour. Thus, empire became a means of disseminating institutions, language, culture and religion. Legislation passed in Westminster furnished the British with the authority to rule over foreign territories and consolidated this vast network, in some cases disregarding almost entirely those subject to such rule, and leaving in its trail an enduring legacy. However, not only did Britain have a lasting impact upon the countries and people that she colonized, the empire itself had a significant impact upon Britain and her people too and its legacy continues to be a contentious subject for historians (Ferguson 2003, 371). Although often portrayed as 'ruthless and rapacious' and the root of much racism and xenophobia, there remain those that support the altruistic argument, that 'Britain's empire was a moral force and one for the good' (James 1998, 638).

In the formal British Empire, the settler colonies, such as Canada, Australia and New Zealand, were self-governing and had a permanent white population. The non-settler colonies, including India, the West Indies and some African countries such as Nigeria, had a mainly transient white population and were ruled by governors appointed in London. By the late 1880s, the British had laid claim to vast territories in East Africa and by the early twentieth century, British soldiers, administrators and businessmen were resident (sometimes temporarily) in Kenya colony and many others,

1. In 1890 the British Parliament passed the Foreign Jurisdictions Act declaring sovereignty over Eastern and Central Africa. The British created two states in the area, the Protectorate of Uganda in 1894 and the British East Africa Protectorate in 1895. The latter became the Colony and Protectorate of Kenya in 1920.

induced by British government policy, emigrated to establish more permanent communities on land that had previously belonged to the indigenous African Kenyans (Marshall 1996, 69). Settlement in Kenya was on a permanent basis and was accompanied by large-scale land dispossession and alienation of the majority black population. During their term of rule, the British also encouraged large numbers of migrant workers from the Asian subcontinent to provide labour in many parts of East Africa;[2] indeed it is argued that 'the use of Indians across the Empire was itself a symbol of Britain's success' (Johnson 2003, 85). As a result, colonial Kenya's social anatomy was forged from three main racial groups: the ruling Europeans, the immigrant Asians and the indigenous Africans.

In Kenya, the achievement of independence in 1963 was viewed initially by most African Kenyans as the 'triumph of nationalism over imperialism' (Ogot and Ochieng 1995, xi) and it was anticipated that *Uhuru* (Freedom) would go hand in hand with political independence, economic growth and the re-establishment of indigenous culture. However, as in the case of many other ex-colonies, Kenya was not able to execute a decisive departure from its colonial past, a legacy that pervaded many aspects of post-colonial society. The country relied heavily upon and even expanded the old administrative and economic structures inherited from the colonial state, exhibiting forms of neocolonialism.[3] A single-party system effectively replaced the old authoritarian colonial government, capital accumulation in the hands of the indigenous people was encouraged (although limited) and long-term economic growth erratic. Despite a vigorous programme of 'Africanization', post-colonial Kenya remained burdened with the legacy of foreign occupation and rule, and remained enmeshed within the networks of a dissolving empire for a protracted period. The institutions and structures inherited by the *Uhuru* government had originally been established to economically exploit the country rather than develop it and those that assumed political leadership were encumbered with (or perpetuated) an establishment that concentrated economic power, authority and privilege[4] in the hands of the elite (Ogot and Ochieng 1995, 14).

---

2. The colonial government had encouraged the migration of workers from the Indian subcontinent at the turn of the century in order to meet the requirement for a disciplined work force for large projects, such as the Uganda Railway. Others that followed were already experienced in trade and began businesses in the coastal areas and eventually moved inland. Since the Asian community in Kenya was denied access to much of the productive farmland, they were left with little option other than to direct their capital into trade and later industry.

3. Neocolonialism has been defined as 'the survival of the colonial system in spite of the formal recognition of political independence in emerging countries which become victims of an indirect and subtle form of domination by political, economic, social, military or technical means' (the Proceedings of the All-African People's Conference held in Cairo, 1961 cited in Leys 1975, 26).

4. For instance, British expatriates in the public sector had been offered high salary levels in an attempt to lure them to 'an inhospitable and distant' colony and to maintain a higher standard of living than would be required for the local Africans. After independence, salary structures in the public sector remained at these relatively high levels (Ogot and Ochieng 1995).

Within the imperial network, the professionalization of accountancy became yet another vehicle for the dissemination of British institutions and practices. Like many other colonies, Kenya represented a new market for the services of British accountants and the form of political rule[5] that was established in the colony influenced the processes of professionalization. Aspirations to capture this market by the established chartered British bodies, along with the expansionist activities of the lower-tier British accounting bodies[6] and the accumulation of capital in the hands of the British and other Europeans in Kenya resulted in a preponderance of British qualified accountants. In Kenya, a professional body led by local, indigenous accountants did not emerge until after political independence in 1963, although a white-dominated professional organization (the Association of Accountants in East Africa [AAEA])[7] did exist, perhaps a direct consequence of the permanent nature of settlement in the colony.[8] Therefore, as the title of this chapter suggests, the case of accountancy in Kenya falls 'between the lines'. That is, it neither conforms to the model found in the white self-governing settler colonies, where the professionalization of accountancy occurred at the turn of the last century, nor does it entirely conform to the general case of the non-white, non-self-governing, non-settler colonies, where professionalization did not commence until after political independence had been granted.[9]

The accounting history of Kenya is divided into distinct time phases. It begins with the arrival of the earliest known British accountants at the turn of the twentieth century and their absolute predominance in the colony as their numbers increased. After political independence was achieved in 1963, the Kenyatta government established programmes for the education of indigenous Africans in subjects such as accountancy as part of their Africanization policy to facilitate the hand over of economic power to the indigenous Africans. Despite such moves to increase the participation of

---

5. The British Empire evolved in an uneven manner as different territories were acquired for different reasons (economic or politically strategic) and were also subject to different forms of rule, ranging from the formal to the informal and self-rule to the installation of governors appointed in London. It was 'internally dynamic' and was subject to change through wars, rivalry and changing economic conditions (Johnson 2003).

6. Bodies such as the Society of Incorporated Accountants and Auditors (SIAA) and later the Association of Certified and Corporate Accountants (ACCA).

7. The AAEA was established during colonial rule in 1949. Initially members were mainly expatriate accountants who had already qualified with one of the recognized British professional accountancy bodies. The Institute of Certified Public Accountants of Kenya (ICPAK) was formed post-independence via legislation passed in 1977.

8. The white minority population was a permanent feature in this colony. The local legislative body was dominated by the white minority and assumed an advisory role, effectively denying the indigenous Africans a substantive voice until after independence.

9. With the exception, perhaps, of India (see Chapter 9 in this volume). In the case of Jamaica, local associations representing the interests of the British professional bodies were also present in the colonial period.

non-whites in the profession, the creation of national institutional arrangements for professional accountancy did not take place until the late 1970s. This chapter sets out to examine these events, from the turn of the twentieth century to 1978 (the inaugural meeting of the Kenyan institute) against the contextual backdrop of colonial rule and its enduring legacy.

## THE NETWORKS OF EMPIRE—THE KENYA EXTENSION

This section evaluates the importance of Kenya colony to the British Empire by assessing the motivations for the historical occupation of Kenya and the economic links that so closely bound the colony to the mother country. Since accountants have an important role to play as the guardians of the financial probity of capitalist expansion, tracing the shifts in capital accumulation can help to explain the changing patterns of demand for the services of professional accountants and help to provide a rationale for the path of professional organization in this country.

### Motivations for British Involvement in East Africa

The motivations for British involvement in East Africa are complex and theorizations by historians are the subject of debate. In essence, such theorizations fall into three categories: economic, political and moral. The Industrial Revolution throughout Europe in the nineteenth century dramatically increased the demand for raw materials to fuel new industries. The search for raw materials such as wood, cotton and palm oil led to enhanced trade with the Americas, Africa and the Indian subcontinent, and ultimately to the acquisition of territories in order to secure supplies (Odhiambo and Wanyande 1989, 89), resulting in the British having a permanent presence in East Africa by 1889. Concurrently, the 'scramble' by European governments to lay claim to territories throughout Africa was partly the result of political developments in Europe and culminated with the International Conference held in Berlin in 1884, at which a resolution was passed which effectively formalized the partition of Africa (Oliver and Fage 1995, 73; Marshall 1996, 69). Britain, it is argued, participated only to defend her economic interests (Cain and Hopkins 2002, 368), although other theorists challenge this (Robinson and Gallagher 1981, 237).[10] In addition to the economic and political drivers, there also existed the paternalistic imperative. The church in Britain, supported by the administration, sent zealous missionaries on a 'civilizing mission' to introduce Christianity and modernity

10. Robinson and Gallagher have contended that the European scramble for Africa was triggered and driven by the British entering Egypt in 1882 to secure control of the Suez Canal, although this too has been countered by other theorists, such as A.G Hopkins. The opening of the Suez reduced the journey time to India, a key British colony, from three months to 17 days (Johnson 2003).

to Africa, whilst condemning and denigrating existing culture and religion (Smith 1998, 369). Missionaries and explorers, such as David Livingstone and Joseph Thompson, also fuelled interest in imperial ambitions in Africa through their writings (Johnson 2003, 365).

## The Organization of Kenyan Colonial Society

By the turn of the century, Britain had initiated a deliberate policy of white settlement in East Africa (Hazlewood 1979, 90) augmented by the Empire Settlement Acts of 1922 and 1937.[11] In practice, settlement resulted in the creation of a race-based hierarchy comprising separate living areas, living standards and opportunities for the three main groups (Mutungi 1974; Swainson 1980; Ogot and Ochieng 1995; Sian 2006a, 2006b, 2007a). The colonizing Europeans operated a system of monopoly (Leys 1975, 3) over the best farmland and housing and occupied positions of influence both within industry and the civil service.[12] A 'colour bar' excluded Africans and Asians from services and opportunities enjoyed by the Europeans. As a community, the Asians cornered the retail and wholesale markets, established businesses in manufacturing and construction, and later many were employed in clerical work within the civil service and in industry. The disenfranchised indigenous Africans were mainly subsistence farmers with strong tribal allegiances (the two largest tribes being the Kikuyu and the Luo). In order to ensure an adequate supply of African labour for the growing European farms, the colonial administration introduced taxes forcing Africans to seek employment on the white farms in order to be able to afford to pay these taxes (Ogot and Ochieng 1995, 14).[13]

This three-way racial divide permeated all aspects of colonial society and, in particular, was evident in the provision of education. In this society, the highest standards of education were restricted very much to the elite white community, although many of the Asian communities were able to establish local schools, whilst the earliest schools for Africans were the 'bush schools' or schools established by missionaries. It was not until the 1950s

11. The 1902 Crown Lands Ordinance allowed settlers to claim the best farming land, giving birth to 'the White Highlands'. By 1906 the Protectorate was being administered by the Colonial Office (CO) and an Executive Council and a Legislative Council had been established (RCS, Colonial Office Report on the Colony and Protectorate of Kenya 1962).

12. Class divisions existed in the colony, reflecting societal structure in Britain at the time. Thus, there was the civil servant cadre, an agricultural upper class of estate owners, an urban middle class, a professional class (lawyers, doctors, accountants), a skilled workers group, those working for multinational companies and missionaries (adapted from Ogot and Ochieng 1995, 111).

13. African trade was restricted by the Credit Trade with Natives Ordinance, 1903 (Mutungi 1974), although by 1922 the Africans were permitted to grow cash-crops as long as the estates continued to be well supplied with labour and they did not compete with the settler farms. By 1933 coffee growing was also permitted in some African areas.

that technical and trade schools were established for African Kenyans, specializing in preparing students to become carpenters, masons, plumbers, shoemakers, tailors, fitters and clerical trainees. As will be shown, such differentials in education meant that Africans were, in the main, unable to attain the standards required for entry to the professions, and in particular accountancy.

## Economic Links with Britain and Capital Accumulation in the Colony

Economically, Kenya was tightly linked to the capitalist system that was dominated by the Europeans and, in particular, the British (Ogot and Ochieng 1995, 14). By the early twentieth century, land incentives encouraged the settler farmers to grow and export cash-crops back to the United Kingdom, as Kenya began to play 'the classic role of a country at the periphery of the capitalist system, exporting primary commodities and importing manufactures' (Leys 1975, 28). As in other parts of the empire, much of the financial capital for non-industrial ventures was provided by 'gentlemanly capitalists' from England (Cain and Hopkins 2002, 368), and in Kenya colony the employment of such capital changed significantly through the twentieth century in line with the changing economic and political climate.[14] Several large British merchant houses operating in East Africa at the time, such as Smith Mackenzie and Mitchell Cotts, facilitated the exchange of goods between the colony and the metropole.

Prior to 1939 estate capital was prevalent in Kenya and the white settler farmers and estate owners were the dominant political force by the early 1920s through participation in the legislative council and local councils (Ogot and Ochieng 1995, 14), despite constituting less than 1 per cent of the population (Swainson 1980, 92, 6). The concentration of capital in the hands of the settlers and estate owners was further reinforced in a number of different ways.[15] Firstly, the operations of British banks in the colony facilitated trading activities and provided capital for many settler ventures. Secondly, the establishment of marketing organizations, such as the Kenya Farmers' Association, ensured that settlers maintained their monopoly over distribution within Kenya. Thirdly, the imposition of tariffs in the colony protected the settler agricultural monopoly. And finally, settler involvement

14. The 'gentlemanly capitalists' were only one of many sources of imperial capital (for a comprehensive analysis, see Johnson 2003). Such capital was employed initially in the establishment and maintenance of the large estates and later in the manufacturing, distribution and retailing of produce and goods. After World War II, international companies poured capital into the colony in their attempts to gain market share.

15. Whilst capitalists invested with a view to profiting from imperial ventures, the empire also required subsidies (mainly for defence) which resulted in high taxation in Britain at the time (Davis and Huttenback 1988).

in new company formations facilitated capital accumulation and greater exercise of influence.[16] The British government did provide some aid to Kenya under the Colonial Development and Welfare Act, 1929, in the hope that it would promote trade with Britain and help alleviate unemployment in the UK by stimulating exports (Swainson 1980, 92).

In the pre-war period over 70 per cent of Kenya's exports were destined for either Britain or some part of the British Empire. The colonial administration also invested in infrastructure projects (such as harbours, railways, communications and roads) and enterprises that were necessary for the smooth administration of the colony or likely to produce easy and immediate profits without excessive risk. Kenya's main trading partners at the time were Britain and other British colonies.[17] Local branches of British banks also closely linked the colony to the Western capitalist system by providing finance capital and gathering local deposits and remitting them back to the head office in Britain (Hazlewood 1979, 90). Commercial penetration was accelerating and in the pre-war period public companies which required larger amounts of capital tended to be owned by Europeans.[18]

With a history of exclusion from agriculture, the Asian capitalists[19]embarked upon manufacturing ventures. Despite having restricted access to credit from banks, they were better suited to such ventures as they were mostly family-run businesses and were more competitive as they were more willing to accept lower margins (Langdon 1976, 185). Asian capital, therefore, played an important role in the development of the Kenyan economy, transforming from merchant capital to production capital over time (Himbara 1994, 91). This was assisted by the entry of Indian commercial banks, such as the Bank of Baroda in 1945, which provided the Asians with better access to credit.

After World War II the entry of British firms (and later non-British multinationals) into the Kenyan economic environment reached its apogee, encouraged by the government, with a view to promoting local manufacture of goods previously imported. This period therefore witnessed a shift from a primarily agriculture-based economy to one that was also driven by

---

16. For instance, Lord Delamere, a prominent early settler, owned large shareholdings in three important early companies: Unga Ltd. (a grain-mill), Nyama Ltd. (a cattle ranch) and *The Times of East Africa*, which gave voice to the settlers on political issues (Swainson 1980).

17. Import trade with Britian and her colonies (mainly Tanganyika, South Africa and India) amounted to 63.42 per cent of total import trade in 1933 and 77.7 per cent of total export trade was destined for Britain and her colonies in the same year. The key exports were tea, coffee, sisal, gold, sugar, cotton, sodium carbonate, hides, maize, sugar and tobacco (Kenya Administrative Report, 1937 CO544/52 National Archives, London).

18. These included: British East Africa Co., East African Tobacco Co., East African Breweries, African Highlands Produce Co. (tea), Anglo-French Sisal Co., Kenya Tea Co., East African Tanning & Extract Co., East African Meat Co., Bird & Co. Africa Ltd. (shipping), Magadi Soda Co., East African Power and East African Portland Cement (Swainson 1980).

manufacturing ventures. Whereas previously the main providers of capital had been the gentlemanly capitalists and British banks, post–World War II Indian banks entered the market along with international companies which established and financed their own operations in the colony. In tandem, the number of expatriates in the colonial administration also rose significantly in the post-war period and there was a trend towards expatriate-run businesses being taken over by Asians (Swainson 1980, 92). As will be shown in this chapter, such capital movements were paralleled by shifts in the demand for accounting services and accountants in the colony.

During the post–World War II period, the colonial government removed some of the barriers that prevented Africans becoming involved in business. Leys (1975) notes how the 1950s witnessed a change in colonial policy to help encourage the emergence of a commercial petty bourgeoisie amongst the African Kenyans.[20] Some funding was provided for training and education schemes, which resulted in the establishment of many small businesses, particularly by African ex-soldiers with pensions to invest in small hotels, restaurants, general merchandise kiosks and shops. The provision of education and training resulted in the emergence of a small class of elite educated Africans, many of whom sought employment in urban areas or were involved in cash-crop farming or fledgling businesses where restricted credit was available (Ogot and Ochieng 1995, 14). Africans, too, became consumers of imported British goods and services (subject to affordability), perhaps lending weight to the argument that imperialism could only be maintained and explained through acquiescence and the collaboration of the subjugated (Robinson and Gallagher 1981; Johnson 2003).

The post-war period also witnessed the rise of international capital in Kenya, in particular an increase in the number of manufacturing firms, although British firms continued to exert a dominant influence. In the 1950s and early 1960s many foreign firms attempted to encourage partnerships with African enterprises to distribute their goods, ensuring that their products were reaching African markets in more rural areas. These attempts resulted in the emergence of powerful African traders in each distribution district (Swainson 1980, 92), and in undertaking such an exercise many foreign firms were effectively preparing for independence.

---

19. Medatally Manji, founder of the House of Manji Group, began trading as a general merchant in 1905 in Nyeri. Muljibhai Madhvani, founder of the Madhvani Group, first began growing coffee in 1908 before moving into sugar plantations and processing in the early 1920s (Himbara 1994). P.P. Chandaria began business as a hawker in 1914 (Murray 1978) and the Chandaria family moved into retail and later into wholesale, although they were also involved in tanning, wattle, cotton ginning and aluminium production in the late 1920s.

20. Leys (1975, 40) suggests that the war had created a sustained demand which could only be satisfied by changes in policy. This action also recognized the potential value of utilizing the growing African population in the 1940s and 1950s in order to meet such demand and was partly the result of political agitation by African leaders.

This analysis of (race-based) capital accumulation in Kenya colony and the links to the capitalist system of the British Empire provides an important foundation for the study of the development of accountancy in this country. In much of the colonial period, capital was concentrated in the hands of the British expatriate farmers, settlers, entrepreneurs and the administration. These entities were serviced by expatriate British accountants acting alone or attached to branches of British firms that had followed their clients to the colony. It was not until after World War II that Asian businesses were developed enough to warrant the services of professional accountants, and it is also at this time that the first Asian professional accountants began to offer their services in Kenya. The first, Manohar Lall, was registered with the Association of Certified and Corporate Accountants (ACCA) in 1949.[21] Independence was the trigger for the increased participation of the indigenous Africans in commerce and industry and also was a period that witnessed the entry of Africans into the professional arena, albeit in the public sector initially.

## THE PROFESSION IN COLONIAL KENYA

The linkages between the colony and the mother country were strong and institutions and structures established in the colony by the expatriates (such as the judiciary, the civil service, legislation and institutional arrangements for the professions) mirrored those 'back home'. Accountants arrived in the colony in the wake of commercial activity and capital flows. Reflecting the race-based social hierarchy that existed in colonial society, accountancy was a profession that was dominated by expatriate British accountants, some of whom were posted to the colony to support the administration or as employees of British companies, whilst others arrived to establish firms to serve the needs of British businesses operating in the colony. The earliest British practice in the colony can be dated to 1907, when E.B Gill co-founded Gill and Johnson in Nairobi.

Increasing commercial activity in the colony brought with it the need for enhanced financial disclosure. Demonstrating the strength of the connexion with the empire, many of the earliest regulations relating to accountancy in Kenya were drawn from similar acts already in operation in other colonies, such as India. The Companies Ordinance, 1921, set out to regulate companies operating in the colony through requirements for accounts and audit. It also empowered the governor to make 'rules' (as advised by the Institute of Chartered Accountants in England and Wales [ICAEW]) for the granting of certificates for auditors and for the recognition of (British) accounting societies.

---

21. The ACCA was renamed the Association of Certified Accountants in 1971, then the Chartered Association of Certified Accountants (CACA) in 1984 and latterly the Association of Chartered Certified Accountants.

Although auditors were governed by companies' legislation, accountants effectively remained unregulated and the colony presented a new market for services for both professionally qualified accountants and those without recognized qualifications offering accountancy services other than audit. In an attempt to close off opportunities for work and differentiate themselves from the non-qualified individuals, the British expatriate qualified accountants established a local professional association, the AAEA (or the 'Association'), in 1949. Membership was restricted to those with specified qualifications,[22] although this list was subject to amendments as the Association saw fit.

## The AAEA—Designations, Credentials and Tactics

The main objective of the AAEA was to act as an interest group for British accountants throughout East Africa, as a source of advice to the colonial administration on matters relating to commerce and taxation and latterly to establish local examinations and regulate training. Evidence from the early minutes of meetings held by the Association suggests that the group intended to replicate the characteristics and exclusionary behaviours of their qualifying parent bodies: 'We feel that to maintain the highest possible standard considerable discrimination must be used' (AAEA, Minutes 29/4/49:.4). Rather than competing with the British parent bodies, as had been the case in other settler colonies such as Australia, Canada and South Africa, the Association did not bestow members with any further designations or require them to submit to entrance examinations and training. The AAEA's membership was drawn from a variety of existing (mainly British) professional associations (who were competitors back home and also in other parts of the empire) and they were reliant upon the use of entry filters by the parent bodies to serve as indicators of professional suitability. Also, unlike their counterparts in Canada, South Africa and Rhodesia,[23] there appears to have been no intention to use the 'chartered' designation, without royal assent. This was perhaps a reflection of the esteem in which the 'chartered' designation was held by the expatriates, in particular by the chartered accountants (CAs) in the colony who formed the majority within the AAEA. By allowing all AAEA members

22. There was a requirement for members to be recommended in writing by at least two existing members and entrants had to hold a recognized qualification from one of the following bodies: the Society of Accountants in Aberdeen (SAA), Society of Accountants in Edinburgh (SAE), the Institute of Accountants and Actuaries in Glasgow (IAAG), the ICAEW, the Institute of Chartered Accountants in Ireland (ICAI), the Society of Incorporated Accountants and Auditors (SIAA), the ACCA, the Societies of Chartered Accountants in South Africa and the Institute of Chartered Accountants in Australia.

23. Other than Australia (1928), no colony has been granted a royal charter. Many ex-colonies did adopt the chartered title through legislation after independence: India (1949), Sri Lanka (1959), Ghana (1963), Jamaica (1965) and Nigeria (1965) (Johnson and Caygill 1971). Although the Kenyan institute was not formed until 1978, the CPA designation had already been used in the title of the local professional examinations since the early 1970s, almost a decade after independence.

to continue to use their original parent body designations, the British CAs retained a marketplace advantage over other non-chartered members within the colony and even within the AAEA.

Initially, the membership had included members in Uganda and Tanganyika, although by 1952 the Association had authorized members in these countries to self-regulate. Unlike expatriate accounting associations in countries such as Trinidad and Tobago (T&T), which were mainly 'social', the AAEA was proactive in raising its profile and that of its members throughout the colony and it set out to differentiate its members from non-members for commercial advantage by promoting membership as a badge of professional competence to prospective clients.[24]

## Motivations for Professionalization and Sponsorship of the Accountants (Designations) Ordinance 1950

In Kenya, the white expatriate accountants exercised a virtual monopoly in the market for the provision of accounting services mainly as other races lower down in the social hierarchy were unable to meet the educational standards required for entry to the elite professions. However, in line with shifts in capital accumulation by the different races, by the mid-1940s a handful of Kenyan Asians were training as accountants with British associations whilst others possessed Indian qualifications.

It may be speculated that motivations for the creation of the AAEA at this particular time arose from the desire to differentiate not only qualified accountants from non-qualifieds, but also, initially at least, to attempt to close off opportunities to competing non-whites, particularly in the growing market for services to Asian capitalists. The AAEA objected to members of the Institute of Chartered Accountants of India using the ACA and FCA designation (Kapadia 1973; Sian 2006b) and they initiated legislation which would require Indian members operating in Kenya to identify themselves as Indian CAs by using the 'CA (India)' designation. Such a geographical qualification would ensure that British CAs were easily identifiable to potential clients, who might hold them in higher esteem. The Accountants (Designations) Ordinance (Cap. 524), 1950, sponsored by the Association, set out to define appropriate initials and designations and restrict their use to those individuals belonging to the stated (mainly British) professional bodies.[25]

---

24. This was achieved in a number of way through various activities: by exposure in articles in the *East Africa Standard*; by the Association hosting debates, discussions, lunches and dinners; the publication of a broadsheet (the *Ledger*) to keep members updated on the activities of the Association and decisions made by council; sponsoring the formation of a library (housed within a section of the McMillan Library in Nairobi); sending out pamphlets to commercial firms; giving talks and providing literature for the local technical college on 'Accountancy as a Career'; and awarding prizes to students taking the Association's examinations.

25. As defined by the act, the recognized bodies were: the Society of Accountants in Edinburgh (CA), the Institute of Accountants and Actuaries in Glasgow (CA),

The Association developed book-keeping examinations (rather than full local professional qualifying examinations) and facilitated the formation of a Students' Society, possibly as a means of encouraging future support for the Association by capturing potential members early on. The book-keeping examinations were open to all races and this suggests that the AAEA considered the entry of suitably educated Africans and Asians into the lower echelons of the profession to be acceptable. However, there is evidence to indicate a general reluctance to accept non-whites into the upper echelons of the profession (Sian 2006b, 364), and aspiring non-white trainee accountants needed to approach disinclined white firms in order to secure professional training and employment. In particular, concerns were aired by the AAEA, in meeting minutes in the late 1950s, about the reaction of clients to non-whites, especially African trainees. A colonial government publication at the time noted that 'in spite of the local need for more accountants, it is not easy for an Asian or an African to find an opportunity of entering into service as either an articled pupil or an apprentice, whether in Great Britain or Kenya' (RCS, Careers in Kenya 1957).

The registration of professional accountants, which has a long history both in Britain and throughout the empire, was another area in which the AAEA sought to emulate the British parent bodies. Although various attempts to create a national register in Britain failed, similar attempts in various corners of the empire were more successful.[26] In Kenya, several discussions were held within the AAEA council, over a period of time beginning in 1953, on the issue of the registration of auditors, in order to restrict access to the lucrative audit market to its own members. By 1959, the Kenya Companies Ordinance was already progressing through the legislative process and added to the urgency of the passage of the Registration of Auditors legislation.[27] By 1960, the Association was also considering the

---

the Society of Accountants in Aberdeen (CA), the Institute of Chartered Accountants in England and Wales (CA), the Institute of Chartered Accountants in Ireland (CA), the Society of Incorporated Accountants and Auditors (incorporated accountant—ASAA), the Association of Certified and Corporate Accountants (certified accountant—ACCA), the Societies of Chartered Accountants in South Africa (CA [SA]) and the Institute of Chartered Accountants in India (CA [India]).

26. Attempts to register accountants in Victoria, Australia, in 1899 also failed. However, the activities of the SIAA in South Africa resulted in the passage of local legislation for the registration of accountants (Johnson and Caygill 1971). In many countries, moves towards registration were linked with growing nationalist sentiment in British colonies, e.g., the New Zealand Registration Act 1908, the Rhodesian Registration Act 1917, the Indian Chartered Accountants Act 1949 (ibid., 169). See also other chapters in this volume.

27. Recommendations for the Registration of Auditors:

- That an 'approved auditor' should be defined as any person granted a Certificate of Registration by the Statutory Registration Board as

a) Being a member of the Association of Accountants in East Africa; or

b) Being a person who could show to the satisfaction of the Board that he was in public practice as an auditor for a period of not less that three years preceding the enactment of the legislation and that he possessed the necessary skill, experience and integrity.

establishment of a local institute (of 'Chartered Accountants [East Africa]') administering its own professional examinations. However, these initiatives were superseded by looming political independence.

As in the case of many other non-settler British colonies (Wallace 1992; Chaderton and Taylor 1993; Annisette 1999; Uche 2002), in Kenya, moves towards political independence proved to be the catalyst for the change in attitude towards the training and recruitment of non-whites, and in particular Africans, in accountancy. By the late 1950s and early 1960s the number of Asian and African book-keepers and accountants began to increase as a result of training initiatives in both the public and private sector. In the face of imminent independence, the colonial government itself became an early proponent of change, encouraging training schemes. Ultimately, the civil service became an early point of entry into the profession for black Africans (Sian 2007b, 854).

However, opportunities for most non-whites to progress remained relatively scarce, although some attempted to study on their own or through correspondence courses for examinations of British bodies that did not require training and examinations to be undertaken in the UK. Those that were able to afford it paid for their own accounting education on realizing the potential economic benefits, often taking other jobs to help to pay for courses and books. Perhaps because of their elevated position in the social hierarchy and the availability of potential clients, Asians were able to enter the profession much earlier than African Kenyans.[28] However, those that did qualify as accountants (mainly through the ACCA and ICAEW) found it almost impossible to obtain employment with the expatriate firms and many eventually began to set up their own practices, serving the needs of Asian businesses (Sian 2007a, 25).

## POLITICAL INDEPENDENCE AND THE POST-COLONIAL REACH OF EMPIRE

Following unrest in the African colonies after World War II, the British government began to consider the deconstruction of what was left of the empire, with a view to maintaining its political interest by transferring power to moderate nationalists and thereby securing a form of continuity by voluntary membership of the Commonwealth (Smith 1998; Johnson 2003). In Kenya, such ambitions were thwarted to some extent by the Mau Mau, who had engaged in terrorist activity from 1952 to 1956 (Odhiambo and Wanyande 1989, 89) demanding political freedom, which was not

---

- That the Statutory Registration Board should consist as to over half its number of persons appointed by the Council of the Association of Accountants in East Africa. (AAEA, Minutes Extraordinary General Meeting 9/1/59: 3)

28. The first Kenyan Asian ICAEW member was registered in 1957 (Sian 2007a).

granted until 1963 when the government of Jomo Kenyatta was sworn in.[29] A corner-stone policy of the post-independence Kenyatta administration was the 'Africanization'[30] of the economy and public services, as articulated in Sessional Paper Number 10, 1965 (*African Socialism and its Application to Planning in Kenya*). Economic development and the empowerment of the suppressed black African were key goals of the new government and the entry of foreign capital was encouraged to facilitate the former. In order to avoid overseas influence foreign companies were required to make shares and managerial positions (as appropriate) available to Kenyan (African) nationals. Declarations of independence notwithstanding, imperial links were maintained as Britain remained an important trading partner (Swainson 1980, 92) and supplier of expert expatriate personnel.

Many British expatriates and other Europeans returned home after independence and whilst some of the Asians also left, mainly those with rights to British citizenship, others remained. As British and European capital took flight, the Asian entrepreneurs were particularly important in plugging the gap that appeared and 'by 1971 almost two-thirds of non-farm private assets in Kenya were still in Asian hands' (Leys 1975, 3). However, residual African hostility towards the Asians encouraged the post-independence government to foster policies which prevented the Asians from increasing longer-term investments in the country. The government also acted to try and stop large-scale disinvestment by passing the Foreign Investment Protection Act, 1964, which encouraged foreign-owned enterprises to apply for a 'Certificate of Approved Enterprise' in order to undertake business in the country, and new companies such as Union Carbide, Del Monte, Nomura, Schweppes and Lonrho entered the Kenyan market (Leys 1975; Swainson 1980). Although companies such as Shell and British American Tobacco (BAT) had been recruiting locally and training since the 1950s and were some of the first to employ Africans in management positions, by the early 1970s it was still the case that most companies retained expatriates in key positions.

---

29. The British retaliated against Mau Mau activities by enforcing a state of emergency, banning the Kenya African Union (KAU) and imprisoning its leader Jomo Kenyatta in 1953 for alleged Mau Mau involvement. Following two Lancaster House Constitutional Conferences, held in 1962 in London, a new constitution was drawn up for Kenya and elections were held in May 1963. Jomo Kenyatta was released from prison, leading his political party to power, and independence was declared on 12 December 1963.

30. Africanization refers to the transfer of jobs, businesses, the management of resources and decision-making from expatriate personnel to indigenous peoples. The transfer was partially effected through a number of new initiatives. Firstly, several new laws were introduced to help improve opportunities for the previously disenfranchised indigenous population (the Immigration Act of 1967 and the Trade Licensing Act of 1967). Secondly, the Kenyatta government extended credit to Africans through various organizations. Thirdly, large land transfers were made from previous European owners to Africans. Finally, there was a massive government-sponsored training initiative so that positions left vacant as the colonizers returned home, particularly in the public sector, could be filled locally by Africans (Ogot and Ochieng 1995).

Despite the establishment in 1965 of organizations such as the Industrial and Commercial Development Corporation and the Kenya National Trading Corporation (established to promote the interests of Africans in trade and industry), the extent of African involvement in commerce remained small in the 1960s. Additionally, many of the national organizations, which had been established to nurture African business, were very slow in countering the shortage of entrepreneurial skills and African capital (Himbara 1994, 91). Foreign capital originally invested directly in production in Kenya eventually moved into other areas such as technology. Although, industrialization in the 1970s was dominated by import substitution manufacturing, as in many other parts of the world, Kenya witnessed a shift towards service and consumer goods industries. Despite restrictions upon their activities, the Asian entrepreneurs continued to play an important role within the Kenyan economy (Mangat 1969, 322) and the new breed of African entrepreneurs were encouraged and supported in business through various government initiatives.

The flight of British personnel and capital and the radical change in government policy after independence had consequences for developments in accountancy in Kenya. It was the declared intention of the government that the economy should pass into the hands of the indigenous people and this was to be reflected in all aspects of Kenyan life. However, even after political freedom had been achieved, the profession continued to be dominated by British expatriate accountants for some time[31] and it became apparent to professional firms and commercial companies that they, and the country, would face an acute skills short-fall and efforts by the government to encourage the entry of indigenous Africans to the profession would have to be supported.

## ACCOUNTANCY AFTER INDEPENDENCE

### The Africanization of Accountancy

The new post-independence government implemented aggressive affirmative action programmes with the intention of removing discriminatory practices and righting the moral injustices suffered by Africans under colonialism. The application of the government's Africanization programme to accountancy had three key aims: firstly, to train new African accountants in order that they could eventually replace the expatriates in key positions

---

31. At the time of independence, the majority of accountants in Kenya were British expatriates holding British accountancy qualifications. In 1963 the number of accountants registered with key British bodies were: ICAEW (132 expatriates and 11 Asians); ACCA (34 expatriates and 17 Asians); the Institute of Cost and Works Accountants (ICWA—27 expatriates); Institute of Municipal Treasurers and Accountants (IMTA—43 expatriates and three Asians) and The Institute of Chartered Accountants of Scotland (ICAS—34 expatriates and one African) (source: membership directories of relevant associations).

in the civil service; secondly, to avert the high financial costs of continuing to employ expatriate qualified accountants and the expense involved in sending trainees abroad to undertake training (Silcock 1977, 101); and, thirdly, to reverse the extant exclusion of Africans such that they would lead the profession in the future.

With this in mind, the government further developed the Kenya Institute for Administration (KIA)[32] as a source for training African accountants. The Adu Committee had been established in 1964 to investigate training needs in accountancy and recommended that training should be directly linked to the promotion of African Kenyans to identified positions within the civil service. The department of executive training at the KIA offered the first courses in accounts and office management and the local government department also offered accountancy courses leading to the Institute of Municipal Treasurers and Accountants (IMTA) examinations which were moderated by the IMTA in Britain. The training initiatives in the public sector met with some success as the IMTA members' register shows nine African members listed (as students) in 1966.[33]

Following the lead of the public sector, the private sector (companies and accounting firms) also realized that the training of local accountants would be of significant economic importance in the newly independent country and took steps to initiate new training programmes. Many began to sponsor African Kenyans to study for accountancy qualifications in Kenya and in some cases sponsored students to study in Britain. However, the continued dominance of the profession by expatriate British accountants gave rise to a number of key issues that would influence the potential development of a new local professional body. Firstly, expatriates continued to control access to accountancy jobs and Africans often found it difficult to find suitable training opportunities.[34] Secondly, tensions were created as some expatriates, aware that they would eventually be replaced by locals in the private sector, proved to be resistant to change and some indeed attempted to thwart attempts by local practising accountants in competition for clients (Sian 2007b). Thirdly, Africans who did manage to train or qualify found themselves still having to

32. The KIA was established in 1961 with funding from the United States' Agency for International Development. It developed five teaching departments offering intensive, practical training courses: public administration, executive training, local government, community development and co-operatives.

33. By 1968 the number of expatriate members listed in the IMTA year-book was 25 and there were also 25 African Kenyans listed.

34. It was easier for non-whites to undertake the ACCA examination rather than those of the chartered bodies, which required them to take examinations in Britain. Asian Kenyans had access to higher levels of education and were able to undertake training for accountancy much earlier than African Kenyans, who do not appear in the ACCA handbooks until 1970. In that year there were 44 expatriate members listed, 31 Asian members listed and only one African Kenyan. John Mwangi was the first African CA in Kenya, qualifying with the ICAS in 1959 in Britain.

surmount race-based barriers to advancement in their careers and continued to suffer discrimination in the job market throughout the 1960s (Sian 2007b, 858).

## Towards an Indigenous Profession and Beyond

By 1968 the KIA was authorized by the government to begin developing the syllabus for local examinations, with assistance from the AAEA. The Kenyan Accountants and Secretaries National Examination Board (KASNEB) was formally inaugurated on 24 July 1969, with the aim of administering the Kenyan professional examinations for accountants.[35] The historical connexions with Britain remained and funding for KASNEB derived from the Commonwealth Fund for Technical Co-operation.

In recognition of the acute shortage of trained professionals[36] and following discreet lobbying by a group of African accountants, a working party[37] was established in 1970 by the government under the chairmanship of the accountant-general, a senior civil servant in the treasury, to draft legislation facilitating the creation of a professional body for accountants. The deliberations of the working party have been well documented (Sian 2006a, 303). Its 1973 report proposed a three-tier structure for the accounting profession: the examination board (KASNEB) to continue setting examinations; a registration board (the RAB) to register qualified accountants and the ICPAK to co-ordinate and regulate the profession and exercise primary disciplinary control over members. The institute was authorized to set accounting standards and have an input into the examination process co-ordinated by KASNEB.

---

35. Students switching from the examinations of other professional bodies to KASNEB examinations were granted exemptions from part 1 of the new Kenyan examinations. A commercial stream was not introduced until 1970, at the request of the Association who then agreed to withdraw their own book-keeping examinations, and was first examined in March 1971 (Gitau 1999).

36. In late 1969/early 1970 there were 335 accountants in possession of recognized qualifications in Kenya. About 60 unqualified accountants were practising with a registrar's certificate and a further 100 were employed but had qualifications that were not recognized by the Accountants Designations Act (Cap. 524). Of this total of 495, an estimated 240 were European (mainly British expatriates), 177 were Asians and only 38 were African Kenyans. All of the Africans possessed foreign (mainly British) qualifications and it was estimated that only six were in practice (Report of the Working Party on Accountants Legislation, 1973).

37. The members were: Mr. P.A.S.A. Dennis (chairman, Ministry of Finance and Planning), Mr. M.J. Njenga and Mr. W.B. Akatsa (KASNEB), Mr. H.J. Nyamu and Mr. C. Maina (KIA), Prof. D.I. MacDonald and Prof. R. Dinman (University of Nairobi), Mr. I.R. Leslie (AAEA), Mr. J. Mwangi (co-opted member), Mr. J.B. Storey (co-opted member), Mr. C.H. Webb (registrar general), Mr. A.W. Mungai (exchequer and audit department), Mr. S. Kiwanuka and Mr. E Cropper (East African Income Tax Department), Mr. F.C. Kamau (Kenya Chamber of Commerce), Mr. J.G. Johnston (honorary secretary).

Although no longer under British rule, British concepts of professionalism pervaded the various discussions in the creation and passage of Accountants' legislation. As in other ex-colonies, in Kenya, the use of the 'chartered' designation was vigorously debated. Although KASNEB had adopted the term 'CPA' for the examinations, 'chartered' was better known in the country and the working party had recommended that the institute retain it in its title. However, this was not reflected in the final version of the legislation. There is some evidence that the model and the name (ICPAK) were selected exactly because they did not reflect the colonial imprint (Sian 2006a). This is in direct contrast to the outcome in other colonies (such as Australia, Canada, South Africa and Nigeria) where 'chartered' was a much coveted title. Although the British influence was strong, so too were the moves for a decisive departure from their British inheritance resulting in the adoption of the CPA designation.

The Accountants Bill was tabled before Parliament in 1976 and came into effect on 1 July 1977 as the Accountants Act. The act brought into legal existence the three bodies that were recommended by the *Report of the Working Party* (1973). Although the AAEA had been involved in promoting the Accountants Act, it was felt that the Association's own examinations should be withdrawn and the Association itself was liquidated in 1980.

The preponderance of accountants with foreign qualifications in Kenya meant that the proposed single professional institute would have to incorporate under one umbrella organization not only those with local KASNEB qualifications but also those with existing foreign (mainly British) accounting qualifications. The *Report of the Working Party* (1973) had recommended that members of institutes already recognized under the Accountants Designations Ordinance be eligible for membership of the ICPAK, along with those qualifying through KASNEB and those admitted at the discretion of the RAB (or 'qualified by experience').[38] There is evidence of significant tension at this time and debates surrounding the issue of who should and who should not be permitted to register (Sian 2006a, 307); for instance, some of the Kenyan Africans who had undertaken the local exams felt reluctant to accept those with foreign qualifications (mainly expatriates and others with British qualifications). However, the general remit for the RAB was to pursue a policy of inclusion, to bring together all practising accountants under the ICPAK umbrella and to avoid the potential formation of competing associations.

---

38. The bodies on the approved list were: KASNEB; ICAS; ICAEW; ICAI; ACCA; Chartered Institute of Public Finance and Accountancy (CIPFA); Institute of Cost and Management Accountants (ICMA); American Institute of Certified Public Accountants (AICPA); Canadian Institute of Chartered Accountants (CICA). For those with qualifications not appearing on this list, the RAB was required to use its discretion to determine whether that individual should be offered membership in the institute. After the passage of the act, accountants would have to pass the ICPAK examinations in order to qualify.

The ICPAK held its inaugural meeting on 17 November 1978 to elect the first chairman and council and many saw it as an opportunity to rid the profession of the vestiges of imperialism. Observers identified three lobby groups, split effectively along old racial lines: firstly, the locally qualified Kenyan Africans, who wanted ultimate control of the new profession and were keen to ensure that an African, rather than an expatriate, was elected chairman; secondly, the Kenyan Asians, who were keen to retain a high-profile presence in the proceedings, although they did not really expect the chairman to be an Asian; and thirdly, the expatriates who were willing to back an African candidate as long as he was 'their man' (Sian 2006a, 314). Ultimately, the elected chairman, and the government's preferred candidate for the job, was Mr. Stanley Mbugua, a CIPFA qualified accountant[39] working in the civil service as inspector of statutory boards, who was a close personal friend (and former student) of the then minister of finance, Mwai Kibaki.

ICPAK became the sole national representative of professional accountants in Kenya. It was responsible for the regulation of accountancy through the issue of accounting standards and became adviser to the government on issues concerning commerce and taxation. It was also the country's representative on the international stage, as a member of the International Accounting Standards Board (IASB) and International Federation of Accountants (IFAC). Although Britain was the colonizing power and British concepts of profession remained an influential force post-independence, ICPAK has in recent years decidedly steered a course towards internationalization through the adoption of international accounting standards. It has been suggested that the activities of the IASB and the global spread of International Financial Reporting Standards (IFRSs) represent a new form of imperialism, although one that the Kenyans have actively sought and which is not just an accident of history.

## CONCLUSION

Kenya was subject to the rule of British law in the colonial period and remained a member of the Commonwealth after political freedom had been achieved. The economy of the colony was directly connected with Britain, who remained a key trading partner after independence. Socially, too, the British influence was strong, as society within the colony mirrored the hierarchical stratification to be found in Britain, although the class determinant was perhaps superseded by race in Kenya. The British presence left a legacy that has manifested itself in the organization of professional accountancy

---

39. Mbugua was also the chairman of the Registration of Accountants Board and had held the prestigious position of chair of the trustees of the Kenya Government Officers Superannuation Fund.

in Kenya in a number of ways, almost predisposing a particular developmental trajectory: firstly, consequences for professionalization resulting from transfers between the colony and the imperial centre; secondly, consequences for professionalization resulting from social ordering in colonial Kenya; and, finally, consequences for professionalization following the granting of political freedom by Britain.

Transfers between the centre and the colony were key determinants of the mode of professional development adopted in this colony and fall into four general categories. Firstly, the transfer of British accounting personnel to the colony in large numbers to satisfy the need for specialists to document growing economic activity in the first half of the nineteenth century. This had a very strong influence on accounting development as the expatriates virtually controlled entry to the profession both before and to some extent after independence. Although, by the late 1950s and early 1960s there were also some transfers in the opposite direction as, in the face of looming independence, some firms sent non-white trainees to the UK for training purposes. Secondly, the transfer of British accountancy qualifications, as the ACCA established examination centres in Nairobi and other parts of East Africa as a means of capturing those unable to satisfy the conditions the training and examinations of the British chartered bodies. Thirdly, with the dominant presence of so many British qualified accountants for so long, it was inevitable that British ideals and concepts of professionalism would also be transferred and engrained within the professionalization process in Kenya. And finally, the transfer of accounting practices and legislation as Kenya became the recipient of early companies' legislation that had been tried and tested either in Britain or elsewhere in the empire, namely India. On its creation in 1978, ICPAK was tasked with the responsibility of setting Kenyan Accounting Standards, which too drew heavily from equivalent UK standards, although it has been suggested that the choice of the CPA designation was a clear reaction to the empire experience.

Social ordering in Kenyan colonial society also had significant implications for the development of accountancy. Race-based stratification effectively meant that political and economic power rested in the hands of the ruling British, to the exclusion of non-whites. This was reflected in accountancy, too, as white accountants were the main providers of services to (mainly) white clients. However, as the Asian community accumulated wealth in the 1940s and 1950s, Kenya witnessed the rise of Asian accountants, partly the result of better access to the required standards of education. Similarly after independence, the passage of capital and economic power to the indigenous Africans coincided with the emergence of the first African accountants (see Sian 2007a). As suggested by the title of this chapter, a unique feature of the Kenyan story was the initiation of professional organization during the colonial period. This is different from the scenario in other racially diverse British colonies and can be attributed to the different forces that were operative in this country. Firstly, many of the white expatriates were permanent residents in the colony rather than transient public servants. Secondly, the expatriate/resident CAs were by far the majority group, ensuring that intra-professional rivalry remained insignificant as the umbrella AAEA was formed. Thirdly, in Kenya there were significant numbers of unqualified 'accountants' and Indian professional accountants who potentially posed a threat to the white qualified accountants. Indeed, the intervention of the Indian authorities and their support for the Indians in Kenya is testament to the interconnected nature of the empire network (Sian 2006b). Finally, because this was a colony of permanent white settlement, the settlers were directly affected by legislation passed by the colonial administration and as such the Association was the unified voice of the profession in the face of legislation on taxation and commerce.

The consequences of political freedom for Kenyan accountancy were also far-reaching. By the 1960s the sun was officially setting on the British Empire as it quietly transformed into the more politically acceptable Commonwealth. In the colonial aftermath, the objective of the new government in Kenya was to deconstruct the edifices to colonialism without damaging the fabric of a newly free and reorganized society. Its Africanization policy facilitated the construction of a framework that created opportunities for African Kenyans with a view to a more equitable distribution of benefits in society. In accountancy, the new government set out to operationalize its social policy by introducing affirmative action in the education, training and employment of indigenous accountants. Driven by both the moral imperative to allow freedom of opportunity for the indigenous Africans and by the economic need to replace the departing expatriate accountants, firms operating in Kenya were required to recruit suitably qualified local African Kenyans wherever possible. This approach in alliance with legislation for a new professional body instigated a slow but steady change within the profession itself as barriers to African entry and advancement began to crumble.

The historical emergence of the accounting profession in Kenya has been characterized by its unique embrace of certain attributes of both the settler and non-settler colony models of professional organization and by the indelible imprint of its colonial encounter, both with Britain directly and with the wider empire. Despite urges for more dramatic post-colonial reinvention, the Kenyan profession has been unable to cast aside the shadow of its inheritance. However, it has been relatively successful, particularly compared with other ex-colonies cited in this volume, in metamorphosing into an autonomous, indigenous-led profession, headed by an institute that has assumed responsibility for its own entry criteria via examinations and for the regulation of accountancy.

## REFERENCES

### Primary Sources

*Accountants Act*. (1977) Nairobi: Government Printers.
Association of Accountants in East Africa
Minutes of the Meetings of Pre-formation Committee, the Council, Ordinary General Meetings and Extraordinary General Meetings of the Association of Accountants in East Africa, ICPAK library, Nairobi.
Colonial Office
CO533/378/3 Letter to the Colonial Office from the Kenya Office concerning the status of auditors in Kenya, 21 May 1928, National Archives, London.
CO544/52 Kenya Administrative Report, 1937, National Archives, London.
Kenya Institute for Administration. (1961–1971) *Ten Years of Progress*. KIA Library, Nairobi, Kenya.
KNA/AE/20/2. (1919) Companies Ordinance, 1918, Ministry of Commerce. Various correspondences circa 1919, Kenyan National Archive, Nairobi.
RCS, Colonial Office Report on The Colony and Protectorate of Kenya. (1962) Royal Commonwealth Society, Cambridge University Library.
RCS, Careers in Kenya. (1957) Published by the Director of Education in consultation with the Establishments Division of the Kenya Government, Government Printer, Nairobi (RCS: Special Reports L46), Royal Commonwealth Society, Cambridge University Library.
*Report of the Working Party on Accountants Legislation*. (1973) Nairobi: Government Printer.
Sessional Paper Number 10. (1965) *African Socialism and its Application to Planning in Kenya*. Nairobi, Kenya: Government Printer.

### Secondary Sources

Annisette, M. (1999) 'Importing accounting: The case of Trinidad and Tobago'. *Accounting, Business & Financial History* 9:103–33.
Cain, P.J., and Hopkins, A.G. (2002) *British Imperialism: 1688–2000*. London: Pearson Education Ltd.
Chaderton, R., and Taylor, P. (1993) 'The accounting systems of the Caribbean'. *Research in Third World Accounting* 2:45–66.
Davis, L.A., and R.A. Huttenback. (1988) *Mammon and the Pursuit of Empire: The Economics of British Imperialism*. Cambridge: Cambridge University Press.
Ferguson, N. (2003) *Empire: How Britain Made the Modern World*. London: Penguin.
Gitau, E. (1999) Speech by the Secretary and Chief Executive (of KASNEB) to the members of the Association of Business Studies Students (ABSS) of the University of Nairobi on 8 April (sourced from Gitau's personal papers).
Hazlewood, A. (1979) *The Economy of Kenya: The Kenyatta Era*. Oxford: Oxford University Press.
Himbara, D. (1994) *Kenyan Capitalists, the State and Development*. London: Lynne Rienner Publishers.
James, L. (1998) *The Rise and Fall of the British Empire*. London: Abacus.
Johnson, R. (2003) *British Imperialism: Histories and Controversies*. Basingstoke, UK: Palgrave Macmillan.
Johnson, T.J. and M. Caygill (1971) 'The development of accountancy links in the Commonwealth'. *Accounting and Business Research* 1(2): 155-173.

Kapadia, G.P. (1973) *History of the Accountancy Profession in India—Volume 1, The Institute of Chartered Accountants of India.* New Delhi, India: ICAI.

Langdon, S.W. (1976) 'Multinational corporations in the political economy of Kenya'. Unpublished PhD Thesis, Sussex University.

Leys, C. (1975) *Underdevelopment in Kenya.* Nairobi: East African Educational Publishers.

Mangat, J.S. (1969) *A History of the Asians in East Africa, c.1886 to 1945.* Oxford: Clarendon Press.

Marshall, P.J. (1996) *British Empire.* Cambridge: Cambridge University Press.

Murray, R. (1978) 'The Chandarias: the development of a Kenyan multinational'. In R. Kaplinsky (ed.) *Readings on the Multinational Corporation in Kenya.* East Africa: OUP.

Mutungi, O.K. (1974) 'Business organisations and the Africanisation of commerce and industry in Kenya'. Unpublished PhD Thesis, Yale Law School.

Odhiambo, E.S.A., and Wanyande, P. (1989) *History and Government of Kenya.* Nairobi, Kenya: Longman.

Ogot, B.A., and Ochieng, W.R. (1995) *Decolonisation and Independence in Kenya: 1940–1993.* London: James Currey.

Oliver, R., and Fage, J.D. (1995) *A Short History of Africa.* London, Penguin.

Robinson, R., and Gallagher, J. (1981) *Africa and the Victorians: The Official Mind of Imperialism.* London: Macmillan Press.

Sian, S. (2006a) 'Inclusion, exclusion and control: The case of the Kenyan accounting professionalization project'. *Accounting, Organizations and Society* 31:295–322.

———. (2006b) 'Operationalising closure in a colonial context: The Association of Accountants in East Africa, 1949–1963'. Cardiff Accounting and Finance Working Paper A2006/2, Cardiff University.

———. (2007a) 'Patterns of prejudice: Social exclusion and racial demarcation in professional accountancy in Kenya'. *Accounting Historians Journal* 34:1–42.

———. (2007b) 'Reversing exclusion: The Africanisation of accountancy in Kenya, 1963–1970'. *Critical Perspectives on Accounting* 19:831–72.

Silcock, T.H. (1977) *Professional Structure in South East Asia.* Canberra: Australian National University.

Smith, S. (1998) *British Imperialism: 1750–1970.* Cambridge: Cambridge University Press.

Swainson, N. (1980) *The Development of Corporate Capitalism in Kenya 1918–77.* London: Heinemann.

Uche, C.U. (2002) 'Professional accounting development in Nigeria: Threats from the inside and outside'. *Accounting, Organizations and Society* 27:471–96.

Wallace, R.S.O. (1992) 'Growing pains of an indigenous accountancy profession: The Nigerian experience'. *Accounting, Business & Financial History* 2:25–51.

# 11 Accountancy and Empire

## Connexions, Patterns and Suggestions

*Chris Poullaos and Suki Sian*

## INTRODUCTION

In this chapter we draw upon the contributions made elsewhere in this volume to sketch briefly, and in broad terms, the various ways in which the organization of accountancy has been affected or constituted by the (British) empire experience, in both the colonial periphery and imperial centre. We seek to identify broad patterns and variations within them as well as to make suggestions for future research.

In doing so we acknowledge the specificity of both the British Empire and British models of professionalization and professionalism. We do not, that is, presume that the former is the ideal-typical model for all empires or that the latter plays the equivalent role in theorizing the organization of expertise along occupational lines. Even within the British Empire we do not envisage British models of accountancy organization as being necessarily or naturally applicable in a standard mode with relatively uniform effects across different parts of the empire at different times (including after formal independence); nor do we, in keeping with the cautions in Johnson (1973, 1982) and Poullaos (2009b) regard their movement across the large expanses of space as either inevitable, effort-free or unquestionably benign. Indeed, previous chapters in this volume highlight the tensions and complications arising in respect of, for example, the movement of chartered accountancy to the colonial periphery. They have shown that the 'continual effort to maintain and if possible enhance the position of the group' (Macdonald 1995, 188) has particular twists in an imperial context and it is these that we will highlight here.

We also reiterate, however, that contributors had considerable discretion as to the focus and scope of their chapters and as a result detailed comparisons of one locale with others are not always feasible. Nor is every part of the British Empire included in the volume—another reason why the remarks that follow are illustrative and suggestive rather than systematic and comprehensive.

## HOW HAS THE ORGANIZATION OF ACCOUNTANTS IN THE COLONIES BEEN AFFECTED BY THE EMPIRE EXPERIENCE?

This section addresses the 'how' question in two related senses. It comments first on the specific impacts on professional organization in the colonies and, second, on the specific 'empire' factors that produced them. The latter group includes: British capital; mobile British accountants; British laws, education and other institutions; the structuring of colonial economies; the construction of colonial social hierarchies (including stratification based on 'race'); the collaboration of local elites; the activities of British accounting associations; the absorption by colonial accountants of British models of professional accountancy; and imperial and local state agents. The former, broadly speaking, include: the structuring of colonial professional organizations, in particular relative positioning in colonial markets for accountancy services of various groupings of accountants; the emergence of exclusionary arrangements locally in conjunction with an integrative tendency in the imperial accountancy arena; the frustration of the ambitions of post-independence state agents for the role of accountancy and the limitations of the social contributions of accountants to post-colonial nations.

Nearly four decades ago, Johnson and Caygill (1971) observed that British accountants followed British capital throughout the empire; a theme pursued in Parker (1989), Briston and Kedslie (1997) and by the contributors to this volume. In the self-governing white settler colonies (in this volume, Canada, South Africa and Australia) the drive by locally born and trained white colonial accountants to gear themselves to compete with British immigrant accountants for lucrative 'British audits' (of local subsidiaries or branches/divisions of British-based enterprises) and/or to establish a competitive position locally, was a factor in the mimetic trend in training regimes, entry rules, designations and other forms of symbolic capital, and the governance and constitution of local accounting associations (see also Chua and Poullaos 2002; Parker 2005). Indeed, British immigrant accountants could themselves 'go native' in the colonies, adopting local identities and attitudes that were at times inimical to the newly arrived Briton and, more particularly, to their 'home' associations. In the white settler colonies the locals had the confidence that came from shared cultural capital (the Britons) and/or a robust alternative (the Afrikaaners); in contrast to at least some of the non-settler colonies. The former group, having the advantage of 'self-government,' became decoupled from the imperial centre much earlier than the latter (see also Parker 1989, 18). It is no coincidence that Canada, South Africa and Australia were producing 'chartered accountants' (CAs) long before the other colonies studied in this volume, notwithstanding that the paths to CA taken by the former group were different. In terms of formal control over accountancy they were 'decolonized' early. Nevertheless, they had not managed to achieve a meaningful form of mutual recognition from the British CA bodies by the end of the 1920s. (Subsequent centre–periphery relationships involving the white self-governing colonies have received little scholarly attention to date.)

In general terms, it seems clear that British capital underpinned the emergence of colonial professional organization, that colonial accountants were to some degree frustrated by the preference of British companies for their accounts to be audited by CAs (or incorporated accountants) and that British accountants tried to leverage this argument when responding to colonial attempts to restrict their access to work locally (Johnson and Caygill 1971; Chua and Poullaos 2002). Nevertheless, the nuances of the capital/professionalization relationship are still fuzzy. As Parker (1989, 18) has noted and the previous paragraph also implies, the specifics of the latter cannot be readily read off from the quantum of the former alone. While British accountants may have continued to argue well into the twentieth century that British capitalists should be able to employ British accountants to monitor their offshore investments (Johnson and Caygill 1971, 169–70), there is surprisingly little suggestion in the primary sources on which Chapter 2 of this volume is based that British capitalists were seriously perturbed about the quality of the accounting work done by locals (especially when they were Britons) even in the 1920s. This point may be qualified, in its turn, by the observation that British accountants were, in the end, not prevented from taking on work in the colonies, reflecting, perhaps, a residual anxiety on the part of local state agents that the accountancy preferences of British capitalists could not be ignored entirely. And while, furthermore, it is tempting to attribute Canadian resistance to the Institute of Chartered Accountants in England and Wales (ICAEW) supplemental charter to the availability of American capital, it is noticeable that the Canadians were more accommodating of the ICAEW's desires than the more capital-dependant South Africans, who were also much more aggressive than the Australians. Arguably, these variations can be explained by tactical considerations reflecting local specificities (including the Afrikaaner culture). Furthermore, the extent, timing and mechanisms through which the accountancy 'requirements' of British capital were adopted by local enterprises could all do with further unpicking. At the same time, the chapters on Canada, Trinidad and Tobago (T&T) and Kenya in this volume emphasize that eventually American and other non-British capital supplanted the dominance of British and took a variety of forms (intellectual/technical rather than just financial or cultural).

One way in which the 'requirements' of British capital, mediated through political processes *in Britain*, were localized, in the non-self-governing (mostly) non-settler colonies in particular, was the passing of local ordinances or legislation with mandatory reporting and audit provisions modeled on British legislation supplemented by local provisions, in various forms, that allowed members of British bodies recognized by British authorities *in Britain* to take on audit work in the colonies. These moves not only provided an entrée to British accountants to structure the colonial professional status hierarchy in their own image; they also potentially expanded the demand for audit services and encouraged local elites to join British accountancy bodies, thereby feeding into processes of professional exclusion both before and after formal independence, which were further supplemented by the operation of other transplanted British institutions, modes of education in particular (as discussed below). It is worth noting here, however, that the interests and agendas of both (a) local (pre-independence) colonial administrators and (b) state agents in the imperial centre leading up to, during and after the decolonization of the non-settler-colonies, with regard to the regulation and organization of colonial accountancy, remain unexamined. Closer analyses of this kind might provide further insight into why forms of state control over (or state sanction of particular groups of) accountants that proved not to be feasible in the imperial centre were deemed permissible, if not desirable, in the periphery. Johnson (1982, 202) writes that in contrast to state hostility to registration in Britain, 'in many colonies the administration was to develop a positive attitude towards registration as a means of controlling and standardising accounting practice, particularly as it related to the needs of international capital'.[1] Arguably, the plausibility of this statement would be further enhanced if the unresolved issues raised earlier in relation to capital-related explanations were researched more fully in conjunction with the attitude of colonial administrations to, and their relationship with, 'international capital' (which in Johnson's context includes British capital).

Contributors to this volume have, nevertheless, highlighted that the controversial structuring of the pre-independence economies of T&T, Jamaica, Kenya, Malaysia, India, Sri Lanka and Nigeria as producers/exporters of agricultural products and raw materials and importers of British manufactures and services arguably limited not only economic growth but also the prospects of an indigenous-led accounting profession (although India's long business history may have ameliorated this tendency to some degree). This outcome was contributed to by policies of colonial governance in (for example) Malaysia, Kenya and Sri Lanka which strengthened 'traditional' compartmentalizations of economic actors such that, for example, those from agricultural backgrounds tended to remain in agriculture. Pre-independence accountancy (the more lucrative end of the market for accountancy services especially) was largely dominated by immigrant British accountants who had no urgent 'need' to collectively organize themselves to establish or maintain their position and little to fear from locally trained accountants (Annisette 1999; Sian 2007), in sharp contrast to the Canadian, Australian and South African cases.

1. The same might be said for Canada and Australia, though not South Africa or New Zealand (which adopted Transvaal-style accountancy legislation in the first decade of the twentieth century). These variations within the white settler colonies could do with further investigation.

As implied already, the effect of empire on local social structures worked in conjunction with the preceding factors to impact upon colonial profession formation. One of the more striking of these effects derives from the movement of non-Britons (including non-empire non-Britons, namely, those of Chinese background) throughout the (formal) empire and their subsequent appearance in the profession at their destination locales. When combined with the exclusion of indigenous populations or non-indigenous locals of African lineage through the enforcement or enhancement of local stratification patterns *via* unequal access to education, English-language instruction in particular, the political sphere and business opportunities, the result has been that Chinese professional accountants are more numerous than *Bumiputra* accountants in Malaysia and well represented in some sectors of accountancy in T&T (Annisette 2003), while accountants of Indian extraction have played a significant role in T&T and Kenya and, seemingly, a lesser role in Sri Lanka. The efforts of the Indian government to protect the interests of accountants of Indian origin in Kenya provide a counterpoint to the features of the imperial accountancy arena resulting from the interaction of South Africa, Canada and Australia with the imperial centre. We suspect that closer examination of the Indian and Chinese accountancy diaspora would provide a contrasting view of the imperial accountancy arena.[2] The overall impression is that imperial accountancy professionalization has distinct (but not simple) 'racial' elements in its history, albeit less overt in Britain and the self-governing colonies than in the other locales examined in this volume; probably adding an edge to the sometimes determined efforts to localize accountancy in the early independence period.[3] The racial legacy included, or was reflected in, (as Marcia Annisette puts it in Chapter 8 of this volume) in the subjugation of colonial minds, a factor noted in regard to Malaysia, Jamaica and India as well as T&T (and possibly applicable elsewhere).

A factor that complicates the race story is that typically exclusion was not total during the whole of the pre-independence era. The collaboration

2. Other instances of cross-border but within-empire interactions include the copying of the legislation of one colony by another (e.g., Malaysian and Singaporean accountancy legislation being based on New Zealand legislation, in the first-mentioned case, upon the advice of an Australian adviser; the spread of Transvaal-style legislation to other provinces in Southern Africa and Australia, as reported in Chua and Poullaos 2002, 427, 432–33, 435; and the use of the Indian Companies Act of 1913 as a template for similar legislation in Kenya in 1918 and Tanzania, among other African colonies; the Indian institute's promoters looking to Australia, Canada and South Africa for organizational or rhetorical inspiration and the transplantation of Australian accountancy feuds to Malaysia).

3. Annisette's contention (2003, 665) that accountancy in T&T before independence was 'coloured white and raced British' can be extended to most other racially diverse colonies. As a result professional bodies through which non-Britons could train or qualify as professional accountants were, on the whole, not formed until after independence. The exception was India where, although a national association did not exist until after independence, regional associations were formed before then and both Indian and British accountants were active members.

of local elites in colonial governance has been highlighted in the chapters in this volume on Sri Lanka, Kenya, Jamaica, T&T and may be implicit elsewhere, for it is typical for a small cadre of local accountancy pioneers to have travelled to the UK to gain professional qualifications from the British chartered bodies before independence and to play a prominent role upon their return. While it is no doubt inappropriate to label all British-trained locals as avid collaborationists, this volume nevertheless points to a tendency for the British-trained to put forth the message that 'British is best' even while being disadvantaged in comparison to British accountants practising locally; seek to initially remove or mitigate this advantage after independence but, nevertheless, to ultimately eschew attempts to localize education and training (that is, to make them responsive to local specificities).

The last point supports Parker's (1989) contention that it wasn't just British accountants or British accounting associations or British qualifications that were exported from Britain to her colonies. The very *idea* of professional accountancy—more particularly, British models thereof (of entry rules, training, designations, etc.)—were widely adopted by the promoters of local associations. Even the conscious efforts in Kenya and Nigeria (and elsewhere) to overcome the proliferation and competition so evident in Britain are testimony to the power of those models. Not surprisingly, organizational mimesis operating in conjunction with the factors noted earlier played into the hands of British associations *per se*. Not only did it give them something to complain about (and to use to enlist the support of imperial state agencies such as the Colonial Office [CO] and the Privy Council Office [PCO]), it also emphasized that if 'British was best' then it was the British bodies and their members that were the most British. It has also contributed to the integrative tendency in the imperial accountancy arena which finds expression in today's 'Global Accounting Alliance' (GAA), consisting overwhelmingly of CA bodies based in Britain or in former British colonies.[4]

The Scottish chartered bodies were never seriously interested in setting up training facilities in the colonies and the ICAEW seems to have lost interest by the end of the 1920s; thereby forcing colonials seeking CA status to incur considerable costs that would, nevertheless, mark them out as part of the professional and (most likely) socio-economic elite upon their return. As Johnson and Caygill (1971) and Owolabi Bakre's chapter in this volume (among others) have highlighted, however, British CAs had the ear of colonial administrations before independence while locally born members of those bodies appear to have been influential after independence. It may thus be misleading to assess their offshore influence purely on membership numbers alone (cf. Johnson and Caygill 1971, 160). The extent to which the British chartered bodies were 'using' colonial

4. At the time of writing, the GAA consists of CA bodies in Australia, Canada, England and Wales, Ireland, New Zealand, Scotland and South Africa; CPA bodies in Hong Kong, Japan and the US; and the Institut der Wirtschaftsprüfer in Germany. See http://www.globalaccountingalliance.com/.

members (British born or otherwise) to do their bidding and/or their members were using the prestige of their 'home' bodies to further their own interests offshore could usefully be explored in further research (cf. Chua and Poullaos 2002, 438). As noted by Johnson and Caygill (1971, 170) and further supported by Chua and Poullaos (2002) and Chapter 2 of this volume, it was the British-based international firms that did much of the heavy lifting when it came to political lobbying in South Africa (and possibly other self-governing colonies). Their subsequent efforts throughout the empire/Commonwealth could usefully be examined in more detail, especially as they are predecessors to today's 'Big Four' who, as Marcia Annisette (Chapter 8, this volume) points out, have a dominant role in the production of standardized technical methodologies used throughout the world. And if, furthermore, those firms are now 'better known than' their original 'home' associations (Parker 2005, 39), then shifts in the relationship between associations and firms in the imperial (and subsequent global arena) over the last century are of interest. In any case, the chartered bodies have continued to steadily expand their offshore (including empire/Commonwealth) membership after decolonization, albeit not as spectacularly as the Association of Chartered Certified Accountants (ACCA) or the Chartered Institute of Management Accountants (CIMA) and their predecessors (Briston and Kedslie 1997).

As Johnson and Caygill (1971) and others have noted, the Society of Incorporated Accountants and Auditors (SIAA) had an active 'empire' policy in the early decades of the twentieth century, with colonial branches running local examinations and schemes for training under articles until its 'amalgamation' with the ICAEW in 1957.[5] As such it could compete directly with local accounting associations for membership, political influence and the favour of the business community, diminishing the effectiveness of South African bodies but not Australian or Canadian ones. The more interesting proponent of the 'empire' policy in the non-white parts of the British Commonwealth during and after decolonization has been the ACCA (and its predecessors). The number of ACCA members in the empire/Commonwealth rose from 375 in 1939 to 1,376 in 1969 and 10,250 in 1989. The equivalent numbers for British CAs *plus* incorporated accountants in (or around) those years were, respectively: 1,892,

5. Johnson and Caygill (1971, 159) are probably correct when they state that the SIAA tended to lose interest in the colonies once it became more established in Britain. In the early 1900s there were 287 incorporated accountants in the empire (outside Britain) compared to 88 CAs (Scottish plus English and Welsh). In the early 1920s the equivalent numbers were 382 and 434, respectively, and in the late 1930s, 758 versus 1,134 (Briston and Kedslie 1997, 179). Johnson and Caygill (1971, 161–62) also note that the handful of bodies formed by British CAs resident in various parts of the empire in the first half of the twentieth century were tolerated rather than encouraged by their home societies. They were not formal branches of those societies through which locals could qualify as CAs. Johnson and Caygill (1971, 162) claim that 'they were locally influential' but there is little evidence that they influenced events in South Africa.

3,763 and 9,671 (Briston and Kedslie 1997, 178–79).[6] In this period it has been the ACCA which has been the spoiler as far as nationalist local associations seeking to assert themselves in the feisty early years of formal independence were concerned, as the chapters in this volume on Jamaica, T&T (see also Annisette 1999, 2000) and Nigeria suggest. (It is a moot point as to whether Malaysia is a contrary case.) Tensions between colonial certified accountants and CAs (being in part tensions between public accountants on the one hand and commercial and government accountants on the other) were a prime means through which the divisiveness within British accountancy was reproduced in the colonies; while after independence, in the Caribbean in particular, the ACCA played the role of the 'international' body standing in contradistinction to bodies formed locally. Given the difficulties which the ICAEW and the Scots created for colonials seeking 'CA', the folding of the SIAA into the ICAEW and the lack of interest on the part of the American Institute of Certified Public Accountants (AICPA) in expanding its operations offshore, it was the ACCA which, in conjunction with the multinational accounting firms (MAFs) (see Annisette, Chapter 8 of this volume) stepped into the vacuum to provide the training and qualifications on the basis of which local accountants could acquire and manifest their allegiance to the international/global accountancy arena rather than the local and, therefore, to the application of standardized accounting/audit methodologies generated offshore to solve the local problems of international clients and their local networks, rather than to the development of local methodologies (e.g., through local universities) to serve the needs of those several steps removed from those networks.[7] Senarath Yapa makes an additional point with respect to Sri Lanka, namely, that the closing off of public practice for Sri Lankan elites who have nurtured and been nurtured by the local version of imperial milieu has been achieved using closure techniques adapted from the ICAEW; while the replication of the ICAEW's public practice orientation has distracted the Institute of Chartered Accountants of Sri Lanka (ICASL) from providing leadership in other areas of accountancy, leaving a vacuum happily filled by British-based bodies such as CIMA and the ACCA (see also Yapa 2006). The claim that the post-colonial elites embodying British models of professional organization are not producing 'enough' accountants and/or providing enough accountancy

---

6. Unlike Jamaica, which had significant numbers of both CAs and certified accountants (ACCA members), in Kenya the CAs significantly outnumbered the non-CAs and dominated the combined body (of British accountants) formed there prior to independence.

7. Nevertheless, there are variations in the ACCA's success in the ex-colonies. It has been notably successful in Jamaica, T&T and Nigeria, where locals have seen it as their entrée to the international accountancy arena. In Kenya and India, however, the supremacy of the national organization has remained essentially unthreatened. In Sri Lanka, the local CA body dominates public practice but the ACCA is now actively competing for influence over other areas of accountancy.

opportunities to locals has been made in respect of Nigeria, Kenya and Malaysia as well. Also worthy of mention here is the desire of the promoters of Institute of Chartered Accountants in India (ICAI) to construct a British-style 'autonomous but nationalist' profession at the very time that the Indian government was experimenting with central planning as a way of overcoming the problems created by years of imperial rule. These analyses, while not necessarily predicted in detail in Johnson (1973), are broadly consistent with his general argument that the claims by development theorists that the social impact of the emerging professional classes in Britain's 'underdeveloped' colonies/new states would be socially beneficial, are best taken with a grain of salt.

The importance of the state–profession relationship to profession formation has been noted across the whole range of the accountancy professionalization literature (Poullaos 2009b) and it has also been highlighted within this volume. While state agents in Canada, South Africa and Australia may have helped their accountancy communities to gain or maintain 'CA'[8] it is also notable that their counterparts in newly independent non-white former colonies have been frustrated in their efforts to create unified local professions that might contribute to (forms of) national development decoupled from the yoke of imperialism; and provided ample opportunities for locally born citizens to enhance their life-chances. As the previous paragraph implies, part of the explanation lies in the internalization and replication by local accountants of British models of professional organization and patterns of behaviour. Also significant has been the ongoing dependence of the 'new states' on British and other 'international' capital (financial and intellectual); and, in the case of Malaysia, British arms. Even where British influence has been supplanted, it may reasonably be argued that, with respect to professional accountancy, the British Empire experience has prepared her former colonies for the era of globalization (or American informal empire, depending on one's point of view; see, for example, Held et al. 1999; Hopkins 2002; Alan Richardson's analysis

8. The non-white non-settler colonies varied in their designation preferences after independence. While some sought to invoke their British inheritance (by choosing 'CA') others sought to decisively disconnect from it. As noted in Chapter 9 of this volume, the Indian profession deliberated extensively over the issue, undertaking intense negotiations with the Indian government. In this case, the continuing economic links with the British remained strong and the issue became political, although ultimately agreement to adopt 'CA' was reached. Similarly the post-independence professional bodies in Nigeria, Jamaica, Sri Lanka and T&T all appropriated 'CA' via local legislation but without perhaps the extensive soul-searching of the Indians. However, in Kenya and Malaysia, the state-legislated associations adopted the CPA designation (drawn from the US). Whilst American hegemony might explain the use of the CPA designation in some parts of the world (Parker 2005), in the case of Kenya it most likely had more to do with the powerful modernizers who adopted the designation as a symbol of Africanization and freedom from British rule (Sian 2006), while Malaysia turned to 'CPA' only after it was 'not allowed' to use 'CA' (Chapter 5, this volume).

of Canada in Chapter 3 of this volume). Even here, however, there are likely to be differences in the capacity of, say, Canada (as a former white-dominated, settler, self-governing colony) to play a 'middle power' role in international standard-setting, using its involvement in international standard-setting as a bulwark against American influence, in comparison to non-white and/or non-settler colonies such as Sri Lanka, Malaysia, Nigeria, Jamaica, India and Kenya.

## HOW HAS THE ORGANIZATION OF ACCOUNTANCY IN BRITAIN BEEN AFFECTED BY THE EMPIRE EXPERIENCE?

This particular trajectory of influence has received less scholarly attention. Johnson and Caygill (1971) observed that the second-tier British associations (the SIAA and the ACCA's predecessor, the London Association of Accountants [LAA]) used offshore membership as a means of bolstering their resources and status in Britain (see also Parker 1989; Briston and Kedslie 1997; Chua and Poullaos 2002). While it would be helpful to have a more thorough analyses of the mechanisms through which those outcomes were achieved, it seems reasonable to posit that the wealth associated with the sheer weight of membership numbers would have been helpful in promoting the SIAA and the LAA in Britain. Chapter 2 of this volume provides some evidence of ICAEW concern about the SIAA's relative membership numbers in South Africa while the same concerns may have applied to (at least) India as well (Poullaos 2009a, 452). The extent to which state agents and market participants in Britain were impressed by the SIAA's and LAA's activities offshore is a subject crying out for further research. In any case, the posited effects in Britain are contingent upon the willingness on citizens of the empire/Commonwealth to join. There is also evidence that the unsolicited efforts by some of those citizens to apply directly to Britain for membership of the British CA bodies during the 1920s provoked a measure of 'race anxiety' in the imperial centre (Poullaos 2009a). Again, further research on subsequent applications of this kind and, more particularly, into the impacts on British accountancy of the migration of empire/Commonwealth citizens to Britain are to be welcomed.[9]

The resistance of accountants and state agents in the self-governing colonies to the domination of British state agents, accounting associations and accountants came through various means: the appropriation of 'CA', the threat or actuality of local legislation (either registration or designation

9. More recent migration has significantly altered the racial demographics in countries such as Canada, Australia, New Zealand and Britain itself (Annisette 2003). The relevant professional associations have, as a result, incorporated more members from racially diverse backgrounds and to date little research has been directed at this phenomenon, other than perhaps Kim's (2004) study of the experience of Chinese accountants in New Zealand.

bills/acts) restricting the access of British accountants to local markets for accountancy services, the pressure for mutual recognition—measures at times instigated or supported by British CAs domiciled in the colonies themselves—and have been highlighted in Chapter 2 of this volume and previous literature.[10] With respect to the self-governing colonies, the particular aspect of cross-border mutual state–profession formation (Johnson 1982) at play—with profession and state in both centre and periphery being mutually affected—was the (re)negotiation of the autonomy of those colonies from the imperial centre. The outcome of the negotiations was that the spread of British designations, accounting firms, modes of training (etc.), and the construction of an imperial accountancy arena generally, thus took place on terms which were more satisfactory to colonial accountants than would otherwise have been the case. For example, the British CA bodies would certainly have preferred that their members, and only their members, could use 'CA'. And, as noted in Chua and Poullaos (2002) and further highlighted in Chapter 2 of this volume, operating in the imperial accountancy arena bought the British CA bodies (in particular) into the purview, and onto the agenda, of imperial state agencies such as the CO, Dominions Office (DO) and PCO, making them vulnerable to the at times unpredictable logic of empire relations. Further research on subsequent compromises (e.g., with regard to mutual recognition) made by British state agencies, accounting societies and accountancy firms in response to pressure from their counterparts in the periphery would, we believe, provide insights into the current global accountancy arena.

As the chapters (and other work by their authors) on Jamaica, Kenya, Nigeria and T&T have noted, the period immediately after independence represented the high point of 'accountancy nationalism' in the non-white/non-settler (former) colonies with pressure being put on British accountants there to either leave or change their *modus operandi* (see also Johnson and Caygill 1971). The response of British accountancy firms, capital and state agents could do with closer examination, not only with respect to those countries but also to the specificities of India, Malaysia and Sri Lanka (not to mention other parts of the empire/Commonwealth). We suspect that there may have been impacts on the imperial (and subsequent global) accountancy arenas that vary markedly, in either kind or degree, from those resulting from the engagement of the white settler colonies with the imperial centre.

This volume has identified a myriad of ways in which the organization of accountants throughout the British Empire has been affected by the empire experience. We suspect that the impact on Britain's former colonies has been more stark than on the imperial centre itself, but this judgment perhaps understates the importance of the empire to Britain; and may either

10. See Johnson and Caygill (1971), Creighton (1984), Parker (1989, 2005), Chua and Poullaos (1993, 1998, 2002), Poullaos (1994, 2008), Carnegie and Parker (1999), Carnegie and Edwards (2001) and Carnegie, Edwards and West (2003).

understate or overstate the importance of accountancy to the maintenance of empire. Whether the overall impact of the empire experience is to be lauded or condemned is also a moot point; although our contributors have raised concerns significant enough to raise the broader question of whether the organizations of accountants in Britain's ex-colonies serve the needs and interests of post-Britannia neo-imperialism rather than those of their local communities, whatever their designation or associational affiliation or cultural heritage might be. This is a particularly pertinent issue if the long-term impact of the empire experience extends beyond Britain's sphere of influence to today's increasingly integrated global accounting community characterized by both support for and resistance to global training and practice regimes.

## REFERENCES


Annisette, M. (1999) 'Importing accounting: The case of Trinidad and Tobago'. *Accounting, Business & Financial History* 9:103–33.

———. (2000) 'Imperialism and the professions: The education and certification of accountants in Trinidad and Tobago'. *Accounting, Organizations and Society* 25:631–59.

———. (2003) 'The colour of accountancy: Examining the salience of race in a professionalisation project'. *Accounting, Organizations and Society* 28:639–74.

Briston, R.J., and Kedslie, M.J.M. (1997) 'The internationalization of British professional accounting: The role of the examination exporting bodies'. *Accounting, Business & Financial History* 7:175–94.

Carnegie, G.D., and Edwards, J.R. (2001) 'The construction of the professional accountant: The case of the Incorporated Institute of Accountants, Victoria (1886)'. *Accounting, Organizations and Society* 26:301–25.

Carnegie, G.D., Edwards, J.R., and West, B.P. (2003) 'Understanding the dynamics of the Australian accounting profession. A prosopographical study of the founding members of the Incorporated Institute of Accountants, Victoria, 1886 to 1908'. *Accounting, Auditing & Accountability Journal* 16:790–820.

Carnegie, G.D., and Parker, R.H. (1999) 'Accountants and empire: The case of co-membership of Australian and UK accountancy bodies, 1885 to 1914'. *Accounting, Business & Financial History* 9:77–102.

Chua, W.F., and Poullaos, C. (1993) 'Rethinking the profession-state dynamic: The case of the Victorian charter attempt, 1885–1906'. *Accounting, Organizations and Society* 18:691–728.

———. (1998) 'The dynamics of closure amidst the construction of market, profession, empire and nationhood: An historic analysis of an Australian accounting association, 1886–1903'. *Accounting, Organizations and Society* 27:409–45.

———. (2002) 'The empire strikes back? An exploration of centre–periphery interaction between the ICAEW and accounting associations in the self-governing colonies of Australia, Canada and South Africa, 1880–1907'. *Accounting, Organizations and Society* 27:409–45.

Creighton, P. (1984) *A Sum of Yesterdays*. Toronto: ICAO.

Held, D., McGrew, A., Goldblatt, D., and Perraton, J. (1999) *Global Transformations*. Cambridge: Polity Press.

Hopkins, A.G. (ed.) (2002) *Globalization in World History*. London: Pimlico.

Johnson, T.J. (1973) 'Imperialism and the professions: Notes on the development of professional occupations in Britain's colonies and the new states'. In *Professions and Social Change (Sociological Review Monograph 20)*, ed. P. Halmos. Keele: University of Keele.

———. (1982) 'The state and the professions: Peculiarities of the British'. In *Social Class and the Division of Labour*, ed. A. Giddens and G. McKenzie. Cambridge: Cambridge University Press.

Johnson, T.J., and Caygill, M. (1971) 'The development of accountancy links in the commonwealth'. *Accountancy and Business Research* (Spring): 155–73.

Kim, S.N. (2004) 'Imperialism without empire: Silence in contemporary accountancy research on race/ethnicity'. *Critical Perspectives on Accounting* 15:95–133.

Macdonald, K.M. (1995) *The Sociology of the Professions*. London, Thousand Oaks, CA, and New Delhi: Sage.

Parker, R.H. (1989) 'Importing and exporting accounting: The British experience'. In *International Pressures for Accounting Change*, ed. A. Hopwood. Hertfordshire: Prentice Hall International and ICAEW.

———. (2005) 'Naming and branding: Accountants and accountancy bodies in the British Empire and Commonwealth, 1853–2003'. *Accounting History* 10:7–46.

Poullaos, C. (1994) *Making the Australian Chartered Accountant*. New York and London: Garland.

———. (2008) '"Independence with a vengeance!"—maintaining Canadian accountants' symbolic capital, 1908–1912'. Paper presented at the Critical Perspectives on Accounting Conference, New York, 24–26 April.

———. (2009a) 'Profession, race and empire: Keeping the centre pure, 1921–1927'. *Accounting, Auditing & Accountability Journal* 22:429–68.

———. (2009b) 'Professionalisation'. In *Routledge Companion to Accounting History*, ed. R. Edwards and S. Walker. London and New York: Routledge.

Sian, S. (2006) 'Inclusion, exclusion and control: The case of the Kenyan accounting professionalisation project'. *Accounting, Organizations and Society* 31:295–322.

———. (2007) 'Patterns of prejudice: Social exclusion and racial demarcation in professional accountancy in Kenya'. *Accounting Historians Journal* 34:1–42.

Yapa, P.W.S. (2006) 'Cross-border competition and the professionalization of accounting: The case of Sri Lanka'. *Accounting History* 13:328–39.

# Contributors

**Marcia Annisette** is an Associate Professor and Chair of the Accounting Area at the Schulich School of Business, York University, Canada. Her major research interest is in the area of accounting and financial history with specific focus on the diffusion of accounting institutions and practices under imperialism. She has published extensively in leading journals and has won best paper awards for her work on the accounting profession in Trinidad and Tobago and the Republic of Ireland. She is co-editor of *Critical Perspectives on Accounting* and is on the editorial board of eight journals.

**Owolabi M. Bakre** holds a PhD in accounting from the University of Essex and is currently a senior lecturer in accounting at Brunel Business School, Brunel University, London, UK. His work on the accounting profession in Jamaica has appeared in *Critical Perspectives on Accounting*. His other research interests include accounting in developing countries; globalization, culture and accounting; tax avoidance; underdevelopment of emerging economies; and accounting and crime.

**Chris Poullaos** is an Associate Professor in Accounting at the University of Sydney, Australia. His work on the professionalization of accounting in Australia, Britain, Canada, the Philippines and South Africa has appeared in international journals and several monographs. He is on the editorial boards of five international journals and looks forward to pursuing the suggestions for further research contained in this volume.

**Alan J. Richardson** is a Professor at the Schulich School of Business, York University, Canada. He has published extensively on the regulation of practice rights and standard-setting processes. His recent work concerns the role of accounting in global communications networks and the effect of global governance networks on domestic accounting phenomena. He is on the editorial board of eight journals including *Accounting, Organizations and Society*, *Contemporary Accounting Research*, *Accounting, Business & Financial History* and *Accounting Historians Journal*.

**Suki Sian** is a chartered accountant and holds a PhD from the University of Aberdeen and an MSc in Accounting and Finance from the London School of Economics. She most recently lectured at Cardiff University, UK. Her main research interests include accounting history, professionalization, globalization, accounting and empire. She was awarded the Vangermeersch Manuscript Award in 2006 for her paper on the professionalization of accountancy in Kenya. She has also led international research projects on financial reporting by small businesses on behalf of both IFAC and UNCTAD.

**Devi S. Susela,** a member of the Malaysian Institute of Accountants and the Malaysian Institute of CPAs, obtained her PhD in the area of Accounting Standard-Setting in Malaysia from University of Waikato, New Zealand. She served as technical adviser to the Malaysian delegation in the International Accounting Standards Committee in 1998. She is an Associate Professor at the Faculty of Business and Accountancy, University of Malaya. Currently she serves as Executive Director of the Malaysian Accounting Standards Board.

**Chibuike U. Uche** trained as a chartered accountant with Coopers and Lybrand (now PricewaterhouseCoopers) in Nigeria and holds a doctorate degree in accounting and finance from the London School of Economics. He is Professor of Banking and Financial Institutions at the University of Nigeria. He was Dean, Faculty of Business Administration, University of Nigeria Enugu Campus (2006–2008) and has recently completed sabbatical leave at Humboldt University Berlin where he was an Alexander von Humboldt Georg Forster Fellow (November 2008–September 2009).

**Shraddha Verma** is a lecturer at the York Management School, University of York. After graduating from the University of Birmingham, she trained as an accountant and then returned to academia, completing an MSc in Accounting and Finance at the London School of Economics and a PhD at the University of Warwick. Her main research interests include the professionalization of accounting, imperialism and accounting and accounting change in India. Her research on India has been published in *Critical Perspectives on Accounting* and the *Accounting Historians Journal.*

**P.W. Senarath Yapa** is an Associate Professor in Accounting at the School of Accounting and Law, RMIT University, Australia. He has published in the areas of accounting education, accounting history and the professionalization of accounting in developing countries. He is on the editorial board of the *Asian Journal of Finance and Accounting.* Prem has had teaching and research experience in Sri Lanka and Brunei. He had also actively involved as a consultant on accounting projects with the public and private sectors in Sri Lanka, Singapore, Brunei, Malaysia, Hong Kong and the Philippines.

# Index

Note: Page references for tables are in *italics*.

## D



## E